ARROYO CENTER

GW00467849

WILL to FIGHT

Analyzing, Modeling, and Simulating the Will to Fight of Military Units

Ben Connable
Michael J. McNerney
William Marcellino
Aaron Frank
Henry Hargrove
Marek N. Posard
S. Rebecca Zimmerman
Natasha Lander
Jasen J. Castillo
James Sladden

Prepared for the United States Army

Approved for public release; distribution unlimited

For more information on this publication, visit www.rand.org/t/RR2341

Library of Congress Cataloging-in-Publication Data is available for this publication.
ISBN: 978-1-9774-0044-4

Published by the RAND Corporation, Santa Monica, Calif.
© Copyright 2018 RAND Corporation
RAND® is a registered trademark.

Cover design by Eileen Delson La Russo; photo by Dang Van Phuoc/AP Photo

Limited Print and Electronic Distribution Rights

This document and trademark(s) contained herein are protected by law. This representation of RAND intellectual property is provided for noncommercial use only. Unauthorized posting of this publication online is prohibited. Permission is given to duplicate this document for personal use only, as long as it is unaltered and complete. Permission is required from RAND to reproduce, or reuse in another form, any of its research documents for commercial use. For information on reprint and linking permissions, please visit www.rand.org/pubs/permissions.

The RAND Corporation is a research organization that develops solutions to public policy challenges to help make communities throughout the world safer and more secure, healthier and more prosperous. RAND is nonprofit, nonpartisan, and committed to the public interest.

RAND's publications do not necessarily reflect the opinions of its research clients and sponsors.

Support RAND
Make a tax-deductible charitable contribution at
www.rand.org/giving/contribute

www.rand.org

Preface

This report documents research and analysis conducted as part of a project entitled *Influencing Will to Fight*, sponsored by the U.S. Army G-3/5/7. The purpose of the project was to explain will to fight at the unit level and to develop a model designed to support assessment of partner forces and analysis of adversary forces.

The Project Unique Identification Code (PUIC) for the project that produced this document is HQD167560.

This research was conducted within RAND Arroyo Center's Strategy, Doctrine, and Resources Program. RAND Arroyo Center, part of the RAND Corporation, is a federally funded research and development center (FFRDC) sponsored by the United States Army.

RAND operates under a "Federal-Wide Assurance" (FWA00003425) and complies with the *Code of Federal Regulations for the Protection of Human Subjects Under United States Law* (45 CFR 46), also known as "the Common Rule," as well as with the implementation guidance set forth in DoD Instruction 3216.02. As applicable, this compliance includes reviews and approvals by RAND's Institutional Review Board (the Human Subjects Protection Committee) and by the U.S. Army. The views of sources utilized in this study are solely their own and do not represent the official policy or position of DoD or the U.S. government.

Contents

Figures

Tables

Summary

In 2016 the U.S. Army recognized the need for deeper and clearer understanding of will to fight. Headquarters Department of the Army G-3/5/7 engaged the RAND Arroyo Center to address this gap with a series of research projects that will continue through at least late 2018. This report provides a flexible, scalable model of tactical to operational will to fight that can be applied to all sizes and types of units in any military ground combat organization; we reserve analysis of air and naval will to fight for future research. The purpose of the model is to provide a logical, research-grounded template for case-by-case advisor assessment of partner or allied military forces and the intelligence analysis of adversary forces. This report also provides a theoretical and experimental basis for adding will to fight to military war gaming and simulation.

Both the U.S. Army and the U.S. Marine Corps argue that will to fight is the single most important factor in war. Whether or not it is most important, it is the essential human factor in what is a fundamentally human endeavor. Will to fight helps determine whether a military unit stays in the fight and also how well it fights. Will to fight should be fully incorporated into all aspects of military planning, training, assessment, analysis, and operations.

Will to fight is *the disposition and decision to fight, to act, or to persevere when needed*. Soldiers, and collectively units, have the *disposition* to fight or not fight. Influenced by this disposition, they make *decisions* in the moment to fight or not fight. This is a simple proposition hiding extraordinary complexity. There is no concrete, predictable formula that can determine whether a soldier or unit will fight. Soldiers can have very low disposition to fight and still choose to fight in certain circumstances. For example, many soldiers with low disposition to fight will fight hard if they are cornered. Soldiers with very high disposition to fight can choose not to fight for a variety of reasons. While we cannot predict will to fight, we can significantly improve our understanding of its meaning, its factors, and its value in war. We can assess and analyze disposition, which allows for estimation of overall effectiveness and forecasting of behavior.

Modeling of will to fight helps explain *why* a unit is more or less likely to fight, and whether it is likely to fight aggressively. It identifies both weak and strong points in a unit's will to fight, both of which can be shored up or exploited. Modeling gives leaders, advisors, and intelligence analysts a common starting point for deeper understanding of each case. Modeling of will to fight opens the door for better planning, operations, advising, intelligence, war gaming, simulation, and, with further research, improved training and education of U.S. military forces.

Key Findings

Findings emerged from a nine-part multiple-method (multimethod) research approach described in Chapter One and in the appendixes. Research confirmed our central assumption: American understanding of will to fight needs significant improvement. Our findings stem from this requirement and apply to all parts of this report series. Note that this research focuses on U.S. understanding of partner and adversary will to fight; follow-on research into U.S. will to fight is warranted. A summary of the model follows these findings and the recommendations.

There Is No Generally Accepted Definition, Explanation, or Model of Will to Fight

Our literature review of 202 published works, U.S. and allied military doctrine, 68 subject matter expert interviews, and several hundred additional sources on specific historical cases, war gaming, and simulation revealed no generally accepted military or scientific definition, explanation, or model of will to fight. Further, there are no commonly accepted definitions or explanations of some of the key terms associated with will to fight, including *morale*, *cohesion*, and *discipline*. Our proposed definitions, explanations, and model are intended to help remedy this gap in general knowledge.

Will to Fight Is Vital to Understanding War, but It Is Often Ignored or Misunderstood

Canonical literature on war, the most prominent generals in the history of warfare, and the current doctrines of both the U.S. Army and the Marine Corps argue that will to fight is the most important factor in war. Our work explores and builds from this widely accepted premise. It is impossible to prove true: No claim of single factor causality across all cases of war is defensible. Worse, will to fight is a frustratingly hard-to-quantify factor in an otherwise highly quantifiable endeavor: War can be more easily—but only partly—broken down into tangible units of soldiers, weapons, tanks, planes, gallons of fuel, and rounds fired. Absent a clear understanding of will to fight, American advisors, intelligence analysts, and leaders have struggled to describe and influence ally and adversary will to fight in the Vietnam War, in Iraq, and in Afghanistan. There is a clear need to understand the will to fight of prospective adversaries like Russia, North Korea, China, and Iran, and also the will to fight of allies across Europe, Asia, and the Middle East.

> **Shortfalls in practice:** Because will to fight cannot be neatly or precisely quantified, military leaders, advisors, and analysts often ignore it or give it short shrift

in practice. Because it has not been adequately modeled, its interpretations are uneven and appear to be unanchored from objective facts. In some cases it is studied but then misunderstood or misinterpreted in ways that contribute to tactical and even strategic defeat in war.

A dangerous gap: These oversights and missteps are dangerous and should be considered unacceptable: Will to fight is an inescapable and essential part of war. Failure to prioritize and constantly seek to improve our understanding of will to fight represents an ongoing threat to American military success and American security.

Will to Fight Is Essential for Assessing or Analyzing Holistic Combat Effectiveness

Describing combat effectiveness means estimating the ability of a military unit to accomplish its mission, which may include defeating an opposing force. Estimates of combat effectiveness are used to inform critical changes in training, equipment, and operations, and to help target enemy capabilities. *Holistic* estimates seek to determine a unit's overall (not narrow, technical) effectiveness. Our research shows that will to fight matters, but that it is not possible to know the precise degree to which it matters in understanding holistic unit combat effectiveness in a general model or in any one case.

A fundamental requirement to fight: Basic physical functioning and will to fight are the only two absolute prerequisites to fighting: People can fight without equipment or training, but no person can fight without the will to do so. A panicked, cowering soldier hugging the world's most advanced rifle is no fighter.

Unavoidably necessary: If will to fight matters *to some degree* or, arguably, *most* to determining the outcomes of wars, and we do not know the degree of its importance from case to case, then we must assume and accept that will to fight is *at the very least* one necessary part of holistic combat effectiveness in *all* cases. Ignoring will to fight invites damaging consequences. Will to fight should be included in all holistic estimates of combat effectiveness.

To Understand Tactical-Operational Will to Fight, All Factors Should Be Considered

Some experts on war propose various unitary theories that seek to explain will to fight, often centering on leadership, cohesion, discipline, or morale. Others argue that many factors should be considered together to develop a holistic understanding of will to fight. We find unitary theories of will to fight to be unreliable. At the very least they are insufficiently proven. Our model of will to fight offers a holistic roadmap for what must be a sui generis factor-by-factor assessment in each case. Two of the most oft-proposed unitary factors—cohesion and morale—are no more or less important than any other factor in the general model.

Cohesion alone does not explain will to fight: The most prominent unitary factor is unit cohesion. Unit cohesion encompasses the social and task bonds created between unit members and between members and unit leaders. There is sufficient evidence to show that cohesion is an important factor that influences will to fight; existing analyses show that it may be very important in many cases. But there is no accepted empirical proof that it is the most important factor in every case. Nor is there irreproachable proof that cohesion, by itself, fully explains will to fight even in one single case.

Morale does not explain, or by itself indicate, will to fight: Other experts offer the ill-defined term *morale* as a unitary theory: The way soldiers feel is equated with their disposition and decision to fight. This is not provable, nor is there any consistent definition of morale. Some use it to represent all aspects of will to fight—that morale is will to fight. We find that morale is instead a transient, partial indicator of will to fight that often has counterintuitive and misleading meanings. This term requires further analysis before it can be usefully modeled.

Ground Combat Force and Joint Doctrine on Will to Fight Is Inconsistent, Inadequate

The U.S. Army and Marine Corps—the ground combat forces of the U.S. military— have alternatively embraced and ignored the concept of will to fight for over a century. Lack of continuous emphasis on will to fight in doctrine undermines its emphasis in training, education, assessment, and analysis. U.S. Joint Force doctrine is similarly inconsistent. Figure S.1 shows the ebb and flow of doctrinal emphasis on will to fight starting with the Army's 1895 *Organization and Tactics*, versions of its *Field Service Regulations*, which morphed into Field Manual (FM) 100-5. It also shows the Marine Corps' *Small Wars Manual*, the Marine Corps' Doctrinal Publication 1, *Warfighting*, and most recently the Army Doctrine Publications (ADPs).

There is no consistent, common definition of will to fight, and there is no common model of will to fight in U.S. ground combat force doctrine or in U.S. joint doctrine.

Will to fight is elevated when it is mentioned: When greater emphasis was placed on will to fight, the ground combat services described it as very important or most important in determining the outcome of war. When it was ignored, it was ignored almost completely. As of late 2017, both the Army and the Marine Corps describe will to fight as the most important factor in war.

An existing Joint Force gap: Joint capstone doctrine (Doctrine for the Armed Forces of the United States, 2013) establishes "fundamental principles and overarching guidance" for the Joint Force.[1] Joint doctrine accepts the Clausewitzean premise of war as a clash of opposing wills and therefore acknowledges the fundamental importance of will to fight. However, as of late 2017, joint doctrine does not define, explain, or integrate will to fight into military planning and operations.

---

[1]   Signed comment by then-chairman of the U.S. Joint Chiefs of Staff GEN Martin E. Dempsey, in U.S. Joint Staff, *Doctrine for the Armed Forces of the United States*, Joint Publication 1, Washington, D.C.: Joint Staff, March 25, 2013, page not numbered.

Figure S.1
Varying Ground Combat Service Emphasis on Will to Fight in Doctrine

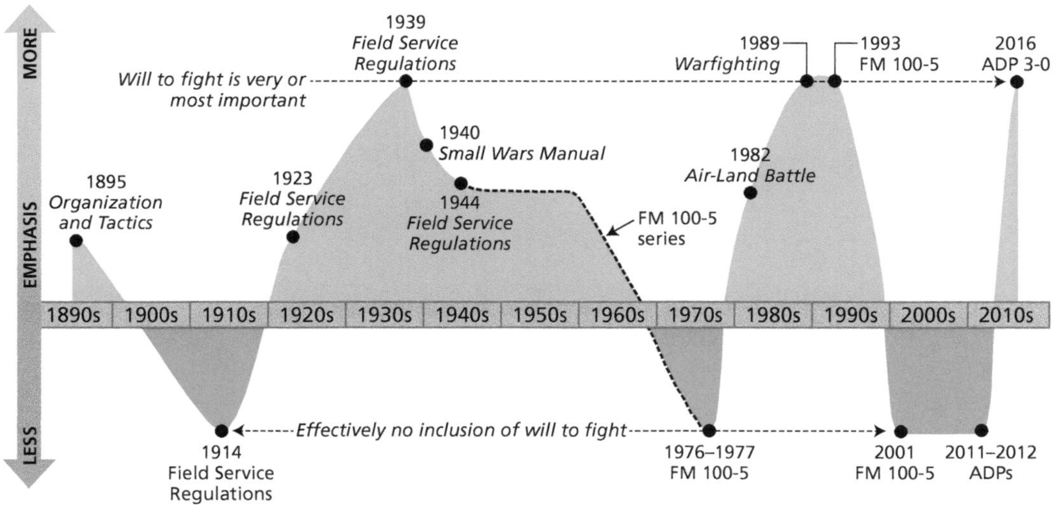

RAND RR2341A-S.1

The 2016 Joint Concept for Human Aspects of Military Operations (JC-HAMO) notes this gap and seeks better understanding of will to fight.

Adding Will to Fight Changes Combat Simulation Outcomes— Sometimes Significantly

Our analysis shows that as of late 2017 most U.S. military war games and simulations of ground combat and combined arms combat—including representation of aerospace and naval units—either do not include will to fight or include only minor proxies of will to fight (e.g., suppression, or the fear and reaction generated by near misses) that are useful but inadequate to convey its full complexity. Existing published research shows that adding will-to-fight factors contributes to changing the outcomes of force-on-force ground combat in games and simulations.

Building from existing research and modeling, and in collaboration with the Natick Soldier Research Development and Engineering Center (NSRDEC), we conducted experimental testing of will to fight using the U.S. Army's Infantry Warrior Simulation (IWARS). Our 7,840 simulated runs applying a suppression proxy and then a complex will-to-fight model across eight experimental scenarios showed that (1) adding will-to-fight factors always changes combat outcomes, and (2) in some cases, outcomes are significantly different. For example, we tested Blue versus Red (friendly versus enemy) squads and platoons in IWARS. To examine the effect of will to fight on combat outcomes, we added the effect of delaying reloading and firing due to suppression on the Blue side only. Adding suppression-induced delay significantly increased the likelihood of a Blue defeat.

Figure S.2
Example of IWARS Squad-Level Simulation Adding Suppression

SOURCE: NSRDEC
RAND *RR2341A-S.2*

Figure S.2 depicts one of the squad-level suppression simulations in IWARS. It shows equal Red and Blue squads firing at each other from 200 meters apart. Soldier 5 is fleeing from enemy fire after suffering suppression-induced panic.

Our more detailed experiments—described in Chapter Three—integrated an existing soldier-level will-to-fight psychological model into IWARS. Adding the Silver Combat Psychological Model (CPM, or Silver Model) also influenced changes in combat outcomes, including odds ratios of defeat and percentages of soldiers fleeing. While further testing across a variety of simulations and scenarios is necessary to develop scientific proof that adding will to fight always changes simulation outcomes, our initial research—which included analysis of 62 commercial and military games and simulations, interviews with game and simulation designers, literature review, and experimentation—suggests that its influence is frequently strong and that any game or simulation of force-on-force ground combat that does not include will to fight would be misleading, and perhaps dangerously so.

A Model of Tactical-Operational Will to Fight

Our model is explanatory, exploratory, and portable. We synthesized it from our nine-part multimethod research effort. It explains the factors in will to fight, but it does not provide a quantifiable formula. It should be used to explore the meaning and relevance of each factor, to better understand will to fight, and to support a wide array of further modeling and simulation efforts. This portable model requires unique application: It provides an empirically derived guide for the necessary hard work of understanding will to fight in each prospective case. There are many ways to arrange and describe this model. We offer three here: (1) a table of categories, factors, and subfactors; (2) a system-of-systems depiction to help visualize the factors and subfactors in the table; and (3) a concentric factors visualization.

Table S.1 contains the layered arrangement of factors and subfactors that influence the will to fight. It reflects five levels of analysis: (1) individual, (2) unit, (3) organization, (4) state, and (5) society. The purpose of the model is to better inform understanding of unit will to fight from the squad level through the division level. There are three categories of factors: *motivations, capabilities,* and *culture.* Motivations are drivers of will to fight that help form individual disposition. Capabilities are the competencies and physical assets available to soldiers and the support they receive from the unit level through the societal level of assessment. Culture includes behavioral

Table S.1
Factors and Subfactors Constituting Will to Fight

Level	Category	Factors	Subfactors	Durability
Individual	Individual motivations	Desperation		Mid
		Revenge Ideology Economics		High
		Individual identity	Personal, social, unit, state, organization, and society (including political, religious)	High
	Individual capabilities	Quality	Fitness, resilience, education, adaptability, social skills, and psychological traits	High
		Individual competence	Skills, relevance, sufficiency, and sustainability	High
Unit	Unit culture	Unit cohesion	Social vertical, social horizontal, and task	Mid
		Expectation		Low
		Unit control	Coercion, persuasion, and discipline	Mid
		Unit esprit de corps		Mid
	Unit capabilities	Unit competence	Performance, skills, and training	High
		Unit support	Sufficiency and timeliness	Low
		Unit leadership	Competence and character	Mid

Table S.1—Continued

Level	Category	Factors	Subfactors	Durability
Organization	Organizational culture	Organizational control	Coercion, persuasion, and discipline	High
		Organizational esprit de corps		High
		Organizational integrity	Corruption and trust	High
	Organizational capabilities	Organizational training	Capabilities, relevance, sufficiency, and sustainment	High
		Organizational support	Sufficiency and timeliness	Mid
		Doctrine	Appropriateness and effectiveness	High
		Organizational leadership	Competence and character	High
State	State culture	Civil-military relations	Appropriateness and functionality	High
		State integrity	Corruption and trust	High
	State capabilities	State support	Sufficiency and timeliness	Mid
		State strategy	Clarity and effectiveness	High
		State leadership	Competence and character	High
Society	Societal culture	Societal identity	Ideology, ethnicity, and history	High
		Societal integrity	Corruption and trust	High
	Societal capabilities	Societal support	Consistency and efficiency	Mid

norms, control measures, and influences that affect individual and unit disposition and decisions to fight. Factors are major influences on will to fight, while subfactors provide further points of examination for portable assessment and analysis. Durability describes the degree to which a factor is likely to change during the course of a single battle or short series of battles. Durability ratings are intended to help advisors and analysts focus on what can be changed, or might change quickly, and which factors might provide immediate indication of changes in will to fight.

We arrange these factors using a system-of-systems model. Each node, or circle, is a factor, while each link is a connection between the factor and a level of analysis. For example, individual identity is a node linked to the individual soldier. Solid black links (lines) show connections that are generally consistent in each case: Individual soldiers

Figure S.3
Individual Will-to-Fight Model

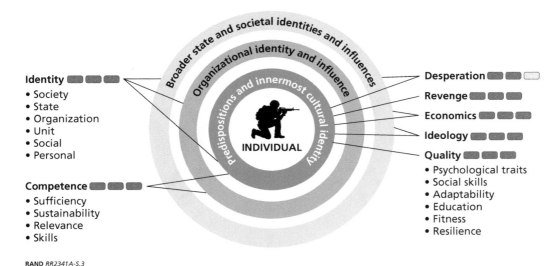

Broader state and societal identities and influences
Organizational identity and influence
Predispositions and innermost cultural identity
INDIVIDUAL

Identity ▭▭ ▭▭ ▭▭
• Society
• State
• Organization
• Unit
• Social
• Personal

Competence ▭▭ ▭▭ ▭▭
• Sufficiency
• Sustainability
• Relevance
• Skills

Desperation ▭▭ ▭▭ ▭
Revenge ▭▭ ▭▭ ▭▭
Economics ▭▭ ▭▭ ▭▭
Ideology ▭▭ ▭▭ ▭▭
Quality ▭▭ ▭▭ ▭▭
• Psychological traits
• Social skills
• Adaptability
• Education
• Fitness
• Resilience

RAND *RR2341A-S.3*

always have individual identity. Because this is a portable model, it cannot show clear, consistent relationships *between* factors. In other words, we cannot say that state leadership always affects individual identity, or how it might do so in every case. It will not always be necessary to understand these links, but in some cases it might be useful; this will require case-specific assessment or analysis.

Figure S.3 is the individual system-of-systems model of will to fight. It depicts an individual soldier at the center of three concentric circles. The internal circle reflects the soldier's predispositions and innermost cultural identities, many of which preexist entry into the military. The second circle represents organizational identity and influence, while the outermost circle represents broader state and societal identities and influences. Each individual can be assessed across three factors—*quality*, *identity*, and *competence*—and their associated subfactors. Individuals may also be influenced by desperation, revenge, economic drivers, and ideology. Finally, each individual is influenced by unit, organization, state, and societal factors listed in Table S.1.

Building from this individual model, Figures S.4 and S.5 present two versions of the entire will-to-fight model through the societal level. In Figure S.4 each factor and subfactor is incorporated and connected with either the individual soldier or a figure representing leadership or organizational structure at each level. Each factor and subfactor has a durability rating: low as a single dark bar, mid as two dark bars, or high as three dark bars. This rating indicates the likelihood that the factor will change over the course of a single battle or short series of battles, and it is intended to focus the model for combat behavior. A fully realistic model would be an infinitely complex, multidimensional spider web of factors, subfactors, and links of varying weight and meaning.

Figure S.4
Will-to-Fight Model from Individual to State and Society: Systems Visualization

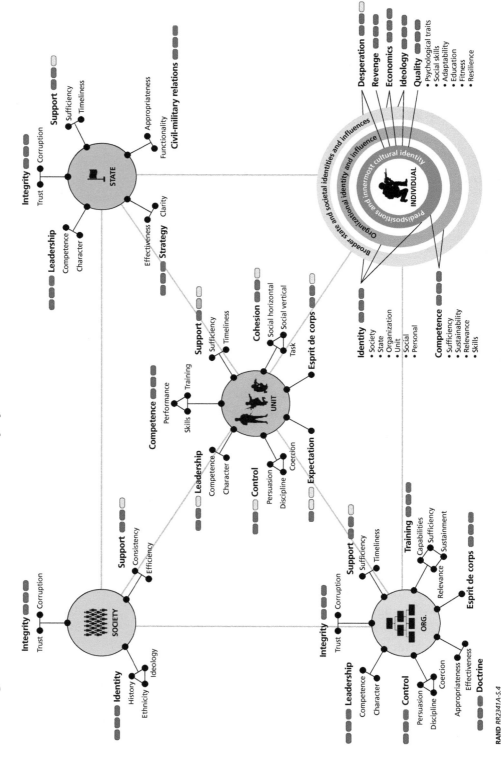

RAND RR2341A-S.4

Figure S.5
Will-to-Fight Model from Individual to State and Society: Wheel Visualization

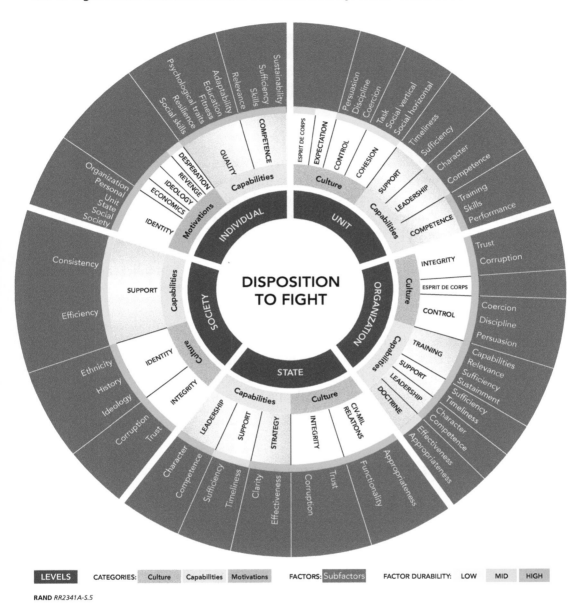

LEVELS   CATEGORIES: Culture   Capabilities   Motivations   FACTORS: Subfactors   FACTOR DURABILITY: LOW   MID   HIGH

RAND RR2341A-S.5

It could include thousands of relationships. We argue that this simpler explanatory model—in which factors are understood and a few well-substantiated general links are suggested—is both more realistic and sufficiently grounded in empirical research to give it practical credibility. It can and should be used, studied, and, if necessary, modified and applied to understand military unit will to fight in any prospective case.

Figure S.5 presents an alternative visualization of the model. In this version, the factors are arranged in a wheel indicating their influence on the disposition to fight. We provide this second visualization in order to demonstrate the flexibility of the model and to provide users with alternative approaches for analysis and assessment. Durability ratings, from low to high, describe the degree to which the factor is likely to change during combat: low durability suggests it is highly vulnerable to change, while high durability suggests it changes gradually for reasons other than enemy action or immediate environmental impact.

How to Apply the Model

Each factor and subfactor should be *considered* for each case, then either explored in greater detail, set aside for future analysis, or discarded. Every assessment or analysis of will to fight requires different levels of detail, has different objectives, and must be accomplished with different resources and on different timelines. Further, each of the factors that influence will to fight is complex: Each could be broken apart into a separate system, or even another system of systems. We do not seek to explain the infinite complexity of individual will or of societal culture. Instead, the model points leaders, advisors, and analysts to the factors and subfactors that our research showed to be most important to understand will to fight.

There is no objective value or general rule that can be applied to any factor in this model. Both quantitative and qualitative methods and data can be applied to understand any of these factors, including measurement of performance, training surveys, intelligence information reports, and individual advisor observations. Anyone attempting to develop and apply a general rule to this model should do so with great caution.

Recommendations for the U.S. Army and the Joint Force

The following recommendations are intended to help improve U.S. Army and Joint Force ground combat plans, operations, assessments, intelligence analyses, games, and simulations. They should also inform combined (allied) understanding of will to fight in Europe, Asia, and the Middle East.

Integrate Will to Fight into Doctrine, Training, Education, and Application

It is unlikely that much progress will be made in improving the application of will to fight absent a definition and model that are accepted and used across the Joint Force. While this research was conducted for the U.S. Army, one service alone cannot shape the way the United States prepares for and prosecutes war. Both Army and joint doctrine and practice should fully incorporate will to fight in clear and detailed terms.

Develop and integrate an Army will-to-fight definition and model: The Army should publish a definition and model of will to fight in capstone doctrine. The model should be published in both written and visual formats to support a wide array of activities. The RAND Arroyo Center definition and model in this report are intended to support this effort.

Integrate will to fight into Army doctrine and application manuals: All ADPs, Army Doctrine Reference Publications, applicable Army Tactics, Techniques, and Procedures, and FMs should define will to fight and integrate practical applications to help soldiers and leaders apply improved understanding of will to fight. Combat tasks should be tailored to help shore up ally and defeat adversary will to fight. Will to fight should be central to the way the Army thinks about and executes warfare.

Make will to fight central to Army training and education: Building from the improvements to doctrine and training manuals, Army leaders at all levels should be trained and educated to understand and incorporate the practical aspects of will-to-fight knowledge into planning and operations. Training exercises simulating force-on-force combat should make will to fight a central consideration for execution and a metric for success.

Integrate will to fight into joint doctrine and education: Joint doctrine should define will to fight, explain how it applies to each aspect of warfighting, and describe ways to incorporate will-to-fight considerations into joint planning and operations. Capstone doctrine should cement will to fight as an enduring and central factor of warfare. Our definition and model are intended to serve as a starting point for Joint Force development of a universal standard.

Include Will to Fight in All Holistic Estimates of Ground Combat Effectiveness

If will to fight is an important, or perhaps the most important, factor in war, and if it is a necessary component of holistic combat effectiveness, then all efforts to assess or analyze the holistic combat effectiveness of a partner or adversary ground combat unit must include will to fight. This recommendation has significant implications for military planners, advisors, intelligence analysts, and commanders seeking to understand the likelihood of success in prospective combat. Methods and standards for determining holistic ground combat unit effectiveness should be changed accordingly.

Integrate will to fight into assessments of partner effectiveness: Assessment of partner effectiveness should include grounded estimates of disposition to fight derived from a universal definition and model. Advisors should be trained to assess will to fight, and forms used to estimate potential combat effectiveness should include a structured, clearly explained section on will to fight.

Integrate will to fight into analyses of adversary effectiveness: Analyses of adversary, or potential adversary, effectiveness should be similarly grounded in order to meet standards for analytic integrity. Intelligence order of battle (OOB) analyses should include estimates of unit will to fight. Our research focused on ground combat, but this recommendation should also be considered for estimates of aerospace and naval units.

War Games and Simulations of Combat Should Include Will to Fight

If will to fight is a necessary and important part of determining holistic ground combat effectiveness, and if war games and simulations of force-on-force combat are intended to represent and understand relative combat effectiveness, then will to fight should be included in any war game or simulation that seeks to replicate or determine the outcome of force-on-force ground combat. Games and simulations that fail to consider will to fight, or do not seek to model it in sufficient detail, risk generating misleading play and results. Commercial games and simulations have demonstrated some useful models, and we show how will to fight can be incorporated into military simulation with IWARS. Our model is intended to provide a basis for incorporating will to fight into tabletop games as well as verified, validated, and accredited military simulations.

Add will to fight to OneSAF and WARSIM: The U.S. Army should incorporate will to fight into its current combat simulations. Will to fight should be integrated into the behavior of individual agents and collective military units. Will to fight should also be integrated into all future simulation design considerations for force-on-force ground combat simulations.

Add will to fight to all joint ground combat simulations: The Joint Force should incorporate will to fight into all current and prospective simulations of force-on-force ground combat. Further analysis should examine the relevance of will to fight in joint and service-specific air and naval simulations.

Abbreviations

ADP	Army Doctrine Publication
ARL	Army Research Laboratory
ARVN	Army of the Republic of Vietnam
CIA	Central Intelligence Agency
CPM	Combat Psychological Model (Silver Model)
CQA	Continuous Quality Assurance
CUAT	Commanders Unit (or Update) Assessment Tool
C-WAM	Center for Army Analysis Wargame Analysis Model
DoD	Department of Defense
DPRK	Democratic People's Republic of Korea
DRV	Democratic Republic of Vietnam
IWARS	Infantry Warrior Simulation
JCATS	Joint Conflict and Tactical Simulation
JC-HAMO	Joint Concept for Human Aspects of Military Operations
JFCOM	Joint Forces Command
JICM	Joint Integrated Contingency Model
JWARS	Joint Warfare System
KIA	killed in action
NATO	North Atlantic Treaty Organization
NGIC	National Ground Intelligence Center
NSRDEC	Natick Soldier Research Development and Engineering Center
ODA	Operational Detachment Alpha
OOB	order of battle
PAVN	People's Army of Viet Nam (Vietnam)
PCA	principal component analysis

RMA	Revolution in Military Affairs
RVN	Republic of Vietnam
STORM	Synthetic Theater Operations Research Model
VBS3	Virtual Battlespace 3

Acknowledgments

We greatly appreciate the support of our sponsor, U.S. Army Deputy Chief of Staff, G-3/5/7, Major General William Hix. We thank Tony Vanderbeek, MAJ Ben Weakley, Mark Calvo, and MAJ Erhan Bedestani for monitoring the study and providing helpful feedback during its course.

We also recognize the invaluable contributions of the experts who helped us reach our findings and develop the model of will to fight. These experts are too numerous to mention here, but include U.S. and UK flag officers, esteemed faculty, modeling and simulation experts, game designers, and other military leaders from several North Atlantic Treaty Organization nations.

Kerry Fosher, the Director of Research at the U.S. Marine Corps' Center for Advanced Operational Cultural Learning, served as our government academic advisor. Her guidance was instrumental to our research design and methodology.

Erik Villard at the U.S. Army Center of Military History provided support and archival access for our Vietnam War research. Center leaders, including Jon Hoffman, were welcoming and supportive of our work.

Manny Diego from the Army Research Laboratory helped us think through some of the gaps in current military simulation and offered enthusiastic support for our work.

RAND Arroyo Center supported our research by sponsoring a Continuous Quality Assurance team. Our reviewers, Jennifer Kavanagh and Henry Leonard at RAND, and sociologist Meredith Kleykamp at the University of Maryland, provided expert and timely feedback throughout the research period. Lynn Davis, also at RAND, provided crucial guidance and mentorship during the initial phase of project design.

Erin-Elizabeth Johnson provided graphic design support, helping to translate our description of the model into a visually stimulating and compelling set of graphics.

Our simulation team offers special thanks to Steven Silver, the designer of the Silver Combat Psychological Model featured in Chapter Three of this report; to Wayne Zandburgen, Phil Sabin, and COL David Hudak; and to our colleagues at NSRDEC, Michael J. Statkus, Dean M. Sutherland, and Robert J. Auer.

We thank Tim Bonds, RAND vice president of the Army Research Division, and Sally Sleeper, the Arroyo Center's director for strategy, doctrine, and resources, for their leadership and guidance. Modeling and simulations expert Paul K. Davis provided detailed and thoughtful comments during our quality assurance review.

We also thank RAND colleagues Marcy Agmon, Francisco Walter, Gina Frost, Jessica Bateman, Katrina Griffin-Moore, Susan Straus, Todd Helmus, Chris Schnaubelt, Eugene Han, Anika Binnendijk, Miranda Priebe, Mark Cozad, Catherine Dale, Aidan Winn, Christopher Paul, Gian Gentile, Scott Savitz, Angela O'Mahony, LTC Brent Williams, Ed Donnelly, Dung Huynh, Marta Kepe, Inhyok Kwon, and Eric Larson.

We owe a special debt of gratitude to RAND Communications Analyst and graphics artist Yvonne Crane. Yvonne designed the concentric wheel model of will to fight in this report. More importantly, she helped us conceptualize the most effective ways to convey our research findings: expert visualization is only the most obvious output of a much longer and more demanding process. Yvonne's tireless efforts were essential to our collective success.

CHAPTER ONE

Introduction and Historical Background: Will to Fight Matters

In all matters which pertain to an army, organization, discipline and tactics, the human heart in the supreme moment of battle is the basic factor. It is rarely taken into account; and often strange errors are the result. . . . We must consider it!
—Colonel Ardant du Picq,
Battle Studies: Ancient and Modern Battle

The use of force demands that we should understand our own natures, for the most basic and the most complicated weapon system is man.
—Brigadier General Shelford Bidwell,
Modern Warfare: A Study of Men, Weapons and Theories

In the spring of 2000 a company of elite Russian paratroopers set in to what would be their final defensive position on Hill 776 in Chechnya's remote Argun Gorge.[1] Chechen rebels, including some hyperaggressive foreign fighters, had maneuvered through a dense fog to cut off the Russians and surround them. Only the men who fought on the hill know for sure what happened next: who was brave, who cowered in fear, and whether (as it was reported) the Russian commander actually called artillery down on his own position as the Chechens closed in. What is clear is that the Russians fought hard, almost to the last man. The Chechens fought just as hard, pressing home their attack under withering artillery, machine-gun, and rifle fire and suffering over 100 casualties. In the end the Russian company was destroyed. Many factors shaped the outcome of the Battle for Hill 776, including poor Russian decisionmaking, a huge numerical advantage for the Chechens, and bad weather. But one factor was critically important: the will to fight. Why did the Russians fight almost to the last man? Why did the Chechens press home their attack even as they suffered staggering casualties? These questions about *will to fight* get to the heart of combat, and to the enduring nature of war. Our report seeks answers.

---

[1]   Descriptions of this battle are drawn from Michael D. Wilmoth and Peter G. Tsouras, "ULUS-KERT: An Airborne Company's Last Stand," *Military Review*, July–August 2001, pp. 91–96. There are conflicting reports regarding this battle, but it is generally accepted that the 6th Company fought hard and was destroyed.

Arguably, *will to fight is the single most important factor in war.* This is the official position of the U.S. Army and the U.S. Marine Corps as of late 2017.[2] With few exceptions, this is also the firm stance of prominent military strategists and historians, including Ardant du Picq, George C. Marshall, B. H. Liddell Hart, Vo Nguyen Giap, and James N. Mattis.[3] Unfortunately for military analysts there is no way to prove which factor matters most in determining the outcome of wars. Therefore, these official and expert statements reflect informed opinion rather than empirically defensible fact. Nonetheless, these opinions matter. If the U.S. military believes that will to fight is the most important factor in war, then at the very least it demands far more attention than it has so far received.

Failure of will has signaled the ending of almost every military conflict in world history. Russian paratroopers on Hill 776 may have fought almost to the last man, but battles and wars tend to end in some form of capitulation rather than total annihilation.[4] Even the most fanatical military forces can lose the will to fight: In World War II tens of thousands of Japanese soldiers surrendered, as did the emperor of Japan.[5] It is equally important to understand the reasons why the Russian paratroopers and many Japanese soldiers fought to the bitter end. Historian John Keegan wrote a compelling summary of will to fight, of its many complexities, and its critical importance to the understanding of war:[6]

> The study of battle is . . . always a study of fear and usually of courage, always of leadership, usually of obedience; always of compulsion, sometimes of insubordination; always of anxiety, sometimes of elation or catharsis. . . . [A]bove all, it is a study of solidarity and also of disintegration—for it is towards the disintegration of human groups that battle is directed.

Will to fight encapsulates and represents all of these intricate human aspects of warfare, and many more. It is *the disposition and decision to fight, to act, or to persevere*

---

[2]   U.S. Army, *Operations*, ADP 3-0, Washington, D.C.: Headquarters, Department of the Army, November 2016b; U.S. Marine Corps, *Warfighting*, MCDP-1, Washington, D.C.: Headquarters, U.S. Marine Corps, 1997.

[3]   We list and explain these positions later in this chapter and throughout the report.

[4]   This conclusion is derived from a summary assessment of seventeenth- to twenty-first-century conventional military conflicts from a variety of sources, including the Correlates of War database and a range of military history literature cited herein.

[5]   Approximately 50,000 Japanese surrendered to Allied forces during World War II. For example: Benjamin P. Hegi, *Extermination Warfare? The Conduct of the Second Marine Division at Saipan*, thesis, Denton: University of North Texas, 2008; Ikuhiko Hata, "From Consideration to Contempt: The Changing Nature of Japanese Military and Popular Perceptions of Prisoners of War Through the Ages," in Bob Moore and Kent Fedorowich, eds., *Prisoners of War and Their Captors in World War II*, Washington, D.C.: Berg Press, 1996, pp. 253–276.

[6]   John Keegan, *The Face of Battle*, New York: Viking Penguin Incorporated, 1976, p. 303.

when needed.[7] Our research describes will to fight at the tactical and operational levels of war. We analyze many aspects of individual will, but our focus is on military units from the squad level to the division level, and on the military organizations that build and sustain these units.

Fighting is generally understood as attacking an enemy force or defending against one. It is a classical act of survival, and also the physical manifestation of political and military direction. Soldiers fight because they must, and in many cases because they want to. But on a modern battlefield most soldiers—whether they are in an infantry platoon or a transportation platoon—rarely make contact with the enemy.[8] Even for frontline soldiers, will to fight is tested in the tense days, hours, and minutes between instances of combat. Therefore, will to fight must address combat, but it must also account for every expression of perseverance and dedication to mission in war. This could mean firing a rifle at an enemy soldier or driving a truck in a combat area or holding fast in a freezing trench while awaiting an inevitable enemy artillery barrage and infantry assault, knowing all the while that help might not be on the way.

Hence, will to fight is more accurately the will *to fight, to act, or to persevere.* We use the term *fight* to encapsulate all of these terms. We focus on the act of combat because it is there, in the life-and-death struggle between soldiers, that will is most clearly tested and revealed.

This all assumes physical capability. Weak and wounded bodies can be made to fight, but if a body is broken it cannot fight: A soldier cannot will a shattered arm to bear the weight of a rifle. Disposition to fight is far more complex. If capacity is present, is the soldier disposed to fight? What is the *likelihood* a soldier will choose to fight? No analyst can confidently predict behavior in war. But if the Army and Marine Corps can assess likelihood to fight and understand *why* fighting is more or less likely for a given military unit, then they can estimate performance and influence disposition: improve it for allies, degrade it for adversaries. Disposition is the result of individualized factors like psychological characteristics, motivation, and expectations for support.[9] Individual disposition is closely bound to group dynamics, including social cohesion, discipline, leadership, and organizational culture.

Human agency—the inalienable role of choice in human behavior—activates the disposition to fight, to avoid fighting, or to flee: If the body and mind are functioning,

---

[7]   We expand on this brief summary throughout the report. This definition is derived from a nine-step multiple-method approach to modeling will to fight. This includes a coded literature review of 202 sources.

[8]   American ground combat forces typically have more than five soldiers in support roles for every combat arms soldier. For example: Stuart E. Johnson, John E. Peters, Karin E. Kitchens, Aaron Martin, and Jordan R. Fischbach, *A Review of the Army's Modular Force Structure*, Santa Monica, Calif.: RAND Corporation, TR-927-2-OSD, 2012, p. 22.

[9]   We provide definitions for these terms below.

then *fighting is a choice*. Lord Moran, a firsthand observer of the trench fighting in World War I, described the will to fight as a "cold choice between two alternatives, the fixed resolve not to quit; an act of renunciation which must be made not once but many times by the power of the will."[10] Disposition influences and underwrites that choice. Soldiers can have some disposition to fight and still decide to sit out or flee. Soldiers will never fight if they have absolutely no disposition to fight. Both disposition and decision are necessary. This is a simple formula summarizing why soldiers fight or do not fight. It has two overarching elements:

disposition to fight + **decision to fight** = the act of fighting

The purposes of this report and the model are to improve understanding of *disposition* to fight.[11] Individual and unit will to fight is the combined effect of the influences of many factors that tend to preexist combat. But will to fight is also affected and tested by immediate concerns in combat, like ceaseless barrages of enemy artillery, lack of sleep, extreme weather, and the constant fear of death.[12] Lord Moran wrote, "The acid test of a man in the trenches was high explosive; it told each one of us things about ourselves we had not known till then."[13] Endogenous factors like enemy action must be addressed, but they can be understood only if one of the two core aspects of will to fight—disposition—is demystified. This is no small task.

Quantification of will to fight would be efficient and useful for the military. In an ideal world an allied or adversary unit could be assigned a precise number of "wills" that could then be built up or degraded. But disposition to fight and human agency defy meaningful quantification. Will to fight can be *assessed* and *analyzed* using a range of guiding factors: Military advisors assess the effectiveness of allied units, and intelligence professionals analyze adversary unit capacity.[14] It can be quantified in simulation for notional battles. But will to fight cannot be *measured* the way that one measures a vehicle's speed or a weapon's range or a ship's carrying capacity. Political

---

[10]   Lord Moran (Charles McMoran Wilson), *The Anatomy of Courage*, New York: Carroll and Graf Publishers, 2007 (1945), p. 67. The official author listing is Lord Moran. This source will be referred to as Moran, 2007 (1945).

[11]   Understanding the decision to fight would require considerable additional research on individual decision-making, and it is unlikely that findings would ever be generalizable to all individual soldiers. There is a wealth of existing literature describing individual decisions to fight or not fight, but this literature is often autobiographical or filtered through semistructured interview protocols with different objectives. For example, RAND's interviews with Vietnamese prisoners during the Vietnam War offer considerable insight into the decision to defect or desert, but less into the decision to fight in any one instance or across a range of instances.

[12]   We list a range of these factors in Chapter Three.

[13]   Moran, 2007 (1945), p. 67.

[14]   For an explanation of the differences between assessment and analysis, see Ben Connable, *Embracing the Fog of War: Assessment and Metrics in Counterinsurgency*, Santa Monica, Calif.: RAND Corporation, MG-1086, 2012.

scientist and retired U.S. Army Lieutenant Colonel Sam C. Sarkesian makes a sound argument about the limits of quantitative measurement and human behavior:[15]

> Measuring subjectivity using quantitative data in a fashion similar to objective measures is at best spurious and not reflective of the unit's ability to perform in combat nor indicative of the individual's will to fight, his commitment to the mission of the unit, and his acceptance and commitment to the ideology of the larger community.

Will to fight matters, and it *may* be the single most important factor in war. But it is deeply frustrating to understand and explain. Its squishy, intangible nature makes it unloved in the heavily quantitative world of the modern military. For these reasons and perhaps others, will to fight is one of the least discussed and least studied aspects of American military theory. Unwillingness to pursue a firmer understanding of will to fight has left a gap in both knowledge and military practice.

We show in Appendix C how the U.S. military has not maintained an emphasis on will to fight in doctrine or in practice. Both the Army and the Marine Corps have demonstrated only periodic interest in will to fight between the late 1800s and 2017. In some decades it is described as the most important factor in war, and in other decades it is ignored. Lack of a core model of will to fight means that there is no shared understanding of its makeup or meaning. Shortfalls in efforts to assess allied will to fight and analyze adversary will to fight are significant.[16] Failure to put theory into practice has cost the United States and its allies dearly.[17] This should be quickly remedied to help the U.S. military improve efficiency, save lives, and win wars.

Objectives, Definitions, and Report Roadmap

Senior strategists in the U.S. Army are aware of the shortfalls in efforts to assess allied will to fight and analyze adversary will to fight. The U.S. Army sponsored our research to help bridge the gap between will-to-fight theory and practice. Together, this report and our forthcoming report on national will to fight represent the first of a series of planned reports.[18] Our approach was to consolidate and refine the various theories of

---

[15] We address Sarkesian's use of the term *subjective* later in this chapter. Sam C. Sarkesian, "Combat Effectiveness," in Sam C. Sarkesian, ed., *Combat Effectiveness: Cohesion, Stress, and the Volunteer Military,* Beverly Hills, Calif.: Sage Publications, 1980, p. 9.

[16] We provide extensive evidence of these points in this chapter, Chapter Two, and Appendix A.

[17] See Chapter Two for examples.

[18] The report on national will to fight describes and models the will to fight of individual national leaders. Findings and model factors in the national report are related to, but distinct from, the findings and model factors in this report. The term *national* refers to the nation, which is associated with, but distinct from, the state and society

Table 1.1
Outputs from the Will-to-Fight Research Project

Output	Brief Description
Model of will to fight	An explanatory, portable model focusing on military units
Assessment and analysis guide	A guide to assess, analyze, and influence will to fight
Simulation experiment	Demonstration of will to fight in an existing military simulation

will to fight into a working model and then translate this model into practical assessment and influence methods. We are also developing a process for incorporating will to fight into gaming and simulation. This report builds from a wealth of existing literature and from original multiple-method (multimethod) research to help the U.S. ground combat forces—the U.S. Army and U.S. Marine Corps—understand adversary and ally will to fight.[19] Table 1.1 shows the outputs of our research.

Definitions

We define will to fight as *the disposition and decision to fight, to act, or to persevere when needed.* Our model of will to fight is made up of 29 factors and 61 subfactors derived from a nine-part multimethod research effort. A section on methodology later in this chapter explains our approach. Detailed descriptions and analysis are in Chapters Two and Three and the appendixes. Several terms closely associated with will to fight emerge in the discussion. Our research team developed the following definitions as an output of the research. Each of these is explained in greater detail throughout the first two chapters of the report.

> *Morale*: a transient, partial indicator of will to fight that often has counterintuitive and misleading meanings[20]
>
> *Cohesion*: social and task bonding within and between military units[21]

---

in the tactical-operational model. These models serve separate purposes. They cannot, and should not, be merged, nor should the factors be correlated for assessment or analysis.

[19]   While this project focused on ground combat, many of the principles and findings are relevant to air and naval combat.

[20]   Morale is a particularly difficult term to define. See Chapter Two for a detailed explanation of morale. Note that we do not include morale as a factor in the model.

[21]   Collective tasks build instrumental bonding that in turn builds a commitment to collective goals and also a willingness to sacrifice to achieve the mission.

Horizontal (soldier-to-soldier) and vertical (soldier-to-leader) bonding, amity, comradeship, trust, and mutuality form social cohesion. Nodes of social cohesion are often called "peer" and "leader" in military cohesion models.

Motivation: individual and sometimes group or organizational drivers of will to fight[22]

Discipline: a product and indicator of control[23]

Esprit de corps: group spirit[24]

Leadership: the act of a single person in authority directing and encouraging the behavior of soldiers to accomplish a military mission[25]

Ideology: commitment to a cause or belief system

Culture: transmitted behaviors, habits, and beliefs of groups of people

Report Roadmap

Chapter One of this report explains the relevance of will to fight and sets a firm basis for the model. It describes will to fight and its relevance to the U.S. military, identifies gaps in capability, and lays out the research approach. In order to move quickly to the model, we reserve a detailed examination of will to fight in U.S. Army and Marine Corps doctrine for Appendix C. Chapter Two presents the model of unit-level will to fight, describing all of the factors and subfactors that influence unit disposition to fight in war. This model is the centerpiece of the report. Our war gaming and simulation analysis and experimentation on will to fight were conducted in parallel with the development of the model. Both efforts informed the model. Chapter Three presents the gaming and simulation results, as well as an extant will-to-fight model that we call the Silver Model. Chapter Four presents key findings and recommendations. Appendix A describes our literature review and the literature coding process. Appendix B describes our case study process. Appendix D summarizes results from our interviews. Appendix E provides detail on the simulation of the Silver Model intended to support replication of our experiments.

---

[22] Motivations are individual drivers of will to fight, like desperation and ideology. Individuals adopt motivations from culture and from environmental pressures like desperation to survive. Unit and organizational motivations grow organically and are imposed on individuals in a concerted effort to generate will to fight.

[23] Control is the approach an organization or unit takes to build and sustain will to fight and accomplish missions. Discipline reflects the cultural approach to control and defines the relationships between leaders and soldiers. It consists of a mix of persuasion and coercion.

[24] Members of a particular unit develop part of their individual identity in relation to the unit and to the organization. Identity shaping takes into account unit history, success or failure on the battlefield (or in training), interunit competition, and external opinions of the unit.

[25] Leadership is constituted of many subfactors, but competence and character matter most for will to fight. Competence is the leader's ability to accomplish tasks and a demonstrated ability to win. Character is the leader's integrity, willingness to sacrifice for soldiers, adherence to rules and regulations, and the ability to adapt in order to succeed and whenever possible ensure soldier safety.

Arguing for Relevance

Theories of will to fight are in perpetual competition for the attention of American military leaders distracted by more concrete and technical explanations of war. This means we have to first present expert testimony and evidence that will to fight matters. The remainder of this chapter explains the importance of will to fight, describes the gap between Western theory and practice, and sets a baseline for the suggested improvements that follow. Appendix C describes the ebb and flow of will to fight in American military thought and doctrine.

Will to Fight Matters but Is Hard to Incorporate into Practice

As this report was published, American ground combat forces and the U.S. Joint Force clearly and unequivocally subscribe to the theoretical preeminence of will to fight. This central assumption about the nature of war is primarily derived from Prussian strategist Carl Von Clausewitz's early 1800s treatise *Vom Kriege*, or *On War*. Clausewitz's name evokes a variety of responses from American military officers ranging from loving obeisance to eye-rolling dismissal. Even in early twentieth-century German military circles his name had been repeated so often that hearing it made the chief of the general staff "sick."[26] Whether he is loved, hated, or accepted with a shrug, Clausewitz is consistently the single greatest influence on modern Western military theory. War historian and political scientist Beatrice Heuser wrote, "By the end of the twentieth century, the heritage of Clausewitz's contest of wills was so widespread as to be taken for granted."[27] He defines war for the entire U.S. Joint Force.[28] His broader work is partly flawed and sometimes contradictory, but his explanation of will to fight is axiomatic.

Clausewitz wrote: "War is thus an act of force to compel the enemy to do our will."[29] In nearly word-for-word acceptance of Clausewitzean theory, both the U.S. Army and the U.S. Marine Corps argue that war is, at its essence, a contest of opposing, independent wills.[30] Both the Army and the Marine Corps accept—*in theory*—

---

[26]   Beatrice Heuser, *Reading Clausewitz*, London: Pimlico, 2002, p. 22.

[27]   Heuser, 2002, p. 84.

[28]   U.S. Joint Staff, 2013, pp. I-2 to I-4. Chinese general-scholar Sun Tzu provides lesser included contributions to this definition and discussion.

[29]   Heuser, 2002, p. 84. There are several translations of *On War* and many different interpretations of his writings. There may be different interpretations of this quote or any other listed throughout our report. See Christopher Bassford, *Clausewitz in English: The Reception of Clausewitz in Britain and America, 1815–1945*, Oxford: Oxford University Press, 1994; and, for example: "The compulsory submission of the enemy to our will is the ultimate object [of war]," in Carl Von Clausewitz, *On War*, trans. Colonel J. J. Graham, 1873.

[30]   U.S. Joint Chiefs of Staff, *Major Combat Operations Joint Operating Concept*, Version 2.0, Washington, D.C.: Joint Staff, December 2006; U.S. Army, 2016b; U.S. Marine Corps, 1997. Historical examples and other literature references are presented throughout this chapter and the remainder of this report. Allied military forces also

that violence is a necessary means to break enemy will and not an end unto itself.[31] In 2016 U.S. Army doctrine writers staked this claim:[32]

> War is a human endeavor—a fundamentally human clash of wills often fought among populations. It is not a mechanical process that can be controlled precisely, or even mostly, by machines, statistics, or laws that cover operations in carefully controlled and predictable environments. *Fundamentally, all war is about changing human behavior.*

The Army goes on to explain that military force is necessary to deny the objectives of the enemy and to win the continuous struggle to maintain the advantage of tempo. But the ultimate purpose of force is to defeat the enemy's will to fight, thereby ending the conflict:[33]

> Operational art formulates the most effective, efficient way to defeat enemy aims. Physically defeating the enemy deprives enemy forces of the ability to achieve those aims. Temporally defeating the enemy anticipates enemy reactions and counters them before they can become effective. *Psychologically defeating the enemy deprives the enemy of the will to continue the conflict.*

The Army's interpretation of war is built on strong foundations. It is rooted in both Western and Eastern military theory and reinforced by literature on military history, psychology, sociology, and, specifically, the literature on will to fight.[34] The U.S. Marine Corps has adopted a "philosophy of warfighting" that closely agrees with the Army's understanding of war:[35]

> The essence of war is a violent struggle between two hostile, independent, and irreconcilable wills, each trying to impose itself on the other. . . . While we try to impose our will on the enemy, he resists us and seeks to impose his own will on us.

---

accept this premise. For example, see UK Ministry of Defence, *Army Doctrine Primer*, AC 71954, Swindon, UK: Development, Concepts, and Doctrine Centre, 2011.

[31] Heuser and others point out that Clausewitz contradicts himself regarding the necessity for the use of force. Early parts of *On War* all but ignore will to fight, emphasizing instead the physical annihilation of the enemy force. But in Books VI and VII, which represent his more developed thinking, he emphasizes the role of force in the context of breaking enemy will. There is no way to fully disentangle *On War*; that is not the purpose of this report. Instead, it is important to understand how it may have been interpreted or, arguably, misinterpreted by American readers.

[32] U.S. Army, 2016b, p. 1–4; emphasis added.

[33] U.S. Army, 2016b, p. 2–3; emphasis added.

[34] Not including several hundred historical case study sources and uncoded books and articles that informed the researchers, the literature review for this project encompassed 202 scientific articles and books from a wide array of sources and fields of expertise. This literature review is presented in Appendix A.

[35] U.S. Marine Corps, 1997, pp. 3–4. As of mid-2018, MCDP-1 is still in effect as written in 1997.

Appreciating this dynamic interplay between opposing human wills is essential to understanding the fundamental nature of war.

Building from the writings of historian Ardant du Picq, French Marshal Ferdinand J. M. Foch, and many others, the Marine Corps goes on to argue that any doctrine failing to prioritize will to fight is failed doctrine:[36]

> No degree of technological development or scientific calculation will diminish the human dimension in war. Any doctrine which attempts to reduce warfare to ratios of forces, weapons, and equipment neglects the impact of the human will on the conduct of war and is therefore inherently flawed.

Long-standing and well-documented expert analysis and opinion reinforce these conclusions. While expert opinion does not establish fact, the best-known military theorists and accomplished officers attest to the foremost value of will to fight. It is safe to say there is a general expert consensus on the subject. A small sampling of this expert consensus on will to fight is informative.

Expert Consensus on the Importance of Will to Fight

In 1903 Marshal Foch, an avid follower of Clausewitzean theory and an icon in early twentieth-century French strategic thought, wrote, "No victory without fighting."[37] Yet in Foch's view, fighting was a means to win the predominant contest of wills. He described this fundamental principle in the form of simple equations:[38]

> War = the domain of moral force.
> Victory = moral superiority in the victors; moral depression in the vanquished.
> Battle = a struggle between two wills.

Foch's writings were fed into French military training and doctrine, which in turn had a powerful influence on concurrent American training and doctrine.[39] In his memoirs, the premier military commander of the United Kingdom's forces in World War II, British Field Marshal Viscount Bernard Law Montgomery wrote, "The morale

---

[36] U.S. Marine Corps, 1997, p. 14.

[37] Ferdinand Foch, *The Principles of War*, trans. Hilaire Belloc, New York: Henry Holt and Company, 1920, p. 32.

[38] Foch, 1920 (1903), p. 287. Foch's use of equations to explain the value of will to fight was intended as a retort to French military instructors who sought to explain war as a technical and tactical calculation absent will to fight.

[39] For example, in 1917 both the U.S. Army and the Marine Corps used French manuals to guide their training. For a detailed analysis of French influence on American military thought, see Michael A. Bonura, *French Thought and the American Military Mind: A History of French Influence on the American Way of Warfare from 1814 Through 1941*, thesis, Tallahassee: Florida State University, 2008.

of the soldier is the greatest single factor in war."[40] Contemporaneously, U.S. General of the Army George C. Marshall stated, "It is not enough to fight. It is the spirit which we bring to the fight that decides the issue. It is morale that wins the victory."[41] Nearly half a century later, U.S. General H. Norman Schwarzkopf stated, "[I]f you don't have the will to fight, then, you are not going to have a very good army."[42] Fifteen years after the Gulf War, then–Lieutenant General and (as of mid-2018) Secretary of Defense James N. Mattis stated, "It is mostly a matter of wills. . . . Whose will is going to break first? Ours or the enemy's?"[43] Clausewitz's fundamental premise that will is the most important factor in war endured in Western military discourse on the nature of war even as the character of warfare changed over nearly two centuries.[44]

Eastern generals and scholars came to the same fundamental conclusions about the importance of will to fight. Articulations varied, but the themes were remarkably consistent across both time and space. In the late sixth century BC, Chinese general-scholar Sun Tzu wrote, "In battle, a courageous spirit is everything."[45] After World War II, Soviet Field Marshal Georgy Konstantinovich Zhukov wrote, "It is a fact that under equal conditions, large-scale battles and whole wars are won by troops which have a strong will for victory, clear goals before them, high moral standards, and devotion to the banner under which they go into battle."[46] After defeating the United States and the Republic of Vietnam (RVN), Vietnamese general Vo Nguyen Giap stated: "Our intention was to break the will of the American Government to continue the war. . . . In war there are the two factors—human beings and weapons. Ultimately, though, human beings are the decisive factor. Human beings! Human beings!"[47] It has been difficult to find a substantial group of modern analysts or military leaders who disagree or hold a starkly opposing viewpoint.

---

[40]   Bernard Law Montgomery, *The Memoirs of the Field-Marshal the Viscount Montgomery of Alamein, K.G.*, Cleveland, Ohio: World Publishing Company, 1958, p. 83.

[41]   George C. Marshall, quoted in H. A. de Weerd, ed., *Selected Speeches and Statements of General of the Army George C. Marshall*, New York: De Capo Press, 1973 (quotes dated from 1945), p. 122.

[42]   H. Norman Schwarzkopf, quoted in Reuters, "War in the Gulf: Commander's Briefing; Excerpts from Schwarzkopf News Conference on Gulf War," *New York Times*, February 28, 1991.

[43]   James N. Mattis, quoted in Mark Walker, "Mattis: Success in Iraq Now a Test of Wills," *San Diego Union Tribune*, August 22, 2006.

[44]   We address this uneven discourse in the following sections.

[45]   There is ongoing debate over the date of original publication and even authorship of Sun Tzu's work. *The Art of War* may have been originally published in the fifth century BC. This quote is from Lionel Giles, trans., *Sun Tzu on the Art of War: The Oldest Military Treatise in the World*, London: Luzac, 1910, p. 70.

[46]   Georgy Konstantinovich Zhukov, *The Memoirs of Marshal Zhukov*, trans. Jonathan Cape, London: Jonathan Cape Ltd., 1971 (1969), p. 301.

[47]   Vo Nguyen Giap, quoted in Stanley Karnow, "Giap Remembers," *New York Times*, June 24, 1990.

Proponents of a mechanistic approach to understanding warfare certainly exist and have existed throughout recorded history; see Appendix C. But there is no broadly accepted school of theory or practice making a convincing argument that will to fight is irrelevant or that it is less important than other factors when all other things are equal. Even tactically focused theories like those espoused in Clausewitz's early writings, and contemporary mechanistic theories like those associated with the Revolution in Military Affairs (RMA) avoid claiming that will to fight is *unimportant*. Theories that emphasize the so-called hard aspects of war tend to ignore will to fight rather than argue it away.[48] Will to fight has endured as a central theme or at least a strong undercurrent in military theory for centuries. Yet it is also difficult to find examples of modern Western militaries that expertly incorporated and sustained focus on both internal (own force) and external (enemy or allied force) will-to-fight considerations over time.[49]

Western Failure to Fully Incorporate Will to Fight into Military Practice

For over a century the foremost experts on will to fight have bemoaned the inability of Western military organizations to remain focused on its premises and practices. They see instead a center-rest return to the more tangible and intellectually obtainable aspects of war like technology, training, and battlefield tactics. Or they focus on internal will-to-fight issues but fail to concentrate on the issues most relevant to this report: the will to fight of allies and adversaries. These experts warn of the potentially disastrous impact of such discordant military practice.

Some of the first written complaints emerged less than half a century after the publication of *On War*.[50] In 1870 Ardent du Picq warned that the emphasis on "mathematical and material dynamics" at the expense of the moral factors in war—will to fight—resulted in stubborn and persistent illusions about the real nature of war.[51] At the same time that Marshal Foch proposed his will-to-fight formula for war (1903) he complained that French military instructors failed to convey the importance of moral factors.[52] Foch, writing at what may have been the zenith of European fixation on the

---

[48]   It is not clear that John Keegan suggested this argument in *The Face of Battle*, though he did suggest that modern warfare might entirely obviate the need for battle; Keegan, 1976. Former director of the Defense Advanced Research Project Agency Robert Cooper offered an alternative viewpoint in 1983: "We don't have the resolve to support a many-millions-of-men army with all of the equipment required to stand the Soviets off. And so consequently we have no other alternative but to turn to high technology. That's it." This argument was one of the early signals of the impending effort to develop an RMA, a concept that generally eschewed human factors. Michael Schrage, "The Sword of Science," interview with Robert Cooper, *Washington Post*, October 9, 1983.

[49]   As we discuss in the following chapters, the Chinese and Vietnamese have been quite successful in centralizing and leveraging will to fight.

[50]   Clausewitz wrote *On War* in the early 1800s, probably between 1815 and 1830. The volume was originally published in 1832.

[51]   Du Picq, 1921 (1870), pp. 40–41.

[52]   Foch, 1920 (1903), p. 3.

importance of will to fight, had seen these shortcomings firsthand as an instructor and as the commandant at the French *École de Guerre*.[53] British Lieutenant Colonel John Baynes's 1967 analysis of morale in World War I begins with the words "This book is an attempt to fill a gap."[54] In 1978, British Major General F. M. Richardson wrote:[55]

> Napoleon's dictum that the mental is to the physical as three is to one is constantly chanted like a magic mantra in military circles. Much more than mere lip service is paid to morale in every aspect of military training. It is, however, questionable if quite enough is done in a really positive way.

The drumbeat of warnings continued: In a 1982 study of tactical-operational will to fight for the Canadian armed forces, Anthony Kellett warned that the overemphasis on internal will to fight to maintain *peacetime* armies meant that "the human requirements of *combat* have been given rather less consideration."[56] In his 1985 comparative analysis of American, Israeli, Russian, and North Vietnamese cohesion, American Army Lieutenant Colonel William Darryl Henderson argued that the "failure to consider the human element in war adequately and an overemphasis on weapons capabilities, number of troops, and other concrete factors" needed remedy; he purposed his book for an American land forces audience in the aftermath of the Vietnam War.[57] In his 1991 introduction to a book on British and Argentinian combat cohesion in the Falklands War, the Technical Director of the U.S. Army Research Lab lamented American overemphasis on technology at the expense of human factors in war. He wrote:[58]

> [T]echnology is not a "silver bullet" capable of solving or neutralizing any military problem. As Vietnam reminded a nation, wars are fought and won by men, not machines. In the final analysis, the outcome of war is decided by men on the battlefield.

---

[53]   Charles W. Sanders, Jr., *No Other Law: The French Army and the Doctrine of the Offensive*, Santa Monica, Calif.: RAND Corporation, P-7331, 1987, p. 6.

[54]   John Baynes, *Morale: A Study of Men and Courage*, Garden City Park, N.Y.: Avery Publishing Group, Inc., 1988, p. 8. Baynes was referring to the gap in analysis of will to fight in World War I. In later chapters he explains how this gap is relevant to contemporaneous military organizations.

[55]   F. M. Richardson, *Fighting Spirit: Psychological Factors in War*, New Delhi, India: Nahtraj Publishers, 2009 (1978), p. 139.

[56]   Anthony Kellett, *Combat Motivation: The Behavior of Soldiers in Battle*, Hingham, Mass.: Kluwer Boston, Inc., 1982, p. xvii; emphasis added.

[57]   William Darryl Henderson, *Cohesion: The Human Element in Combat*, Washington, D.C.: National Defense University Press, 1985, p. 3.

[58]   Edgar M. Johnson, quoted in Nora Kinzer Stewart, *Mates and Muchachos: Unit Cohesion in the Falklands/ Malvinas War*, McLean, Va.: Brassey's (U.S.), Inc., 1991, p. xi.

Similar complaints about Western militaries attended every interwar period of the twentieth century, and they have emerged again as focus on the wars in Afghanistan and Iraq—where soldiers from Britain, France, Netherlands, Norway, Germany, Italy, and other Western nations served—has waned.[59]

There is a pattern in the wavering emphasis on will to fight.[60] A major war occurs and Western literature on the will to fight dribbles forth. A few aspects of will to fight are incorporated into military practice, some are ignored, and some are embraced only after a decade or more of debate. Gradually the most painful lessons of war fade as combat veterans retire. Practicalities of technique, technology, and tactics shove the seemingly esoteric considerations of will to fight into the background. A new war erupts, painful lessons are briefly and only partly relearned, and then are again gradually forgotten.[61] The consequences of this ebb and flow stand testament to the pressing need to improve and normalize the study of will to fight in American military practice and to make its lessons useful.

Consequences of Misjudging or Failing to Influence Will to Fight

Western military history is replete with failures and triumphs in the effort to understand will to fight. Because will to fight matters in every case, each historical case should offer lessons. Most cases, though, offer only a murky middle ground for researchers seeking causal evidence: Where was it absolutely clear that strong or weak will to fight caused success or failure? Clarity is hard to sustain in the absence of a stark event like a rout or surrender. Quantifiable comparison of all the factors of war to determine a firm causative outcome in any one battle, let alone in a set of large case studies, is a fool's errand.

Still, there are clear lessons to be found, particularly for the focus of this study: assessment and influence of ally and adversary will to fight. This section describes the disastrous consequences of German failure to assess French will to fight at Verdun. The next section provides cases specific to the American experience with assessing ally and adversary will to fight.

---

[59] For example: Anthony King, "On Combat Effectiveness in the Infantry Platoon: Beyond the Primary Group Thesis," *Security Studies*, Vol. 25, No. 4, 2016, pp. 699–728; Peter van den Aker, Jacco Duel, and Joseph Soeters, "Combat Motivation and Combat Action: Dutch Soldiers in Operations Since the Second World War; A Research Note," *Armed Forces and Society*, Vol. 42, No. 1, 2016, pp. 211–225.

[60] Kellett sees this pattern as well in his observation beginning with World War II. Kellett, 1982, p. xiv. Anthony King made the same observation in 2015. Anthony King, "On Cohesion," in Anthony King, ed., *Frontline: Combat and Cohesion in the Twenty-First Century*, Oxford: Oxford University Press, 2015, p. 6.

[61] Many examples of this ebb and flow are readily accessible. A notable example is the shift in French military doctrine and application from a will-to-fight centric to a technology-and-fortification-centric military between World War I and World War II. See Barry R. Posen, *The Source of Military Doctrine: France, Britain, and Germany Between the World Wars*, Ithaca, N.Y.: Cornell University Press, 2014; Elizabeth Kier, "Culture and Military Doctrine: France Between the Wars," *International Security*, Vol. 19, No. 4, Spring 1995, pp. 65–93.

Falkenhayn at Verdun

World War I German Chief of Staff Erich von Falkenhayn is a testament to the ability of Western military officers to understand, appreciate, and incorporate will to fight into the planning and execution of military operations.[62] Falkenhayn interpreted every move through the lens of moral force: Attack would most likely succeed when enemy will to fight was low, and stood a good chance of failure if enemy will to fight was high.[63] Falkenhayn also provides a case study in the failure of tactical-operational intelligence to accurately assess opponent will to fight and a testament to military hubris. While he tried to put Clausewitz's theories of will to fight into practice, he erred badly at Verdun.

In late 1915 Falkenhayn and the rest of the general staff planned a large offensive near the Meuse River. Their intent was to break French state will to fight. According to Falkenhayn's plan, French military defeat would be so terrible and irrecoverable that France would quit the war. This would leave the British at the mercy of what would be a correspondingly larger German Army. Falkenhayn selected the French position at Verdun as the focal point of the offensive. Here the French had unintentionally extended their lines in a broad salient centered on the Meuse heights. This position left the French flanks exposed, and only narrow routes for reinforcement and counterattack. Figure 1.1 depicts the battle lines at Verdun between the beginning of the German offensive in 1916 and the limit of German advance. The general direction of the German attack was north to south, or top to bottom in the map.[64]

The German plan called for massive artillery bombardments followed by a multi-division ground assault intended to trigger a crushing rout. German intelligence backed Falkenhayn's assessment of French will to fight:[65]

> Many French deserters spoke of the war-weariness of the French soldiers and particularly of the adverse effect on French morale of the failure of and the high casualties suffered during the offensives in [1915]. . . . When the French began instituting a defense in depth and leaving their first trench line only lightly defended, German intelligence interpreted this to mean that the French command feared that their troops would break under the German *Trommelfeuer* [drumfire].

---

[62]   This summary of the German assessment of French will to fight at Verdun is drawn from Robert T. Foley, *German Strategy and the Path to Verdun: Erich Von Falkenhayn and the Development of Attrition, 1870–1916*, Cambridge: Cambridge University Press, 2005; Robert Chamberlain, "The Mud of Verdun: Falkenhayn and the Future of American Landpower," *Military Review*, July–August 2016, pp. 78–87; Erich von Falkenhayn, *The German General Staff and Its Decisions, 1914–1916*, New York: Dodd, Mead, and Company, Inc., 1920 (1919); and Alistair Horne, *The Price of Glory: Verdun 1916*, New York: St. Martin's Press, 1962.

[63]   Falkenhayn, 1920 (1919), p. 197. He specifically referred to military and moral condition. Also see page 223.

[64]   Francis J. Reynolds, Allen L. Churchill, and Francis Trevelyan Miller, *The Story of the Great War: History of the European War from Official Sources*, New York: P. F. Collier and Sons, 1916, Book Six, p. 85. This is a copyright-free book available through Project Gutenberg.

[65]   Foley, 2005, p. 185.

Figure 1.1
The Battle of Verdun

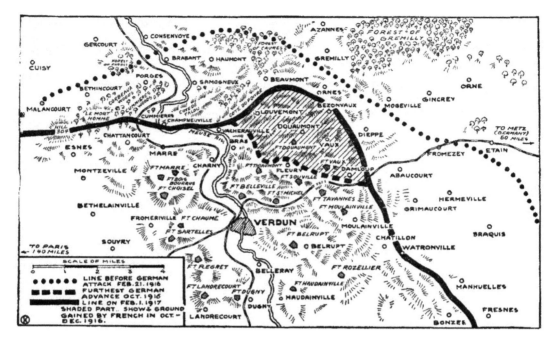

SOURCE: Churchill, Reynolds, and Miller, 1916

RAND *RR2341A-1.1*

While French will to fight was indeed suffering, the German assessment of French tactical-operational will to fight at Verdun was dangerously exaggerated and arguably wrong. German intelligence officers made two mistakes. First, they failed to account for the French *noria* system.[66] French *Général de Division* Philippe Pétain, then commander of the Second Army's Verdun salient, recognized that French soldiers were suffering from exhaustion. His *noria* reserve rotation plan was designed to provide soldiers rest, to rebuild their will to fight, and to ensure the Germans would face only fresh troops with strong will to fight.[67] To the German intelligence officers, this rotation—designed to improve French will to fight—gave the appearance of thinned lines and weak will.

Second, the Germans assessed that the poor morale (or temporary feelings) of captured French troops amounted to poor will to fight among all French troops. It is generally unwise to extrapolate the unsurprisingly sour disposition of prisoners to the

---

[66]   *Noria* refers to a system of connected, rotating buckets designed to pull water from a well.

[67]   Peter Edwards, "Mort pour la France: Conflict and Commemoration in France After the First World War," *University of Sussex Journal of Contemporary History*, Vol. 1, 2000, p. 5.

will to fight of active, armed soldiers, at least not without solid corroboration. More importantly, the Germans took poor individual morale to be an indicator of weak unit cohesion and the unwillingness of the Second Army to hold the line or counterattack. Yet it is possible—even common—to have poor individual will and *strong* collective, unit-level will to fight. Despite the external appearances given by poor prisoner morale, the French at Verdun were more than ready to hold the line against withering German artillery fire and bayonets. Falkenhayn's entire plan rested on a false assumption about French will to fight, and the plan failed.

Both sides suffered tremendous losses. French casualties exceeded 300,000. But the Second Army held and Falkenhayn's plan cost the Germans an equivalent number of casualties: over 300,000.[68] German casualties over ten months at Verdun may have amounted to approximately two-thirds of the entire U.S. Army's active duty force in early 2018.[69] Many other factors contributed to German failure, including bad weather that bogged down German artillery. Whatever the proximate cause of their tactical defeat, the Germans did not achieve their objectives: Falkenhayn failed to seize Verdun, failed to break French tactical-operational will to fight in 1916, and failed to break French state will to fight.[70] The war went on for another two years, and the losses at Verdun contributed to Germany's strategic defeat.

Writing about Verdun in his 1919 memoirs, Falkenhayn describes "powerful German thrusts" that had "shaken the whole enemy front in the West very severely" and that had placed doubt in the minds of the Entente partners. French counterattacks were "desperate," made up of troops collected in "extreme haste."[71] He estimated German to French casualties at an unrealistic 2:5 ratio.[72] He follows with paeans to German will to fight, and it is abundantly clear throughout his memoir that he had little respect for French fighting spirit.[73] Falkenhayn is to be commended for his genuine appreciation for will to fight as a central factor in war. If he had had a better analysis method to help him understand French will to fight, he might have altered

---

[68] Horne, 1962, p. 327. Estimates of total casualties vary by source.

[69] As of February 2018, the total active force was 471,513. See the U.S. Department of Defense website, March 29, 2018. This website is periodically updated.

[70] Alistair Horne argues that while the French may have survived Verdun, the *noria* system fed so many soldiers through the front lines that, as a whole, the Army came away traumatized. Horne believes Verdun fed French defeatism in World War II. Alistair Horne, "The Legend of Verdun," *NewStatesman*, February 17, 2016. Building from Horne's work and from Richard Watt's *Dare Call It Treason* (New York: Simon and Schuster, 1963), Bruce Allen Watson argues that French tactical-operational will to fight degenerated for a whole host of mostly internal military, political, and social reasons in the year after the battle for Verdun. Bruce Allen Watson, *When Soldiers Quit: Studies in Military Disintegration*, Westport, Conn.: Greenwood Publishing Group, 1997, Chapter Four.

[71] Falkenhayn, 1920 (1919), p. 266.

[72] Falkenhayn, 1920 (1919), p. 270.

[73] Lack of respect for French will to fight and tactical prowess was common among members of the German officer corps, dating back to at least the early Prussian era.

his plans. His hubris and jingoistic vision of Teutonic will to fight made the defeat at Verdun far more likely.[74] Nothing can be done about hubris. Much can be done about will-to-fight analysis.

Impact of American Will-to-Fight Assessment and Analysis Failures

In Appendix C we describe the wavering and generally inadequate efforts by American ground combat forces—the Army and Marine Corps—to consistently incorporate will to fight into doctrine, assessments, and analyses. It is no surprise, then, that in case after case following World War II, American political and military leaders failed to take full measure of either ally or adversary will to fight.[75] They misjudged, discounted, or purposefully ignored will to fight even as they were presented with convincing evidence that will to fight might be their undoing. Compounding, and perhaps in some cases justifying, this unwillingness to act is the lack of credible assessment methods or even a widely agreed-on definition of will to fight. Some blame must fall on military theorists and the scientific community.

Whatever the cause, from at least the early 1950s through today, the military, political, economic, and social costs of this dissonance between accepted theory and practice have been extraordinary: Failure to assess Arab will to fight in the 1973 Yom Kippur War nearly led to the destruction of Israel, and it pushed the United States and the Soviet Union to the brink of war. Successful analyses of North Vietnamese will to fight from 1954 to 1974 were effectively ignored, leading to strategic defeat. Failure to assess Iraqi Army will to fight in 2011 contributed to the rise of the Islamic State and the continuation of a war that the United States had declared to be over in 2011.[76]

1973 War: Adversary Analysis Failure

Israel's resounding defeat of the Arab armies in the 1967 Six-Day War left Israeli military leadership and intelligence analysts with a false sense of invulnerability. They built their post-1967 defensive preparations on the belief that Arabs had poor tactical-operational will to fight. One Israeli general reportedly stated, "We're fighting Arabs, not Germans."[77] A U.S. Army historian later noted the Israelis' "arrogant and patron-

---

[74]   In his assessment of Falkenhayn's hubris at Verdun, Paul Jankowski wrote, "No battle punctured his illusions more violently, or assured his downfall more inexorably, than the battle for Verdun." Paul Jankowski, *Verdun: The Longest Battle of the Great War*, New York: Oxford University Press, 2013, p. 82.

[75]   Cases are presented later in this report.

[76]   We did not identify any obvious examples of success.

[77]   Abraham Rabinovich, "Yom Kippur War: Against the Odds," *Jewish Journal*, September 11, 2013.

izing attitude toward the Arabs" after 1967.[78] Israelis believed that Arabs had little or no will to fight. This Israeli perspective informed American perceptions of Arab military forces. Misconstrued lessons from the Six-Day War led Central Intelligence Agency (CIA) analysts to conclude that the relative will to fight of Israeli versus Arab soldiers would offset any foreseen Arab threat and even deter war.[79] Arabs could not fight aggressively so they probably would not fight at all. These mistaken assumptions would underpin the wider intelligence failure that nearly led to the defeat of the Israeli military.

In October 1973 Egypt and Syria conducted a massive dual-front surprise attack across the Sinai Peninsula in the west and the Golan Heights in the east. American intelligence agencies were caught off guard: They had published a number of firm analytic arguments stating that Egypt and Syria would not attack.[80] Initial Arab victories shocked the Israelis and the world. Egyptian columns penetrated the vaunted Bar-Lev defensive line in the western Sinai and decimated the Israeli Sinai Division.[81] Israeli president Golda Meir may have been on the brink of launching a nuclear strike to prevent total collapse.[82] Israeli forces regrouped and eventually defeated the Egyptian and Syrian armies. Israeli violations of an ensuing ceasefire nearly pushed the United States and the Soviet Union into a conventional and perhaps nuclear war. One historian called this "the most dangerous moment of the Cold War since the Cuban missile crisis of 1962."[83] War between the superpowers was thankfully averted.

A scathing internal assessment of this American intelligence failure stated that the analysts were "quite simply, obviously, and starkly—wrong."[84] Their main failure was in misinterpreting the decisionmaking of Egyptian president Anwar al-Sadat. But the report noted that a key component of this failure was the "impact of preconceptions" and specifically those about Arab tactical military will to fight:[85]

---

[78]   George W. Gawrych, *The 1973 Arab-Israeli War: The Albatross of Decisive Victory*, Leavenworth Papers Number 21, Fort Leavenworth, Kan.: Combat Studies Institute, U.S. Army Command and General Staff College, 1996, p. 52.

[79]   Director of Central Intelligence, *The Performance of the Intelligence Community Before the Arab-Israeli War of October 1973: A Preliminary Post-Mortem Report*, declassified intelligence assessment, Washington, D.C.: Intelligence Community Staff, December 1973, p. 14.

[80]   Director of Central Intelligence, 1973.

[81]   Uri Bar-Joseph, *The 1973 Yom Kippur War*, Israel Studies: An Anthology, Jewish Virtual Library Publications, May 2009.

[82]   Avner Cohen, "The Last Nuclear Moment," *New York Times*, October 6, 2003.

[83]   Elizabeth Stephens, "Caught on the Hop: The Yom Kippur War," *History Today*, October 2008, p. 44.

[84]   Director of Central Intelligence, 1973, p. 14.

[85]   Director of Central Intelligence, 1973, p. 14.

There was . . . a fairly widespread notion based largely (although perhaps not entirely) on past performances that many Arabs, as Arabs, simply weren't up to the demands of modern warfare and that they lacked understanding, motivation, and probably in some cases courage as well.

On the same page it states: "There is no question that the effect of errors of judgment concerning Arab military capabilities on the [Intelligence] Community's political estimates was significant." Mistaken assumptions about Arab tactical will to fight corrupted analysts' assumptions about the will to fight of Arab leaders, preventing the United States from warning its allies or stepping in to prevent a war that might in turn have escalated the Cold War.[86]

1954–1974 Vietnam War: Some Analytic Success but Political Failure

The case of the Vietnam War shows that even accurate intelligence analyses of will to fight are meaningless if they are ignored by decisionmakers. Table 1.2 presents selected quotes from 20 years of CIA intelligence assessments of the will to fight of the leaders of the Democratic Republic of Vietnam (DRV).[87] Each report folds in a range of tactical-operational reports just as the state-level analyses of Arab will to fight derived in part from tactical-operational input. This table shows a consistent series of straightforward analytic conclusions: The DRV had a deep reservoir of will to fight.

In this case the CIA analysts got it right. But despite their persistent warnings—echoed by some senior administration officials behind closed doors—the United States sought to break the will of DRV leaders through measured escalation and by imposing casualties.[88] The analysts were right, but they failed to convince policymakers or to influence a meaningful change in policy. The United States failed to break DRV will to fight, lost its own political will to fight, and fled Vietnam in 1975 having lost nearly 60,000 Americans. Defeat in Vietnam continues to haunt American political decisionmaking today.

Much has been written about decisionmaking in the Vietnam War. Instead of looking at the decisionmaking fed by the analysis, for our purposes it is more useful to look at the analysis that fed the decisionmaking. The narratives about will to fight

---

[86]   This will necessarily remain speculation. However, on October 17, at the height of the escalatory tensions with the Soviet Union, President Richard M. Nixon made the following statement to his cabinet members: "The Soviets have got to choose: will they risk our whole relationship in order to test us in the Middle East? They have got to know we won't be pushed around in our support of any nation anywhere." Richard M. Nixon, quoted in U.S. Central Intelligence Agency, *WSAG Principals: Middle East War*, declassified memorandum, Washington, D.C.: The White House, October 17, 1973.

[87]   For overviews of U.S. intelligence activities in Vietnam, see Bruce Palmer, Jr., "U.S. Intelligence and Vietnam," declassified article, *Studies in Intelligence*, Vol. 28, Special Edition, 1984; Michael B. Petersen, *The Vietnam Cauldron: Defense Intelligence in the War for Southeast Asia*, Washington, D.C.: Defense Intelligence Agency, 2012.

[88]   See H. R. McMaster, *Dereliction of Duty: Lyndon Johnson, Robert McNamara, the Joint Chiefs of Staff, and the Lies That Led to Vietnam*, New York: HarperCollins, 1997.

Table 1.2
CIA Assessments of DRV Will to Fight from 1954 to 1974

Year	Analysis
1954	In sum, we believe that the Communists will not give up their objective of securing control of all Indochina but will . . . pursue their objective by political, psychological, and military means. [The DRV] will seek to develop strong overt Communist political groups where possible and will generally use all available means towards the eventual unification of the country under Communist control.
1964	We believe that the North Vietnamese leaders look at Communist prospects with considerable confidence. In South Vietnam, they probably feel that GVN [Government of Viet Nam] will to resist is waning and may feel that the same is true of the US.
1966	For thirty-six years the Vietnamese Communist Party has struggled unrelentingly to acquire political control in Vietnam. During this period the Vietnamese Communists have often altered their strategy but never their objective, which remains today what it was when the Party was founded in 1930. . . . The Communists almost certainly do not have any fixed or rigid timetable for victory. . . . The wearing effects of the war are causing some decline of civilian morale in North Vietnam. . . . The decline, however, has not had any meaningful impact upon the determination of the regime to continue with the war. . . .
1968	North Vietnam, with Bloc aid, has the will and the resources to continue fighting for a long time.
1970	Hanoi still considers that it has the will and basic strengths to prevail. . . . Despite Hanoi's obvious concerns with its problems, the Communists almost certainly believe that they enjoy some basic strengths and advantages which will ultimately prove to be decisive.
1974	Hanoi continues to demonstrate its determination to impose Communist control on the South. There has been no apparent curtailment in Hanoi's support for [the war]. . . . Finally, even if there is not a major offensive during the next year, it is clear that at some point Hanoi will shift back to major warfare in its effort to gain control of South Vietnam.

SOURCES: U.S. Central Intelligence Agency, *Post-Geneva Outlook in Indochina*, National Intelligence Estimate Number 63-5-54, Washington, D.C.: Director of Central Intelligence, August 3, 1954, pp. 3, 5; U.S. Central Intelligence Agency, *The Outlook for North Vietnam*, SNIE 14.3-64, Washington, D.C.: Director of Central Intelligence, March 4, 1964, p. 1; U.S. Central Intelligence Agency, *The Vietnamese Communists Will to Persist*, memorandum, Director of Central Intelligence, August 26, 1966; U.S. Central Intelligence Agency, *Special Assessment on Vietnam*, Washington, D.C.: CIA, May 24, 1967; U.S. Central Intelligence Agency, *The Attitudes of North Vietnamese Leaders Towards Fighting and Negotiating*, Washington, D.C.: CIA, March 25, 1968, p. 47; U.S. Central Intelligence Agency, *The Outlook from Hanoi: Factors Affecting North Vietnam's Policy on the War in Vietnam*, Special National Intelligence Estimate 14.3-70, Washington, D.C.: Director of Central Intelligence, February 5, 1970, pp. 1, 6; U.S. Central Intelligence Agency, *The Likelihood of a Major North Vietnamese Offensive Against South Vietnam Before June 30, 1975*, National Intelligence Estimate 14.3-1-74, Washington, D.C.: Director of Central Intelligence, May 23, 1974, pp. 5, 9.

were thorough and should have been convincing. But they lacked the kind of structural backbone necessary to sway policymakers. Without a model of will to fight, intelligence analyses seeking to explain it came across as subjective. *Subjective* is unfortunately a pejorative term in policy.[89] A model would have helped in this case, in the 1973 War case, and, as the next section shows, in Iraq.

---

[89] For a discussion of the use of the term *subjective* in assessment see Connable, 2012.

2011 Iraq Withdrawal: Ally Assessment Failure

In 2011 the United States withdrew from Iraq in what was intended to be the end of an eight-year war. Official assessments by the U.S. Forces-Iraq in 2011 claimed that, despite some shortcomings, the Iraqi Security Forces were ready to take over the responsibility for securing Iraq.[90] Some expert observers lamented the hurried nature of the time-driven ending. But in 2011 RAND interviewed American officers in Iraq who believed that "the ISF had achieved the capabilities necessary to maintain internal security and address threats from violent extremist organizations."[91] Lieutenant General Babaker Zebari, Iraq's Army chief of staff, disagreed: He stated publicly that the Iraqi Army would not be ready until 2020.[92] These concerns did not halt the withdrawal.

Just three years after the last U.S. Army unit left Iraq, small groups of irregular, lightly armed Islamic State fighters defeated the Iraqi Army, seized over one-third of the entire country, and threatened to invest the capital. Four Iraqi Army divisions disintegrated without fighting. They abandoned their equipment and left fellow soldiers to face brutal execution.[93] After these dramatic defeats, U.S. Secretary of Defense Ashton B. Carter complained that "the Iraqi forces just showed no will to fight."[94] American military advisors and combat aircraft had to return to prevent the country's total collapse. As of mid-2018 Iraqi forces had recaptured all territory from the Islamic State, but vast sections of the country's infrastructure had been destroyed.[95]

Will to Fight, American Military Power, and the Need for Improvement

There is an odd dichotomy in U.S. ground combat service application of will-to-fight theories. Focus on will-to-fight factors like leadership, training, discipline, esprit, and motivation in the development of Army and Marine Corps *internal* combat effectiveness assessments has been fairly consistent from the interwar period through 2017.[96]

---

[90]   Richard R. Brennan, Jr., Charles P. Ries, Larry Hanauer, Ben Connable, Terrence K. Kelly, Michael J. McNerney, Stephanie Young, Jason Campbell, and K. Scott McMahon, *Ending the U.S. War in Iraq: The Final Transition, Operational Maneuver, and Disestablishment of the United States Forces-Iraq*, Santa Monica, Calif.: RAND Corporation, RR-232-USFI, 2013, p. 288.

[91]   Brennan et al., 2013, p. 309.

[92]   British Broadcasting Corporation, "Iraq General Says Planned U.S. Troop Pullout 'Too Soon,'" August 12, 2010.

[93]   Yassir Abbas and Dan Trombley, "Inside the Collapse of the Iraqi Army's 2d Division," *War on the Rocks*, July 1, 2014.

[94]   Greg Jaffe and Loveday Morris, "Defense Secretary Carter: Iraqis Lack 'Will to Fight' to Defeat Islamic State," *Washington Post*, May 24, 2015.

[95]   The first withdrawal occurred in 1991 after the Persian Gulf War. We address this case later. For an alternative viewpoint on Iraqi will to fight, see Adam Scher, "The Collapse of the Iraqi Army's Will to Fight: A Lack of Motivation, Training, or Force Generation?" *Army Press Online Journal*, February 19, 2016.

[96]   For example: Thomas M. Camfield, "'Will to Win'—The U.S. Army Troop Morale Program of World War I," *Military Affairs*, Vol. 41, No. 3, October 1977, pp. 125–128; Jennifer Diane Keene, "Intelligence and Morale

This is evident in service emphasis on strong leadership, adaptability, and motivation, and in providing critical support like rapid medical evacuation. It follows that if will to fight is essential to building American ground combat power, then it is also essential in understanding ally and adversary combat power.

Yet *external* assessments and analyses focused on allies and adversaries have not followed theory. Neither service can show much effort toward assessing, analyzing, or influencing ally or adversary will to fight. This gap applies to the Joint Force as well. Capstone joint doctrine acknowledges the critical importance of will to fight, but joint doctrine fails to provide clear guidance to help the services and combatant commands apply its principles. As of mid-2018 joint doctrine does not define or explain will to fight. The U.S. Joint Chiefs of Staff recognize this gap. In 2016 the Joint Staff published a concept paper identifying a gap across the Department of Defense (DoD) in the understanding of partner and adversary will to fight.[97] Reasons for this dichotomy are manifold. Arguably, the constant pursuit of a tactical or technological solution to the enduring nature of war prevents a wholehearted acceptance of will to fight as an internal and external priority. The Joint Staff made this argument in the JC-HAMO:[98]

> Recent failure to translate military gains into strategic success reflects, to some extent, the Joint Force's tendency to focus primarily on affecting the material *capabilities*—including hardware and personnel—of adversaries and friends, rather than their *will* to develop and employ those capabilities. . . . A failure to grasp human aspects can, and often will, result in a prolonged struggle and an inability to achieve strategic goals.

As the Joint Chiefs point out, these shortfalls are evident in the recent historical record. Failure to assess and act on will to fight may not have been causal in each case, but the American military track record since World War II has been poor. Various failings in Korea, Vietnam, Afghanistan, and Iraq have led to a general decline in American strategic performance: America is now a country that fails to win wars decisively. This decline in strategic performance happened even as American military technology and tactical acumen have advanced. Something is missing.

Improving understanding of will to fight might not be a panacea. But if it is the most important factor in war—or just *an* important factor in war that is routinely overlooked or misunderstood—then improvement is absolutely necessary. It is clear that American

---

in the Army of a Democracy," *Military Psychology*, Vol. 6, No. 4, 1994, pp. 235–253; Mark Vaitkus and James Griffith, "An Evaluation of Unit Replacement on Unit Cohesion and Individual Morale in the U.S. Army All-Volunteer Force," *Military Psychology*, Vol. 2, No. 4, 1990, pp. 221–239.

[97]   U.S. Joint Chiefs of Staff, *Joint Concept for Human Aspects of Military Operations (JC-HAMO)*, Washington, D.C.: Joint Staff, October 19, 2016.

[98]   U.S. Joint Chiefs of Staff, 2016, pp. 1–2.

political and military leaders should do more to incorporate will-to-fight assessment and analysis into planning, training, operations, and strategic decisionmaking.

Prospective Applications for U.S. Army Recruitment, Training, and Education

Our explanation and model of will to fight are focused on partners and adversaries. However, they are universal and have prospective applications for U.S. Army recruitment, training, and education. In 1980 William L. Hauser, former Army officer and director of the Army Research Institute for the Behavioral and Social Sciences, asked three questions about will to fight: (1) Where do soldiers (and collectively, units) get the will to fight? (2) Can the will to fight be measured in an individual soldier? and (3) If the will to fight can be and is measured, and is found to be lacking, can it be acquired?[99] Hauser believed at the time that the Army had not done enough to understand the will of its own soldiers and implored focused effort: "Improvement of the will to fight *must* become one of our highest defense priorities."[100] The Army has done considerable work to achieve this objective since Hauser issued his admonition and appeal. We cite a number of post-1980 officially sanctioned field studies that demonstrate these efforts. However, we have neither studied nor determined whether the Army's work on internal will to fight has been sufficient. Hauser's admonition may or may not remain valid, but his appeal is still worth considering 37 years later.

Research Purposes, Methodology, and Limitations

This report presents findings addressing the three central objectives of our research for the U.S. Army: (1) to create a working model of tactical-operational will to fight, (2) to develop ways for the U.S. Army (and also the U.S. Marine Corps) to assess and influence ally will to fight and adversary will to fight, and (3) to incorporate will to fight into U.S. military war games and simulations. The initial literature review suggested two further purposes: to reinvigorate discussion and focus on will to fight in the U.S. military and to further general knowledge on will to fight for the U.S. military, the scientific community, and the general public.

What is tactical-operational *will to fight*, and how can it be assessed and influenced to help the United States and its allies win wars? The term *tactical-operational* refers to the levels of war. Levels are ephemeral constructs that help military professionals focus on challenges like training or fighting at an appropriate scope and scale. In general terms, the strategic level of war is equated with state decisionmaking and resources, the operational level is where the military strings together battles to accom-

---

[99] William L. Hauser, "The Will to Fight," in Sarkesian, 1980, p. 187.

[100] Hauser, 1980, p. 200. Sarkesian offered a four-part model of individual will to fight, consisting of submission, fear, loyalty, and pride. These generally align with our more detailed model.

plish strategic objectives, and the tactical level is where each battle takes place.[101] The organization, the state, and the society affect the development and use of all levels of military units and all levels of war.

Delineations between these levels are fuzzy rather than explicit, and they are intrinsically linked. In simple terms, tactical-operational will to fight is *military* will to fight represented in the individuals, units, and organizations that fight wars. Figure 1.2 shows the levels-of-war concept developed by our research team to help guide our analysis.[102]

Note that this figure includes the individual at the lowest level. This seemingly obvious inclusion belies an acute and long-standing research challenge: How can we understand the value and decisionmaking of an individual, or of all individuals, in the context of collective action?

The Levels of Analysis Challenge: Unit, Organization, Society, and the Individual

Empirical research studies targeting singular aspects of will to fight, like cohesion or morale, tend to focus on one or at most two levels of analysis. Political scientist Jasen Castillo's *Endurance and War* focuses on the state and the organization. Historian Kenneth Pollock's *Arabs at War* also focuses on the state and organizational levels of war. Sociologist Anthony King makes a strong argument for studying combat effectiveness and will to fight at the platoon level.[103] We seek to aggregate many targeted analyses—Castillo's, Pollock's, King's, Kellett's, Siebold's, and so on—into a holistic will-to-fight model.[104] This broader mandate relieves us from the necessity to narrow our analysis to a single level, but it demands that we assess them all. Some focus was necessary: The majority of our effort centers on military units from the squad through the division levels.[105]

Levels of analysis are intrinsically related and, for the purposes of understanding will to fight, inseparable. Our research describes the complex relationships between the individual, the unit, the organization, the state, and the society. Individuals are the building blocks of military units, organizations, and societies. They also represent the most difficult and controversial level of analysis for will to fight. Individual-level

---

[101] U.S. Joint Staff, 2013, pp. I-7 and I-8.

[102] This figure represents an aggregation of many different levels of war explanations by independent authors (including Trevor N. Dupuy) and by various organizations in the U.S. military. It is intended for general orientation and broad differentiation rather than as a means for fixed calculation.

[103] Jasen J. Castillo, *Endurance and War: The National Sources of Military Cohesion*, Stanford, Calif.: Stanford University Press, 2014; Kenneth M. Pollock, *Arabs at War: Military Effectiveness, 1948–1991*, Lincoln: University of Nebraska Press, 2002; King, 2016.

[104] A holistic assessment or analysis of combat effectiveness would have to include determinations of firepower, maneuverability, and other quantifiable factors not included in the will-to-fight model.

[105] Assessment and analysis often do not look below the battalion level, but understanding squads and platoons can help describe the disposition to fight at higher echelons.

Figure 1.2
The Levels of War for Will-to-Fight Analysis

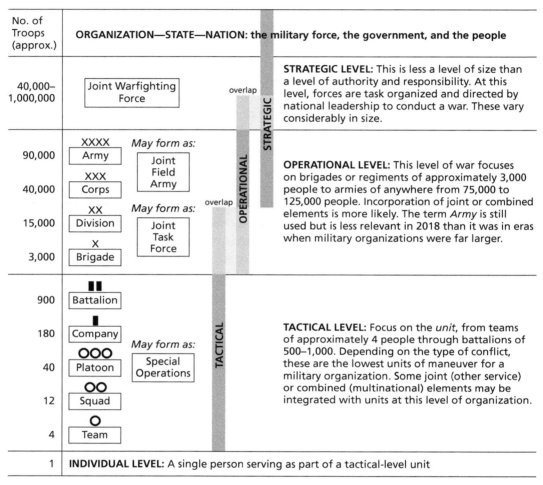

No. of Troops (approx.)	ORGANIZATION—STATE—NATION: the military force, the government, and the people		
40,000–1,000,000	Joint Warfighting Force	overlap	**STRATEGIC LEVEL:** This is less a level of size than a level of authority and responsibility. At this level, forces are task organized and directed by national leadership to conduct a war. These vary considerably in size.
90,000	XXXX Army — May form as: Joint Field Army		**OPERATIONAL LEVEL:** This level of war focuses on brigades or regiments of approximately 3,000 people to armies of anywhere from 75,000 to 125,000 people. Incorporation of joint or combined elements is more likely. The term *Army* is still used but is less relevant in 2018 than it was in eras when military organizations were far larger.
40,000	XXX Corps	overlap	
15,000	XX Division — May form as: Joint Task Force		
3,000	X Brigade		
900	∎∎ Battalion		**TACTICAL LEVEL:** Focus on the *unit*, from teams of approximately 4 people through battalions of 500–1,000. Depending on the type of conflict, these are the lowest units of maneuver for a military organization. Some joint (other service) or combined (multinational) elements may be integrated with units at this level of organization.
180	∎ Company — May form as: Special Operations		
40	⭘⭘⭘ Platoon		
12	⭘⭘ Squad		
4	⭘ Team		
1	INDIVIDUAL LEVEL: A single person serving as part of a tactical-level unit		

RAND RR2341A-1.2

analysis poses a special challenge for will-to-fight research. Understanding *an* individual requires direct, individual-level observation. Findings are valid only for that individual. We are not conducting research on specific individuals. Some general understanding of *individuals* and their will to fight is absolutely necessary to understand units. Psychologists advising our research cautioned against pursuing a quantitative or predictive model of individual will to fight. We have generally heeded this advice.[106] Instead, we examine the general factors of individual will to fight in the context of unit

---

[106] In Chapter Three we describe our experimentation with an existing quantified individual model designed to help us demonstrate the importance of individual will and its connections to unit will. We do not intend this model to be used for quantitative analysis or prediction.

will. We are not modeling the will of *an* individual—we are not saying that the will of a single individual can be determined without individual-level, face-to-face engagement—but instead are modeling the will of *individuals* with the intent of informing unit-level assessment and analysis.[107]

After the unit, our next emphasis is on organizations. These are military services like the Iraqi Ground Forces or the People's Army of Viet Nam (PAVN). Organizations are the institutional groups that generate and sustain units down to the team level. Organizational esprit de corps, integrity, support, training emphasis, and leadership all influence will to fight. At the next higher (and outer) plane we separate the state and the society to help differentiate between those aspects of will to fight that are endogenous and those that are exogenous to direct government control.

The state and the society sustain or weaken the organization, the unit, and the individual. The state consists of government leaders and organizations above and outside of the military organization. States provide direction and support to organizations and units. The society represents supergovernmental aspects of collective will to fight, including economic power and popular support. What some describe as *societal culture* influences all aspects of will to fight.[108] Societal ethnic and sectarian similarities and differences can affect unit cohesion. Organizational culture is strongly influenced by societal culture.

Holistic Combat Effectiveness: How Important Is Will to Fight?

Combat effectiveness is the ability of a military unit to accomplish its mission, which often focuses on defeating an opposing force. Being effective is a relative state: A unit can be very good at getting things done but not as good as an enemy unit, with predictable results. Will to fight is a critical part of *holistic* combat effectiveness.[109] Holistic assessments or analyses are those that seek to determine the overall effectiveness of the unit and not its ability to conduct a narrow or technical task. Yet it is difficult to model or calculate effectiveness even before adding the complexities of will to fight. Military

---

[107] Multilevel analyses of individual and unit will to fight have already been performed, albeit with different parameters and objectives from the present study. See James Griffith, "Multilevel Analysis of Cohesion's Relation to Stress, Well-Being, Identification, Disintegration, and Perceived Combat Readiness," *Military Psychology*, Vol. 14, No. 3, 2002, pp. 217–239; Boas Shamir, Esther Brainin, Eliav Zakay, and Micha Popper, "Perceived Combat Readiness as Collective Efficacy: Individual- and Group-Level Analysis," *Military Psychology*, Vol. 12, No. 2, 2000, pp. 105–119.

[108] The term *national culture* is hotly contested. For analysts who follow the work of Geert Hofstede, national culture is effectively a concrete, self-contained island of cultural factors. For many anthropologists, national culture is an oversimplification of a complex, dynamic, heterogeneous, and unbounded phenomenon that defies neat categorization. We seek a middle ground between simplistic reification and inarticulate diffusion.

[109] Other assessments or analyses of combat effectiveness might seek to answer limited or technical questions about a unit. For example, they might seek to determine a unit's ability to provide logistics support in an effective and timely manner in a training scenario that does not include simulated combat. These limited or technical questions do not address holistic will to fight.

Figure 1.3
Will to Fight as a Component of Holistic Combat Effectiveness

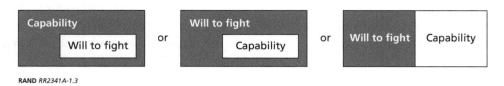

RAND RR2341A-1.3

skepticism of measurement efforts is sometimes considerable and especially so for its intangible, human aspects. U.S. Navy Admiral Hyman G. Rickover said, "I have no more faith in the ability of the social scientists to quantify military effectiveness than I do in numerologists to calculate the future."[110] Whatever the challenges, will to fight should be considered part of any holistic assessment or analysis of combat effectiveness for any manned unit.

How much will to fight matters in each case is another question. This question can never be answered with scientific reliability. For the purposes of our research it is enough to consider the three possible balances in Figure 1.3. Will to fight is compared with technical and tactical capabilities: weapons, vehicles, and other tangible factors that can be quantitatively measured. Capability affects will to fight, and will determines in part how equipment is used and tactics are applied. There is some unknown balance between the factors of will and capability. Will to fight is more important, less important, or equally important in each prospective case.

There is no fixed formula to determine this balance. Three issues with combat effectiveness are relevant here: (1) Will to fight matters to some unknown extent in every case, so *any* valid assessment of holistic combat effectiveness should include an assessment of will to fight; (2) it is possible to assess or analyze the value of will to fight as a critical element of combat effectiveness, but only on a case-by-case basis; and (3) relevant combat effectiveness analysis must also be relative to tasks and the adversary. We seek to provide the assessment and analysis tools to help determine the value of accounting for will to fight as a component of combat effectiveness.

Methodology

We adopted a multimethod research approach to obtain our findings. Multimethod research is most appropriate for complex problems that have historically defied both quantitative formulation and acceptable qualitative results.[111] What follows are *brief*

---

[110] As quoted in Roger A. Beaumont and William P. Snyder, "Combat Effectiveness: Paradigms and Paradoxes," in Sarkesian, 1980, p. 29.

[111] See Janice M. Morse, "Principles of Mixed Methods and Multimethod Research Design," in Abbas Tashakkori and Charles Teddlie, eds., *Handbook of Mixed Methods in Social and Behavioral Research*, Thousand

descriptions of each of the nine parts in the multimethod research approach for readers most interested in the content, findings, and recommendations that follow. Chapters Two and Three and Appendixes A and B provide a detailed explanation of selected methods, focusing on the literature review and the case study and coding effort. All research was conducted in partnership with the RAND team assessing national will to fight for the U.S. Army.

Will-to-Fight Literature Review and Coding

Our initial effort was to read and code both the canonical and lesser-known literature on will to fight. We read and coded 202 books, journal articles, and conference papers addressing a wide array of will-to-fight concepts, theories, and cases.[112] This international, but primarily English-language, review also addressed points of agreement and difference across political science, sociology, psychology, and military history. Coding was completed using Dedoose, a software package designed to help analysts find and describe trends in large bodies of qualitative literature. Coding results fed the tentative will-to-fight model. See Appendix A for a detailed explanation of the coding process and both Chapter Two and Appendix A for its results.

Gaming and Simulation Literature Review

Efforts to model war require a careful assessment and best-effort replication of will to fight. Designers who address will to fight often conduct extensive theoretical and historical research. Their written work should inform any effort to develop a gaming and simulation system for will to fight. Our team conducted a literature review of 75 rule sets (coding 62 of them), model descriptions, and designer notes from both commercial and military games and simulations, as well as published analyses on game design. Findings and descriptions are presented in Chapter Three.

Subject Matter Expert Interviews and Discussions

Throughout the course of our research we engaged subject matter experts to obtain insight and recommendations. From October 2016 through September 2017 our team engaged 68 experts including historians, political scientists, sociologists, psychologists, game designers, and military officers from the United States, Ukraine, the Republic of Korea, the United Kingdom, and elsewhere. Our purpose was to elicit expert understanding of will to fight and to obtain recommendations for how it should be modeled, assessed, analyzed, and incorporated into gaming and simulation. See Appendix D for a list of questions posed to our interviewees and a sample of responses.

Oaks, Calif.: Sage Publications, 2003, pp. 189–208; Delbert C. Miller and Neil J. Salkind, *Handbook of Research Design and Social Measurement*, 6th ed., Thousand Oaks, Calif.: Sage Publications, 2002.

[112] We generated data from 110 sources while reviewing, applying coded questions to, but not formally coding 92 sources that did not fit our final criteria. See Appendix A.

Exploratory Vietnam War Case

We conducted exploratory research into the Vietnam War case to develop an inductive, case-specific assessment of will to fight. The purposes of this exploratory case were to inform the development of the model and to provide an exemplary will-to-fight case in a stand-alone report. We selected the Vietnam War case for this effort because it provides sharp, contrasting will-to-fight insights at all levels of analysis (including societal) and for both sides of the war. This case is well known, relevant, and accessible to the U.S. military officers who are the primary audience of this research. Finally, the Vietnam War offers the single most robust set of unclassified data of any war case relevant to this study. As of mid-2018, this research is ongoing. The Vietnam case will be published in a separate report.

Case Study Coding

We coded 14 war cases to assess both societal and tactical-operational will to fight in order to improve on the tentative model derived from the initial literature review and exploratory case. We selected conventional cases from World War I onward to concentrate our analysis on modern conventional will to fight (see "Bounding the Study" below, and Appendix B for more detail on selection).[113] Our team conducted an inter-coder reliability test using the Vietnam War case. We engaged published subject matter experts for 7 of the 14 total cases. These included Vietnam War historians Gregory Daddis and Kevin Boylan, Middle East expert Andrew Parasiliti, World Wars expert Jasen Castillo, and Koreas expert In Hyo Seol, a National Defense University Fellow from the Republic of Korea and a researcher at the Korean Institute for Defense Analyses. We derived findings from 10 of the 14 coded cases. Appendix B provides details on our coding process and results.

Literature Review on Military Assessment and Analysis Methods

We reviewed historical and current literature on advising and intelligence analysis of will to fight to help translate the will-to-fight model into a useful tool for advisors and intelligence analysts. We emphasized examination of tools and methods used to assess and describe partner and adversary will to fight. See Appendix C for references to several existing tools and methods.

Game and Simulation Coding

Building from the gaming and simulation literature review, we surveyed 75 and coded 62 commercial and military games and simulations. Coding was a structured assessment process to determine the degree to which games and simulations incorporated will to fight and made the will-to-fight model as realistic as possible, and to determine their relative success at achieving some realism while remaining playable. At some point, complexity overwhelms the utility of many games and simulations. Coded

---

[113] We selected cases using the Correlates of War database list of cases. We did not incorporate any analysis from the database.

material ranged from tabletop games with figures to commercial tactical games to full-scale military simulations currently in use by the DoD. Findings from this coding process informed our will-to-fight model design and our ongoing gaming model design. Results are presented in Chapter Three.

Experimental Will-to-Fight Simulations

RAND Arroyo Center engaged the developers of two DoD simulations: the Infantry Warrior Simulation (IWARS) and the Joint Conflict and Tactical Simulation (JCATS). Our team collaborated with the IWARS team at the U.S. Army Natick Soldier Center to experiment with incorporating will to fight into military simulations. We collaborated with the Army Research Laboratory (ARL) team seeking to model human factors in military combat simulations. We also incorporated Steven Silver's existing individual-level will-to-fight model into the NetLogo modeling software and IWARS to determine the feasibility of incorporating an individual-level model into military simulation. Chapter Three presents our results.

Analysis of Russian Will to Fight

In parallel to our primary research we conducted a separate analysis of Russian will to fight derived from both English- and Russian-language sources. It includes our interpretation of Russian self-assessments of will to fight, many of which appeared in Russian-language sociological literature. It also includes case study analysis on Russian will to fight in World War I, World War II, and Chechnya. Findings from this research were incorporated into the model in this report and presented separately to the sponsor.

Bounding the Study: Modern, Conventional, Non-U.S. Cases

We view this research as the first step toward developing a universal Joint Force model for will to fight. With this limited objective we narrowed our case studies and analyses to modern, conventional warfare using non-U.S. cases. Our objective is to describe will to fight in national armies and in a way that is relevant to contemporary cases. Follow-on research should address will to fight in irregular warfare and in air and sea warfare, and the will to fight of U.S. forces.

Continuous Quality Assurance

This was a complex project addressing a subject that has persistently defied clear findings. We knew from the outset that our objectives and methods would demand rigorous review. To help ensure success we engaged a RAND Continuous Quality Assurance (CQA) team. Reviewers worked with the research team throughout the project, offering guidance to help avoid early misdirection. Our CQA team consists of senior RAND researchers Jennifer Kavanagh and COL (USA, Ret.) Henry Leonard, and Meredith Kleykamp at the University of Maryland. Our government advisor on the project is Kerry B. Fosher, an anthropologist and the Director of Research at the U.S. Marine Corps' Center for Advanced Operational Cultural Learning.

A Note on Subjective-Objective and Qualitative-Quantitative Methods and Data

Lack of objective, quantifiable modeling and data is a broad deterrent to deeper invest-ment in will-to-fight research. Sam C. Sarkesian described the analysis of the human factors of war—including will to fight—as subjective. While he did not intend this to be pejorative, many others take the same position with pejorative intent.[114] West-ern debate over the meaning and value of information in war has centered on two dyads: subjective-objective and qualitative-quantitative. In some of the literature on combat effectiveness and in some official U.S. military doctrine, subjective and quali-tative information is often considered unanchored, not provable, opinion driven, and therefore less reliable (or in some cases useless).[115] Anything that is viewed as objective or quantitative is assumed to be inherently good and valuable and therefore inherently better than anything subjective or qualitative. This assumption is inherently flawed, and it directly undermines the study of human aspects of war like will to fight. It flies in the face of the Joint Chiefs of Staff 2016 JC-HAMO, which decries a persistent and undue faith in the quantification of war. This JCS argument in turn echoes the same arguments made by experts on war beginning (at least) in the late 1800s.

In a published 2012 RAND report, the lead author of this study made a detailed argument that in war nearly all seemingly objective and quantifiable information masked extensive subjectivity and qualitative analysis.[116] *No method or type of informa-tion is inherently better than another in the study of war.* There is value to be had from all types of information. It is incumbent on leaders, advisors, and analysts to seek and apply information and methods appropriate to the problem at hand. Certainly there are instances where qualitative and subjective research is conducted without necessary rigor and so produces misleading or inaccurate results. However, the same is true of poorly designed quantitative research. Rigorously designed and conducted qualitative or subjective research can provide important insights that might be missed with a purely quantitative approach. In this case the problem reasonably defies a solely quan-titative approach. All types of methods and data should be considered on their merits to inform assessments and analysis of will to fight. Accordingly, this multimethod research sought to draw from all types of data, including narrative histories, quantita-tive empirical studies, and long-standing efforts to structure subjective or qualitative information.[117]

---

[114] Antulio J. Echevarria II argues that this debate started with Clausewitz. Antulio J. Echevarria II, "War, Poli-tics, and the RMA—The Legacy of Clausewitz," *Joint Forces Quarterly*, Winter 1995–1996, pp. 76–80.

[115] For example: U.S. Joint Forces Command, *Commander's Handbook for an Effects-Based Approach to Joint Operations*, Suffolk, Va.: Joint Warfighting Center, February 24, 2006, pp. iv–15.

[116] Connable, 2012.

[117] See Jim Storr, *The Human Face of War*, London: Continuum UK, 2009; Gregory Belenky, ed., *Contemporary Studies in Combat Psychiatry*, New York: Greenwood Press, 1987; Sarkesian, 1980.

CHAPTER TWO

A Model of Will to Fight

A useful model approximates reality and gives people a tool for thinking through complex problems and, in some cases, understanding systems. Simpler and more concrete problems and systems are easier to model with convincing realism. Tangible systems like trucks and weapons can be modeled with great accuracy. But any model of will to fight will be far less accurate or precise than any technical model: Integrating individual motivations and behavior, units, culture, and combat defies precision and accuracy. Even without replicable accuracy, though, a model of will to fight can be very useful. More importantly, a model is needed to serve as a baseline for effective assessment, analysis, estimation, forecasting, and influence.

This chapter presents a military unit will-to-fight model for the tactical-operational levels of war. First we explain the objectives of the model. Next we describe the model, taking a step-by-step approach with each factor and subfactor, building from the individual up to the unit. We then explain how to apply the model. In Chapter Three we describe how factors exogenous to the model can and do affect and expose will to fight in practice.

Our model is intended to serve as a holistic representation and resolution of existing theories and models of will to fight. It synthesizes, modifies, and condenses a wide array of descriptions of the key elements of will to fight from a wide array of sources. It is important to note that in Chapter Three we show results from the use of a second, existing model to experiment with will to fight in simulation. We call this the Silver Model, derived from Steven Silver's combat psychological model originally developed for a Microsoft gaming division in the 1990s.

Objectives and Parameters of the Model

We built an explanatory, exploratory, portable model at the tactical and operational levels of war, synthesizing factors and descriptions of the model from all nine parts of our multimethod research effort.[1] The model is explanatory rather than explicit

---

[1]   For a useful explanation of the difference between causality and causation, see Menno Hulswit, "Causality and Causation: The Inadequacy of the Received View," undated manuscript; H. M. Blalock, Jr., ed., *Causal*

because will to fight can be *assessed* but not *measured*: As we argued in the previous chapter, will to fight is a factor of war that fundamentally defies accurate and precise quantification.[2] An explanatory model is a generalized model with limited objectives. It seeks to describe factors and subfactors, allowing advisors and analysts to link them in ways that might be useful. It does not try to scientifically prove links or argue that they are, and must be, the same in every case. Complexity makes the development of a general causal model of will to fight unwise. Most of the factors we describe will probably matter in most cases. All of the factors we describe should be considered for every case. Links between factors should be explored on a case-by-case basis.

This model is exploratory because it is intended to serve as the starting point for the development of a universally applicable Army and possibly Joint Force model. It should be continually improved on, and parts of the model should be investigated in greater detail for specific applications. Tools to apply the model should be developed, tested, used in practice, and then used to modify the model as necessary. Most importantly, the model should be used to examine the various theories of will to fight that we cite here in order to improve and consolidate general knowledge on war.

A model that is not replicable must be applied anew to every case. This model is a tool for facilitating and structuring deeper analysis. Therefore, our model is *portable* but not scientifically *replicable*: Assessing partner forces or analyzing adversary forces will still require some modification, possibly some new modeling, and extensive effort in each case.[3] In fact, if it works as intended, the model might make assessment and analysis of will to fight more challenging than current, mostly unstructured approaches. But it will also make these efforts more practicable and rewarding. Table 2.1 summarizes the differences between a causal, replicable model and an explanatory, portable model.

There is ample precedent for this approach. General modeling of complex social systems and behaviors tends to be explanatory rather than explicit. When models of complex social systems and behaviors are explicit, they are also riskier and more likely to be misleadingly precise.[4] Another purpose for this model is exploration: It should be

---

Models in the Social Sciences, 2nd ed., New York: Aldine de Gruyter, 1985; Rom Harré and Fathali M. Moghaddam, eds., *Questioning Causality: Scientific Explorations of Cause and Consequence Across Social Contexts*, Santa Barbara, Calif.: Praeger, 2016.

[2]   Assessment is an overarching process that can, but does not necessarily, include measurement. See Connable, 2012, Chapters One and Two.

[3]   Portability is often used to describe software modeling that can be applied across systems or even disparate programs. In many cases software is both portable and replicable; the terminology for software applications is slightly different from our use. Generally, a central model can be applied through a wide array of applications, with specific meaning applied in each case. Portability may extend to applications our model might generate. See Jim Pivarski, Collin Bennett, and Robert L. Grossman, *Deploying Analytics with the Portable Format for Analytics (PFA)*, River Forest, Ill.: Open Data Group, Inc., undated.

[4]   For a discussion of these trade-offs, see Harré and Moghaddam, 2016.

Table 2.1
Differences in Modeling Objectives

Objective	Description
Causal	Claims cause-and-effect relationship between variables, and variables and outcomes
or Explanatory	Describes variables and possible causes and effects in general terms
Replicable	One explicit model exists and can be applied without modification in all cases
or Portable	A general model exists but it must be modified for each case

used to further research and analysis into the factors and relationships that constitute will to fight. RAND has done extensive work in exploratory modeling, including for combat effectiveness. Paul K. Davis and Donald Blumenthal explain this approach:[5]

> For both research and applications, combat models should be viewed less as answer machines than as frameworks for summarizing and communicating objective and subjective knowledge . . . and as mechanisms for *exploration*. This view, which is especially important in designing complex research models, establishes stringent requirements for model transparency, comprehensibility, and flexibility.

Explanation and exploration are the practical limits for general modeling of the will to fight. Building a precise, causal model would require one of two approaches: (1) precisely and accurately modeling all of the subcomponents that influence will to fight (including cohesion, leadership, individual psychological traits, and motivations), resolving all competing theories across the fields of psychology, sociology, political science, and history, and then proving the replicability of the model across military units; or (2) finding a unitary theory of will to fight. We briefly analyze both of these options in the next section and argue against both. Our research suggests that the best approach is to identify and explain the most consistently important factors of will to fight.

A Brief Note on the Literature Behind the Model

This model is derived from the sources and findings used for all nine parts of our multimethod research. Of these many sources, the literature on will to fight is most accessible to the reader. This literature is both broad and deep. Broad literature seeks to describe many factors and their interactions, while deep literature focuses on a single or very small set of factors often at a specific level of war. Anthony Kellett's *Combat*

---

[5]   Paul K. Davis and Donald Blumenthal, *The Base of Sand Problem: A White Paper on the State of Military Combat Modeling*, Santa Monica, Calif.: RAND Corporation, N-3148-OSD/DARPA, 1991, p. vii. Davis and Blumenthal go on to argue, "Models should be consistent with and reinforce the principles of war" (p. 30).

Motivation is a broad, aggregate assessment of will to fight, while Guy Siebold's "Military Group Cohesion" is a deep analysis. All of these sources were needed to help build the model, but broad sources are most helpful to understand will to fight as a holistic model.

This list, presented in no particular order of relative importance, is both a general guide to these broad sources and a recommended reading list. It represents a helpfully closed circle of citation: Baynes cites Moran, Kellett cites Baynes and Moran, and so on.[6]

1. Carl Von Clausewitz, *On War*
2. Anthony Kellett, *Combat Motivation*
3. Lord Moran, *The Anatomy of Courage*
4. John Baynes, *Morale*
5. F. M. Richardson, *Fighting Spirit*
6. Sam C. Sarkesian, ed., *Combat Effectiveness*
7. Richard Holmes, *Acts of War*
8. Anthony King, *The Combat Soldier*
9. William Darryl Henderson, *Cohesion*
10. John Keegan, *The Face of Battle*

Any well-researched, well-written book on military history is a good source for understanding ways to model will to fight. Each of these ten books includes historical examples in context.

Modeling Will to Fight Using a System-of-Systems Approach

As long as it is understood to be explanatory, exploratory, and portable, a model of will to fight is best visualized in a systems approach or, in modern terms, a system-of-systems approach. The systems approach was pioneered by RAND analysts such as Herman Kahn and Irwin Mann, made practical for tactical-operational analysis by military analysts such as Jim Storr, and applied extensively by the U.S. military.[7] A system-of-systems model is literally a system containing many other systems, all of which are interconnected.[8] Everything from culture to unit cohesion to leadership to

---

[6]   All of these sources are cited in the reference section of this report. Here we use the primary title for brevity.

[7]   Herman Kahn and Irwin Mann, *Techniques of Systems Analysis*, Santa Monica, Calif.: RAND Corporation, RM-1829-1-PR, 1957; Storr, 2009, pp. 44–82. See Connable, 2012, p. 287, for a depiction of six system-of-systems models in U.S. doctrinal publications. RAND has also previously warned against attempting to apply this approach literally to highly complex problems with many variables. See E. S. Quade, *Military Systems Analysis*, Santa Monica, Calif.: RAND Corporation, RM-3452-PR, 1963, p. 10.

[8]   See Russell Ackoff, "Towards a System of Systems Concepts," *Management Science*, Vol. 17, No. 11, 1971, pp. 661–671; Nirav B. Shah, Donna H. Rhodes, and Daniel E. Hastings, *Systems of Systems and Emergent System*

training works together to influence will to fight. Each of these dynamic factors is a complex subsystem. Individual soldiers and units are the critical nodes in a network of interwoven relationships ranging up and out to the societal level. Each soldier is also a system reflecting cultural influences, motivations, fears, expectations, and other factors.[9] Visualizing this conceptual system of systems may be the best way to demystify the complexity of will to fight. This is the first step in distilling simpler, more practical tools for advisors and analysts.

Will to fight resides in both individuals and military units. It is impossible to delink the two: We cannot understand individual will to fight without understanding unit dynamics, or unit will to fight without the individual. We address both, but we tailor the model toward the unit because units are the focus of effort for military advising and intelligence analysis.[10] Former Army officer William Darryl Henderson argued that cohesion and, more broadly, will to fight are best studied at the unit level. In units, "the organization, the small group, and the leader come together."[11] Units exist in one of three states: in a ready training state, in a combat state, or in a recovery state that might or might not be in a combat zone. Core elements of will to fight are fairly consistent, but each of these states requires some distinct analysis; see Chapter Three.

Set aside all of the exogenous events and conditions that affect and reveal will to fight. Think now about a military unit before it enters combat. For the purposes of understanding will to fight we call this a *ready state*. There is no enemy, no weapon fire, and there are no other challenges to influence or test will to fight. Think about ready-state will to fight as an intricate, multilayered set of influencing factors and relationships: leaders, led, cohesion, training, and so on, unaffected by combat. From the ready state, units enter *combat state*, then go into *recovery state*. Combat state is when the unit is exposed to factors exogenous to the model that affect will to fight: enemy fire, weather, and so on. During the recovery state, changes accrued in the combat state can rebound or solidify, and factors like veterancy—the effect of extended combat

---

Context, occasional paper #85, Cambridge, Mass.: Massachusetts Institute of Technology, undated; James E. Campbell, Dennis E. Longsine, Donald Shirah, and Dennis J. Anderson, *System of Systems Modeling and Analysis*, SAND2005-0020, Albuquerque, N.M.: Sandia National Laboratories, 2005.

[9]   We considered ways to isolate units, or even individuals, from aspects of this model. The most logical step would be to eliminate the state and national factors to focus on the unit. Essentially, the unit would become a cultural island. But the concept of cultural islands is impractical. Culture and knowledge are never bounded by artificial constructs like units. Individuals can rarely, if ever, be separated from their existing relationships with family, the state, the nation, and the organization. Our meta-analysis of the literature showed that all factors, from society to unit, affect will to fight, all the time. Individual ideology linked to the society and the state—for example, a World War II–era Japanese soldier's dedication to the empire—may be one of the most significant factors in will to fight.

[10]   Our approach borrows in part from Paul Davis's concept of multiresolution modeling. Paul K. Davis and James H. Bigelow, *Experiments in Multiresolution Modeling (MRM)*, Santa Monica, Calif.: RAND Corporation, MR-1004-DARPA, 1998.

[11]   Henderson, 1985, p. 9.

over long periods of time—take hold. The best way to think about will to fight is to assemble the unit piece by piece, from the individual to the unit, and then describe how the unit and its will to fight might change as the unit moves from ready state to combat state to recovery.

A Recognition of Risk

There are some inherent dangers in applying system-of-systems visualization to an imprecise, complex human condition riven by case-specific idiosyncrasies. Using systems terminology suggests precision normally associated with engineering diagrams. It might encourage users of the model to pursue unobtainable causal meaning or misleading precision. However, our review of the literature convinced us that the lack of visualization has undermined the relevance of will to fight for practitioners. Narrative descriptions are difficult to translate into useful tools, and they are particularly difficult to transform into war gaming and simulation models. Using system-of-systems visualization is a calculated risk that we deem necessary to help move will to fight from a vague concept toward practical application.

Two Visualizations: Nodes and Links, and Concentric Wheel

We offer two visualizations of the model. Both represent the same factors, subfactors, and durability ratings, which we explain below. There are two purposes to offering different visualizations of the same underlying model: (1) to provide more than one option for advisors and analysts seeking to apply the model, and (2) to support follow-on efforts to develop and integrate a model into U.S. military doctrine. This section describes a node-and-link model and a concentric wheel model. Throughout this chapter we present side-by-side visualizations of both models.

A Node-and-Link Model

System-of-systems models are generally organized around *nodes* and *links*. In the system-of-systems approach to modeling, a node is an entity like a person, a building, or a variable, while a link is a relationship between nodes. For our model, nodes are the factors that influence will to fight. We use the term *factor* rather than *variable* because we cannot quantify will to fight: *Variable* suggests the existence of a mathematical formula. In this explanatory model we identify the most important factors that influence will to fight, arrange them at the individual, unit, organization, and state-society levels, and use visualization to help organize the factors.

Nodes are represented by circles. Links are represented by lines. A few relationships allow us to ascribe clear links. For example, it is clear that training and skills are obtained from at least the unit and the organization. Both training and skills reside in the individual. We can group factors (nodes) together. For example, we can say that both ideology and economic needs are individual-level motivators of will to fight and

Figure 2.1
Notional Example of Nodes and Links

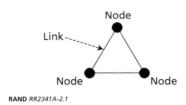

RAND *RR2341A-2.1*

that these are commonly connected to societal culture and economy. But we cannot identify common, recurring relationships *between* nodes in a general model. For example, we cannot say that a strongly held ideological belief always combines with leadership or discipline or training in a commonly recurring way. Figure 2.1 shows an example of nodes and links.

Case-specific assessment or analysis will need to be conducted to determine links in each case, if it is necessary. Advisors and intelligence analysts should use this model as a guide to help describe the nodes and links for each case. If factor-to-factor relationships can be shown through direct observation or intelligence reports or other sources, then the chances of successfully influencing will to fight improve considerably.

Factors: The Basic Elements of the Model

Factors of will to fight are organized on two vertices. First, they are arranged in ascending order of scale from individual to unit to organization, to the state, and to the society. Next, factors are arranged horizontally by *categories* that emerged in the literature: motivations, capabilities, and culture. Motivations are individual drivers of will to fight, like desperation and ideology. Individuals adopt motivations from culture and from environmental pressures like the desperation to survive. Unit and organizational motivations grow organically and are imposed on individuals in a concerted effort to generate will to fight. For example, esprit de corps, or pride and belonging to a unit, grows from unit success in battle (and other reasons), and leaders try to foster esprit de corps to motivate individual soldiers. Leadership is present and consistently relevant at all levels. Highly competent leaders with good character—those who are viewed as honest, moral, and thoughtful—are most likely to facilitate strong will to fight. Capabilities are things that facilitate will to fight. These are provided by units, organizations, states, and societies. Culture organizes will to fight at the unit level and above, describing ways that individuals interact, norms for behavior, and the critical factor of cohesion. Table 2.2 describes these three categories of factors and subfactors focusing on disposition to fight.

This table is a basic key to assessing and analyzing will to fight. We also assign relative durability ratings to each factor.

Table 2.2
Categories of Will-to-Fight Factors

Category	Description
Motivation	Individual drivers of will to fight, like desperation or ideology
Capability	Assets and abilities to accomplish missions that can improve confidence
Culture	Behavioral norms, identities, social constructs, and sentiment that affect will

Relative Durability Ratings

We attach one additional marker to each factor as we build the model: *relative durability*. All factors may be important in every case, but some factors are more susceptible to change during combat than others. The purpose of adding durability ratings is to help advisors and analysts isolate factors that have immediate consequence in combat from factors that tend to change more gradually or are unlikely to be directly affected in one battle. For example, a unit leader who had a good peacetime reputation might fall apart in combat, leading to an immediate change in the unit's will to fight. However, tactical combat is unlikely to change the leadership of a state leader and unit will to fight is unlikely to change during combat due to some distant shift in state leadership. Therefore, unit leadership is less durable than state leadership for the purpose of understanding unit will to fight. Factors in the model have low, mid, or high durability. Low-durability factors are more likely to change during a single combat engagement and have immediate impacts on will to fight. Figure 2.2 depicts the simple scale that is applied to each factor in the node-and-link model. Figure 2.3 depicts the same scale in the concentric wheel model. From left to right these connote low, mid, and high durability.

For the sake of simplicity we assign only one of these three possible qualities to each factor. We assigned these ratings based on our interpretation of each factor

Figure 2.2
Relative Durability Rating in the Node-and-Link Model

Low   Mid   High

RAND *RR2341A-2.2*

Figure 2.3
Relative Durability Rating in the Concentric Wheel Model

RAND *RR2341A-2.3*

within the multimethod research process. *Rating assignments resulted from informed expert opinions of the RAND Arroyo Center research team.* We determined durability ratings from our review of the literature on will to fight and a review of historical cases relevant to will to fight. We assessed each factor and subfactor based on the likelihood it would or would not change over the course of a single battle or series of battles based on this informed expert opinion.

The durability rating is intended as a guide to assessment and analysis rather than a fixed scale. While it is unlikely that competence would change dramatically during combat, it is possible. Leadership may generally have low durability, but in any one case it might be quite durable. Any portable assessment or analysis could refine these ratings or simplify them into a binary scale.

A Factor Model of Will to Fight

Table 2.3 constitutes a simple factor-level model of will to fight. It is the basis for the visual system-of-systems model that follows. Even without the visual model this table can be used to improve understanding of partner and adversary forces. Detailed explanations of the categories and factors follow in the next sections. This table reflects five levels of analysis: (1) individual, (2) unit, (3) organization, (4) state, and (5) society. The purpose of the model is to better inform understanding of unit will to fight from the squad through the division levels. This table is the basis for both the node-and-link and concentric wheel visualizations.

Individuals in a military unit and the units as collectives can be affected by all of these factors, with every factor having different meanings, values, and relationships from case to case. Portability places the onus of understanding the value of each factor and its relationships on the advisor and analyst.

Table 2.3
Factor Model of Tactical-Operational Unit Will to Fight

Level	Category	Factors	Subfactors	Durability
Individual	Individual motivations	Desperation		Mid
		Revenge Ideology Economics		High
		Individual identity	Personal, social, unit, state, organization, and society (including political, religious)	High
	Individual capabilities	Quality	Fitness, resilience, education, adaptability, social skills, and psychological traits	High
		Individual competence	Skills, relevance, sufficiency, and sustainability	High

Table 2.3—Continued

Level	Category	Factors	Subfactors	Durability
Unit	Unit culture	Unit cohesion	Social vertical, social horizontal, and task	Mid
		Expectation		Low
		Unit control	Coercion, persuasion, and discipline	Mid
		Unit esprit de corps		Mid
	Unit capabilities	Unit competence	Performance, skills, and training	High
		Unit support	Sufficiency and timeliness	Low
		Unit leadership	Competence and character	Mid
Organization	Organizational culture	Organizational control	Coercion, persuasion, and discipline	High
		Organizational esprit de corps		High
		Organizational integrity	Corruption and trust	High
	Organizational capabilities	Organizational training	Capabilities, relevance, sufficiency, and sustainment	High
		Organizational support	Sufficiency and timeliness	Mid
		Doctrine	Appropriateness and effectiveness	High
		Organizational leadership	Competence and character	High
State	State culture	Civil-military relations	Appropriateness and functionality	High
		State integrity	Corruption and trust	High
	State capabilities	State support	Sufficiency and timeliness	Mid
		State strategy	Clarity and effectiveness	High
		State leadership	Competence and character	High
Society	Societal culture	Societal identity	Ideology, ethnicity, and history	High
		Societal integrity	Corruption and trust	High
	Societal capabilities	Societal support	Consistency and efficiency	Mid

No model of a complex social phenomenon is exhaustive. These are the factors that emerged from our research. It is distinctly possible that other factors matter in any individual case. Portability also requires assessors and analysts to look for factors that might be relevant but that do not appear in this model.

Morale: An Inconsistent and Potentially Misleading Indicator of Will to Fight

> Morale . . . is like life itself, in that the moment you undertake to define it you begin to limit its meaning with the restrictive boundaries of mere language.
> —BG James A. Ulio, "Military Morale"

Morale is noticeably absent from Table 2.3. It is one of the two most commonly used terms to describe will to fight.[12] Yet our research shows that to understand will to fight it is necessary to treat morale as a special case. Our conclusion is that morale is an impractical term that, as of mid-2018, is not useful for assessing will to fight. There is no way to explain morale without oversimplifying it or reverting to awkward complexity. We chose a middle-ground approach: Morale is *a transient, partial indicator of will to fight that often has counterintuitive and misleading meanings.*[13] We have set it aside until it can be better defined and its value can be more clearly described.

Our definition of morale requires explanation and careful consideration. Morale has been used to explain everything from feelings about the availability of off-duty recreation to a comprehensive stand-in for will to fight.[14] It is often taken to reveal the way soldiers feel from moment to moment, a wispy sentiment reflected in complaints or smiles. Visible and often nonmilitary metrics for happiness, like "job satisfaction," are equated with will to fight. This is a dangerous misunderstanding of the complexity of soldier sentiment.

Another approach is to elevate the meaning of morale. Many analysts, historians, and gaming and simulation designers instead use morale to aggregate and holistically represent will to fight. In this interpretation, morale *is* will to fight, it is durable, and it is not always visible. War historian Kaushik Roy argues, "The 'will to war' is directly

---

[12]   The other word is *cohesion*.

[13]   The American philosopher William Ernest Hocking defines morale as "a character of the will in reference to a particular undertaking. . . . [I]t is a measure of one's disposition to give one's self to the objective at hand." William Ernest Hocking, "The Nature of Morale," *American Journal of Sociology*, Vol. 47, No. 3, November 1941, p. 303. Hocking suggests that only democracies can have high collective morale at the societal level.

[14]   In one study, researchers simply asked soldiers to rate "unit morale" on a scale of 1–5 without further explanation. See Karmon D. Dyches, James A. Anderson, and Kristin N. Saboe, "Modeling the Indirect Association of Combat Exposure with Anger and Aggression During Combat Deployment: The Moderating Role of Morale," *Military Psychology*, Vol. 29, No. 4, 2017, pp. 260–270. It is also commonly used to assess human behavior in fields other than warfare. For example: Ben Hardy, *Morale: Definitions, Dimensions, and Measurement*, doctoral thesis, Cambridge: Cambridge Judge Business School, 2009.

proportional to good discipline and strong morale amongst troops."[15] Psychiatrist Joost
A. M. Meerloo offered a thoughtful and concise discussion of morale viewed through
this analytic lens.[16] He saw complex (as opposed to a happy-sad indicator) morale as
a "rather vague concept," and he tried to rectify this gap by breaking it down into 47
factors including ideology and motivation.[17] John Baynes offers his interpretation:[18]

> High morale is the most important quality of a soldier. It is a quality of mind
> and spirit which combines courage, self-discipline, and endurance. It springs from
> infinitely varying and sometimes contradictory sources, but is easily recognizable,
> having as its hallmarks cheerfulness and unselfishness. In time of peace good
> morale is developed by sound training and the fostering of *esprit de corps*. In time
> of war it manifests itself in the soldier's absolute determination to do his duty to
> the best of his ability in any circumstances. At its highest peak it is seen as an
> individual's readiness to accept his fate willingly even to the point of death, and to
> refuse all roads that lead to safety at the price of conscience.

Baynes sees morale as a quality, a disposition, and an indicator. It derives from all
of the factors we list above and perhaps more. Looking at Baynes, Meerloo, Kellett, and
all of the other literature on will to fight suggests a different interpretation of morale.
Baynes was describing will to fight rather than morale. "Will to fight" can be logically
transposed for "morale" in Meerloo's article and in Baynes's book. *Morale* is not the
right operative term.

By itself, morale does not constitute will to fight. Nor is it a distinct factor that
influences will to fight or an absolute reflection of disposition to fight. We propose that
morale is instead the moment-by-moment sentiment reflecting *some of* an individual's
and a unit's collective feelings about immediate conditions. As Meerloo and others
argue, it is both an individual and a unit indicator, and it is only one of many including discipline, esprit de corps, and training.[19]

Morale derives from all of the factors that affect will. Even though it is transient it
relates to the durable factors like training, ideology, and esprit de corps. An individual
soldier with excellent training, strong ideological beliefs that align with the military
mission, and a powerful connection to an elite unit is more likely to have high morale

---

[15]   Kaushik Roy, "Discipline and Morale of the African, British and Indian Army Units in Burma and India
During World War II: July 1943 to August 1945," *Modern Asian Studies*, Vol. 44, No. 6, 2010, p. 1255.

[16]   Meerloo was a twentieth-century Dutch psychiatrist and psychoanalyst.

[17]   Joost A. M. Meerloo, "Mental Danger, Stress and Fear: Part II. Man and His Morale," *Journal of Nervous and
Mental Disease*, Vol. 125, No. 3, July–September 1957, pp. 357–379.

[18]   Baynes, 1988 (1967), p. 108.

[19]   We do not specify individual indicators, although our follow-on research focuses on identifying ways to
observe unit and national will to fight. Any of the factors or subfactors in the model might be applied as an indicator through either direct or proxy observation.

at any given point in time. Conversely, lower will-to-fight factor values make individuals more vulnerable to low morale. But even this rather clear binary distinction (stronger will means generally better morale) does not explain will to fight.

Taken at face value, morale can be dangerously deceptive. It is possible to appear miserable while possessing intense disposition to fight, and it is possible to appear happy and content while having poor disposition to fight. Outermost reflections of morale are extraordinarily difficult to read. A highly trained, well-prepared infantry unit might have low morale until it is thrust into combat because the soldiers desperately want to fight. A relatively unprepared unit might be quite satisfied away from combat, giving the deceptive appearance of strong will to fight. It is not sufficient to look at soldiers, determine their immediate, relative happiness or sadness, and determine that they do or do not have will to fight.

Previous efforts to measure morale are informative. A 1981 study measured U.S. Army soldier morale using a survey instrument derived from business literature. Soldiers were asked how they felt about their "supervisors" and "co-workers."[20] This kind of peacetime, ready-state measurement might be useful for understanding job satisfaction, but there is no generalizable morale measurement that translates into consistently accurate assessments of will to fight in combat.[21] In 1942 the U.S. Pacific Fleet translated a quantitative internal Japanese assessment of their morale problems. The American editor of the report wrote, "The entire report is a study in disaffection."[22] Yet despite their recorded morale and discipline problems, the Japanese Army proved to have extraordinary will to fight for most of the war. Neither job satisfaction nor martinet obedience is a consistent indicator of high morale or will to fight.[23]

A simple paradox also undermines the usefulness of morale in determining unit will to fight. Our research showed that it is common to see cases of low individual morale and high unit morale, which might (or might not) correspond with low individual and high collective will to fight. Remember the French prisoners at Verdun from the vignette in Chapter One. Their low morale convinced the German intelligence staff that the entire French Second Army had low morale and therefore low will to fight. German soldiers suffered the consequences of this misinterpretation of morale. This

---

[20] John P. Allen and John T. Hazer, *Development of a Field-Oriented Measure of Soldier Morale*, Fort Benjamin Harrison, Ind.: Army Research Institute for the Behavioral and Social Sciences, December 1981.

[21] Much of the empirical analysis of morale focuses on ready-state units because they are generally stable and always easier to study than units in combat. This emphasis on ready-state, or peacetime, studies appears to have skewed scientific understanding of morale toward a noncombat definition.

[22] U.S. Pacific Fleet, *Japanese Army Discipline and Morale*, Special Translation Number 76, Pearl Harbor, Hawaii: Commander in Chief Pacific, July 7, 1945. Also see Douglas Ford, "British Intelligence on Japanese Army Morale During the Pacific War: Logical Analysis or Racial Stereotyping," *Journal of Military History*, Vol. 69, No. 2, April 2005, pp. 439–474.

[23] Also see Henry Durant, "Morale and Its Measurement," *American Journal of Sociology*, Vol. 47, No. 3, November 1941, pp. 406–414.

also proved true in the Soviet Army during the Winter War against Finland from 1939 to 1940, where individual Soviet soldier morale was often quite low but unit will to fight held together:[24]

> Although Soviet soldiers did retreat, desert, surrender, shirk, and inflict wounds on themselves to get out of combat, and units were often deployed in disarray, none of these factors escalate to the point that they threatened to destroy the overall military effectiveness of the Soviet forces. . . . [D]espite tens of thousands of men killed, wounded, and captured, and vast losses of materiel, Soviet forces remained on the field of battle and continued to fight, although, with a few notable exceptions, more fiercely than well.

Marine Private First Class Hector Cafferata offers another example of the potential differences between happiness, orderliness, and the disposition and decision to fight. Cafferata was part of the First Marine Division in the Korean War. In 1950 his unit was surrounded on a hilltop outpost above the Toktong Pass, fighting a desperate holding battle to allow the outnumbered U.S. ground units to escape a massive Chinese offensive.[25] Temperatures plummeted at night to −33°F. Dead bodies were piled up around the Marines. Water was in short supply. Every Marine was exhausted from constant fighting. Most of them were suffering from chronic diarrhea. Few were clean-shaven. They were all eating half-thawed, gelatinous canned food. The Marines' *feelings* about their situation—surrounded, frozen, sick, thirsty, malnourished, exhausted, and terrified—manifested in expressions, postures, and statements that might have given the impression of low morale.[26]

But when the Chinese executed a human wave attack in the middle of the night, Cafferata and his entire unit fought hard. Cafferata came out of his cold sleeping bag and killed over a dozen enemy soldiers. He batted away a grenade with his rifle and lost part of his hand throwing back another grenade. His Medal of Honor citation credits him with helping to hold the line and win the battle. Why did Cafferata choose to fight under such conditions? In his own words, he fought because of his pride in being a Marine, because his identity as a Marine conveyed a sense of duty, and because of his cohesion with his comrades. Cafferata made the following comment after the war:[27]

---

[24]   Roger R. Reese, "Lessons of the Winter War: A Study in the Military Effectiveness of the Red Army, 1939–1940," *Journal of Military History*, Vol. 72, No. 3, July 2008, p. 831. Also see James Venceslav Anzulovic, Jr., *The Russian Record of the Winter War, 1939–1940: An Analytical Study of Soviet Records of the War with Finland from 30 November 1939 to 12 March 1940*, dissertation, College Park, Md.: University of Maryland, 1968.

[25]   This description is taken from multiple sources, including Bob Drury and Tom Clavin, *The Last Stand of Fox Company*, New York: Atlantic Monthly Press, 2009; Martin Russ, *Breakout: The Chosin Reservoir Campaign, Korea 1950*, New York: Fromm International Publishing, 1999; Congressional Medal of Honor Society, "Cafferata, Hector A., Jr."

[26]   Drury and Clavin, 2009.

[27]   Hector Cafferata, "Commandant's Message: 235th Birthday of the Marine Corps."

I did my duty, I protected my fellow Marines, they protected me, and I'm prouder of that than the fact that the government decided to give me the Medal of Honor.

Reading morale in cases like the Korean War is complicated. An outsider might have looked at Fox Company the night before the Chinese assault and seen miserable Marines on the verge of collapse. But a more astute observer might have seen the emergence of a different, deeper reflection of morale stemming from unit identity, expert competence, organizational esprit de corps, cohesion, and leadership. Exogenous conditions that portend low morale can indeed degrade will to fight, but they can also make it stronger by causing individuals to hew closer to the factors that matter most in times of crisis. U.S. Army Brigadier General James A. Ulio wrote:[28]

> [I]t is when rations are lowest, privations sharpest, and every physical and emotional strain the hardest to bear that the quality of military morale may rise to its truest and best, even to the highest plane of spiritual dignity.

This expert insight highlights rather than resolves the complexity of the term. Because it is thus far unresolved, morale is not a factor in the RAND Arroyo Center model. Users can apply Baynes's approach by using the term *morale* to mean holistic will to fight, they can ignore it, or they can seek to define and apply it in ways that we have not envisioned.

How to Read and Apply the Model: A Guide, Not a Formula

The RAND Arroyo Center model is a guide to assessment and analysis. Each factor and subfactor should be *considered* for each case, then either explored in greater detail, set aside for future analysis, or discarded. Every assessment or analysis of will to fight requires different levels of detail, has different objectives, and must be accomplished with different resources and on different timelines. For example, an Army Special Forces Operational Detachment Alpha (ODA) team leader tasked with assessing the will to fight of an allied military platoon may use it to quickly fine-tune a field training plan or deliver a rapid narrative assessment to higher headquarters.[29] A team of intelligence analysts at a national intelligence agency might apply the model with great rigor

---

[28] Ulio, 1941, p. 324.

[29] Special Forces ODAs, or SFOD-As, operate in teams of 12 in remote areas, often semi-independently, and almost always focused on tactical training and operations. ODA team leaders are periodically required to send reports to higher headquarters describing events in the field, and often describing the capabilities and competencies of the foreign military units they may be advising. These reports are sometimes disseminated as Special Operations Debrief and Retrieval System (SODARS) reports. SODARS reports are typically narrative reports with minimal structure. A simple will-to-fight tactical assessment model would probably facilitate the ODA team leader's ability to quickly, concisely, and effectively describe the will to fight of a partner military force. For explanations of the ODA, see U.S. Army, "Special Forces" (website). For an explanation of SODARS, see Thomas Newell, *The Use of Special Operations Forces in Combating Terrorist Financing*, thesis, Monterey, Calif.: Naval Postgraduate School, 2006, Chapter Three.

over time, examining each factor and generating a series of narratives, charts, tables, and a rating scale tailored just for a fixed set of adversary military units. There is no one-size-fits-all approach to understanding or using this model. Instead, the model should be used to craft a unique process and output tailored to the interests, requirements, capabilities, and timelines of the user. Applying the model to gaming and simulation requires differentiation. No two applications of this model should be exactly the same.

The model points leaders, advisors, and analysts to the factors and subfactors that our research showed to be most important to understand will to fight. For example, at the individual level it is not necessary to understand the identity or educational experience or psychological profile of each individual soldier in a unit to better understand that unit's will to fight. Instead, it is important to consider these subfactors, to think about how they collectively contribute to individual will to fight, and then use this analysis as a guide to develop a collective profile for each unit. If the subfactor of *skills* is important to building a soldier's factor of *competence*, and high competence in turn gives the soldier confidence—and perhaps increased disposition—to fight, how skilled, collectively, are all the soldiers in the unit? How do the soldiers perceive their skills? Holistic findings can be derived from an application of the model without explaining all details of an individual soldier and the entire social system of a unit, an organization, a state, and a society.

What, then, does the model offer in terms of output? What would a reading of the model look like for an advisor in the field or an intelligence analyst? Our research team will continue to develop tools to apply the model through at least the end of 2018. However, the model can be used to generate any type of result in any format. It can contribute to an overall narrative assessment: A notional unit x has poor will to fight because of weaknesses in factors y and z. Or it can generate a color-coded chart or table for quick and easy assessment by senior leaders. Or it can be used to identify and target individual factors or groups of factors for practical application like improved training or, against an adversary, psychological operations or well-placed and well-timed kinetic strikes. It can and should be used to address the gaps identified in the JC-HAMO.

How should each factor be rated and weighted? For example, what is the objective value of *unit cohesion*? There is no objective value or general rule that can be applied to any factor in this model. Both quantitative and qualitative methods and data can be applied to understand any of these factors, including measurement of performance, training surveys, intelligence information reports, and individual advisor observations. Possible approaches are effectively limitless. Anyone attempting to develop and apply a general rule to this model should do so cautiously. While it is true that better unit esprit de corps, better organizational leadership, and better state support can usually be equated with better will to fight, it is not true that more desperation, higher expectations for support, or more coercion necessarily improves will to fight. In some cases, more unit cohesion might help an otherwise weak unit refuse orders to fight. Each factor must be examined separately and then considered collectively in a way that fits the objectives and format of the assessment or analysis.

The next sections in this chapter build the model step-by-step, from the individual to the unit, organizational, state, and societal levels. The chapter concludes by presenting the holistic explanatory, exploratory, and portable will-to-fight model.

Individual-Level System-of-Systems Model of Will to Fight

The first way to think about a realistic system-of-systems model of will to fight is to build it from the individual level to the unit level. Here we are following a recruit from civilian life, through indoctrination, through basic training (where the recruit becomes a soldier), and out to his or her unit. Each individual carries with him or her all of his or her life experiences and learned approaches to deciding behavior. These are called cognitive schemas. Basically, schemas are roadmaps for action that each individual learns through cultural transmission and by trial and error.[30] The individual also brings with him or her a series of motivations—for example, idealism, economic need, or existential fear.[31] Table 2.4 is a list of individual factors derived from the list in Table 2.3.

Table 2.4
Individual Factors of Will to Fight

Level	Category	Factors	Subfactors	Durability
Individual	Individual motivations	Desperation		Mid
		Revenge Ideology Economics		High
		Individual identity	Personal, social, unit, state, organization, and society (including political, religious)	High
	Individual capabilities	Quality	Fitness, resilience, education, adaptability, social skills, and psychological traits	High
		Individual competence	Skills, relevance, sufficiency, and sustainability	High

[30] See Roy G. D'Andrade, "Schemas and Motivation," in D'Andrade and Strauss, 1992, pp. 23–44; Claudia Strauss, "Models and Motives," in D'Andrade and Strauss, 1992, pp. 1–20; and Deborah Kendzierski and Daniel J. Whitaker, "The Role of Self-Schema in Linking Intentions with Behavior," *Personality and Social Psychology Bulletin*, Vol. 23, No. 2, 1997, pp. 139–147.

[31] We explain motivation later in this chapter. D'Andrade writes about the ways in which schemas can be motivating. D'Andrade, 1992. Also see Kellet, 1982; and Fernando Rodrigues-Goulard, "Combat Motivation," *Military Review*, November–December 2006, pp. 93–96.

It includes the categories of *individual motivations* and *individual capabilities*, 7 factors, and 16 subfactors relevant to understanding individual will to fight. All of these are explained below.

Individuals enter organizations with existing cognitive schemas. Organizations indoctrinate individuals and attempt to change these schemas and motivations: Instead of fleeing gunfire—a logical and common civilian schema for survival—they are often retrained to run toward the sound of gunfire. Once they are indoctrinated and trained, soldiers are sent out to their units, where they meet their leaders, learn about local expectations for behavior, receive unit training, and form bonds with fellow soldiers. Each soldier is both a system and an interrelated part of the unit, organizational, state, and societal system of systems.

Figure 2.4 depicts this process, building the system-of-systems model of compounding, interrelated factors from one level to the next. Circles represent the additive layers of factors from deeper internalized factors like ideology, to organizational culture and training, and then to the unit. In the first box to the left (light tan circle), each individual incorporates culture and experience into his or her cognitive patterns prior to joining the military. In the center, the individual joins the military organization (light green circle) and adds organizational cultural influences to the set of factors that influence disposition to fight. On the right, the individual enters the unit (dark green circle) and joins other individuals. The unit becomes more important to the individu-

Figure 2.4
Individuals as Parts of Organizations and Units

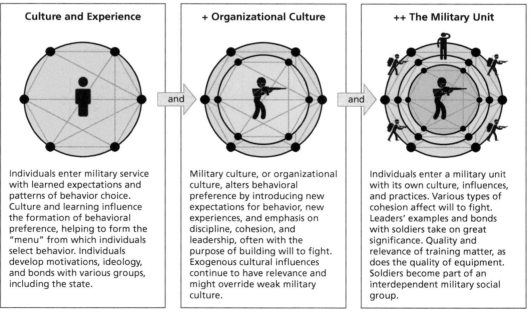

Culture and Experience	+ Organizational Culture	++ The Military Unit
Individuals enter military service with learned expectations and patterns of behavior choice. Culture and learning influence the formation of behavioral preference, helping to form the "menu" from which individuals select behavior. Individuals develop motivations, ideology, and bonds with various groups, including the state.	Military culture, or organizational culture, alters behavioral preference by introducing new expectations for behavior, new experiences, and emphasis on discipline, cohesion, and leadership, often with the purpose of building will to fight. Exogenous cultural influences continue to have relevance and might override weak military culture.	Individuals enter a military unit with its own culture, influences, and practices. Various types of cohesion affect will to fight. Leaders' examples and bonds with soldiers take on great significance. Quality and relevance of training matter, as does the quality of equipment. Soldiers become part of an interdependent military social group.

al's disposition to fight than the organization (light green circle), reflected in its closer placement to the center. Black circles represent factors, while gray lines notionally represent the many interrelated, additive links that build at each level. This figure is a stylized way of thinking about the complex and layered development of the overall model.

Each individual soldier carries internalized *motivations* to fight and *individual capabilities* to fight. Motivations are reasons an individual is more or less disposed to fight, before layering in any aspect of military culture or training. Capabilities, including *quality* and *individual competence*, affect disposition to fight. Our literature review showed that better educated, more stable, more sociable, and more capable soldiers who are confident of performing in combat are generally more disposed to fight, with all other factors being equal.[32]

Motivations

Motivations are obtained from cultural interactions with family members, friends, and groups; from formal or informal learning at home and in school; and from social and material needs including desire to succeed and the need to survive.[33] Motivations weigh heavily on the decision to fight but they do not stand alone. They are only part of the interconnected latticework that forms both individual and unit will to fight. We identified five categories of individual motivation to fight.[34] Some *or* all of these might be relevant for any individual, but all should be considered (identity is always present). With the exception of desperation, these factors are highly durable: They are not sharply affected within the scope of a single battle and they are generally resistant to rapid change.

Desperation can be immediately existential, or it can describe a fear of genocide or the desire to protect families threatened by war. It reflects the idea that combatants will fight to survive. We found examples of this at the level of the person (literally fighting for your life and personal safety) and at a higher social level—for example, the survival of the Confederacy during the American Civil War.[35] Desperation can

---

[32] There is some controversy behind these assumptions. See Keene, 1994, pp. 235–253.

[33] While this report does not directly draw on or address the collective research on military air crews, we found the research presented by Roy R. Grinker and John P. Spiegel on American air crews in World War II to be highly informative, and particularly so for individual factors. Roy R. Grinker and John P. Spiegel, *Men under Stress*, Philadelphia: The Blakiston Company, 1945.

[34] All factors described in this chapter were derived from our coding of relevant literature and cases, as well as a wide array of supporting literature cited throughout this report. Some of the best aggregated explanations of these factors can be found in Baynes, 1988 (1967); Bidwell, 1973; Richardson, 2009 (1978); Sarkesian, 1980; Kellett, 1982; Henderson, 1985; King, 2015; and Richard Holmes, *Acts of War: The Behavior of Men in Battle*, New York: The Free Press, 1985.

[35] Mark Clodfelter, "Aiming to Break Will: America's World War II Bombing of German Morale and Its Ramifications," *Journal of Strategic Studies*, Vol. 33, No. 3, 2010, pp. 401–435; Keegan, 1976; Joseph Allan Frank and George A. Reaves, *Seeing the Elephant: Raw Recruits at the Battle of Shiloh*, Urbana: University of Illinois Press, 2003; James M. McPherson, *For Cause and Comrades: Why Men Fought in the Civil War*, New York: Oxford Uni-

be tactical or strategic, personal or societal, and sometimes a mixture of these typologies. Tactical desperation is almost always personal: If the battle is lost, the individual soldier will be faced with maiming, death, capture, or the humiliation of fleeing in the face of the enemy. Societal desperation obtains when the individual believes that the strategic-level war presents an existential threat to the soldier's homeland. Sometimes this also means a physical, and therefore personal, threat to the soldier's family. Tactical desperation can change quickly during the course of a single battle or series of battles, while societal, strategic desperation is more constant during these short time periods.[36]

Revenge-fueled will to fight can also be an immediate motivator, or it can reflect deeper anger. For example, oppression of minorities over time can generate a deep desire for revenge that exists beyond the battlefield. Revenge emerged as a motivator in the scholarship about the U.S. Civil War and World War II.[37] Soldiers often speak or write about the desire for revenge at the small unit level. They experience a loss at the hands of the enemy, observe enemy atrocities, or are convinced of the need for revenge through organizational or state information campaigns. Dramatic increases in American military recruitment after the Japanese attack on Pearl Harbor in 1941 and the al Qaeda attack on the World Trade Center in 2001 reflected desire for revenge.

Ideology is a commitment to a cause or belief system. This could include general ideas of patriotism, religious commitment, explicitly political ideologies such as strong belief in communism or Nazism, or abstract concepts like peace or freedom.[38] In a 1916 monograph containing his exhortations to new officers, British Lieutenant Colonel W. Shirley attempted to draw a distinction between revenge and the ideologi-

---

versity Press, 1997; Andrew F. Lang, "Upon the Altar of Our Country: Confederate Identity, Nationalism, and Morale in Harrison County, Texas, 1860–1865," *Civil War History*, Vol. 55, No. 2, 2009, pp. 278–306.

[36] This is true even if the single battle or short series of battles decides the outcome of a war. The existential strategic threat is more pressing but still constant throughout the course of the battle or short series of battles.

[37] Frank and Reaves, 2003; Jacob Neufeld and George M. Watson, Jr., "A Brief Survey of POWs in Twentieth Century Wars," *Air Power History*, Vol. 60, No. 2, 2013, p. 34; Omer Bartov, "The Conduct of War: Soldiers and the Barbarization of Warfare," *Journal of Modern History*, Vol. 64, 1992, pp. S32–S45.

[38] Kellett, 1982; Scott Atran, Hammad Sheikh, and Angel Gomez, "Devoted Actors Sacrifice for Close Comrades and Sacred Cause," *Proceedings of the National Academy of Sciences*, Vol. 111, No. 50, 2014, pp. 17702–17703; Rune Henriksen and Anthony Vinci, "Combat Motivation in Non-State Armed Groups," *Terrorism and Political Violence*, Vol. 20, No. 1, 2007, pp. 87–109; David W. P. Elliott and Mai Elliott, *Documents of an Elite Viet Cong Delta Unit: The Demolition Platoon of the 514th Battalion: Part Four: Political Indoctrination and Military Training*, Santa Monica, Calif.: RAND Corporation, RM-5851-ISA/ARPA, 1969; Neufeld and Watson, 2013; Roger D. Markwick and Euridice Charon Cardona, *Soviet Women on the Frontline in the Second World War*, New York: Palgrave Macmillan, 2012; T. W. Britt, *Responsibility, Morale, and Commitment During Military Operations*, Heidelberg, Germany: Army Medical Research Unit Europe, 1996; T. M. Chacho, "Why Did They Fight? American Airborne Units in World War II," *Defence Studies*, Vol. 1, No. 3, 2001, pp. 59–94; Paul C. Stern, "Why Do People Sacrifice for Their Nations?" *Political Psychology*, Vol. 16, No. 2, 1995, pp. 217–235.

cal duty to protect free people and right wrongs committed by Germany in World War I.[39]

> I pray you conjure up the horrid vision of Prussian despotism. . . . Think if *your* country were devastated, *your* homes destroyed, *your* women-folk dishonored, and *your* dear ones done to death. . . . Heaven forbid that I should seek to inspire you with the spirit of retaliation. It is true that revenge and hate are calculated to promote courage, but they are also apt to betray you into cruel and dishonorable actions unworthy of the name and character of the British Army. I exhort you to go forth as the Champions of Right, not as the Avengers of Wrong.

Identity is the most varied and perhaps the most complex motivation, and it is always multifaceted. Soldiers typically enter the military with social identities built from their relationships with family and friends, with societal identities, often with ethnic identities, and many others. Academic descriptions of the term *identity* are varied and contested, and not all are relevant to understanding will to fight.[40] Several points are worth drawing from this literature. First, individual identity is never unitary. Will to fight of all individual soldiers will be influenced by various identities from within and outside the military organization. For example, Bruce Allen Watson describes how the influences of communism contributed to the mutiny of some French soldiers during World War I.[41] Second, identity is dynamic but generally not to the point that it would change over the course of a single battle. Finally, identity is both culturally obtained and unique within the individual: Each soldier forms a unique perspective on various influencing identities, and in doing so creates a separate unique identity that influences will to fight.

Ideology, which we treat as a separate motivator in order to aid analysis, can foster identities. All motivators have high durability except for desperation.

---

[39] W. Shirley, *Moral: The Most Important Factor in War*, London: Sifton, Praed & Company, 1916, pp. 6–7.

[40] *Identity* is a relevant term in nearly every aspect of social science and in every field, from anthropology to sociology to psychology. A full review of identity literature would require a separate book. These articles and books might help inform a better understanding of identity as it relates to will to fight: Glen E. Kreiner, Elaine C. Hollensbe, and Mathew L. Sheep, "On the Edge of Identity: Boundary Dynamics at the Interface of Individual and Organizational Identities," *Human Relations*, Vol. 59, No. 10, 2006, pp. 1315–1341; William Bloom, *Personal Identity, National Identity, and International Relations*, Cambridge: Cambridge University Press, 1990; Leonie Huddy, "From Social to Political Identity: A Critical Examination of Social Identity Theory," *Political Psychology*, Vol. 22, No. 1, March 2001, pp. 127–156; Stephen Gibson and Susan Condor, "State Institutions and Social Identity: National Representation in Soldiers' and Civilians' Interview Talk Concerning Military Service," *British Journal of Social Psychology*, Vol. 48, No. 2, June 2009, pp. 313–336; Rachel Woodward and K. Neil Jenkings, "Military Identities in the Situated Accounts of British Military Personnel, *Sociology*, Vol. 45, No. 2, 2011, pp. 252–268; and Sonia Roccas and Marilynn B. Brewer, "Social Identity Complexity," *Personality and Social Psychology Review*, Vol. 6, No. 2, 2002, pp. 88–106.

[41] Watson, 1997, Chapter Four.

Identity	This includes social and personal identity. It is the commitment to an identity (e.g., expectations about what a soldier does) or sense of self-search for satisfaction.
Desperation	Desperation is the fear of death or the need for self-preservation, a sense of utter extremity, or a belief that no other options exist: when you fight because your back is to the wall. Desperation can change within the course of a battle, but for the individual model desperation most often refers to broader fears about the survival of the state, the organization, or family. It is therefore highly durable.
Revenge	Revenge can stem from a number of sources, both long-standing and immediate. Revenge can have historical roots—for example, it can manifest from long-standing disputes between ethnic and sectarian groups—or it can result from observing an enemy attack or atrocity.
Economy	Economic motivations can be tied to self and family. This includes the need for subsistence—literally the need to eat—the need for socioeconomic advancement, and the motivation to earn money to improve quality of life.
Ideology	For this model, ideology is any commitment to a cause or belief system, including religion and political causes—for example, communism, democracy, Islam, Christianity, freedom, and national socialism (Nazism). State patriotism or jingoism is a common motivation.

These motivators are layered across the individual will-to-fight model, showing how they might be derived from unit, organizational, state, and societal factors. Soldier capabilities form the other part of the individual model, depicted in Figure 2.4. Other factors could also be included in this model; it reflects our research but it is not necessarily exclusive.

Individual Capabilities

Individual capabilities fall into two general categories: (1) soldier quality and (2) competence. Quality is *the basic mental and physical capability of the individual*. It consists of *education*, *social skills*, *fitness*, *psychological traits*, *adaptability*, and *resilience*. Each of these six components is derived collectively from the literature: A wide array of books and articles from the disciplines of military history, war studies (or military science), sociology, and psychology show that these six subfactors contribute to an individual soldier's basic capability. Quality is the soldier's ability to understand the often complex reasons that fighting is required, to remain stable and avoid succumbing to panic, to develop meaningful bonds with fellow soldiers and leaders, and to find ways to avoid, overcome, or take advantage of the inevitable chaos, friction, and uncertainty inherent in war.[42] Quality can change over time, but it has generally high durability over the course of a single battle or a short series of battles. The major exception to this is *psychological traits*, which we discuss below. Intense combat action can rapidly alter the psychological profile of an individual soldier.[43]

Quality is the most complex and debatable aspect of individual will to fight, even more than identity. Psychiatrists and psychologists have not settled on a single acceptable, replicable way to understand why someone will or will not fight in combat, or even on a unitary theory of mental constructs or measurement.[44] Some efforts, including a 1957 study titled *Fighter 1: An Analysis of Combat Fighters and Non-Fighters*, were controversial and may have generated misleading conclusions.[45] Thankfully our model does not need to solve the enduring debates over the human mind. There is sufficient literature to show that with all other factors being equal, individuals who are more mentally stable are more resilient and more willing to fight.[46] Collectively, the literature argues that recruiting better-quality people makes for a more willing fighting force.[47] Psychological traits are complex and offer an array of opportunities for analysis and simulation. An individual's aggressiveness, sense of humor, and other factors are

---

[42]   For descriptions of panic and associated terms, see Harry Stack Sullivan, "Psychiatric Aspects of Morale," *American Journal of Sociology*, Vol. 47, No. 3, November 1941, pp. 277–301.

[43]   See Belenky, 1987.

[44]   We describe one of these approaches—trait-state, or state-trait, modeling—in Chapter Four. Also see Meerloo, 1957, pp. 362–363.

[45]   Robert L. Egbert, Tor Meeland, Victor B. Cline, Edward W. Forgy, Martin W. Spickler, and Charles Brown, *Fighter 1: An Analysis of Combat Fighters and Non-Fighters*, Technical Report 44, Monterey, Calif.: U.S. Army Leadership Human Research Unit, December 1957. See Kellett, 1982, pp. 308–309, for an assessment of this report.

[46]   Our model provides a basis for assessing and analyzing unit will to fight, not a key for individual-level psychoanalysis. Gregory Belenky provides an effective survey of empirical analysis on combat psychiatry. Belenky, 1987. Also see Moran, 2007 (1945); Edgar Jones, "The Psychology of Killing: The Combat Experience of British Soldiers During the First World War," *Journal of Contemporary History*, Vol. 41, No. 2, 2006, pp. 229–246; Lorraine B. Davis, ed., "War Psychiatry," in Russ Zajtchuk, ed., *Textbook of Military Medicine*, Washington, D.C.: TTM Publications, U.S. Army Office of the Surgeon General, 1995; Dave Grossman, *On Killing: The Psychological Cost of Learning to Kill in War and Society*, Boston: Little, Brown, and Company, 1995; Reuven Gal and Franklin D. Jones, "A Psychological Model of Combat Stress," in Russ Zajtchuk, ed., *Textbook of Military Medicine, Part I: War Psychiatry*, Falls Church, Va.: Office of the Surgeon General of the United States of America, 1995, pp. 133–148; Juri Toomepuu, *Soldier Capability-Army Combat Effectiveness (SCACE) Study*, Fort Benjamin Harrison, Ind.: Army Soldier Support Center, 1980; Robert H. Ahrenfeldt, *Psychiatry in the British Army in the Second World War*, London: Routledge and Kegan Paul Limited, 1958.

[47]   There are some counterarguments and some arguments for a typology of good fighter–bad fighter. These include Egbert et al., 1957; Trevor N. Dupuy and Gay M. Hammerman, *Soldier Capability—Army Combat Effectiveness (SCACE)*: Volume III, *Historical Combat Data and Analysis*, Dunn Loring, Va.: Historical Evaluation and Research Organization, December 1980; and Rune Henriksen, "Warriors in Combat—What Makes People Actively Fight in Combat?" *Journal of Strategic Studies*, Vol. 30, No. 2, 2007, pp. 187–223.

all relevant to will to fight.[48] However, the literature suggests one central factor: Is the individual soldier stable? Stable soldiers are more likely to successfully process the stress of combat in order to fight or act. Special operations forces are careful to select psychologically stable individuals because they are generally more capable of handling the stress of combat without breaking under fire; breaking under fire is one of the behaviors associated with a loss of will to fight (see Chapter Three for additional behaviors).[49]

Education is both the quality and relevance of individual learning, and its applicability to the combat situation. Education can be a double-edged sword: Both Lord Moran and John Baynes suggest that sometimes knowing too much can weigh on the mind and perhaps exacerbate the impact of combat on stability.[50] However, the majority consensus in the literature review is that higher levels of education equate with greater will to fight: Understanding the context of combat and the rationale for fighting can bolster individual motivation.[51] Literature on cohesion and wartime psychology also addresses the value of individual social skills, physical fitness, and psychological traits to will to fight.

Social skills are the skills to develop cohesive bonds with peers and leaders. In general, a group of soldiers inept at forming social bonds would be less likely to form social cohesion, and therefore somewhat less likely to fight.[52] Fitness is physical ability and conditioning—is the soldier physically capable of fighting or acting as needed? A strong and capable body tends to impart confidence in performance, which contributes positively to will to fight. Fitness has been shown to reduce anxiety, and anxiety generally undermines will to fight.[53] In general, anything that generates confidence in the ability to fight—including quality training, good leadership, and so on—improves will to fight, although even extraordinary confidence can be undone in any one case by any one overriding factor.[54] There is no magical, additive formula of individual qualities that guarantees dependable, mission-focused will to fight.

---

[48]   Belenky, 1987; Moran, 2007 (1945); Baynes, 1988 (1967); Henderson, 1985.

[49]   For example: Paul T. Bartone, Robert R. Roland, James J. Picano, and Thomas J. Williams, "Psychological Hardiness Predicts Success in U.S. Army Special Forces Candidates," *International Journal of Selection and Assessment*, Vol. 16, No. 1, March 2008, pp. 78–81.

[50]   Moran, 2007 (1945); Baynes, 1988 (1967).

[51]   This finding and all of the findings in this section and the remainder of the model are derived collectively from the nine-part multimethod research. The articles in Belenky, 1987, provide considerable insight into psychiatric studies, psychological modeling for combat, and the performance of individual soldiers in combat.

[52]   For example: James Griffith, "Measurement of Group Cohesion in U.S. Army," *Basic and Applied Social Psychology*, Vol. 9, No. 2, 1988, pp. 149–171.

[53]   For example: Marcus K. Taylor, Amanda E. Markham, Jared P. Reis, Genieleah A. Padilla, Eric G. Potterat, Sean P. A. Drummond, and Lilianne R. Mujica-Parodi, "Physical Fitness Influences Stress Reactions to Extreme Military Training," *Military Medicine*, Vol. 173, No. 8, 2008, pp. 738–742.

[54]   For example: Reuven Gal, "Unit Morale: From a Theoretical Puzzle to an Empirical Illustration—An Israeli Example," *Journal of Applied Social Psychology*, Vol. 16, No. 6, 1986, pp. 549–564; Anthony King, "The Word

Adaptability is the capacity and disposition to adjust to unfamiliar and uncomfortable situations to find a way to succeed.[55] Adaptable soldiers have developed the cognitive schemas for rapid adjustment to changing conditions and for general problem solving.[56] They are less dependent on predictability and routine and more capable of handling the unpredictability, friction, and dynamism of combat. Adaptable soldiers are less vulnerable to surprise, which is a significant exogenous factor in depleting will to fight (see Chapter Three). Heroism, a sign of high disposition to fight, appears to be derived in part from adaptability.[57]

Resilience is the capacity and disposition to overcome intense mental strain to avoid weakening or breaking.[58] Like education, adaptability, and some other individual factors, resilience derives from both military and nonmilitary life experience. Higher resilience is generally associated with lower incidents of combat stress and therefore higher will to fight.[59] RAND Arroyo Center conducted a meta-analysis of resilience literature and identified seven evidence-informed factors that make up individual resilience: positive coping, positive affect, positive thinking, realism, behavioral control, physical fitness, and altruism.[60] The team described an additional 13 factors that contributed to these individual qualities. All of these could be studied and used to generate a separate, sub-subfactor resilience model for will to fight.

We identify *competence* as a will-to-fight factor at the individual and unit levels. At the individual level, competence is the application of military skills to quality. All

---

of Command: Communication and Cohesion in the Military," *Armed Forces and Society*, Vol. 32, No. 4, July 2006, pp. 493–512; Frederick J. Manning, "Morale and Cohesion in Military Psychiatry," in Russ Zajtchuk, ed., *Textbook of Military Medicine*, Washington, D.C.: TTM Publications, U.S. Army Office of the Surgeon General, 1995.

[55] For a detailed examination of individual adaptability, see Ben Connable, *Warrior-Maverick Culture: The Evolution of Adaptability in the U.S. Marine Corps*, doctoral thesis, London: King's College London, 2016.

[56] One interesting experiment examines this premise and tests approaches to adaptability: Peder Hyllengren, "Military Leaders' Adaptability in Unexpected Situations," *Military Psychology*, Vol. 29, No. 4, 2017, pp. 245–259.

[57] This factor emerged in almost every combat narrative we reviewed, and that included acts of heroism. There is also some empirical work on the connection between adaptability and heroism. See Brian Wansink, Collin R. Payne, and Koert van Ittersum, "Profiling the Heroic Leader: Empirical Lessons from Combat-Decorated Veterans of World War II," *The Leadership Quarterly*, No. 19, 2008, pp. 547–555.

[58] For example: Ricardo M. Love, *Psychological Resilience: Preparing Our Soldiers for War*, Carlisle, Pa.: U.S. Army War College, 2011; John M. Schaubroeck, Ann Chunyan Peng, Laura T. Riolli, and Everett S. Spain, "Resilience to Traumatic Exposure Among Soldiers Deployed in Combat," *Journal of Occupational Health Psychology*, Vol. 16, No. 1, 2011, pp. 18–37.

[59] Paul T. Bartone uses the term *hardiness* to stand in for resilience, and he associates it with will to fight in selected cases. Paul T. Bartone, "Resilience Under Military Operational Stress: Can Leaders Influence Hardiness?" *Military Psychology*, No. 18 (supplemental), 2006, pp. 131–148.

[60] Lisa S. Meredith, Cathy D. Sherbourne, Sarah Gaillot, Lydia Hansell, Hans V. Ritschard, Andrew M. Parker, and Glenda Wrenn, *Promoting Psychological Resilience in the U.S. Military*, Santa Monica, Calif.: RAND Corporation, MG-996-OSD, 2011.

people have qualities that would be relevant to will to fight. Military indoctrination, acculturation, training, and military education give the soldier the abilities necessary to fight in modern war. Will to fight is derived in part from the way soldiers trust their own competence: Do they believe they have the *skills* necessary to fight effectively or to do their jobs to support those in direct combat?[61] Is their competence *relevant* to the mission and to the enemy they have to fight? Are their skills *sufficient* to allow them to fight or act effectively? Do the soldiers believe that their competence has been sustained over time, or has it been allowed to languish and fade, leaving them less capable of fighting and therefore, perhaps, less disposed to fight?

It is sufficient to say that high-quality and competent soldiers who are capable and confident in their abilities, and who believe that they are prepared for combat will be more disposed to fight when needed than soldiers who are generally incapable and who lack confidence in their abilities.[62]

Soldier quality	Education levels, social skills, physical capabilities, and psychological traits—including the collective traits of resilience and adaptability—all compose quality. Higher-quality soldiers have more disposition to fight. Lower-quality soldiers have less disposition to fight.
Competence	Competence is skills and capabilities developed as an individual or as part of the unit, including fighting, basic soldiering, specialty, leadership, and fitness. Skills and capabilities can preexist training, but they are strongly influenced by military training and combat experience.

Quality and competence have high durability. However, quality is slightly more complex than competence. Soldiers enter battle with certain qualities, including mental stability. But stability can change very quickly in response to trauma. We explore this individual dynamic in Chapter Three as part of the discussion of the Silver Model trait-state dynamic.

Building the Individual Model from the Factors

Figure 2.5 places these individual factors into a systems model. It shows the three layers of influence with the most internalized qualities at the inner circle, the organizational influence at the middle circle, and the state and societal influences on the outer circle. Connections between factors and the circles show how the factor is generally relevant to an individual. In keeping with the purpose of our model, this figure is explanatory rather than explicit. It shows general sources of each factor. It *does not*

---

[61]   Hew Strachan, "Training, Morale and Modern War," *Journal of Contemporary History*, Vol. 41, No. 2, 2006, pp. 211–227.

[62]   For example: Woodward and Jenkings, 2011.

Figure 2.5
Systems Model of Stand-Alone Soldier Will-to-Fight Factors

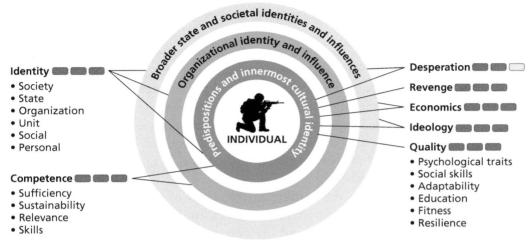

Identity ▭ ▭ ▭
- Society
- State
- Organization
- Unit
- Social
- Personal

Competence ▭ ▭ ▭
- Sufficiency
- Sustainability
- Relevance
- Skills

Broader state and societal identities and influences
Organizational identity and influence
Predispositions and innermost cultural identity
INDIVIDUAL

Desperation ▭ ▭ ▭

Revenge ▭ ▭ ▭

Economics ▭ ▭ ▭

Ideology ▭ ▭ ▭

Quality ▭ ▭ ▭
- Psychological traits
- Social skills
- Adaptability
- Education
- Fitness
- Resilience

RAND *RR2341A-2.5*

argue that these factors have a fixed position, value, or set of relationships, or that these arrangements are replicable. Individuals bring many parts of quality—basic psychological composition, cognitive schemas, physical limitations—with them as they enter the military, but these can be modified by training. Identity is influenced at every level: society, state, organization, and unit. Competence derives from the organization and the unit, and interacts with quality and other factors.

Even at the individual level the complexity of the model stands out. Understanding the actual relationship between these factors even in a single individual is a virtual impossibility. It is enough to understand that these factors do matter and that they interrelate.

Adding the Individual Subfactors of Will to Fight

This section adds the subfactors to the visual models, building them out factor by factor. We identified key subfactors when the top-level factor demanded greater detail and when important associated but subordinate factors existed. Subfactors may provide some of the best opportunities to both understand and influence will to fight. While a military advisor or analyst may never seek to understand the psychological qualities of an individual soldier, understanding soldiers' collective strengths and weaknesses can help military units shape and execute influence operations.[63] Knowing that many

---

[63] U.S. military personnel generally think about influence operations as information operations, or those non-kinetic communications—including psychological operations, deception, civil affairs, public affairs, and computer network operations—that are used to shape human perceptions about military operations. In the broader sense they can also include kinetic actions that are designed to influence behavior rather than just wound or kill.

soldiers in a unit appear to have poor adaptability can inform methods to improve a unit's collective ability to adapt. Or the military can take advantage of a less adaptable enemy unit by increasing the tempo and variety of operations against it: Knowing the precise weaknesses in enemy will to fight can help a commander build precise methods to break it.

Figures. 2.6 through 2.8 depict the components of quality, identity, and competence. There are also many ways to break down desperation, revenge, economy, and ideology, but these variations are too individualized for a general model. Figure 2.6 depicts the component elements of quality, showing *education*, *social skills*, and *fitness*, and then three closely linked characteristics: *psychological traits*, *adaptability*, and *resilience*. These are linked but also distinct. Both adaptability and resilience depend on extant psychological traits, but these can be improved or degraded through acculturation and training, and in combat.

Next, Figure 2.7 depicts the component elements of identity. It generalizes a range of identities that are most important for understanding will to fight, connecting the *society*, the *state*, the *organization*, and the *unit* to the individual. Each individual maintains *personal* concepts of identity as well as a range of *social* identities that may have nothing to do with the military but might be critically important to will to fight. Ethnic and religious identities can and often do affect cohesion at the unit level, and also trust in the state. For example, Russian soldiers from ethnic minorities are often looked down on in the Russian Army. Trust is eroded, resentments build, and the dis-

Figure 2.6
Soldier Quality as a Subsystem at the Stand-Alone Level of Will to Fight

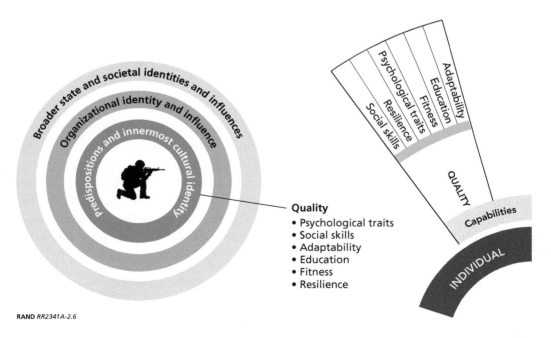

RAND RR2341A-2.6

Figure 2.7
Identity as a Subsystem at the Stand-Alone Level of Will to Fight

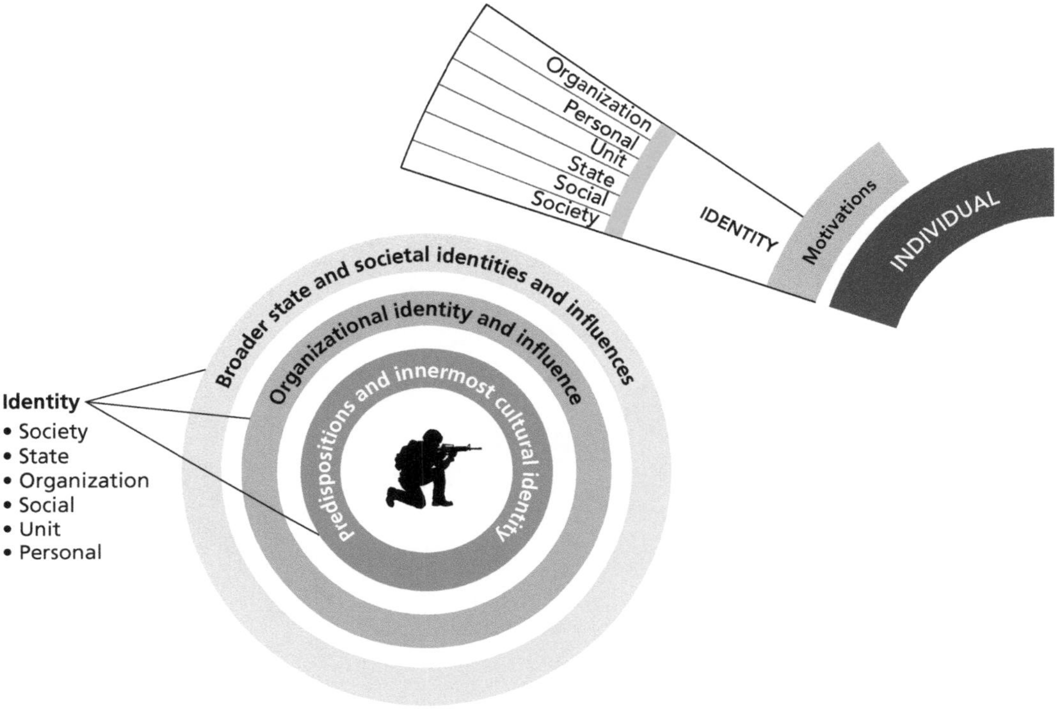

Identity
- Society
- State
- Organization
- Social
- Unit
- Personal

position to fight is hard to build or sustain.[64] All aspects of identity have high durability, and all are influenced by the organization, state, and society.

Figure 2.8 depicts competence as the third factor that influences stand-alone will to fight. At the individual level, competence encompasses skills that are built and enhanced by received training. Competence is durable: Its qualities cannot be changed over the course of an hour of combat. Later in this chapter we describe unit competence and organizational training, and their impacts on individual competence. At the individual level the soldier has *skills*. These are the actual capabilities the individual soldier brings to the fight. Are these skills *relevant* to the tasks the soldier has to perform? Training in hand-to-hand combat is not relevant to rifle fire at 200 meters. Are these skills *sufficient* to prepare the soldier for those tasks, or to win a fight? And finally, are skills *sustained* over time, or are they fading?

---

[64] For example: Dale R. Herspring, "Undermining Combat Readiness in the Russian Military, 1992–2005," *Armed Forces & Society*, Vol. 32, No. 4, 2006, pp. 513–531; Alena Maklak, "Dedovshchina on Trial: Some Evidence Concerning the Last Soviet Generation of 'Sons' and 'Grandfathers,'" *Nationalities Papers*, Vol. 43, No. 5, 2015, pp. 682–699.

Figure 2.8
Competence as a Subsystem at the Stand-Alone Level of Will to Fight

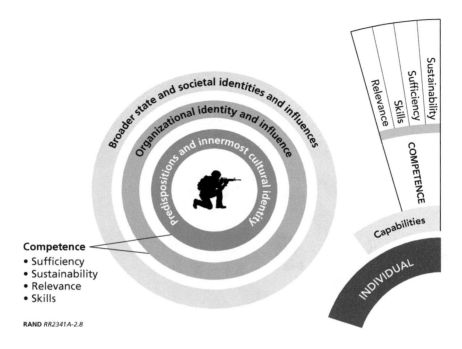

RAND RR2341A-2.8

Figure 2.9 builds from these subsystems to depict the individual soldier as the center of an individual subsystem. Each soldier's will to fight derives from the effects of at least the three constant factors—quality, identity, and competence—and one or more of the potential factors, like desperation, revenge, economics, and ideology.

It would be possible to break down each of the subfactors into more subfactor systems. This is the point at which portability comes into play: With this guide, further exploration and subfactor modeling are not only possible but encouraged. Each user will have to determine a suitable level of detail based on specific requirements. In some cases significant detail will be needed for a small set of factors. For example, a U.S. military advisory unit attempting to screen candidates for a partner military force might apply all 20 of the resilience subfactors that RAND identified in its 2011 study.

With the individual model in place, we must put the soldier back into the unit. In the military, no soldier stands alone. Nearly all relevant military behavior is related to the unit. All of the factors that bear on the individual's will to fight are intrinsically linked to unit factors.

Figure 2.9
Individual Soldier as a Will-to-Fight Subsystem

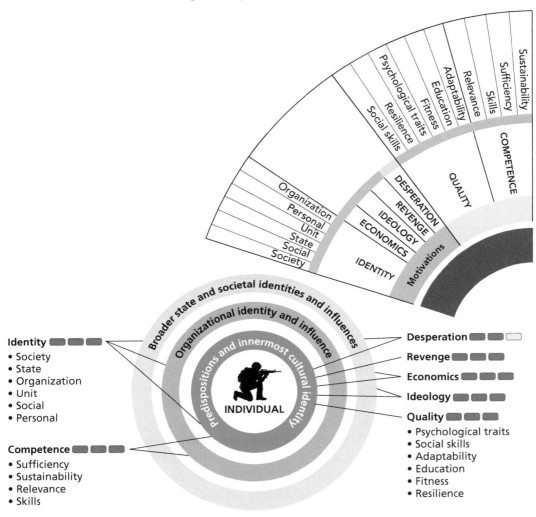

Identity 🔲🔲🔲
- Society
- State
- Organization
- Unit
- Social
- Personal

Competence 🔲🔲🔲
- Sufficiency
- Sustainability
- Relevance
- Skills

Desperation 🔲🔲⬜

Revenge 🔲🔲🔲

Economics 🔲🔲🔲

Ideology 🔲🔲🔲

Quality 🔲🔲🔲
- Psychological traits
- Social skills
- Adaptability
- Education
- Fitness
- Resilience

Unit-Level System-of-Systems Model of Will to Fight

Describing unit-level will to fight risks what scientists call *reification*. This is the process of describing an intangible thing in concrete terms to make it easier to explain. The word *reify* is pejorative. It implies that the analyst took dangerous liberties in giving shape to something that should have remained shapeless. Individual soldiers are real: They exist as entities and can be seen and counted. Individual decisionmaking is also real, and in many ways, observable. Units, however, are social constructs. Table 2.5 depicts the unit will-to-fight factors derived from Table 2.3.

Table 2.5
Unit Will-to-Fight Factors

Level	Category	Factors	Subfactors	Durability
Unit	Unit culture	Unit cohesion	Social vertical, social horizontal, and task	Mid
		Expectation		Low
		Unit control	Coercion, persuasion, and discipline	Mid
		Unit esprit de corps		Mid
	Unit capabilities	Unit competence	Performance, skills, and training	High
		Unit support	Sufficiency and timeliness	Low
		Unit leadership	Competence and character	Mid

For the purposes of assessment and analysis, unit will to fight is a far more amorphous thing than individual will to fight. Individuals within a unit can break and run, but the unit can still hold together. Conversely, units can break apart, but individuals can still decide to stand their ground. Determining where the individual ends and the unit begins is a challenge unto itself. Further, the number of factors affecting unit will to fight compounds so acutely that any effort to describe all of these factors at once becomes impossible. The larger the unit, the greater the analytic problem.

There are effectively three ways to deal with the problem of unit-level reification for modeling. We could accept the dangers of simplifying the unit and assign it human-like characteristics. Units would have stand-alone disposition to fight; individuals would be discounted. Or we could attempt to model every aspect of unit will to fight, showing how all factors from the individual to the state are interrelated. The first option risks oversimplification, while the second risks indescribable complexity and precision without accuracy. For practical purposes we chose a middle ground: Units have some characteristics, but we will seek to explain the individual's role with a reasonable degree of clarity. Seeing the general connections between individual and group will to fight is important for simulation, assessment, and analysis.

Factors Bearing on Unit Will to Fight

For the purposes of general modeling, units are made up of soldiers and leaders. Most military units are hierarchical: A team leader leads a section of two or three soldiers. That team works for a squad leader, who controls a total of three teams. Next, the squad leader works for a platoon leader, who controls three squads. This pyramid-like set of relationships reaches to the company, battalion, brigade, division, corps, and army levels, with a single leader at each level. Rather than try to model each level, our model is scalable from squad to army. It depicts a unit leader and soldiers as nodes in the unit system, each with its own interrelated subsystem of will-to-fight factors. Unit-level factors integrate with individual factors to form a collective system of systems. There are seven unit-level factors that affect will to fight. Adding these seven factors builds out the system-of-systems model from the individual to the unit, and then toward the organization, state, and society.

At the unit level, soldiers and leaders develop interpersonal bonds referred to as *cohesion*. Literature on cohesion dominates the modern discourse on will to fight. For some, cohesion is a unitary theory. We return to this unlikely possibility later. Our model depicts cohesion as one factor influencing will to fight that might or might not be pivotal in any one case.

Cohesion

Our model represents two types of cohesion, both generated at the unit level: *task cohesion* and *social cohesion*. Social cohesion is further broken down into two subfactors: *vertical* and *horizontal*, reflecting soldier-to-leader and soldier-to-soldier bonds. Cohesion with the organization, the state, and the society is reflected in other factors, described below.

The first unit-level subfactor of cohesion is *task cohesion*, or a commitment to collective goals. Soldiers in the unit bond together because they are focused on a collective task, whether that is fighting or building a bridge or setting up a communications network. Robert MacCoun describes a unit with high task cohesion composed of "members who share a common goal and who are motivated to coordinate their efforts as a team to achieve that goal."[65] Task cohesion is distinct from other types of cohesion, but it is an essential part of the social and organizational bonds that foster will to fight.[66]

The second type of cohesion at the unit level is *social cohesion*. Mission accomplishment develops bonds. Social cohesion is bonding based on friendship, trust, and other aspects of interpersonal relationships. The essential argument here is that soldiers fight because of the close interpersonal bonds formed in their primary social group through shared experience and hardship. Social cohesion includes both horizontal (peer) and vertical (leader) bonds in the so-called standard model of military group cohesion.[67] Some research on U.S. military forces after the Vietnam War questioned the primacy of social cohesion, but it is consistently emphasized in contemporary scholarship.[68]

---

[65]   Robert J. MacCoun, "What Is Known About Unit Cohesion and Military Performance," in Bernard Rostker et al., eds., *Sexual Orientation and US Military Personnel Policy: Options and Assessment*, Santa Monica, Calif.: RAND Corporation, MR-323-OSD, 1993, pp. 291.

[66]   King, 2006.

[67]   Guy L. Siebold, "The Essence of Military Group Cohesion," *Armed Forces and Society*, Vol. 33, No. 2, 2007, pp. 286–295.

[68]   Skeptics include Robert J. MacCoun and Elizabeth Kier. See Charles C. Moskos, "The American Combat Soldier in Vietnam," *Journal of Social Issues*, Vol. 31, No. 4, 1975, pp. 25–37; James Griffith, "What Do the

Trust is closely associated with cohesion, although it is not explicitly modeled as a subfactor.[69] It is the confidence that individuals have in their training, in the competence and will to fight of their peers, in their leaders, and in the organization. Trust can exist without cohesion: It is possible to believe that the unit will perform well in combat while still having almost no sense of belonging to that unit. Expectations are both a by-product and a component of trust.

Social cohesion exists on two planes: horizontal and vertical. Horizontal social cohesion exists between members of the unit—soldier to soldier. Vertical cohesion exists between members and leaders—soldier to noncommissioned officer or commander. All types of cohesion have moderate durability because cohesion is at least somewhat vulnerable to the many disruptive factors of combat.

Task cohesion   Collective tasks build instrumental bonding that in turn builds a commitment to collective goals, and also a willingness to sacrifice to achieve the mission.

Social cohesion   Horizontal (soldier-to-soldier) and vertical (soldier-to-leader) bonding, amity, comradeship, trust, and mutuality form social cohesion. Nodes of social cohesion are often called "peer" and "leader" in military cohesion models.

Appendix A describes several previous efforts to model cohesion. Figure 2.10 is a simplified representation of the social and task relationships between soldiers and between soldiers and leaders. Comparisons to chemical diagrams would not be misplaced. Theories of strong and weak chemical bonds have some metaphorical value for understanding unit cohesion. This is a unit-level system-of-systems diagram, with each soldier and leader representing their own subsystemic values and also serving as nodes

---

Soldiers Say? Needed Ingredients for Determining Unit Readiness," *Armed Forces and Society*, Vol. 32, No. 3, 2006, pp. 367–388; MacCoun, 1993; Robert B. Smith, "Why Soldiers Fight. Part I. Leadership, Cohesion and Fighter Spirit," *Quality and Quantity*, Vol. 18, No. 1, 1983, pp. 1–32. Cohesion is spread widely through U.S.-centric literature, including a prominent thread on social cohesion as an important motivating factor in the U.S. Revolutionary War. Robert Middlekauff, "Why Men Fought in the American Revolution," *Huntington Library Quarterly*, Vol. 43, No. 2, 1980, pp. 135–148; McPherson, 1997, p. 13; Baynes, 1988 (1967); Stewart, 1991; Robert S. Rush, "A Different Perspective: Cohesion, Morale, and Operational Effectiveness in the German Army, Fali 1944," *Armed Forces and Society*, Vol. 25, No. 3, 2016, pp. 477–508; Van den Aker, Duel, and Soeters, 2016; Frank H. Denton, *Some Effects of Military Operations on Viet Cong Attitudes*, Santa Monica, Calif.: RAND Corporation, RM-4966-1-ISA/ARPA, 1966; Robert J. MacCoun, Elizabeth Kier, and Aaron Belkin, "Does Social Cohesion Determine Motivation in Combat? An Old Question with an Old Answer," *Armed Forces & Society*, Vol. 32, No. 4, 2006, pp. 646–654.

[69]   Research on Dutch and Israeli military forces also suggests that trust is an important element in cohesion. Bernard M. Bass, Bruce J. Avolio, Dong I. Jung, and Yair Berson, "Predicting Unit Performance by Assessing Transformational and Transactional Leadership," *Journal of Applied Psychology*, Vol. 88, No. 2, 2003, p. 207; S. J. Jozwiak, *Military Unit Cohesion: The Mechanics and Why Some Programs Evolve and Others Dissolve*, Quantico, Va.: Marine Corps University, 1999; Siebold, 2007.

Figure 2.10
Cohesion in a Unit

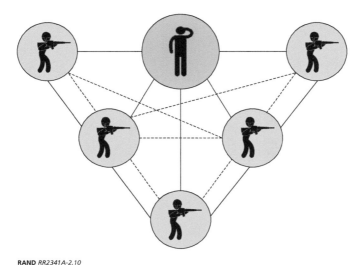

in the unit-level system. Solid lines from the leader to the soldiers represent vertical social cohesion, solid lines between the soldiers represent strong horizontal social cohesion between the nearest teammates, and dotted lines represent weaker social cohesion bonds between more distant teammates. *All* of the lines, collectively, represent task cohesion.

This figure represents one way to visualize unit-level cohesion. We offer this model, the tables of factors, and then a different system-of-systems visualization at the end of this section. Figure 2.11 is the first part of the unit-level will-to-fight model. It depicts a leader and a soldier in the center, representing all members of a unit (from ten to tens of thousands, depending on the level of analysis). Each leader and soldier is composed of individual subsystems described in the previous section.

Cohesion is the first factor in unit-level will to fight. Here it forms a node in what will eventually be a ring of factors.

Expectation

Expectation is the belief that something will happen. It is one of the most diffuse factors, but it recurs as a make-or-break issue in tactical and operational warfare. Expectation is also the only factor in our model that is not explicitly identified by other scholars. It does not appear as a factor in Baynes, Henderson, and Meerloo, and it appears only indirectly in U.S. military doctrine.[70] Our review of will-to-fight literature and

---

[70] It is central to leadership. U.S. military leaders have to set and meet high expectations to maintain will to fight. Leaders are taught to understand the consequences of failure to meet expectations. See the section on lead-

Figure 2.11
Cohesion Added to the Unit Model

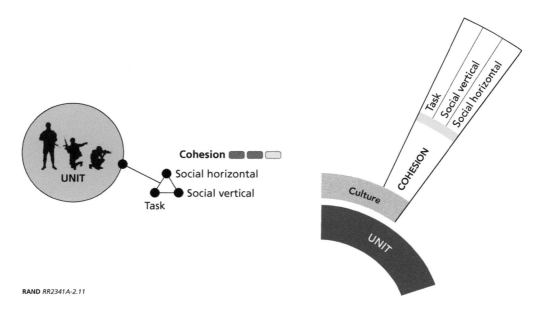

ancillary review of selected military history literature suggests that expectation is an important will-to-fight factor.

In a generally functional and competent military organization, soldiers tend to expect their leaders to be competent, to care for them, and to risk lives only when necessary. They expect units to their left and right to perform their missions and to keep everyone's flanks secure. Soldiers expect the higher units and the organization to provide supplies, medical support, and reinforcements. At the highest levels they expect state leaders to remain committed to their mission, to provide them with clear objectives, and to rally public or moral support. Soldiers also expect the society to provide that support. Sustained expectations correlate with sustained disposition to fight. Broken expectations can weaken and even shatter soldiers' will to fight. Unit-level expectations and individual resilience are closely linked.

For example, American military forces try to apply the so-called golden-hour rule to casualty evacuation. Units forward position helicopters and ambulances to ensure wounded are rapidly evacuated to a surgical facility within one hour. Evidence has emerged from the wars in Afghanistan and Iraq showing that the golden hour saves lives. It also has a perceived effect on will to fight. Then-Secretary of Defense Robert

---

ership, below, for references. In another example, one of the four leadership principles of the U.S. Marine Corps is "Keep your Marines informed." This indirectly suggests that Marines who know what to expect in combat are better prepared for combat. It does not directly address expectation in relation to will to fight. U.S. Marine Corps, *Leading Marines*, MCWP 6-11, Washington, D.C.: Headquarters, U.S. Marine Corps, 2002, p. 105.

M. Gates explained his justification for enforcing the golden-hour rule before the subsequent evidence of effectiveness existed:[71]

> I had no data to support my decision. I simply told them my decision was a matter of morale and moral obligation to the troops. If I were a soldier who had just been blown up, I'd want a helicopter there as fast as possible.

His reasoning, in part, was that soldiers who expected to receive immediate first-class medical attention would be more willing to fight. Providing and building medical capacity for frontline soldiers is done with the explicit purpose of improving partner will to fight.[72] Expectation is closely linked with support at all levels.

Expectation is something of an outlier in comparison with the other factors because it can have positive impact on will to fight even when it is low. If soldiers in a unit do not expect much from their leaders, organization, or each other, they may be less enthusiastic about fighting, but they are also less likely to be let down. This creates an odd dynamic: Low expectations can lower will to fight, but low expectations can also inoculate a unit against disappointment. If soldiers do not expect good performance, leadership, or support, they are less likely to have their hopes dashed in combat at a moment when they are already under significant stress. Assessing expectation will require a careful description of its relevance to will. For example, is it low and therefore good, or low-bad, high-good, and so on?

An example from the Vietnam War helps describe expectation vis-à-vis will to fight. In 1975 the Army of the Republic of Vietnam (ARVN) was falling back toward Saigon as the PAVN conducted its final, massive ground offensive. Some observers contemporaneously expected ARVN leaders to abandon their units, soldiers to break and flee, and the military to suffer a general collapse.[73] But many ARVN units fought tooth and nail to defend southern cities. Along with some attachments the 18th Division—a unit that had been lambasted by American generals in previous years—fiercely defended the city of Xuan Loc as part of what its own commander recognized to be a losing strategic effort.[74] Even though many southern soldiers were resigned to

---

[71]   Robert M. Gates, quoted in Thom Shanker, "Study Says Faster Medical Evacuation Was Lifesaver for U.S. Troops," *New York Times*, September 30, 2015.

[72]   For example: Ramey L. Wilson, *Building Partner Capacity and Strengthening Security Through Medical Security Force Assistance*, thesis, Monterey, Calif.: Naval Postgraduate School, 2013.

[73]   For example: U.S. Department of State, *ARVN Morale Study: November 1974*, Saigon, R.V.N.: U.S. Embassy, November 1974.

[74]   See comments regarding the capabilities of the 18th Division by GEN Creighton Abrams and others in Lewis Sorley, ed., *The Abrams Tapes: 1968–1972*, Lubbock: Texas Tech University Press, 2004. The 18th Division commander's comments are cited in George T. Veith and Merle L. Pribbenow II, " 'Fighting Is an Art': The Army of the Republic of Vietnam's Defense of Xuan Loc, 9–21 April, 1975," *Journal of Military History*, Vol. 68, No. 1, January 2004, p. 213. Also see James H. Wilbanks, *Xuan Loc: The Final Battle Vietnam, 1975*, conference paper, New Orleans, La.: Popular Culture Association, 2000; Democratic Republic of Vietnam, *The Thieu Regime Put*

eventual defeat, they initially fought on for a variety of interrelated reasons: to defend their families, to avoid capture, out of a sense of duty and professionalism, to protect one another, and because many of them held out a genuine or knowingly false expectation that the United States would intervene to save them at the last minute.[75] This expectation was continually reinforced by President Richard M. Nixon and, even through April 10, 1975, by President Gerald R. Ford.[76]

While it would be impossible to tease out the degree to which expectation for U.S. relief strengthened the will to fight of any one ARVN soldier, postwar comments by ARVN leaders make it clear that it figured into their decisionmaking through at least April 21, 1975.[77] On that day, the 18th Division executed a directed retreat from Xuan Loc, and the president of South Vietnam, General Nguyen Van Thieu, publicly acknowledged that the United States would not rescue the government of Vietnam. He then resigned and fled.[78] PAVN tanks seized the palace in Saigon on April 30, 1975.

> **Expectation** Belief that fellow soldiers, unit leaders, other units, the organization, the state, and the society will provide support—or will not provide support—to the unit. If expectations are low, then the impact of failure is low. If expectations are high, then failure to deliver can have a significant impact on will to fight.

In training environments military leaders often test expectations to test resilience. For example, at the very end of a long training march with full combat load a leader might take a sudden turn away from the barracks and add a mile to the route to test soldiers' willingness to continue in the face of broken expectations.[79] Expectation has very low durability because it is dependent on immediate performance: It can be met or dashed at any point in combat by any actor, action, or event. Figure 2.12 adds expectation as a node to the unit model.

---

to the Test: 1973–1975, Hanoi, D.R.V.: Foreign Language Publishing House, 1975; Anthony James Joes, *The War for South Vietnam: 1954–1975*, rev. ed., Westport, Conn.: Praeger Publishers, 2001.

[75]   See both Veith and Pribbenow II, 2004; and Democratic Republic of Vietnam, 1975, for examples and discussions of these sentiments and concerns.

[76]   Nguyen Tien Hung and Jerrold L. Schecter, *The Palace File: The Remarkable Story of the Secret Letters from Nixon and Ford to the President of South Vietnam and the American Promises That Were Never Kept*, New York: Harper and Row Publishers, Inc., 1985; Gerald R. Ford, Address Before a Joint Session of the Congress Reporting on United States Foreign Policy, The American Presidency Project, The White House, April 10, 1975.

[77]   For example: Nguyen Tien Hung and Schecter, 1985; Veith and Pribbenow II, 2004; and Democratic Republic of Vietnam, 1975; Dong Van Khuyen, *The RVNAF*, Washington, D.C.: Center of Military History, 1980.

[78]   British Broadcasting Corporation, "1975: Vietnam's President Thieu Resigns," April 21, 1975.

[79]   This vignette is derived from the personal experiences of two authors of this report.

Figure 2.12
Expectation Added to the Unit Model

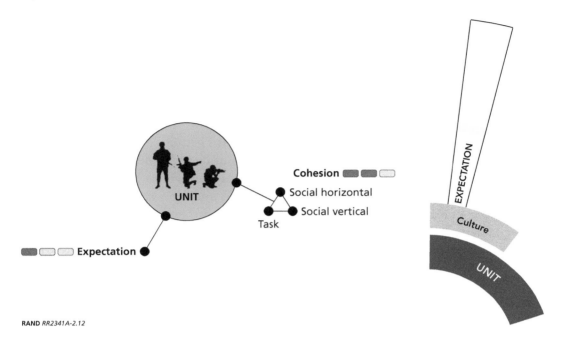

Unit Leadership

Leadership is the act of a single person in authority directing and encouraging the behavior of soldiers to accomplish a military mission. Leadership is often singled out as the most important element of unit-level will to fight.[80] In a 1993 doctrinal publication the U.S. Army equated leadership with will to fight in nearly absolute terms: Success or failure of leadership dictated unit will to fight.[81] Our analysis shows that leadership is better described as an enabler of will to fight. Good leaders can help keep units together, while bad leaders can weaken both individual and collective disposition to fight.[82] But units can and do fight despite bad leadership. Even the best leaders can see the will to fight of their units ebb away as the enemy advances, as individual motivational factors fail to generate sufficient will, or as they are let down by a higher or parallel unit. Death of leaders does not always signal a break in will to

---

[80]   For a description of leadership and its components, see U.S. Army, *Army Leadership*, ADRP 6-22, Washington, D.C.: Headquarters, Department of the Army, August 2012c.

[81]   U.S. Army, *Operations*, Washington, D.C.: Headquarters, Department of the Army, June 1993, p. 6-7. See Appendix C for a full description of Army doctrine on will to fight and specific analysis of this document.

[82]   One Army Research Institute study suggested a complex interaction between leadership and cohesion. See Fred A. Mael and Cathie E. Alderks, "Leadership Team Cohesion and Subordinate Work Unit Morale and Performance," *Military Psychology*, Vol. 5, No. 3, 1993, pp. 141–158.

fight. Leadership is important, but depending on organizational culture, it generally has midlevel durability.[83]

In most armies, leadership is formal: There is one person in charge at every level of command from team through army.[84] For will to fight, the leader's primary role is to build and sustain the disposition to fight of the unit and of each soldier within that unit. Each leader is also an individual soldier, so the starting point for understanding leadership is the stand-alone soldier system-of-systems model. Because leaders have special roles at the head of units, they also have other qualities that have a strong effect on unit will to fight.

The factor of leadership serves three purposes: It identifies an important individual in the unit, it helps explain the qualities of the unit, and it describes an intraunit perception that has strong influence on individual soldier will to fight. Leaders affect the perceptions of soldiers. If leaders are competent and have strong character, they usually have a positive influence on unit will to fight. If they are incompetent or have weak character, soldiers will have a poor perception of their leadership, they may lose confidence, and their vertical cohesion with the leader will weaken. Leadership can be directly influenced in both directions.

The U.S. Army has a leadership requirements model that lists elements of good leadership. Among other things, leaders must have character, confidence, fitness, presence, and intellect, and they must lead by example, build trust, communicate effectively, develop subordinate capabilities, and get results.[85] Literature that describes leadership as an enabler of will to fight focuses on competence and character.[86] Competence is related to task performance and mission accomplishment. John Baynes summarizes the need for competence and success: "Success indeed is the only criterion of a General; that he should achieve it as economically as possible in terms of casualties is important, but less so than the victory itself."[87] Leader competence is similar to individual competence—is the leader physically fit? tactically adept? well trained? capable of making the best use of available resources? Leader competence in the Army model is: "gets results." Even the most hated or personally distant leaders can build and sustain will to fight if they are good at their jobs. In combat, soldiers want to know that they will win battles.

---

[83] Some organizational cultures place great emphasis on the leader's role. For example, Soviet-era military units were highly leader centric. Death of a Soviet unit leader might have had greater impact on will to fight than death of an American leader in a comparable unit across the Fulda Gap.

[84] Some parts of leadership are informal, and sometimes junior soldiers have to take over a unit in combat. This general model focuses on the most formal, ready-state relationships. See U.S. Army, 2012c, p. 1-4.

[85] U.S. Army, 2012c, p. 1-5.

[86] Griffith, 2006; T. R. Fehrenbach, *This Kind of War: The Classic Korean War History*, Washington, D.C.: Brassey's, 1994 (1963); Guy Siebold, "Military Group Cohesion," *Military Life: The Psychology of Serving in Peace and Combat*, Vol. 1, 2006, pp. 185–201; Dupuy and Hammerman, 1980; Paul L. Savage and Richard A. Gabriel, "Cohesion and Disintegration in the American Army: An Alternative Perspective," *Armed Forces and Society*, Vol. 2, No. 3, 1976, pp. 340–376.

[87] Baynes, 1988 (1967), p. 237.

Character reflects the leader's integrity, willingness to sacrifice for soldiers, adherence to rules and regulations, but also willingness to adapt in order to succeed and ensure (to the greatest extent possible) soldier safety. Basically, character tells soldiers whether the leader can be counted on to do what is right.

Unit leadership   Leadership is the act of a single person in authority directing and encouraging the behavior of soldiers to accomplish a military mission. Leadership is constituted of many subfactors, but competence and character matter most for will to fight. Competence is the leader's ability to accomplish tasks and a demonstrated ability to win. Character is the leader's integrity, willingness to sacrifice for soldiers, adherence to rules and regulations, and the ability to adapt in order to succeed and, whenever possible, ensure soldier safety.

Leadership has midlevel durability. A leader's competence and character are likely to change gradually rather than rapidly. The positive and negative effects of leadership can outlast a dead leader, but a leader's visible success or failure in combat can cause an immediate change in soldiers' perceptions and will to fight. Figure 2.13 adds leadership to the unit model.

Figure 2.13
Leadership Added to the Unit Model

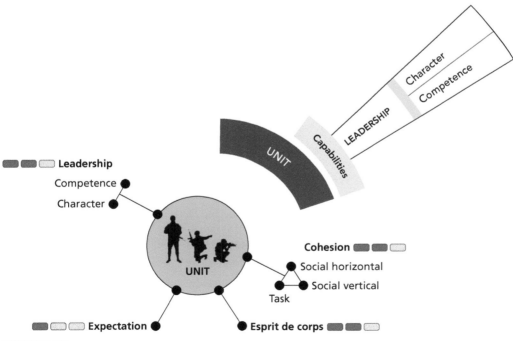

RAND RR2341A-2.13

Unit Control

Leaders and organizations use culturally specific methods to control behavior.[88] *Coercion* and *persuasion* are methods of control, while discipline is a product and indicator of control. Unit control and organizational control are closely linked, but they must be treated as distinct nodes in the model. Units almost always adopt organizational methods of control, and they benefit from organizational support in controlling soldiers. But units within an organization can apply control in very different ways.

There are two general methods to apply control: coercion and persuasion. Coercion is the use of threats, fear, and, if necessary, punishment to encourage soldiers to do their jobs, including staying in the fight when they might have a strong desire to flee.[89] Punishments for battlefield cowardice are usually extreme and sometimes capital. Persuasion is a more complex mix of encouragements to behave within standards, to perform well, and to stay in the fight. Establishing formal and informal behavioral norms, setting high standards for performance, promotions, and pay increases, and rewarding top performers are all common methods of military persuasion.[90]

Some leaders emphasize coercion, while others emphasize persuasion. The concept and practice of discipline can shift dramatically depending on the approach. A manual on U.S. Army leadership includes advice on how to apply *rational persuasion*, an approach seemingly at odds with a more traditional, hierarchical understanding of military control.[91] Lord Moran provides some of the best analysis of control and the trade-offs between coercion and persuasion. Here he describes two different approaches to discipline in the English (British) Army:[92]

> The discipline of the English Army in the early days of the Peninsular War was modeled on the methods of Frederick the Great. It was control from without in its crudest, most brutal shape; men did their job because the fear of flogging was greater than the fear of death. Sir John Moore . . . swept away Frederick's influence. . . . He left a creed in which the English Army still believes, a creed supported by a faith in human nature. He insisted that the men should be treated as human beings. The officers must know their men, be their friend and look after their wants; even orders were to be given in the language of moderation. It was a

---

[88]   Kellett offers an excellent summary of Western military control approaches. Kellett, 1982, Chapter Ten.

[89]   For example: Jason Lyall, "Forced to Fight: Coercion, Blocking Detachments, and Tradeoffs in Military Effectiveness," unpublished research paper, December 15, 2015; Warren Perry, "The Nature and Significance of Discipline," *The Australian Quarterly*, Vol. 13, No. 4, December 1941, pp. 99–103.

[90]   See Kellett, 1982, pp. 201–213, for a discussion of reward and recognition as forms of persuasion.

[91]   "Rational persuasion requires the leader to provide evidence, logical arguments, or explanations showing how a request is relevant to the goal." U.S. Army, 2012c, p. 6-2.

[92]   Moran, 2007 (1945), p. 172. Lord Moran refers to Lieutenant General Sir John Moore, an eighteenth- and nineteenth-century British military general who reformed British Army training programs.

discipline of kindness, an appeal to the heart inspired by mutual respect, affection, and comradeship.

All military units apply a mix of both approaches to build and maintain the disposition to fight. A good example is the PAVN. It was a highly coercive force that also relied very heavily on informal persuasion, ideological encouragement, and praise for performance. It also applied ideological control, a measure that tends to have both coercive and persuasive components. PAVN officers proved expert at applying ideological control through the use of propaganda, small-group discussions, and political loyalty tests. Soviet political officers similarly applied ideological coercion and persuasion at the unit level. Ideological control is directly linked with individual soldier ideology.

Many analysts equate control, and specifically coercion, with *discipline*. In this interpretation, discipline is the application of authority and regulation to obtain obedience. But discipline is in fact something more complex. It is an essential element of military culture, and as Richard Holmes suggests, it is closely related to civilian culture.[93] The ways in which armies conceive of discipline reflect broader norms for social relationships and particularly the cultural acceptance or rejection of self-actualization. Discipline is both an artifact of control and a reflection of the cultural appropriateness and effectiveness of that control. Lord Moran's description of discipline was in fact a description of a shift in British military culture. Soldiers (probably gradually) went from seeing themselves as purely anthropomorphic instruments of the army to somewhat more respected members of a team. Moran goes on to describe the difference between external and internal control, using "discipline" for what we term "coercion," and "high morale" for what we might call "self-discipline" in this context:[94]

> A man under discipline does things at the instigation of someone in authority, and if he doesn't he is punished. A man with a high morale does things because in his own mind he has decided to do them without any suggestion from outside sources.

There are effectively two archetypes of discipline. Absolute control reflects the extreme of externally controlled discipline. Self-motivation is the extreme of internally motivated discipline. Absolute control is top-down coercion met with total obedience. It is leader centric, and therefore heavily dependent on leader competence and character. Individually motivated discipline is soldier centric. Leaders provide guidance and expect soldiers to perform within standards of their own volition. The concept of mission-type orders, or mission command, depends on this kind of devolved responsibility and decisionmaking.[95]

---

[93] Holmes, 1985, pp. 332–342.

[94] Moran, 2007 (1945), p. 176. Also see Richardson, 2009 (1978), pp. 88–92.

[95] Mission-type orders and mission command are generally associated with maneuver warfare. See Appendix C for a discussion of maneuver warfare theory in U.S. ground combat force doctrine. A good survey of mission com-

Neither extreme exists in practice; all units perform a complex mix of both approaches. Neither approach is inherently better. Instead of indicating positive or negative value, the type of discipline that exists in a unit reveals potential strengths and weaknesses in will to fight. A highly controlled unit may be more vulnerable to break-downs in leadership and support, but it might be less vulnerable to measures aimed at breaking down individual soldiers. It would arguably be more capable of addressing gaps in soldier quality and competence. The opposite might be true of a unit that relies more on self-discipline.

Control, then, is both method and form. It is coercion or persuasion applied and then revealed in the ways leaders and soldiers relate to one another, and in the way they perform tasks. Discipline is closely related to vertical cohesion and task cohesion. Discipline is a subordinate factor to control and perhaps a complex indicator of will to fight. However, we found that discipline is necessarily a contested and somewhat generic term. It represents a necessarily unresolved dialectic rather than a factor with singular meaning.[96] We cannot recommend it as a stand-alone indicator or as having special value in the model.

> **Unit control** This is the method of obtaining obedience to orders and pursuit of mission objectives. Control relies on a mix of coercion and persuasion, and it is reflected in discipline. Coercion is a set of unit-imposed motivations that involve fear, compulsion, punishment, and external threats to elicit obedience; these can include cultural norms that result in social punishments, in addition to authoritarian physical threats. Persuasion is encouragement to perform to formal and informal standards of behavior, and can include rewards, discussion, ideological conditioning, and intraunit competition. Discipline reflects the cultural approach to control and defines the relationships between leaders and soldiers. It is one of several indicators of will to fight.

Control has midlevel durability. Under the intense pressures of combat, leaders might change their approach to controlling soldiers, for better or worse. For example, an untested unit that responded well to a more persuasive approach in training might require coercion to move forward under fire. Changing control methods during a fight and applying techniques that normally require months of acculturation might undermine will to fight, or in some cases it might shore it up at a critical moment in time. Figure 2.14 adds control to the unit model.

---

mand issues and cases, all related to the U.S. Army, can be found in Donald Vandergriff and Stephen Webber, eds., *Mission Command: The Who, What, Where, When, and Why*, self-published, 2017.

[96] For more on the idea of discipline as a (perhaps unintentional) dialectic, see Connable, 2016.

Figure 2.14
Control Added to the Unit Model

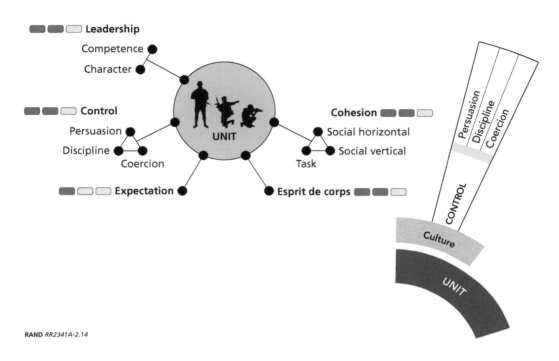

Unit Esprit de Corps

Espirit de corps is a French term generally translated as "group spirit."[97] It is also called *élan* or *pride*, and it is often referred to simply as *esprit* (spirit). Members of a particular unit develop part of their individual identity in relation to the unit and to the organization. Identity shaping takes into account unit history, success or failure on the battlefield (or in training), interunit competition, and external opinions of the unit. Baynes argued that esprit de corps—or in his words, "the pride in belonging to a good battalion, in knowing other people well and being known by them, in having strong roots in a well loved community"—was the single most important aspect of will to fight.[98] Kellett provides a useful distinction between esprit de corps and social cohesion, and also a good definition of esprit:[99]

> Cohesion denotes the feelings of belonging and solidarity that occur mostly at the
> primary group level and result from sustained interactions, both formal and infor-

[97]   Jean Vauvilliers, "Pour une théorie générale de l'esprit de corps," *La Revue Administrative*, No. 347, September 2005, pp. 489–498.

[98]   Baynes, 1988, p. 253.

[99]   Kellett, 1982, pp. 46–47. Also see Richardson, 2009 (1978), pp. 14–22.

mal among group members on the basis of common experiences, interdependence, and shared goals and values. Esprit denotes feelings of pride, unity of purpose, and adherence to an ideal represented by the unit, and it generally applies to larger units with more formal boundaries than those of the primary group. . . . [Esprit] constitutes a filter through which the primary group is linked to the army, and the army is the legatee of informal, face-to-face interactions.

Esprit exists in varying degrees at every unit level, but we concur with Kellett that it is most obvious and perhaps most influential to will-to-fight disposition and choice at levels above the company. In the British system it is most evident at the regimental level, while in the Russian military it seems to aggregate at the corps or army level. For example, the Russian First Guards Tank Army has a long and storied history and a tradition of high esprit de corps.[100] Esprit is often closely linked with competence, cohesion, leadership, and trust.[101]

Unit esprit de corps This includes terms such as *élan* and *unit pride*. These terms point to the fighting spirit of a unit and an ardor or eagerness to pursue a cause or task. It captures a confidence in battle prowess and success, and concepts of elite membership.

Esprit de corps has midlevel durability. While soldiers' perceptions about states and societies are unlikely to change significantly in combat, their perceptions about units can change for better or worse based on immediate combat performance. Organizational success or failure during a fight can affect higher-level esprit, but probably more gradually. Figure 2.15 adds esprit de corps to the unit model.

Unit Competence

Competence derives from all of the other sources of will to fight, but it is also a factor on its own. It reflects the unit's collective ability to successfully perform tasks and defeat enemy forces under most reasonable conditions. No commander would expect a squad to defeat a division in head-to-head combat, but a competent squad should be confident that it could defeat an enemy squad, all other factors being equal. Competence is a value and a perception: The collective skills and performance of the unit's soldiers and leaders generate a collective perception of competence. Historian Hew Strachan

[100] Michael R. Gordon and Eric Schmitt, "Russia's Military Drills Near NATO Border Raise Fears of Aggression," *New York Times*, July 31, 2017.

[101] For insight into esprit de corps, see Fiona Alpass, Nigel Long, Carol MacDonald, and Kerry Chamberlain, "The Moskos Institution-Occupation Model: Effects on Individual Work Related Perceptions and Experiences in the Military," *JPMS: Journal of Political and Military Sociology*, Vol. 27, No. 1, 1999, p. 67; Baynes, 1988; Chacho, 2001; Richardson, 2009 (1978); Kellett, 1982.

Figure 2.15
Esprit de Corps Added to the Unit Model

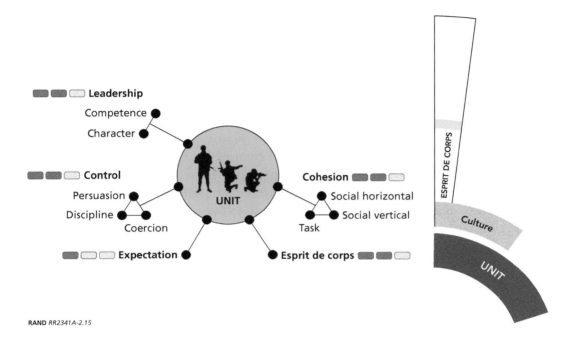

argues that training is perhaps the most effective confidence-building measure and the greatest contributor to the disposition to fight:[102]

> The value of training is therefore in large part psychological: it is an enabling process, a form of empowerment, which creates self-confidence. . . . Surprise can destroy collective cohesion on the battlefield and training is its best antidote.

Retired British Army officer and defense analyst Jim Storr believes, "Most propensity to fight, and to fight well, is about training."[103] In our model, training is not necessarily more important than any other factor. However, in general, highly competent units tend to believe in their ability to succeed. This belief contributes to confidence. In turn, confidence is generally associated with stronger will to fight.[104] It follows that less competent units are also less confident and they tend to have lower disposition

---

[102] Strachan, 2006, p. 216.

[103] Jim Storr, interview with RAND research team, London, September 6, 2017.

[104] Moran, 2007 (1945); Baynes, 1988; Henderson, 1985.

to fight. This lack of confidence in military capability emerged as a central theme in the early failures of the ARVN.[105]

We break competence into three parts: (1) *skills*, (2) *training*, and (3) *performance*. Skills represents the collective version of individual skills. While an individual can fire a rifle, it takes a team working together to effectively fire a machine gun. Individual riflemen are ineffective without collective skills like fire control and unit movement. The subfactor of skills represents both individual and collective skills. Skills have high durability.

Collective training is a durable method of building and sustaining will to fight. Collective training is primarily a function of the organization and the unit, and it has two broad purposes: (1) to improve individual competence and the individual's ability to contribute to unit actions, and (2) to improve collective, unit competence and to build a group that functions smoothly and intuitively.[106] Influencing the methods and means of training can improve or undermine will to fight.

Performance is the demonstration of competence. It can be revealed in training as units are put through collective tests, or it can be revealed in combat. Performance is both a quality and a perception. It is tangible in that it can be seen and measured. Good performance translates to confidence, which in turn is a positive influence on the disposition to fight.

> **Unit competence** Unit skills, training, and performance: skills are resident in individuals and across units, representing the ability to perform tasks. Training is the methods and capabilities used to build and maintain skills. Performance is the demonstration of skills. All components of competence can build or erode confidence, and therefore disposition to fight.

Understanding the links between competence and the other factors is particularly useful for portable assessments and analysis of will to fight. Competence is highly durable, but it is also relative to the situation and task that needs to be performed. Our aforementioned squad can be highly competent and still have a very low disposition to fight a division. Figure 2.16 adds competence to the unit model.

Unit Support

Units need equipment, supplies, weapons, vehicles, medical assistance, fires (artillery, air support), food, water, and other material things to fight effectively. Without sup-

---

[105] Robert K. Brigham, *ARVN: Life and Death in the South Vietnamese Army*, Lawrence: University Press of Kansas, 2006.

[106] For example: U.S. Army, *Training Units and Developing Leaders*, ADRP 7-0, Washington, D.C.: Headquarters, Department of the Army, August 2012e; John A. Boldovici, David W. Bessemer, and Amy E. Bolton, *The Elements of Training Evaluation*, Alexandria, Va.: Army Research Institute, 2001.

Figure 2.16
Competence Added to the Unit Model

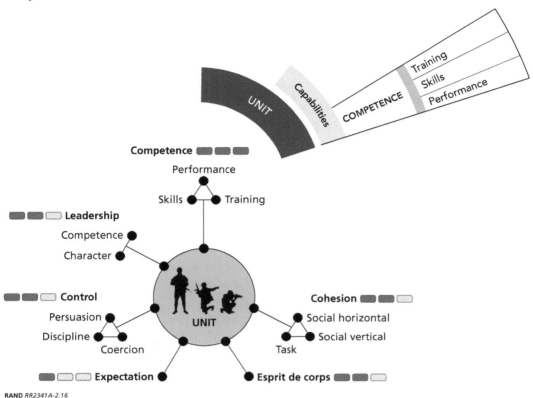

RAND *RR2341A-2.16*

port, confidence in the ability to perform (competence) can drop, trust in leadership can drop, and over time, lack of support can affect esprit de corps.[107] *Support* is a factor at the unit and organizational levels. It consists of two subordinate factors: (1) *sufficiency* and (2) *timeliness*. First, is the support provided to the unit sufficient to help it perform its mission? Do the weapons function, and are they the right kind to defeat the immediate threat? Do boots fall apart after a few miles of marching, or can soldiers rely on them to keep their feet in one piece over time? Is there enough water, food, fuel,

---

[107] We sound a note of caution here. Some units, like the U.S. Marine Corps, pride themselves on performing with limited material support. Griffith, 2006; Brigham, 2006; Catignani, Sergio, "Motivating Soldiers: The Example of the Israeli Defense Forces," *Parameters*, Vol. 34, No. 3, 2004, p. 108. Frank and Reaves, 2003; William Rosenau, Ralph Espach, Román D. Ortiz, and Natalia Herrera, "Why They Join, Why They Fight, and Why They Leave: Learning from Colombia's Database of Demobilized Militants," *Terrorism and Political Violence*, Vol. 26, No. 2, 2014, pp. 277–285; Edward A. Shils and Morris Janowitz, "Cohesion and Disintegration in the Wehrmacht in World War II," *Public Opinion Quarterly*, Vol. 12, No. 2, 1948, pp. 280–315; Don M. Snider, "An Uninformed Debate on Military Culture," *Orbis*, Vol. 43, No. 1, 1999, pp. 11–26.

ammunition, medical supplies, radio equipment, and air support to get the job done? Second, is the unit able to acquire and deliver support on time? If delays in supply are a constant, then the value of quality erodes.

> **Unit support** This is the sufficiency and timeliness of equipment, supplies, weapons, medical assistance, fires, food, water, and other things the unit needs to accomplish its missions. Is the unit able to acquire support in a timely manner, or is it delayed to the point that it affects trust and performance?

Unit support is highly interdependent with units at higher echelons, supporting units, and also with the organization. However, support affects will to fight differently for each unit. Some units are more capable than others of continuing to maintain will to fight without sufficient or timely support. Some units might blame unit-level leaders for failing to provide support, while others will blame the organization. This may be determined by access to information. For example, in a notional case where organizational support falls through, leaving the unit unable to provide support, a soldier may know only that the unit has failed and may blame the unit for the failing of the organization. This can be an endemic problem that affects will to fight across battles, and it requires distinct assessment or analysis. Unit support has low durability because a single dramatic failure like the loss of air support at a critical moment in battle can undermine confidence in a unit or organization that otherwise provided good support.

This is the last factor in the unit-level will to fight system. The next step is to combine these factors with the individual soldier models to produce the unit system-of-systems model. The following sections layer in the organizational, state, and societal factors to generate the complete system-of-systems model. Figure 2.17 is the unit system-of-systems model. Adding unit support, it depicts each factor at the unit level broken into its constituent subfactors. Individuals in the unit continue to reflect the subsystemic factors described in the section on individual will to fight. Societal, state, and organizational factors influence both the individual and the unit; we add these in greater detail in the next section.

This diagram focuses on the factors rather than on the relationship between the factors. Potential links are effectively limitless. In the following sections we add organizational and then state and societal factors to the model.

Organizational Factors: Impact on Units and Individuals

Organizational leadership, culture, and capabilities have strong influences on will to fight at the unit level. Military services train and indoctrinate individual soldiers, imparting organizational cultural norms and patterns of behavior. Most ground forces teach soldiers about the organization's legacy in order to build esprit de corps, which should then carry over to the units within the organization. Discipline is imposed

Figure 2.17
Unit System-of-Systems Diagram Showing Individual Factors

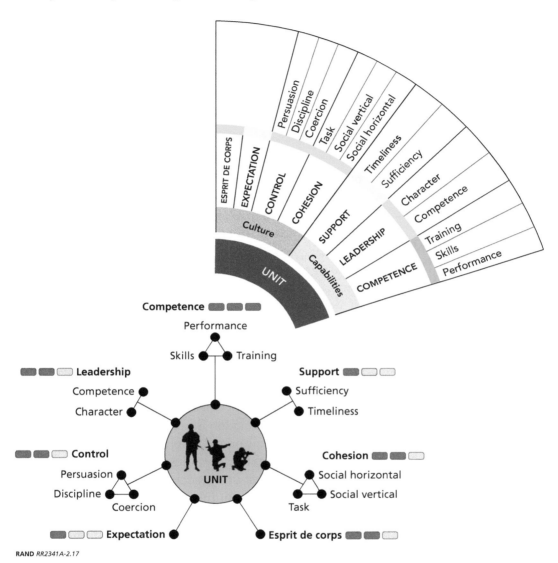

through coercion and persuasion in a way that matches the organization's purpose, its size, the quality of its recruits, and its culture. Every organization manages money and resources, providing support to units while trying to uphold standards for integrity and limiting corruption. Individual soldiers within units remain connected to the organization throughout their terms of service (and beyond), but each organization is more or less effective at maintaining the initial connections formed in recruit training as soldiers move through their careers.

Ground combat organizations tend to look similar in many ways, but each is unique. Variations in history, size, resources, mission, and the relationship with the state and the society all shape organizations in different ways.[108] Consider the similarities and differences between the British Royal Marines and the Chinese People's Liberation Army Ground Force (PLAGF).[109] Both are military services that provide recruitment, training, leadership, organizational culture, doctrine, and support. From there they diverge. The Royal Marines organization is quite small and has a much longer legacy dating back to the mid-eighteenth century. As a long-serving special commando force it probably has more robust esprit de corps than China's approximately 1.5 million soldier ground force. But the Royal Marines are also far less capable of providing combat support to its Marines than the PLAGF is to its soldiers. The sole commando brigade of only a few thousand Marines has a microscopic role in conventional combat in comparison with the PLAGF's multicorps organization. The Royal Marines are able to take a more persuasive approach to control than the PLAGF, leveraging small size and high recruiting standards to encourage tight cohesion and individual self-discipline. Assessing or analyzing these two organizations and their impact on unit will to fight would require significant differentiation.

Table 2.6 depicts the organizational factors that affect unit will to fight drawn from Table 2.3: control, esprit de corps, integrity, training, support, doctrine, and leadership.

Organizational Control

Methods of *control*—coercion and persuasion—are similarly defined at the organizational level and the unit level, but the measures are different. At the unit level a leader chooses how to apply rules, regulations, enticements, and punishments that are designed and codified by the organization. Discipline is a manifestation of control at both levels. Typically, unit leaders seek to mirror organizational standards. When they stray too far from the center they are sometimes forcibly adjusted.[110] However, tailoring control to some degree is necessary to ensure that unit leaders can adapt to local conditions. For assessment and analysis this suggests a requirement to examine both organizational and unit control to identify misalignment and to determine what, if anything, differences in control at the two levels might imply. If they are misaligned, then will to

---

[108] For a sample of organizational cultural literature relevant to this report, see Carl H. Builder, *The Masks of War: American Military Styles in Strategy and Analysis*, Baltimore: Johns Hopkins University Press, 1989; Barbara Czarniawska-Joerges, *Exploring Complex Organizations: A Cultural Perspective*, Newberry Park, Calif.: Sage Publications, 1992; Allan D. English, *Understanding Military Culture: A Canadian Perspective*, Ithaca, N.Y.: McGill-Queens University Press, 2004; Charlotte Linde, *Working the Past: Narrative and Institutional Memory*, Oxford: Oxford University Press, 2009.

[109] For information on the Royal Marines, see the Royal Navy, "Royal Marines." For information on the PLAGF, see the China Military website.

[110] For example, see David J. Bercuson, "Up from the Ashes: The Re-Professionalization of the Canadian Forces After the Somalia Affair," *Canadian Military Journal*, Vol. 9, No. 3, 2009, pp. 31–39.

Table 2.6
Organizational Will-to-Fight Factors

Level	Category	Factors	Subfactors	Durability
Organization	Organizational culture	Organizational control	Coercion, persuasion, and discipline	High
		Organizational esprit de corps		High
		Organizational integrity	Corruption and trust	High
	Organizational capabilities	Organizational training	Capabilities, relevance, sufficiency, and sustainment	High
		Organizational support	Sufficiency and timeliness	Mid
		Organizational doctrine	Appropriateness and effectiveness	High
		Organizational leadership	Competence and character	High

fight might be reduced as soldiers struggle to fit their performance of behavior into an acceptable cultural norm. Or a tailored unit approach to control might offset a culturally misaligned or simply impractical organizational approach to control. No matter how well or misaligned the two levels of control might be, combat will put control to the test. If it is inappropriate to the task or the enemy, then will to fight will suffer. If it is appropriate, then will to fight might be reinforced.

Organizational control has high durability because it is unlikely to change over the course of a single battle or short series of battles. It is not particularly affected by individual combat events. Figure 2.18 depicts control as a factor of organizational will to fight, along with coercion and persuasion as subfactors.

Figure 2.18
Control Added to the Organizational Model

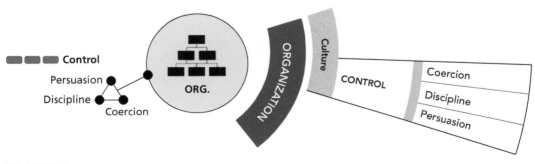

Organizational Esprit de Corps

In the standard Western cohesion model, organizational esprit de corps is referred to as "organizational and institutional" esprit.[111] F. M. Richardson suggests that esprit can be found at every level of the organization, including at coalitions like the North Atlantic Treaty Organization (NATO).[112] *Organizational esprit* has regional and service-specific character, but it is relevant in every case of conventional military will to fight.[113] Organizational esprit can be and often is closely tied in with individual identity. Pride in organizational belonging helps form identity as a professional soldier, and it can establish loyalty to the organization that can influence will to fight. Baynes makes a strong case for the value of regimental esprit in the British Army, but observers of other organizations describe identity formation aligned with organizational esprit more generally.[114]

Organizational esprit de corps has high durability because it is unlikely to change over the course of a single battle or short series of battles. Nor are these isolated events likely to trigger short-notice changes across the entire organization. Figure 2.19 adds esprit de corps to the organizational model.

Organizational Support

Support consists of the same factors at the unit and organizational levels: equipment, supplies, weapons, vehicles, medical assistance, fires (artillery, air support), food, and water.[115] It is represented with the same subfactors: *sufficiency* and *timeliness*. In the U.S. system a military service like the Army or Marine Corps organizes, trains, and equips forces at the institutional level, but combatant commands like the U.S. European Command or joint task forces are responsible for coordinating support during operations. Services in other countries have a more linear and dependent relationship with units in the field. Sui generis assessment and analysis will be required to identify which organization provides field support during combat. Understanding the link between organizational support and the unit might require a layered approach to identify impacts on will to fight from multiple organizations.

---

[111]   Siebold, 2007.

[112]   Richardson, 2009 (1978), pp. 23–39.

[113]   For example: Carlos García-Guiu, Miguel Moya, Fernando Molero, and Juan Antonio Moriano, "Transformational Leadership and Group Potency in Small Military Units: The Mediating Role of Group Identification and Cohesion," *Revista de Psicología del Trabajo y de las Organizaciones*, Vol. 32, No. 3, 2016, pp. 145–152; Robert Kendall Brigham, *ARVN: Life and Death in the South Vietnamese Army*, Lawrence: University Press of Kansas, 2006; Denton, 1966.

[114]   Baynes, 1988 (1967). This is a consistent theme throughout the book, but it is best described in the first chapter. Historians of the U.S. Marine Corps generally associate Marine esprit with identity, and the Marine Corps aggressively seeks to build and reinforce a connection between organizational esprit, individual identity, and will to fight. For example: Terry Terriff, "'Innovate or Die': Organizational Culture and the Origins of Maneuver Warfare in the United States Marine Corps," *Journal of Strategic Studies*, Vol. 29, No. 3, 2006, pp. 475–503.

[115]   This can also include communications, nonorganic transportation, and many other factors.

Figure 2.19
Esprit de Corps Added to the Organizational Model

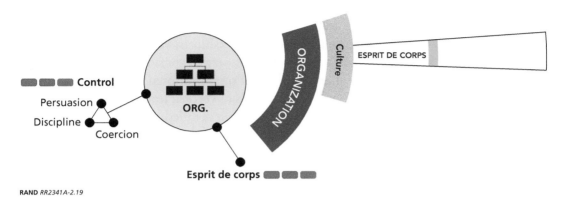

RAND RR2341A-2.19

Organizational support affects will to fight the same way at the organizational level as at the unit level. Organizational support has midlevel durability because it can succeed or falter during the course of a single battle, though it is less vulnerable to significant change than unit support. Figure 2.20 adds support to the organizational will-to-fight model.

Figure 2.20
Support Added to the Organizational Model

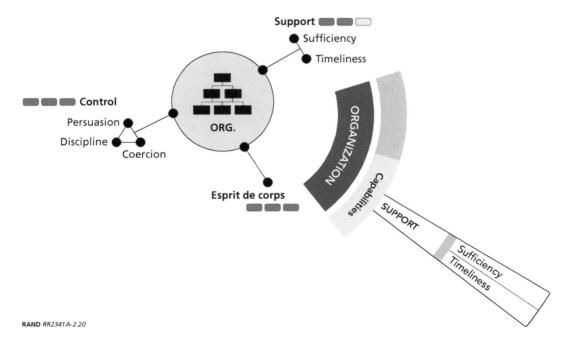

RAND RR2341A-2.20

Organizational Leadership

Leadership is defined, described, and constituted of the same subfactors at both the unit and organizational levels. It depends on both *competence* and *character* as subfactors, and leaders connect with soldiers and other leaders through vertical cohesion. Vertical cohesion between units and the organization's leadership is weaker and more distant than at the small-unit level. Just as it might be necessary to consider multiple organizational levels of support, assessment and analysis of organizational influences on will to fight might require an examination of several levels of vertical leadership. For example, in an army consisting of multiple corps and services, a detailed and holistic estimate of regimental will to fight might require a description of leadership at the division, corps, and service levels.

The relevance of organizational leadership to will to fight in combat is heavily dependent on context. In Western military forces, the leaders of military services like the U.S. Army and Marine Corps play a distant background role in operations, while in other military forces an organizational leader can also be the operational leader. In some militaries, a strong and charismatic leader at the organizational level might play an outsized role at the unit level. U.S. Army historians provide some examples of charismatic organizational leaders in *Great Commanders*.[116]

Organizational leadership has high durability since it is unlikely to change during or—barring a major calamity—due to the events of a single battle or short series of battles. Figure 2.21 adds leadership to the organizational will-to-fight model.

Organizational Integrity

Integrity represents the professional character of the organization. Our review of will-to-fight related literature, our interviews with organizational military leaders and experts, and our case study examinations showed that the most important aspect of organizational integrity for *will-to-fight considerations* is corruption.[117] Corruption can have a profound impact on individual perceptions of the organization and their willingness to fight for it over time. The U.S. Army argues: "Unethical behavior quickly destroys organizational morale and cohesion—it undermines the trust and confidence essential to teamwork and mission accomplishment."[118] Ethical practice is multifaceted, but at the organizational level, for this study, integrity consists of the organization's approach

---

[116]   Christopher R. Gabel and James H. Willbanks, eds., *Great Commanders*, Fort Leavenworth, Kan.: Combat Studies Institute Press, 2012.

[117]   See Saul Fine, Judith Goldenberg, and Yair Noam, "Integrity Testing and the Prediction of Counterproductive Behaviours in the Military," *Journal of Occupational and Organizational Psychology*, No. 89, 2016, pp. 198–218; Shaun Gregory and James Revill, "The Role of the Military in the Cohesion and Stability of Pakistan," *Contemporary South Asia*, Vol. 16, No. 1, March 2008, pp. 39–61; Philip M. Flammer, "Conflicting Loyalties and the American Military Ethic," *American Behavioral Scientist*, Vol. 19, No. 5, May–June 1976, pp. 589–604; Castillo, 2014.

[118]   U.S. Army, 2012c, p. 3-6.

Figure 2.21
Leadership Added to the Organizational Model

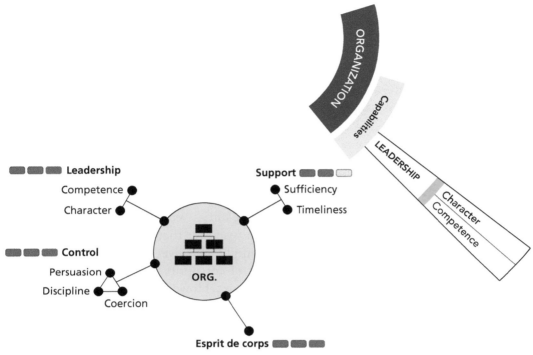

RAND RR2341A-2.21

to corruption—to what degree is it accepted or ferreted out?—and the perception of integrity measured in trust. Organizational integrity is often evinced in the character of military officers.[119] Therefore, organizational integrity is often closely linked to the leadership subfactor of character.

Every military organization in every country has some level of corruption. It would be unrealistic and unhelpfully demure to avoid this discomforting reality. Some leaders and soldiers at every level fall prey to the enticements of extra money or power. This fundamental reality of human nature is and has always been present in all services of the U.S. military.[120] However, U.S. military organizational integrity is exception-

---

[119] U.S. Army, 2012c; Fine, Goldenberg, and Noam, 2016.

[120] For example: Craig Whitlock, "'Fat Leonard' Probe Expands to Ensnare More Than 60 Admirals," *Washington Post*, November 5, 2017; Julia Harte, "The Fraud of War: U.S. Troops in Iraq and Afghanistan Have Stolen Tens of Millions Through Bribery, Theft, and Rigged Contracts," *Slate*, May 5, 2015; Lindell Kay, "Marine Accused of Stealing $1M in Gov't Property," *The Daily News* (Jacksonville, N.C.), March 4, 2013; Jennifer J. Li, Tracy C. McCausland, Lawrence M. Hanser, Andrew M. Naber, and Judith Babcock LaValley, *Enhancing Professionalism in the U.S. Air Force*, Santa Monica, Calif.: RAND Corporation, RR-1721-AF, 2017.

ally high in comparison with that of most other global military forces. It is high not because corruption is absent but because the organization constantly seeks to maintain high standards for integrity and in most cases swiftly and harshly punishes corrupt practices.

In some foreign military organizations, corruption is built into semiofficial or even official promotion policies. For example, between at least 2010 and 2014 the Iraqi Ground Force was shot through with corrupt practices.[121] Both junior and senior leadership positions were often purchased rather than won through merit, or they were assigned as part of a sectarian favoritism campaign. The former chief of staff of the Iraqi Army believed that hundreds of millions of payroll dollars were handed out to corrupt military leaders who claimed to lead soldiers who in fact existed only on paper.[122] Observers of the Iraqi military argue that corruption directly undermined the military's ability to counter the Islamic State in 2014, helped feed the collapse of will to fight in places like Fallujah and Mosul, hindered its efforts to recover from these initial defeats, and was a drag on its efforts to regain the initiative.[123] Deeply corrupt practices typically have a corrosive effect on will to fight wherever they exist.[124]

In some cultures, what U.S. analysts might perceive as corruption might be acceptable practice. Assessments and analyses of corruption will necessarily be case-by-case efforts, taking into account cultural context. However, it is not necessarily true that widespread acceptance of corrupt practices means that these practices are warmly accepted by the rank and file or that they will have no effect on will to fight.

Organizational integrity has high durability because it is unlikely to change over the course of a single battle or short series of battles. Figure 2.22 adds integrity to the organizational will-to-fight model.

Organizational Training

Training aligns with competence at the unit and individual levels, and it links directly to the training subfactor at the unit level.[125] Organizations provide training to both

---

[121] For example: Matt Schiavenza, "Why Iraq's Military Has No Will to Fight," *The Atlantic*, May 25, 2015.

[122] Martin Chulov, "Post-War Iraq: 'Everybody Is Corrupt, from Top to Bottom, Including Me,'" *The Guardian*, February 19, 2016.

[123] Schiavenza, 2015; Jaffe and Morris, 2015; Ishaan Tharoor, "Why the Iraqi Army Keeps Failing," *Washington Post*, May 19, 2015.

[124] For example: Nolan Peterson, "Ukraine's War Against Putin-Backed Rebels Is Being Undermined by Corruption," *Newsweek*, August 13, 2017; Reuters, "Chinese Military Corruption Has Gotten So Bad That It Could Undermine the Country's Ability to Wage War," May 7, 2015; Karolina Maclachlan, "How Corruption Undermines NATO Operations," *DefenseOne*, December 2, 2015.

[125] For example: Allan R. Millett, Williamson Murray, and Kenneth H. Watman, "The Effectiveness of Military Organizations," *International Security*, Vol. 11, No. 1, 1986, pp. 37–71; Johan M. G. van der Dennen, "Combat Motivation," *Peace Review: A Journal of Social Justice*, No. 17, 2005, pp. 81–89; Henriksen, 2007.

Figure 2.22
Integrity Added to the Organizational Model

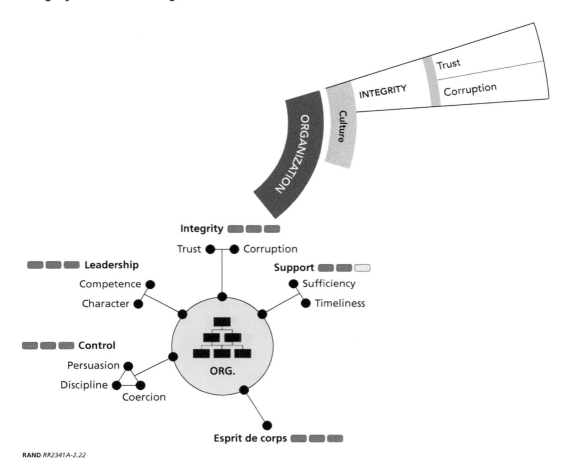

RAND RR2341A-2.22

individuals (e.g., basic training, advanced skills courses) and units, and they provide support to training at the unit level. Units are almost always heavily dependent on the organization for training, so this connection is important. We identified four subfactors within the organizational factor to help identify and describe these dependent capabilities. Each subfactor is also internally interdependent at the organizational level. Does the organization have the *capabilities*—resources, instructional staff, training areas, and other things—necessary to provide and support training across the force? Is the training *relevant* to the mission, is it *sufficient* to accomplish the mission, and does the organization help *sustain* training over time? If these things are not present, then will to fight is likely to be reduced. If these things are present, then will to fight is likely to be supported and sustained.

Figure 2.23
Training Added to the Organizational Model

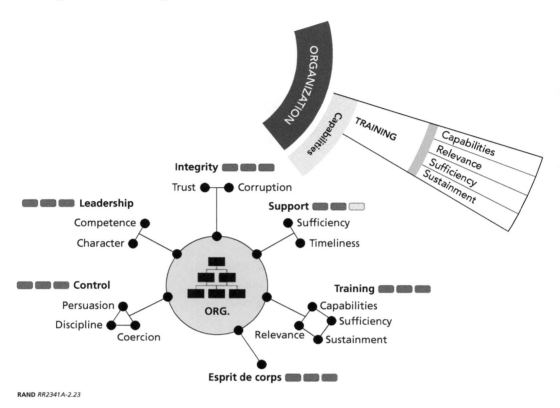

RAND RR2341A-2.23

Training takes place before, between, or after battles, so it is highly durable during battle. Figure 2.23 adds training to the organizational will-to-fight model.

Organizational Doctrine

Doctrine is the organization's approach to everything from organizing to fighting. It provides guidelines for how each unit should prepare itself for combat and how it should fight.[126] Doctrine represents the organization's understanding of war and also some measure of predictive thought. Armies attempt to learn from past wars and to apply lessons to doctrine; in doing so they improve their chances in future wars. But the nature of the next war is always unknown to some extent. Uncertainty in doctrine and some mismatch with operations are inevitable. The closer an organization's

[126] For example: U.S. Joint Chiefs of Staff, *Doctrine for the Armed Forces of the United States*, Joint Publication 1, Washington, D.C.: Joint Staff, March 25, 2013; U.S. Army, *Doctrine Primer*, ADP 1-01, Washington, D.C.: Headquarters, Department of the Army, September 2014.

doctrine matches each situation, and the more effective that doctrine proves to be in combat, the more confidence soldiers and units will have in the organization. Greater confidence coincides with improved will to fight. Misaligned doctrine undermines military effectiveness and erodes confidence. A 2000 RAND study argued, "Ineffective doctrine can negate all the advantages offered by superior equipment and fighting men."[127] This same study advised the military intelligence community to evaluate doctrine as a central element of adversary military capability. Doctrine is rated on *appropriateness* and *effectiveness*. It is more or less appropriate to the task at hand, and it is more or less effective in integrating organizational power and supporting military success.

Doctrine has high durability because it rarely, if ever, changes over the course of a single battle or short series of battles. Figure 2.24 adds doctrine to the organizational will-to-fight model, rounding out the addition of factors and subfactors at this level.

The following definitions and descriptions address only the new factors that occur at this level: integrity and doctrine.

Organizational integrity	Organizational integrity is the organization's approach to maintaining professional standards as they relate to corrupt practices. Corruption exists on a spectrum in every organization; every organization has some level of corruption. The ways in which the organization deals with corruption, and the degree to which the corruption that exists is culturally acceptable, engender or erode trust. High levels of trust are generally equated with improved will to fight, while low levels of trust generally undermine will to fight.
Doctrine	Organizational doctrine codifies the way the organization functions and fights. Doctrine is both a reflection of the organization's culture and an organizing principle for units. To varying degrees it is appropriate to the challenge at hand, and effective in helping the organization and units overcome challenges to succeed in combat.

Organizational factors are the closest to unit factors, but influences on unit will to fight permeate from beyond the organization. Both state- and societal-level factors affect individual identity and motivations, unit capabilities and confidence, and, ultimately, will to fight.

---

[127] Ashley J. Tellis, Janice Bially, Christopher Layne, and Melissa McPherson, *Measuring National Power in the Postindustrial Age*, Santa Monica, Calif.: RAND Corporation, MR-1110-A, 2000, pp. 149–150.

Figure 2.24
Organizational System-of-Systems Diagram Showing Individual Factors

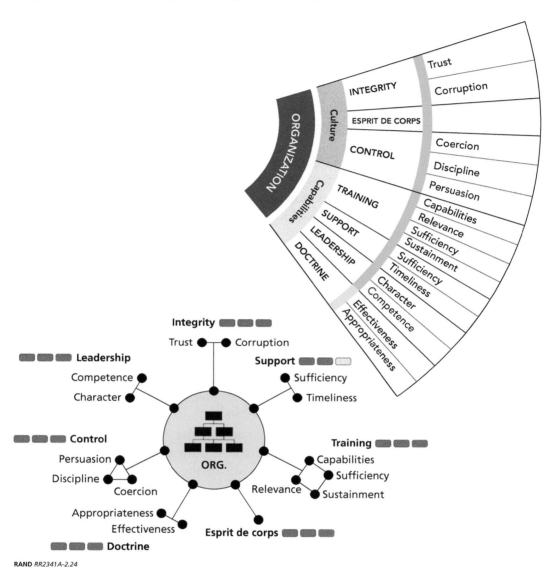

RAND RR2341A-2.24

State and Societal Factors: Impact on Units and Individuals

The state and society are distinct entities in the model but are closely linked. In the model, each state effectively functions as a larger version of the military organization, but it has less specific day-to-day roles in the will to fight of each unit and soldier. For the purposes of this model, a state is a governmental organization that controls the resources and policies—including those related to raising armies and prosecuting war—of a geographically organized society.[128] For example, the Democratic People's Republic of Korea (DPRK, or North Korea) is a state. The society is constituted of all people who identify as members of the state, a loosely bound geographically oriented culture that influences, and is influenced by, the state and the military, and a source of support or dissent in war. All of the North Korean people, together with all of the elements of North Korean culture (history, norms, etc.), constitute the North Korean society.

States provide overarching policy guidance in peacetime. State leadership builds or erodes confidence in the rationale for war. States help generate and inculcate political identities and ideologies that have a direct impact on the way that soldiers and leaders in units view the state, the military, and each specific case of war. States supply and support organizations and units for war. Two factors—leadership and integrity—are effectively the same at the state-societal and organizational levels. Support has a different meaning at this level, while civil-military relations and strategy are relevant only at the state level. Societal identity is closely linked with individual identity. Table 2.7 depicts the state-level factors derived from Table 2.3.

Table 2.7
State and Societal Will-to-Fight Factors

Level	Category	Factors	Subfactors	Durability
State	State culture	Civil-military relations	Appropriateness and functionality	High
		State integrity	Corruption and trust	High
	State capabilities	State support	Sufficiency and timeliness	Mid
		State strategy	Clarity and effectiveness	High
		State leadership	Competence and character	High
Society	Societal culture	Societal identity	Ideology, ethnicity, and history	High
		Societal integrity	Corruption and trust	High
	Societal capabilities	Societal support	Consistency and efficiency	High

---

[128] Societies and culture are not physically limited by geography. This is a necessary simplification for the model. In practice, diaspora populations, hybridity, and other factors make geographic boundaries less relevant to the distribution and sharing of culture.

State Civil-Military Relations

Civil-military relations are the official and practical ways in which the military and civilian authorities interact. Clausewitz placed particular emphasis on the importance of civil-military relations, and particularly on the relationship between statesmen and military leaders. This factor does not require a clear adjudication of Clausewitzean theory.[129] Its only purpose is to set a placeholder for assessment and analysis: The ways in which political and military leaders interact with one another can affect trust and confidence in the organization and the state. Ineffective or inappropriate civil-military relations can undermine will to fight. Relationships between leaders are more or less *appropriate* and *functional*. Appropriate relations fit within societal cultural norms and are generally acceptable to soldiers, while less appropriate relations do not fit and are unacceptable to some degree. Functional relations facilitate effective military activity, while less functional or dysfunctional relations undermine military activity.

Both appropriateness and functionality of civil-military relations affect will to fight differently in every military organization. Like all other citizens of any state, soldiers develop individual beliefs about the appropriateness of the relationships between military and civilian leaders. In some cases these are one and the same. For example, as of mid-2018 Kim Jong-un is both the chair of the Worker's Party of Korea and the supreme commander of the Korean People's Army.[130] Unification of the civil and military parts of the state is long-standing and accepted practice in the DPRK, and it is unlikely that this model undermines the will to fight of North Korean soldiers.[131] Appropriateness is relative.

Functionality is also relative, but generally more straightforward. Either the civil and military leaders work together effectively or they do not. Poor functionality undermines confidence in the state. Since the state is responsible for making war, this loss of confidence would logically affect the confidence—and therefore the will to fight—of individual soldiers. For example, modern Turkey is far more democratic than the DPRK, but a series of coups over the past half century have undermined civil-military relations and affected the functionality of the Turkish Army.[132] Poor civil-military rela-

---

[129] David J. Betz, *Civil-Military Relations in Russia and Eastern Europe*, London: RoutledgeCurzon, 2004; John Binkley, "Clausewitz and Subjective Civilian Control: An Analysis of Clausewitz's Views on the Role of the Military Advisor in the Development of National Policy," *Armed Forces and Society*, Vol. 42, No. 2, 2016, pp. 251–275.

[130] "Profile: North Korean Leader Kim Jong-un," *BBC*, August 29, 2017.

[131] This is an example of a possible conclusion and not a formal, evidence-based conclusion. A formal conclusion would require specific, detailed analysis of the DPRK and the will to fight of its military forces.

[132] According to Halil Karaveli of the Central Asia Caucuses Institute, the 2016 coup in Turkey left the military "broken" and "unable to counter security threats." Considering the ongoing operations in Syria as of late 2017, this is an overstatement. But the effects he describes are relevant to this analysis. Tim Arango and Ceylon Yeginsu, "With Army in Disarray, a Pillar of Modern Turkey Lies Broken," *New York Times*, July 28, 2016. Also

tions directly undermined ARVN will to fight during the Vietnam War.[133] Coups and the eventual merging of civilian and military leadership eroded trust in South Vietnam's democratic process.

Civil-military relations are closely connected with state integrity and they affect will to fight in similar ways. Soldiers have more or less trust in their civil and military senior leaders based on their perceptions of the appropriateness of top-level civil-military relations. If soldiers deem these relationships to be appropriate, then they are unlikely to affect will to fight; there are probably very few cases where appropriate relationships *improved* will to fight. Negative cases like that of the ARVN are likely to have greater impact. In these cases, soldiers perceive something fundamentally wrong with their government. This perception leads to a loss of confidence much in the same way that corruption erodes confidence. In turn, this loss of confidence erodes will to fight, just as it did in many ARVN units during various periods of the Vietnam War.

Civil-military relations have high durability because they are unlikely to change over the course of a single battle or series of small battles due to local combat events. Figure 2.25 adds civil-military relations to the state model of will to fight.

Figure 2.25
Civil-Military Relations Added to the State Will-to-Fight Model

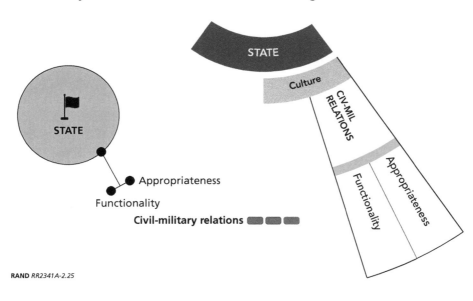

RAND RR2341A-2.25

see Humeyra Pamuk and Gareth Jones, "Turkish Military a Fractured Force After Attempted Coup," *Reuters*, July 26, 2016.

[133] Brigham, 2006; Andrew Wiest, *Vietnam's Forgotten Army: Heroism and Betrayal in the ARVN*, New York: New York University Press, 2008.

State Integrity

For the purposes of understanding will to fight, *state integrity* addresses the way the state maintains standards for behavior and handles corruption. This is effectively the same as organizational integrity but at a higher level of analysis. Strong state integrity can give confidence to soldiers, thereby improving will to fight. Weak state integrity can undermine confidence in the state and in the ultimate purposes of war, thereby reducing confidence and will to fight. These are not hard-and-fast rules, but our case studies generally bore them out.[134]

There is no way to consistently differentiate the degree to which state and organizational corruption affect will to fight in any one case or across a number of cases. Therefore, we cannot offer a generalizable distinction between the two levels. It seems logical that organizational corruption would generally have a greater effect on confidence and will to fight than state corruption because soldiers are closer to and more dependent on the organization than on the state. However, this assumption might not hold in cases of extreme state corruption or in cases where exceptionally high state integrity standards outweighed the impact of military organizational corruption. State and organizational corruption should be assessed or analyzed separately and then viewed in concert. In many historical cases the military is seen as less corrupt than the state; this is often the basis for military coups.[135] In cases like the ARVN and the RVN, state corruption permeated the military and military corruption undercut the state.[136]

State integrity has high durability because it is unlikely to change over the course of a single battle or series of small battles due to local combat events. Figure 2.26 adds integrity to the state will-to-fight model.

State Support

States provide *support* in the same way that organizations do. They deliver (or do not deliver) equipment, weapons, vehicles, medical supplies, and so on through the organization to the unit and the individual. *Sufficient* and *timely* material support is important to sustain military operations, and therefore to sustain will to fight.[137] If the state provides sufficient material to execute strategy, then soldiers are more likely to have confidence in the state and therefore generally higher will to fight. If the state does not

---

[134] See Appendix B. Note that our case study findings were informative but not statistically significant. This portion of our research did not generate meaningful empirical results.

[135] It is also true that some military coup leaders have used accusations of corruption to justify coups without necessarily providing convincing evidence. Literature on coups and civil-military relations is extensive. Clausewitz's *On War* offers a good starting point. Also see Taeko Hiroi and Sawa Omori, "Causes and Triggers of Coups d'état: An Event History Analysis," *Politics and Policy*, Vol. 41, No. 1, 2013, pp. 39–64.

[136] Retired ARVN Lieutenant General Dong Van Khuyen provides one of the best descriptions of the impact of corruption on the ARVN. See Dong Van Khuyen, 1980, pp. 341–374.

[137] Tellis et al. describe in detail the connections between state capabilities, infrastructure, development, and production to military effectiveness. Tellis et al., 2000, Chapters Five and Six.

Figure 2.26
Integrity Added to the State Will-to-Fight Model

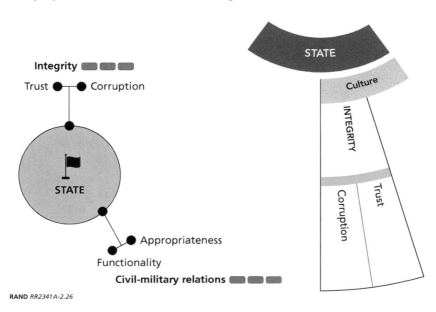

provide sufficient material to execute strategy, or if the delivery of the support is not timely, then soldiers are less likely to have confidence in the state and therefore generally lower will to fight.[138] There is often a strong connection between state integrity and state support. When state leaders undercut military operations by diverting resources to their own pockets, thereby reducing support to soldiers in the field, soldiers tend to lose confidence in state support. Loss of confidence is generally related to reduced will to fight.

State support has midlevel durability. It probably will not change significantly over the course of a single battle or series of small battles due to local combat events, but it can have immediate impact on the course of battle and the confidence that soldiers have in the state. Figure 2.27 adds support to the state will-to-fight model.

State Strategy

Strategy can be general and specific. A general strategy, or grand strategy, describes the way the state conceptualizes geopolitics and war.[139] It can set some general terms for

---

[138] For example: Castillo, 2014.

[139] The lead author of this report summarized the literature on strategic theory and design in a 2016 RAND working paper. See Ben Connable, *Redesigning Strategy for Irregular War: Improving Strategic Design for Planners and Policymakers to Help Defeat Groups Like the Islamic State*, Santa Monica, Calif.: RAND Corporation, WR-1172-OSD, December 2017.

Figure 2.27
Support Added to the State Will-to-Fight Model

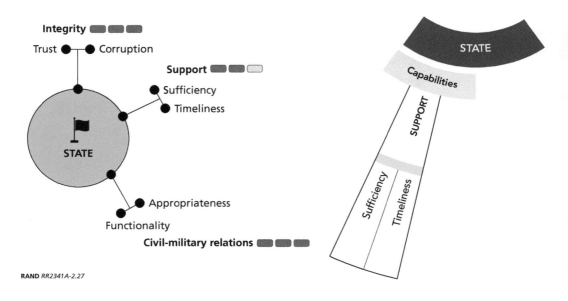

RAND RR2341A-2.27

engaging in war. For example, U.S. national security strategies consistently reiterate the general objective of defending the homeland against foreign attack. Specific strategies are tied to wars. They are the plans, actions, and resources applied to win wars at the level of the state. Strategies that are *clear* and *effective* are more likely to build and sustain will to fight. Soldiers generally want to know what they are fighting for, and they want to know that the state has a good plan to support their efforts and win the war.[140] At the unit level, clear and effective strategies are easier to translate into statements of purpose and action than unclear and ineffective strategies. Clear and effective strategic guidance from the state gives the unit leader a powerful tool to influence the will to fight of the soldiers in the unit.

Strategies that are not clear and effective can undermine confidence in the state's ability to wage war, in the purpose of the war, and in the likelihood of victory.[141] As we

---

[140] For one explanation of these differences, see Connable, 2017.

[141] Paul Robinson argues that NATO strategy in the 1990s' Kosovo campaign undermined operational will to fight by establishing low casualties as the primary operational objective. Operational commanders were reluctant to commit airpower in a way that was risky but obtained the best results, and ground forces were not committed in order to prevent casualties. This was neither a clear nor an effective strategy. Arguably, lack of clear strategy— or perhaps the misalignment of strategy to mission—in Bosnia in 1995 contributed to the disastrous Dutch surrender at Srebrenica. Paul Robinson, " 'Ready to Kill but Not to Die': NATO Strategy in Kosovo," *International Journal*, Vol. 54, No. 4, Autumn 1999, pp. 671–682; Jan Willem Honig, "Avoiding War, Inviting Defeat: The Srebrenica Crisis, July 1995," *Journal of Contingencies and Crisis Management*, Vol. 9, No. 4, December 2001, pp. 200–210.

have previously argued, factors that reduce confidence are likely to have some negative influence on will to fight. Lack of clarity and effectiveness undermines unit leadership, weakens a soldier's connections to the mission, and makes gaps in other factors like state support more glaring and more damaging to unit will to fight.

Strategy can sometimes take major turns, but it tends to shift in gradual increments. It is possible but unlikely that a single battle would lead to a shift in strategy. State strategy is therefore highly durable in the context of a single battle or small series of battles. Figure 2.28 adds strategy to the state will-to-fight model.

State Leadership

Leadership has similar characteristics at each level, and the definition of leadership remains generally consistent here. *State leadership* can be as fragmented and multi-faceted as organizational leadership. In any one case it may be necessary to assess or analyze state leadership at many levels and across many organizations or agencies to understand the ways it affects will to fight at the unit level. Again, the RVN offers a useful example. Top-level RVN leaders had varying levels of character and competence throughout the war, and their behavior had different effects on military will to fight. Catholic leaders' favoritism toward Catholic officers undercut perceptions of the state leaders' character and the loyalty and will to fight of some non-Catholics. Consistent inability to wean the ARVN from U.S. support, to stabilize the government, and to reduce harsh centralized state controls left the competence of state leaders

Figure 2.28
Strategy Added to the State Will-to-Fight Model

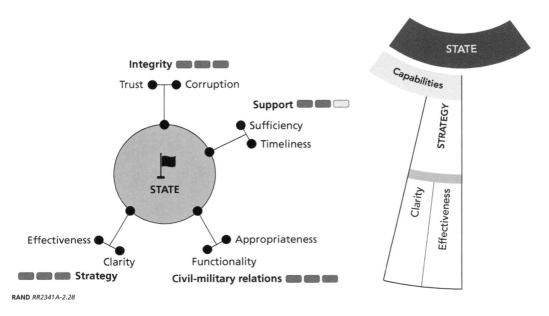

in question.[142] Meanwhile, ministerial officials serving both presidents took different approaches, sometimes mimicking top-level leaders and sometimes deviating from or hewing more closely to the expectations of American advisors. Effects of state leadership on will to fight at the unit level in the ARVN varied considerably from unit to unit depending on unit type and mission.[143]

It is possible that state leadership might fall due to a single dramatic combat defeat, but this kind of event would be quite rare. We assign state leadership high durability. Figure 2.29 adds leadership to the state will-to-fight model.

Figure 2.29
Leadership Added to the State Will-to-Fight Model

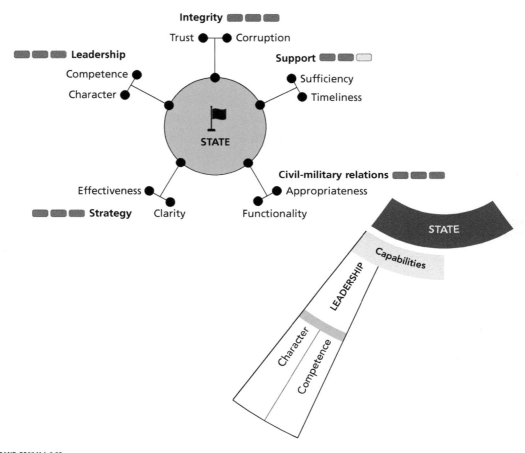

[142] Brigham, 2006; and K. W. Taylor, ed., *Voices from the Second Republic of South Vietnam (1967–1975)*, Ithaca, N.Y.: Cornell University Press, 2014.

[143] For example: Brigham, 2006; Wiest, 2008; Dong Van Khuyen, 1980.

Societal Identity

Identity is one of the most complex and varying societal factors. We offer a simple set of subfactors only to help guide assessment and analysis.[144] *Societal identity* is closely tied to individual identity; both affect the individual's relationship with the unit, organization, and state.[145] For the purposes of understanding unit-level will to fight, societal identity can be *ideological, ethnic,* or *historical.* History plays a role in the development and context of all types of identity; it cuts across the other subfactors. It also stands alone as a catchall for any identity (including societal identity) not clearly ideological or ethnic. Ideological identities include religions, political movements, and other belief systems associated with the state or existing at the societal cultural level of analysis.

Chiara Ruffa describes the role of identity in the military competence and will to fight of the Italian Alpini, a regional military unit located in the northern, mountainous region of Italy.[146] When the Alpini regiment was raised as a regional force in 1872, some state leaders expressed concern that regional recruitment might undermine the power of national identity in the Alpini and more broadly in the Army. The Alpini generated intensive social cohesion from local recruitment and equally intensive task cohesion from their arduous and dangerous mountaineering training. By the middle of the twentieth century the Alpini had also developed a sense of regional and unit-based political autonomy, realizing the fears expressed by some Italian politicians in 1872. Soldiers in the Alpini created a primary political identity associated with but separate from Italian state identity. Ruffa argues that the tight cohesion and political autonomy of the Alpini—presently an elite unit with a diverse deployment record—were a poisonous mix. It eroded their combat effectiveness, led to hesitant performance in combat, and in one case contributed to unit disintegration.[147]

---

[144] A stricter academic interpretation would require a separate volume. Our separate report on national will to fight addresses this factor in more detail.

[145] In the section on individual identity, we wrote that the literature on identity is diverse and often conflicting. There are different theories related to identity, including identity theory, social identity theory, and a range of related psychological theories of self and other types. For example: Jan E. Stets and Peter J. Burke, "Identity Theory and Social Identity Theory," *Social Psychology Quarterly*, Vol. 63, No. 3, September 2000, pp. 224–237; Michael A. Hogg, Deborah J. Terry, and Katherine M. White, "A Tale of Two Theories: A Critical Comparison of Identity Theory with Social Identity Theory," *Social Psychology Quarterly*, Vol. 58, No. 4, December 1995, pp. 255–269; Peter J. Burke, Timothy J. Owens, Richard T. Serpe, and Peggy A. Thoits, eds., *Advances in Identity Theory and Research*, Boston: Springer, 2003; and Steven Hitlin, "Values as the Core of Personal Identity: Drawing Links Between Two Theories of Self," *Social Psychology Quarterly*, Vol. 66, No. 2, June 2003, pp. 118–137. Also see Kreiner, Hollensbe, and Sheep, 2006; Bloom, 1990; Huddy, 2001; Gibson and Condor, 2009; Woodward and Jenkings, 2011; and Roccas and Brewer, 2002.

[146] All information in this paragraph is drawn from Chiara Ruffa, "Cohesion, Political Motivation, and Military Performance in the Italian Alpini," in Anthony King, ed., *Frontline: Combat and Cohesion in the Twenty-First Century*, Oxford: Oxford University Press, 2015, pp. 250–265.

[147] Also see Christie Davies, "Itali sunt imbelles," *Journal of Strategic Studies*, Vol. 5, No. 2, 1982, pp. 266–269.

Figure 2.30
Identity Added to the Societal Will-to-Fight Model

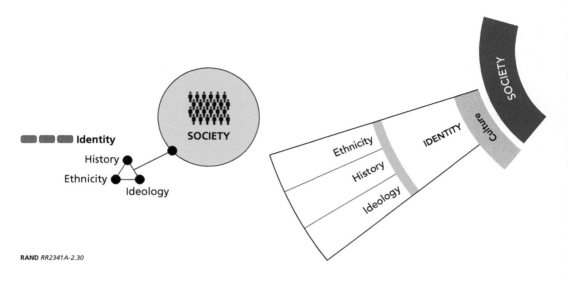

Ethnicity can be homogenous or heterogeneous. Homogenous ethnic identities can be leveraged to generate unity and international feelings of animosity toward other ethnicities. Targeted animosity toward out-groups can backfire when it affects the sense of belonging within a military organization.[148] Heterogeneous ethnicity can be a source of strength or weakness for will to fight. The U.S. military has found heterogeneity to be a source of strength in its units. Other analyses suggest that heterogeneity undermined will to fight in the Wehrmacht during World War II, and it appears to have some negative effect on Russian will to fight today.[149] Identity is a contextual factor: It does not offer more or less valuation.

Societal identity is one of the more static factors in our model. It has high durability. Figure 2.30 adds identity to the societal model of will to fight.

Societal Integrity

Societies are more or less accepting of corruption and more or less vulnerable to corruption. These variations affect the development of individual perceptions about integrity at all levels of analysis, and they affect the ways societies support and interact with the

---

[148] Watson, 1997, Chapter Three; Jason Lyall, "Why Armies Break: Explaining Mass Desertion in Conventional War," unpublished research paper, November 9, 2016.

[149] Kristy N. Kamarck, *Diversity, Inclusion, and Equal Opportunity in the Armed Services: Background and Issues for Congress*, Congressional Research Service, October 24, 2017; Morris Janowitz, *On Social Organization and Social Control*, Chicago: The University of Chicago Press, 1991; Herspring, 2006. Also see MacCoun, 1993.

military.[150] *Societal integrity* is linked to expectation and it generates similar unusual dynamics. Societies that have high levels of corruption and also acceptance of corruption might generate less angst over corrupt practices. In turn, societal corruption might be less likely to undermine will to fight than if a disparity existed between norm and practice.[151] Understanding societal integrity issues can help set the context for assessing or analyzing state and organizational integrity. Our research suggested that understanding societal corruption is important to understanding will to fight; it emerged in the literature review, case studies, and in our analysis of the Russian military and the Vietnam War.

Societal corruption affected will to fight in both the DRV and the RVN. The hierarchical, Confucian-guided, patrilineal, communist, and oligarchical DRV had relatively low levels of societal corruption compared with the RVN.[152] Lower societal corruption facilitated lower corruption in the state, the PAVN, and individual units. Corruption existed, but it was fairly well controlled by the state and by individuals imbued with societal norms for integrity. Some similar cultural dynamics existed in the south, but southern Vietnam was generally more socially diffuse, less hierarchical, and more of an anocracy than a democracy.[153] French colonial influence was stronger in southern Vietnam than in the north, and some effects of colonial abuse and (arguably) emphasis on the Western philosophy of personalism undermined societal integ-

---

[150] Corruption was a factor in Castillo's work on will to fight (Castillo, 2014), and it emerged in many of the other cited works on will to fight. We also accessed the following: Sanjeev Gupta, Luiz de Mello, and Raju Sharan, "Corruption and Military Spending," *European Journal of Political Economy*, Vol. 17, 2001, pp. 749–777; Seini O'Connor and Ronald Fisher, "Predicting Societal Corruption Across Time," *Journal of Cross-Cultural Psychology*, Vol. 43, No. 4, 2012, pp. 644–659; Ji Li, Jane Moy, Kevin Lam, and W. L. Chris Chu, "Institutional Pillars and Corruption at the Societal Level," *Journal of Business Ethics*, Vol. 83, No. 3, 2008, pp. 327–339; and Simon Gachter and Jonathan F. Schulz, "Intrinsic Honesty and the Prevalence of Rule Violations Across Societies," letter, *Nature*, Vol. 531, March 24, 2016, pp. 496–499, with additional data pages.

[151] Or, it might still undercut will to fight. Soldiers sometimes develop standards for integrity that are very different from those of their civilian counterparts.

[152] For example: Shawn Frederick McHale, *Print and Power: Confucianism, Communism, and Buddhism in the Making of Modern Vietnam*, Honolulu: University of Hawaii Press, 2004; Alexander Woodside, "History, Structure, and Revolution in Vietnam," *International Political Science Review*, Vol. 10, No. 2, 1989, pp. 143–157. For further analysis of Confucianism and its relation to the evolution of social order in Vietnam, see John K. Whitmore, "Social Organization and Confucian Thought in Vietnam," *Journal of Southeast Asian Studies*, Vol. 15, No. 2, September 1984, pp. 296–306.

[153] Edward J. Mitchell, "Inequality and Insurgency: A Statistical Study of South Vietnam," *World Politics*, Vol. 23, No. 3, 1968, pp. 421–438; George A. Carver, Jr., "The Real Revolution in South Vietnam," *Foreign Affairs*, Vol. 43, No. 3, 1965, pp. 387–408; U.S. Central Intelligence Agency, *Prospects for North and South Vietnam, 26 May 1959*, National Intelligence Estimate 63-59, Washington, D.C.: Directorate of Intelligence, May 26, 1959. An anocracy is a government that is neither a democracy nor an autocracy but has some characteristics of both. Anocracies are often corrupt and ineffective.

Figure 2.31
Integrity Added to the Societal Will-to-Fight Model

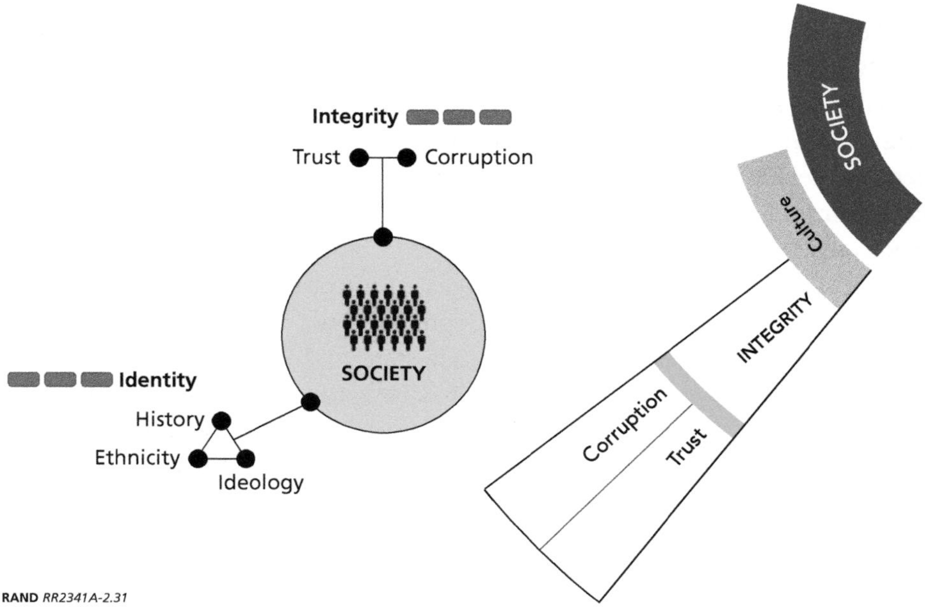

rity and helped set the conditions for corruption.[154] Societal integrity was intertwined with state and organizational integrity on both sides: In the north it often fostered recruitment and positive motivation, while it often had the opposite effect in the south.

Societal integrity is highly durable because it is unlikely to change over the course of a single battle or short series of battles. Figure 2.31 adds societal integrity to the societal will-to-fight model.

Societal Support

Societal support can take many forms. Our analysis suggests that the most common are popular support, material support, and recruiting support. Instead of listing all possible types of support, we maintain *consistency* and *efficiency* as subfactors in order to assess the value of any and all types of support to unit will to fight. People register popular support or dissent through polling, expression in literature and video, and voting, and through other media. Polling and voting should not necessarily be taken at face value when considering their impact on will to fight. American societal support for the post-9/11 wars is an argument for nuanced analysis. Even when overall support

---

[154] Pierre Brocheux and Daniel Hémery, *Indochina: An Ambiguous Colonization 1858–1954*, Berkeley: University of California Press, 2009; Johan De Tavernier, "The Historical Roots of Personalism: From Renouvier's Le Personnalisme, Mounier's Manifeste au service du personnalisme, and Maritain's Humanisme integral to Janssens' Personne et Societe," *Ethical Perspectives*, Vol. 16, No. 3, 2009, pp. 361–392.

for the wars in Afghanistan and Iraq was at low ebb, the popular support for troops fighting those wars remained high. For example, in a 2006 poll 36 percent of Americans supported the war in Iraq while 72 percent of the same sample had a favorable view of troops fighting in Iraq.[155] This dichotomous social perspective may have had material consequences for will to fight. Throughout the war in Iraq from 2001 to 2011 troops fighting and returning home received warm support.[156] One of the most obvious manifestations of this support is "troop greeters," who welcome home returning soldiers, marines, sailors, and airmen passing through U.S. airports. Some of the greeters opposed the wars but supported the troops.[157]

Material support can take the form of volunteer collection and dissemination of packages for soldiers, contributions to war bonds or (as in World War II) scrap metal collection, or perhaps funding for the recovery of wounded soldiers. Recruiting support is generally expressed in the willingness of families to send military-age sons and daughters to war, and the willingness of those sons and daughters to enlist.

Societal support has high durability because it is unlikely to change significantly over the course of a single battle or short series of battles. Figure 2.32 adds support to the societal will-to-fight model.

These definitions address factors that are unique or significantly different from the individual, unit, and organizational levels:

Civil-military relations	The nature, appropriateness, and functionality of the relationships between political and military leaders affect the way that soldiers and, collectively, units view their relationship with the state, their trust in the state as an institution, and their willingness to fight for the state in time of war.
State support to the military	The state is required to provide the organization, unit, and individual with direction, training, manpower, equipment, and, in time of war, material support and aid like air strikes or medical evacuation. Efficient and consistent state support builds and sustains confidence in the state, engendering will to fight. Inefficient and/or inconsistent state support undermines confidence in the state and erodes will to fight.

---

[155] Lydia Saad, "Republicans and Democrats Disagree on Iraq War, but Support Troops," *Gallup News Service*, September 28, 2006. Also see Moni Basu, "Survey: Veterans Say Afghanistan, Iraq Wars Not Worth It," *CNN*, October 5, 2011. It is worth examining the significant differences between these post-9/11 perceptions and Vietnam-era perceptions, although these fall outside the scope of our research. See Frank Newport and Joseph Carroll, "Iraq Versus Vietnam: A Comparison of Public Opinion," *Gallup News Service*, August 24, 2006.

[156] There is no way to measure the impact of this support on will to fight. Instead, it could be assessed or analyzed using multiple data sources with an effort to identify data on troop perceptions of social support.

[157] *The Way We Get By*, film description, *PBS*, November 11, 2009.

Figure 2.32
Support Added to the Societal Will-to-Fight Model

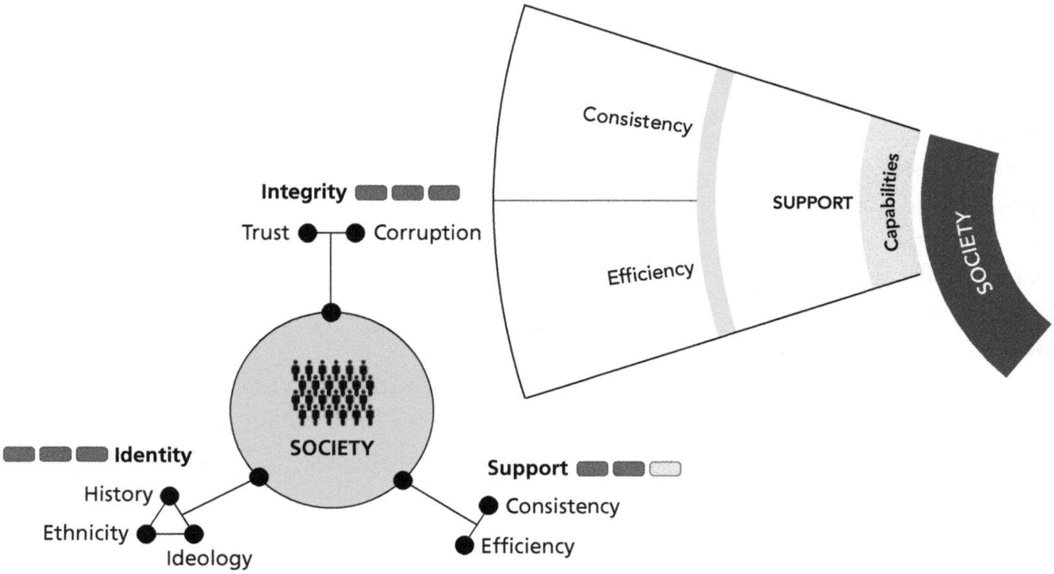

RAND RR2341A-2.32

State strategy	States develop general strategic concepts and specific plans to deal with specific problems. Strategy includes the plan, the resources to effect the plan, and the actions to ensure the plan succeeds. Clear and effective strategies give soldiers confidence in the purpose and direction of the war, thereby reinforcing will to fight. Unclear and/or ineffective strategies reduce confidence in the purpose and direction of the war, thereby reducing will to fight.
Societal support to the military	Societies provide popular, material, and recruiting support to the war effort. High levels of societal support engender will to fight: Soldiers who believe the society is invested in their mission are generally more likely to fight. Soldiers who believe that society is not invested in their mission are generally less likely to fight.
Societal identity	Identity can be ideological, ethnic, or historical, although history plays a role in shaping all types of identity. Historical identity is any identity that is not clearly ideological or ethnic in nature, and it includes the broader concept of national identity. In the literature on foreign military social

cohesion, homogeneity is generally associated with improved will to fight. However, positive experiences in the U.S. military with heterogeneity suggest that there is no hard-and-fast rule to assess or analyze this factor.

Figure 2.33 depicts the entire node-and-link model of tactical-operational will to fight, connecting the individual, the organization, the state, and the society to the unit. Figure 2.34 depicts the entire concentric wheel model of tactical-operational will to fight.

Assessing or analyzing these factors together will give a picture of a unit's disposition to fight in the ready state. Keep in mind that one critical factor might undermine an otherwise positive balance for will to fight or reinforce will to fight even when most other factors are lacking or are working to reduce that will. Assessment and analysis of will to fight requires both a holistic understanding of disposition and a factor-by-factor assessment sufficient enough to reveal potential overriding factors. Assessment and analysis tools should be tailored for specific purposes. There is no right or wrong way to apply the model.

Figure 2.35 depicts the 29 factors in a simple notional Likert Scale rating of 1–5. Scores for each factor would have been determined by detailed factor-by-factor assessment or analysis. Higher scores denote more positive impact on will to fight, while lower scores denote less positive or negative impact on will to fight. In this notional case, 27 of the 29 factors are rated as 3, or average. Desperation and leadership stand out. Desperation is rated as 5, while leadership is rated as 1. For this notional military unit, high levels of individual desperation across most of the soldiers in the unit might overcome all of the other factors, including abysmal unit leadership. This could influence exceptionally high disposition to fight. Or perhaps the abysmal unit leadership would undercut all other factors, including individual soldier desperation. Factor valuation demands specific explanation and differentiation in every case, along with an understanding of the context in which the factors are exercising their influence. Even if 28 of 29 factors were rated at 5 and one factor was rated at 1 or 2, that single factor would have to be closely examined to determine its potentially offsetting value.

This simple notional chart illustrates the value of considering will to fight as a disposition influenced by numerous factors acting together and sometimes against one another. It also shows the importance of considering each factor both individually and in its possible interactions with the others. This illustration also drives home three related points: (1) *Will to fight should never be considered simply as a sum, average, or weighted average of the factors*; (2) applying the will-to-fight model requires both holistic and factor-by-factor assessment or analysis; and (3) there is no fixed approach to assessing or analyzing will to fight. A narrative description, a more detailed subfactor assessment, or a less-detailed approach focusing on a few selected factors might be appropriate for specific military uses in any one case.

Figure 2.33
A System-of-Systems Tactical-Operational Will-to-Fight Model: Node-and-Link

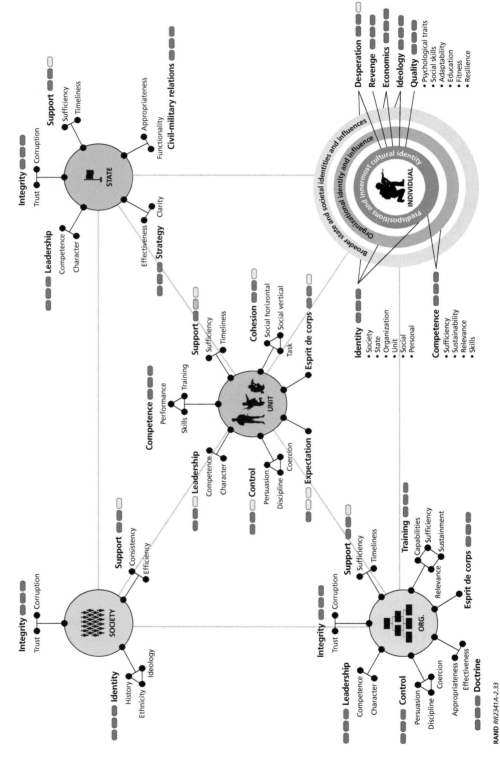

Figure 2.34
System-of-Systems Tactical-Operational Will-to-Fight Model: Concentric Wheel

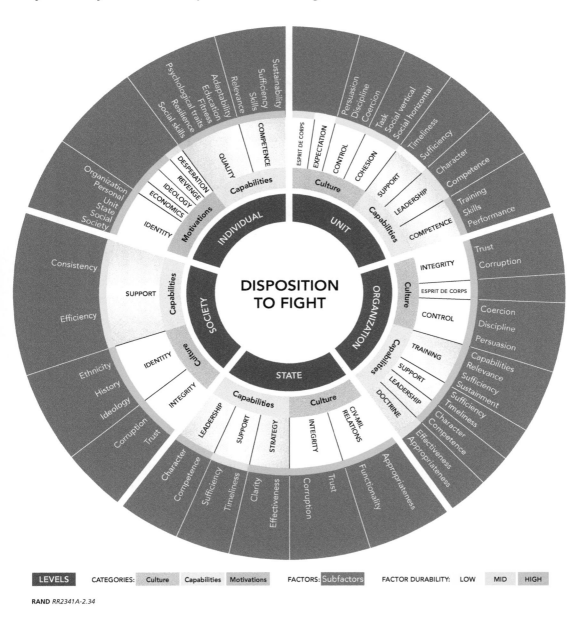

LEVELS   CATEGORIES: Culture   Capabilities   Motivations   FACTORS: Subfactors   FACTOR DURABILITY: LOW   MID   HIGH

RAND RR2341A-2.34

Understanding disposition to fight in the ready state, before combat, is prerequisite to understanding why individuals and units choose to fight in combat. Examining soldiers only in the immediate context of war absent a deeper understanding of their motivations, capabilities, and cultural influences invites dangerous misunderstandings. Similarly, examining disposition absent the immediate context of war tells only part

Figure 2.35
Notional Will-to-Fight Rating Scale with Differentiated Factor Ratings

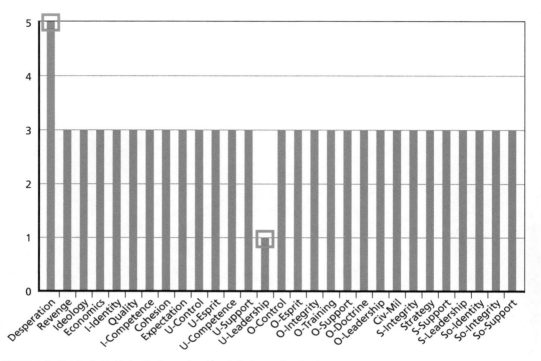

NOTE: I=Individual; U=Unit; O=Organizational; S=State; So=Society

RAND RR2341A-2.35

of the story. Therefore, the next chapter introduces combat factors including enemy actions, the environment, and veterancy. It focuses on developing will to fight as a component of war gaming and military combat simulation. If will to fight is a critical component in war, then it should be a critical component in war gaming and simulation.

CHAPTER THREE

War Gaming and Simulating of Will to Fight

One of the clearest ways to study the major impact of will to fight in war is through war gaming and simulation.[1] War gaming and simulation would be an effective way to explore the RAND Arroyo Center will-to-fight model proposed in Chapter Two or any other model of will to fight. The purposes of examining will to fight in games and simulations are to anchor will to fight to existing practice, to show how will to fight can change combat outcomes in notional situations, and to set a baseline of experimental research to foster a wider use and acceptance of will to fight in military practice.[2] If will to fight can be successfully incorporated into military gaming and simulation, then it might find greater utility and acceptance in other military applications.

War games and simulations are approximations of combat intended to help people think about the nature of war, to help people understand complex military problems without actually fighting, to reduce uncertainty in decisionmaking, and to forecast and analyze notional combat outcomes. War games are played between people, usually across a table, and usually across a flat two-dimensional map. Some games use three-dimensional terrain and figures to represent soldiers and vehicles.[3] War games are "human-in-the-loop" because they are dependent on human decisionmaking and human adjudication of semifixed rules.[4] Simulations are computer representations of combat. Some simulations are also human-in-the-loop, but many run autonomously,

---

[1] For explanations of war games and simulations for military purposes, see Roger Smith, "The Long History of Gaming in Military Training," *Simulation Gaming*, Vol. 41, No. 1, February 2010, pp. 6–19; Robert D. Specht, *War Games*, Santa Monica, Calif.: RAND Corporation, P-1041, 1957; Francis J. McHugh, *Fundamentals of War Gaming*, Newport, R.I.: U.S. Naval War College, March 1, 1966.

[2] Recall that by "outcomes" we mean not just winning or losing but the range of other effects—casualties, fleeing, freezing, and so on—that constitute some of the results of each game or simulation.

[3] There are other types of games, including matrix games and card games. Matrix games are typically discussion based, while card games use playing cards specifically designed to represent some aspect of military equipment, personnel, or activity.

[4] Some commercial game players would argue that rules are always fixed. For example, many hard-core players of the game *Advanced Squad Leader* would never consider bending a rule to speed game play or to account for an unusual situation. Official military tabletop gaming tends to allow for greater flexibility to account for the messy realities of combat and to ensure the purpose of the game is not lost at the expense of hidebound conformity.

playing out combat between computer-generated soldiers—or in simulation jargon, *agents*. In simulations, stochastic (random) determinations of combat outcomes are calculated using fixed rather than semifixed rules. Games are generally more useful in exercising human decisionmaking. Simulations are generally more useful in delivering precise but notional outcomes for analysis.[5]

This chapter presents findings from our review of existing games and simulations and our limited objective simulation experiments in NetLogo and IWARS. While will to fight defies precise quantification in real-world practice, the experiments offer some quantitative evidence of the value of including will to fight in simulated holistic combat effectiveness assessments. This work builds from a wealth of published research dating back to the 1970s. It also serves as a needed step in what should be a more concerted effort to build empirical evidence of the value of will to fight for military war gaming and simulation.[6] We encourage other researchers to replicate our experiments, improve on them, and integrate will-to-fight models into a broader set of military war games and simulations. To that end, all data, modeling, and experimentation results presented in this chapter and Appendix E will be made available upon request once this report has been published.[7]

RAND has played an important role in the development of war games and simulations since at least the early 1950s. Most notably, RAND developed and applied the RAND Strategy Assessment System (RSAS), the Day After methodology, and the Joint Interagency Contingency Model (JICM).[8] In 1967 RAND analyst Marvin B. Schaffer introduced morale and discipline coefficients to the venerated Lanchester Laws central to many quantitative combat effectiveness analyses.[9] In 1988 RAND used analytic war

---

[5]   There are exceptions to this generalization. Some human-in-the-loop simulations are specifically designed to test human decisionmaking.

[6]   Two of the best and most accessible works are Philip Sabin, *Simulating War: Studying Conflict Through Simulation Games*, London: Bloomsbury Academic, 2012.

[7]   We estimate publication in mid-2018. They may be made available to U.S. government personnel prior to publication, depending on RAND quality assurance review requirements.

[8]   For example: Herman Kahn and Irwin Mann, *War Gaming*, Santa Monica, Calif.: RAND Corporation, P-1167, 1957; Paul K. Davis and James A. Winnefeld, *The RAND Strategy Assessment Center: An Overview and Interim Conclusions About Utility and Development Options*, Santa Monica, Calif.: RAND Corporation, R-2945-DNA, 1983; Bruce W. Bennett, Arthur M. Bullock, Daniel B. Fox, Carl M. Jones, John Schrader, Robert Weissler, and Barry A. Wilson, *JICM 1.0*, Santa Monica, Calif.: RAND Corporation, MR-383-NA, 1994; and Stuart Johnson, Martin C. Libicki, and Gregory F. Treverton, eds., *New Challenges, New Tools for Defense Decisionmaking*, Santa Monica, Calif.: RAND Corporation, MR-1576-RC, 2003. Also see Elizabeth Losh, "Playing Defense: Gender, Just War, and Game Design," in Pat Harrigan and Matthew G. Kirschenbaum, eds., *Zones of Control: Perspectives on Wargaming*, Cambridge, Mass.: The Massachusetts Institute of Technology, 2016, pp. 355–369. For more information on RAND gaming and simulation, see Pardee RAND Graduate School, "Methods Centers at Pardee RAND: RAND Center for Gaming."

[9]   Marvin B. Schaffer, *Lanchester Models of Guerrilla Engagements*, Santa Monica, Calif.: RAND Corporation, RM-5053-ARPA, 1967. Lanchester Laws are a series of equations developed in the early twentieth century to

gaming to help narrow uncertainty in the NATO-Warsaw Pact balance, incorporating will-to-fight factors into the game.[10] Research presented here seeks to help further RAND's contribution to Army and Joint modeling and simulation efforts, and to the broader pursuit of improved realism and effectiveness in war games and simulations. Specifically we seek to address the lack of effective will-to-fight modeling in most U.S. military war games and simulations.

Adding Combat Factors and Veterancy

Understanding how the realities of combat affect will to fight is a necessary precursor to assessing and modifying war games and simulations. Chapter Two presented the will-to-fight model in what we are calling a unit's *ready state*, or precombat state.[11] Combat does not add to or take away from the factors or subfactors in the model, but it does help reveal—and may alter—their values at the unit level and individual level both during and after the fact. This section describes some of the exogenous factors in combat that can affect will to fight. It briefly explains how exposure, fear, and fatigue can affect will to fight as time in combat increases, and how combat experience can have a lasting impact on soldier and unit will to fight over time. We label these factors as exogenous because they are exogenous to the model. Combat factors are equally relevant for real-world assessment and analysis and for war gaming and simulation.

Combat State Factors

How does will to fight change when a unit enters combat? How do exogenous factors like artillery fire or fanatical enemy attacks or just cold weather affect a unit's collective disposition to fight over the course of a single battle or short series of battles? Specifically, how does combat affect what we describe as mid- or low-durability factors in the model? These are shown in Table 3.1.

We assembled a common set of combat factors from all of the sources used in this report, from our structured assessment of war games and simulations, and from

---

help calculate the likely outcomes of force-on-force combat. Schaffer explains these in his report. Also see Jerome Bracken, "Lanchester Models of the Ardennes Campaign," *Naval Research Logistics*, Vol. 42, 1995, pp. 559–577; Christopher P. Fredlake and Kai Wang, *EINStein Goes to War: A Primer on Ground Combat Models*, Alexandria, Va.: Center for Naval Analyses, September 2008.

[10] Paul K. Davis, *The Role of Uncertainty in Assessing the NATO/Pact Central Region Balance*, Santa Monica, Calif.: RAND Corporation, N-2839-RC, 1989b; Bruce W. Bennett, Carl M. Jones, Arthur M. Bullock, and Paul K. Davis, *Main Theater Modeling in the RAND Strategy Assessment System (3.0)*, Santa Monica, Calif.: RAND Corporation, N-2743-NA, 1988. Assessments of morale and cohesion were built into the combat effectiveness determination for each unit prior to the onset of gamed combat.

[11] Note that many military units have a mix of veterans and nonveterans. While this is not always true, the idea of separating ready from combat state is to idealize the model, not to set a firm line between the two. Any assessment or analysis should account for existing veterancy in any specific military unit under examination.

Table 3.1
Mid- and Low-Durability Model Factors

Factors	Subfactors	Durability
Individual desperation		Mid
Unit cohesion	Social vertical, social horizontal, and task	Mid
Unit expectation		Low
Unit control	Coercion, persuasion, and discipline	Mid
Unit esprit de corps		Mid
Unit support	Sufficiency and timeliness	Low
Unit leadership	Competence and character	Mid
Organizational support	Sufficiency and timeliness	Mid
State support	Sufficiency and timeliness	Mid

a wider array of historical literature familiar to the RAND Arroyo Center research team. This list is by no means exhaustive. As with the core model of will to fight, each combat factor might be redefined or broken into a more detailed set of subfactors. We address some of these permutations with factor modifiers. Combat factors are separate from the RAND Arroyo Center will-to-fight model: They are factors that affect the model, not factors of the model itself. There is no distinct alignment between any one factor or group of factors in the model and any one combat factor or group of combat factors.

A few exogenous factors are intangible, and many are already reflected in the RAND Arroyo Center model. In the *combat state*, expectation reflects both a perception of support and leadership and the expectation of wounding or death. Before the first rounds of combat are fired, most soldiers experience the fear of unpredictable, intense violence. This intangible fear affects will to fight. We model expectation as a unit-level factor because it occurs within a group context. It is also a deeply personal feeling as the unit enters the combat state. Tables 3.2 and 3.3 break 31 combat factors into two types: *adversary* and *exogenous*.

Adversary Combat Factors

Adversary factors are associated with enemy forces. Each factor is described in relation to the friendly force: It has value only as it impacts friendly will to fight. How aggressive is the enemy? Have they achieved surprise and thrown the friendly unit off-balance? Are they using chemical or flame weapons that tend to play on deep-seated individual fears? Each of the 31 factors has a description and modifiers. Modifiers affect the value of the factor and can be used for assessment. For example, the factor of artillery fire has different types of impact on friendly will to fight depending on the shell type

Table 3.2
Adversary Combat Factors

Factor	Description	Modifiers
Artillery fire	Attack with indirect fire	Shell type, duration, accuracy, suppression
Direct fire	Engage with rifles, machine guns	Accuracy, intensity, volume, duration, suppression
Flee combat	Enemy runs away	Numbers, observed or reported, duration, timing
PsyOp	Hostile messaging	Resonance of message, accuracy of targeting, vector
Close quarters	Pistol range or hand to hand	Offensive or defensive, weapons, ferocity
Air attack	Fixed- or rotary-wing attacks	Accuracy, intensity, volume, duration, defended against?
Surrender	Enemy soldiers surrender	Numbers, reason, observed or reported, frequency, type
Atrocities	Violating the laws of war	Type, nature of victim, frequency, observed or reported
Flank attack	Assault other than frontal attack	Location, timing, intensity, accompanied by fire
Fear weapon	Use of CBRN or flames	Type, vector, accuracy, effectiveness, duration
Sniper fire	Hidden long-range rifle fire	Accuracy, distance, concealment, duration
Mass	Concentrate forces to attack	Timing, position, purpose, duration, type of force
Aggression	More or less ferocious	Reputation, actions, consistency, applied intelligently?
Surprise	Catch friendly force unaware	Timing, follow-through, purpose, type of force
Mines or IEDs	Hidden explosive attacks	Type, concealment, location, density, effect
Fanaticism	Ideological intensity	Type of ideology, reputation, effects on combat behavior
Competence	Capabilities and qualities	Reputation, and observed performance vis-à-vis reputation
Cyberattack	Attack friendly networks	Type, effectiveness, impact, complexity, timing
Armor	Attack with tanks	Mass, type, effectiveness, with or without infantry

NOTE: CBRN = chemical biological radiological or nuclear; IEDs = improvised explosive devices; PsyOp = psychological operations

(heavy artillery? light mortars?), the duration of the attack, its accuracy, and the degree to which it generates suppression of friendly activity.[12] With all other things being equal, a long barrage of large-caliber, accurate artillery fire that significantly suppresses

---

[12] Suppression is the fear effect generated by the near passing or near impact of bullets or shells.

friendly behavior is more likely to reduce will to fight than a short, inaccurate barrage. Surprise is a common modifier that typically exacerbates the negative effect of attacks. For example, a surprise air attack is more likely to degrade friendly will to fight than one spotted by friendly observation ahead of time. We list surprise as a stand-alone factor since it is an essential factor in most theories of effective warfighting, but it can be applied as a modifier to any of the other enemy actions.

The effects of adversary disposition and actions on will to fight are well recorded in military history and codified in modern U.S. ground force doctrine. Lord Moran describes the terrorizing effect of artillery fire and the varying abilities of soldiers to maintain their will to fight under artillery fire over time.[13] The use of chemical, biological, radiological, or even flame weapons like a close-in flamethrower can have equally deleterious effects on will to fight.[14] U.S. Army ADP 3-90 states that surprise "induces psychological shock in enemy soldiers and leaders."[15] The Marine Corps describes surprise as a "state of disorientation resulting from an unexpected event that degrades the enemy's ability to resist."[16] In other words, surprise is specifically designed to reduce will to fight. U.S. Army armored units are purposefully designed to instill shock in the enemy: Fear of an anthropomorphic armored steel beast capable of rending flesh with heavy shells or machine guns or crushing soldiers under its treads is endemic. Fear of armor can reduce will to fight in all but the most experienced, well-trained, and capable infantry soldiers.[17] Observing adversary surrender can have the opposite effect. Surrender generally reduces fear of the enemy, particularly when soldiers see unarmed enemy with their hands over their heads, demoralized and unthreatening.

Exogenous Combat Factors

Exogenous (external) combat factors include any factor not in the endogenous (internal) will-to-fight model and not directly associated with the adversary. Factors that appear in the model, such as support, leadership, and cohesion, are directly impacted by events in combat. In combat, support includes equipment, supply, and medical support. We list food and water as a separate factor because it appears frequently in

---

[13]   Moran, 2007 (1945), various.

[14]   For example: Mark S. Oordt, "The Psychological Effects of Weapons of Mass Destruction," in Carrie H. Kennedy and Eric A. Zillmer, eds., *Military Psychology: Clinical and Operational Applications*, New York: The Guilford Press, 2006, pp. 295–309; James W. Stokes and Louis E. Banderet, "Psychological Aspects of Chemical Defense and Warfare," *Military Psychology*, Vol. 9, No. 4, 1997, pp. 395–415; and John W. Mountcastle, *Flame On: U.S. Incendiary Weapons, 1918–1945*, Mechanicsburg, Pa.: Stackpole Books, 1999.

[15]   U.S. Army, *Offense and Defense*, ADP 3-90, Washington, D.C.: Headquarters, Department of the Army, August 2012f, p. 8.

[16]   U.S. Marine Corps, 1997, p. 41.

[17]   U.S. Army, *Armor and Mechanized Infantry Team*, ATP 3-90.1, Washington, D.C.: Headquarters, Department of the Army, January 2016a, pp. 1–4. Similar publications by the U.S. Army reinforce this argument. Also see John A. English, *A Perspective on Infantry*, New York: Praeger Publishers, 1981, Chapter Four.

Table 3.3
Exogenous Combat Factors

Factor	Description	Modifiers
Fatigue	Rest allowed before, during combat	Quality, timing, duration, under duress
Weather	Effects of heat, cold, rain, snow, etc.	Intensity, duration, prep for inclement weather
Food and water	Available sustenance	Adequacy, quality, temperature, timing
Terrain	Effects of incline, foliage, etc.	Grade or density, effects on movement, prep
Time in combat	How long the unit has been fighting	Total time, time under fire, interval of breaks
Ally wounded	See fellow soldiers hit	Type of wound, proximity, closeness to soldier
Ally killed	See fellow soldier killed	Type of death, proximity, closeness to soldier
Leader killed	Loss of a leader in combat	Type of death, proximity, quality of replacement
Enemy wounded	See enemy soldier with wounds	Observe or wound?, type of wound
Enemy killed	See enemy soldier dead or dying	Observe or kill? existing body? state of body
Unit degradation	Number or percentage of soldiers lost	Speed of loss, closeness to casualties, type of loss
Family threatened	Soldier family members' safety	Proximity to combat, intent of the enemy

descriptions of combat. While fatigue and time in combat are endogenous to the soldiers in the unit, they are imposed as exogenous events of combat.

The impacts of fatigue, weather, sustenance, and harsh terrain on will to fight are also recorded as the effects of enemy disposition and actions.[18] The U.S. military routinely studies fatigue because it is recognized as a source of degraded mental state and performance.[19] Lord Moran devoted a separate chapter to exposure, or the effects of harsh weather conditions on the mental state of soldiers. He wrote: "The harsh violence of winter may find a flaw even in picked men."[20] Lord Moran went on to describe the corrosive effects of long-term exposure to soldiers' will to fight:[21]

---

[18]   Environmental effects are summarized in Rick L. Campise, Schuyler K. Geller, and Mary E. Campise, "Combat Stress," in Kennedy and Zillmer, 2006, pp. 215–240. Also see English, 1981, Chapter Nine.

[19]   For example: Wendy M. Troxel, Regina A. Shih, Eric Pedersen, Lily Geyer, Michael P. Fisher, Beth Ann Griffin, Ann C. Haas, Jeremy R. Kurz, and Paul S. Steinberg, *Sleep in the Military: Promoting Healthy Sleep Among U.S. Servicemembers*, Santa Monica, Calif.: RAND Corporation, RR-739, 2015; and Diana R. Haslam and Peter Abraham, "Sleep Loss and Military Performance," in Belenky, 1987, pp. 167–184.

[20]   Moran, 2007 (1945), p. 87.

[21]   Moran, 2007 (1945), p. 88.

One fellow with a working imagination relapsed into a state of torpor not unlike the condition following intense grief, another drifted into a resentful state not easy to describe, which was the first warning of his defeat. . . . It was not only the mind that was hurt, exposure left the soldier weaker in body and so weaker in purpose, his will has been sapped.

Seeing or hearing about the wounding or death of fellow soldiers or leaders can be shocking and demoralizing, particularly with the first instance.[22] Loss can affect cohesion and leadership, but it can also undermine individual motivation, faith in unit and organizational support, doctrine, strategy, and many other factors.

In addition to all of these adversary and exogenous factors, any event or change in condition that affects any of the factors in the will-to-fight model is relevant to understanding changes in will to fight during combat. It would be impossible to list these or to describe how they might alter will to fight in any one case. We offer a few examples:

- A budget crisis reduces war funds for one side, degrading (at least) unit support, unit expectation, organizational support, and state support.
- One side is clearly losing the war, which affects individual identity, unit expectations, state strategy, and societal support on both sides.
- One side suffers a military coup against the national civilian leadership, affecting state civil-military relations, state leadership, state support, and state integrity.
- A powerful third country adds its support to one side, changing (at least) unit support, unit expectation, organizational support, state support, and state strategy.

Combining all of these factors in real time generates a more complete understanding of their possible influences on combat behavior. A range of these combat behaviors emerges both in the real world and in conceptual models. Calculating the value and relations of all endogenous, adversary, and exogenous factors from moment to moment in the real world is not possible. Replicating these calculations in games and simulations is possible, but never to the point of absolute realism. It is still helpful to understand the range of possible combat behaviors for both real and simulated combat.

Combat Behaviors

Table 3.4 lists and describes a number of combat behaviors, ranging from rout, disobedience, and freezing to aggression, competent assault, and heroism. These are drawn from the literature review and from the review of games and simulations. Each behavior is rated by type as positive, acceptable, or harmful. Positive behavior accelerates the unit's mission, acceptable behavior supports the mission, and harmful behavior undermines the mission. These terms are written in the context of force-on-force combat, but they could be modified for other types of missions. No behavior is fixed: Individuals

---

[22] For example, Belenky, 1987; Moran, 2007 (1945).

Table 3.4
Possible Combat Behaviors Resulting from Decisions Driven by Will to Fight

Factor	Description	Type
Heroism	Hyperaggressive individual behavior that can inspire other soldiers	Positive
Aggression	Attacking or defending vigorously; help degrade adversary will to fight	Positive
Competent assault	Perform offensive mission with a calm, workmanlike attitude	Acceptable
Competent defense	Perform defensive mission with a calm, workmanlike attitude	Acceptable
Hesitation	Delay in following orders or taking action	Harmful
Pinned	Unwillingness to move under fire but may return fire	Harmful
Freezing	Unwillingness to act and a descent into incapacitation	Harmful
Disobedience	Refusal to follow a combat order	Harmful
Panic	Soldier allows fear to dominate resulting in ineffective behavior	Harmful
Rout/Flee/Break	Running away from combat	Harmful
Surrender	Quit fighting and submit to enemy control	Harmful

NOTE: Assault generally requires greater will to fight than defense.

and entire units can exhibit many different behaviors over the course of a single battle. This list is not necessarily exclusive.

Individual soldiers in a unit can exhibit any of these behaviors and perhaps several of them in the course of a single battle. Individual behavior often has a knock-on effect on unit behavior. Heroic actions often trigger heroism or reduce fear in fellow soldiers.[23] Understanding how collective behavioral actions can be triggered and play out is helpful in assessing or analyzing both positive and harmful unit behaviors. Military historians, military psychologists, and other experts who study battle—including modeling and simulations experts—describe trigger points for mass aggression or mass flight or surrender.[24] This is also sometimes referred to as a cascading effect, and it can transfer within a unit and from unit to unit across a battlefield.

---

[23] This dynamic emerged in many of our historical case studies. For a discussion of heroism, see Reuven Gal, "Combat Stress as an Opportunity: The Case of Heroism," in Belenky, 1987, pp. 31–46.

[24] For example: Mark Granovetter, "Threshold Models of Collective Behavior," *American Journal of Sociology*, Vol. 83, No. 6, May 1978, pp. 1420–1443; J. Fennell, "Courage and Cowardice in the North African Campaign: The Eighth Army and Defeat in the Summer of 1942," *War in History*, Vol. 20, No. 1, 2013, pp. 99–122; Craig W. Reynolds, "Flocks, Herds, and Schools: A Distributed Behavioral Model," *Computer Graphics*, Vol. 21, No. 4, July 1987, pp. 25–34; and Watson, 1997.

Applying Combat Factors

Even if we were able to identify and describe all of these factors, it still would not be possible to accurately predict the outcome of combat. However, estimation and forecasting are possible and warranted. Many of the adversary factors and some of the exogenous factors can be known ahead of time and used in a comparative analysis with the unit will-to-fight model. For example, a poorly trained, poorly led allied company low on sleep and food might be preparing to attack uphill against an aggressive adversary platoon supported by tanks and flame weapons. This combination of factors does not guarantee allied defeat, but it does help focus will-to-fight analysis on the factors that might—or might not—help the allied unit overcome this deficit. For example, in this case the allied unit might be collectively driven by strong ideological motivation, or they might be seeking revenge for enemy atrocities, or they might be defending their families against impending attack. Any one of these factors alone might be sufficient to overcome a stacked deck of derogatory factors.

These factors can also be used in historical analysis of will-to-fight cases. Trevor N. Dupuy took a similar approach in his analysis of historical cases.[25] If details are available it might also be possible to improve understanding of unit-level will after the fact. However, the main purpose of Tables 3.1–3.3 is to help assess the realism of war games and simulations. How many of these factors affect soldier or unit behavior, and are they portrayed realistically? If not, then how far is the model from reality, and is that distance acceptable for the sake of playability?

Time in Combat and Recovery State Dynamics

Will to fight is not a static value. It can and does change during battles, over the course of a military campaign, and as soldiers rotate to and from combat areas. All of the factors listed in the previous section can grind down a soldier's will during a single day, a week, a month, or a year. Will to fight can ebb and flow as the nature and intensity of combat change. Will to fight can also increase, resulting in more proficient soldiers, improved leadership, and so forth.

After combat, the military unit enters a *recovery state*. This can be a short period between battles, or it can be a longer period in which the unit is moved away from the combat zone entirely. During this period the aftereffects of battle continue to shape the will to fight of the individuals and, collectively, the unit in many possible ways.[26] Trauma from battle can erode will to fight as post-traumatic stress sets in. Changes in expectations can improve will to fight after soldiers overcome their precombat jitters. Skills and competence can improve with training in safe areas, leading to greater confidence. Or a failure in battle can erode confidence and will to fight. Many of these dynamics are captured in the term *veterancy*, which describes the condition of accrued

---

25   For example: Dupuy and Hammerman, 1980.

26   Examples of these effects are detailed in Belenky, 1987.

combat experience. In most war games and simulations and in many calculations of combat effectiveness, veteran military units are automatically assumed to have greater will to fight. This is a dangerous oversimplification of veterancy. It does not match existing research.

Lord Moran's observations of World War I battlefield veterancy may not have been empirical, but they do coincide with more recent analysis of the longitudinal effects of combat. He described courage as a reserve that can be spent and that is likely to spend out in extended combat. He wrote, "[M]en wear out in war like clothes." But on the same page he argued, "[I]f a soldier is always using up his capital he may from time to time add to it. There is a paying in as well as a paying out." In other words, veterancy can have different value over time. In some cases long breaks between combat or short periods of deep rest, relaxation, or retraining might allow soldiers to "pay in" to their reserves. But combat changes every surviving soldier in different ways, and every instance of combat is different in often meaningful ways.[27]

Existing studies of the impact of veterancy on will to fight can be described only as explanatory and exploratory, not causal and replicable. Michael J. Artelli aggregated a number of longitudinal veterancy analyses in *Modeling and Analysis of Resolve and Morale for the 'Long War.'*[28] These include studies of Royal Air Force pilots in World War II and U.S. Peace Corps volunteers in the late 1960s and early 1970s.[29] They show a similar amplitude change in poststress behavior. Roy L. Swank and Walter E. Marchand wrote a more specific ground combat analysis based on their observations of American Army veterans of the World War II Operation Overlord, or D-Day, focusing on the change in will to fight within a single, intense campaign.

Soldiers in the Swank and Marchand study reported intense anxiety in the first few days of combat as they were in a "constant state of fluctuating fear."[30] This produced physiological change, including increased urination, thirst, and sweating. But after the first week the soldiers adapted. Between day 10 and day 30 from D-Day they reached a period of maximum efficiency as they became used to enemy fire and more

---

[27] Selection bias certainly affects veterancy: Only those soldiers surviving combat classify as living veterans with enduring will to fight.

[28] Michael J. Artelli, *Modeling and Analysis of Resolve and Morale for the "Long War,"* thesis, Wright-Patterson Air Force Base, Ohio: Air Institute of Technology, 2007.

[29] David Stafford-Clark, "Morale and Flying Experience: Results of a Wartime Study," *British Journal of Psychiatry*, Vol. 95, No. 398, 1949, pp. 10–50; W. Walter Menninger, "The Meaning of Morale: A Peace Corps Model," in D.P. Moynihan, ed., *Business and Society in Change*, New York: American Telegraph and Telephone Company, 1975. Collectively these effects look similar to Elisabeth Kubler-Ross's change curve, which describes the five stages of grief. However, as Russell Friedman and John W. James argue, her work lacks empirical validity and it has been applied in ways for which it was never intended. See Russell Friedman and John W. James, "The Myth of the Stages of Dying, Death, and Grief," *Skeptic*, Vol. 14, No. 2, 2008, pp. 25–37.

[30] Roy L. Swank and Walter E. Marchand, "Combat Neuroses: Development of Combat Exhaustion," *Archives of Neurology and Psychiatry*, Vol. 55, No. 3, 1946, p. 237.

Figure 3.1
Swank and Marchand Combat Effectiveness Degradation Curve, 1946

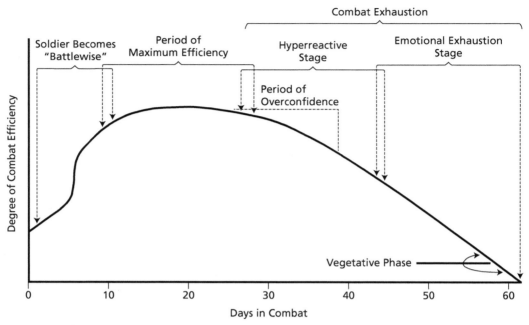

SOURCE: Artelli, 2007, derived from Swank and Marchand, 1946
RAND *RR2341A-3.1*

confident in their own capabilities. From day 30 to day 40 they entered a period of combat exhaustion, beginning with a hyperreactive stage that included a brief period of overconfidence. At this point, short periods of rest became insufficient to reset soldier confidence and capability. This overlapped into a 15-day period of emotional exhaustion, culminating for some in a vegetative state. Figure 3.1 is Artelli's adaptation of Swank and Marchand's original diagram.

While these curves may ring true for many observers of combat forces, they are not replicable or universally applicable. They help us think about veterancy during combat, but they amount to little more than informed observations of specific cases. More recent work focuses on the concept of resilience. The empiricism of the analysis has improved significantly since World War II.[31] RAND analysts Todd C. Helmus

---

[31]   For example: Terri Tanielian and Lisa H. Jaycox, eds., *Invisible Wounds of War: Psychological and Cognitive Injuries, Their Consequences, and Services to Assist Recovery*, Santa Monica, Calif.: RAND Corporation, MG-720-CCF, 2008; Kimberly T. Green, Patrick S. Calhoun, and Michelle F. Dennis, "Exploration of the Resilience Construct in Posttraumatic Stress Disorder Severity and Functional Correlates in Military Combat Veterans Who Have Served Since September 11, 2001," *Journal of Clinical Psychiatry*, Vol. 71, No. 7, July 2010, pp. 823–830; Lynda A. King, Daniel W. King, Dawne S. Vogt, Jeffrey Knight, and Rita E. Samper, "Deployment Risk and Resilience Inventory: A Collection of Measures for Studying Deployment-Related Experiences of Military

and Russell W. Glenn's *Steeling the Mind: Combat Stress Reactions and Their Implications for Urban Warfare* summarizes the long history of combat stress analysis from World War II and builds in more recent work on post-traumatic stress disorder (PTSD), resilience, and the effects of multiple combat deployments on individual soldiers. They offer a range of approaches for improving resilience, but not a replicable veterancy curve.

Collectively this research demonstrates that veterancy is a complex issue. There is no universal description of its characteristics, its longitudinal dynamics, or its value to improving or degrading will to fight. It is clear that placing a constant positive value on veterancy or assuming that it always improves will to fight is an indefensible approach. Nor would it be appropriate to generalize that all veterans suffer from PTSD and therefore must have constantly degraded, and perhaps increasingly degraded, will to fight over time. Adding will to fight to war games and simulations in a thoughtful, effective way demands acknowledgment of the literature and no small degree of nuance.

The next section describes our assessment of a set of existing war games and simulations. It shows that with a few notable exceptions, the requirements for realistic combat and recovery state complexity are rarely met, or they are simplified to the point of abstraction. The following section presents the results from our will-to-fight simulation experiments.

Analysis of Existing War Games and Simulations

> Real conflicts involve masses of individuals, each driven by his own specific goals and fears. Reducing this multiplicity of motivations to a single abstract set of human inputs on each side is obviously very tenuous.
> —Philip Sabin, *Simulating War*

> In real life, much of what wargames reduce to chance is the product of thousands of decisions by individuals at every stage of the action . . . [t]houghts in the head of a private soldier as to whether to run or to fight, decisions where to place a headquarters, and so forth.
> —Stephen P. Glick and L. Ian Charters,
> "War, Games, and Military History"

Lack of progress toward a working model of will to fight was starkly apparent in our assessment of military war gaming, modeling, and simulation. Both U.S. ARL and UK Defence Science Research Laboratory researchers have officially recognized this

Personnel and Veterans," *Military Psychology*, Vol. 18, No. 2, pp. 89–120; and Maria M. Steenkamp, William P. Nash, and Brett T. Litz, "Post-Traumatic Stress Disorder: Review of the Comprehensive Soldier Fitness Program," *American Journal of Preventive Medicine*, Vol. 44, No. 5, May 2013, pp. 507–512.

gap.[32] A 2015 ARL report stated, "The Soldier, as a complex human, is not sufficiently represented in models and simulations."[33] A user of an Army combat simulation went further in describing the stark absence of human factors in each soldier, or agent. Without will to fight or other human behavioral characteristics, the agents behaved unrealistically:[34]

> [They were] Super Soldiers who could stand face to face with a Shark-nado, shed only tears of joy, needed no rest or sleep, and effectively executed tasks after being in [full chemical protective gear] for the duration of the exercise.

Commercial tabletop games and computer simulations were generally more effective at representing will to fight, but focus varied. Our research sought to identify trends and best practices across commercial and military games and simulations to identify trends and to find some best practices that could help bridge the gap between the supersoldier approach and a more realistic will-to-fight model.

Findings from War Games and Simulations Analysis

Our analysis of existing games and simulations consisted of professional discussions with designers, analysis of simulation models, and coding of a nonrandom sample of 62 commercial and military games and simulations drawn from a broader assessment of 75 products.[35] We reviewed the rule sets for each game and simulation, reviewed published literature on the military simulations, and play tested another nonrandom subset of 19 games and simulations within our sample. In some cases, including for *Close Combat* and the Synthetic Theater Operations Research Model (STORM), we interviewed designers. Our analysis of military simulations included U.S. military war game and simulation systems dating from the post–World War II tactical Carmonette simulation to the late 1990s Joint Warfare System (JWARS) simulation to the Center for Army Analysis Wargame Analysis Model (C-WAM) tabletop game in 2016.

---

[32] See Laura Spear and Vincent Baines, "An Initial Conceptual Model for Morale Factors," *Proceedings of the 18th Conference on Behavior Representation in Modeling and Simulation*, Sundance, Utah: Social Computing Behavioral Cultural Modeling & Prediction and Behavior Organization, 2009, pp. 31–38; Joseph S. McDonnell, "Distributed Soldier Representation: M&S Representations of the Human Dimensions of the Soldier," presentation, NDIA Annual Systems Engineering Conference 2015, Orlando, Fla.: 26–29 October 2015: U.S. Army Research Laboratory, 2015.

[33] McDonnell, 2015, slide 4.

[34] McDonnell, 2015, slide 3.

[35] Additional detail is provided in Appendix E. We selected commercial tabletop and computer simulation games that (1) represented ground combat as a core feature and (2) represented scenarios from World War I through the modern era. We did not preselect for will to fight; we examined and coded games without applying any other criteria. Our team identified commercial games and simulations by reviewing the literature on gaming and simulation, talking with game designers, perusing gaming websites, reading gaming weblogs and bulletin boards, and applying the subject matter expertise of team members. We selected any and all military simulations that fit the same two criteria (ground combat from World War I through the modern era).

Coding was inductive: We created a code line for any will-to-fight factor that appeared in any game or simulation, eventually resulting in 24 overall codes ranging from tactical leadership to state and societal morale.[36]

Table 3.5 is a list of the games and simulations we assessed and coded for the characteristics listed previously in this chapter.[37] Coded titles are affixed with an asterisk after the title.[38] Nonshaded cells with black text are commercial products. Gray shaded cells are military products. The date range for the selection is from the early 1960s through 2017. We include two titles—*Ultimate General: Civil War* and *War Games Rules 3000BC to 1485AD*—that fall outside the World War I to 2017 conventional war and time frame brackets. Their explicit focus on will to fight made the rule sets valuable to our analysis, and the will-to-fight systems from these games could easily be replicated for modern combat.

We converted codes to a bit matrix and analyzed the data using nonparametric statistical methods to identify groupings and clusters of results describing the similarities and differences between cases and features.[39] Commercial games and simulations used a variety of approaches to mimic will to fight, focusing on leadership and morale. In most cases, morale was a stand-in for overall will to fight. We assessed four categories of games and simulations:[40]

1. Commercial tabletop games using hexagon maps or model terrain, counters, or figures

---

[36] While we decided not to include morale in our model, it was a common term in war games and simulations. The meaning of morale differed from product to product, and sometimes it differed significantly.

[37] We list three separate types of games and simulations: (1) tabletop, (2) hex map, and (3) Sim. A tabletop game is typically a terrain model using realistic three-dimensional figures, rulers, and turn-based rule sets. A hex map game is typically a two-dimensional (although there are some variations with raised hexes for terrain) game using counters to represent individual soldiers, vehicles, or units. "Sim" represents simulation, or any computer-driven game. Note that simulations can also be two- or three-dimensional, and many replicate hex maps and counters. Our dataset contains detailed coding of the various types of games and simulations, and their representations, scales, and rules.

[38] Some rule sets and models were not readily available, or they provided insufficient information about will-to-fight factors. We examined these 13 products, used them to inform our research, but did not code them or include them in our data. We also examined approximately 50 other commercial and military products but discarded them because they were insufficiently relevant to our research objectives and criteria.

[39] We applied three analytic methods: (1) principal component analysis (PCA), which projected cases into a constructed feature space; (2) Jaccard Similarity, or a comparison of similarities between cases and features; and (3) Community Detection, which clustered cases from the Jaccard Similarity results to better identify groups of data. Results from these three analytic tests helped us group findings in meaningful ways, but they do not constitute predictive analysis.

[40] Few military tabletop games were available. These include TACSPIEL and C-WAM. None of these appear to include a significant will-to-fight component. JICM had (and may still have) a will-to-fight component, but our interviews with experts at RAND suggest that it was not used or even accepted as viable by many consumers of the simulation.

Table 3.5
War Games and Simulations Assessed and Coded

Title	Type	Title	Type	Title	Type
Chain of Command*	Tabletop	Sticks and Stones*	Hex map	EINStein	Sim
Battalions in Crisis!*	Tabletop	Up Front*	Cards	CBS*	Sim
War Games Rules 3000 BC–1485 AD*	Tabletop	Cold War 3d Edition*	Tabletop	IWARS*	Sim
Fistful of TOWs 3*	Tabletop	Fireteam WWII*	Tabletop	OneSAF*	Sim
Tide of Iron*	Hex map	Bolt Action!*	Tabletop	ModSAF*	Sim
Battalion Combat Series v1.0*	Hex map	Modern Spearhead*	Tabletop	SIMNET*	Sim
Tactical Combat Series v4.01*	Hex map	The American Kriegsspiel*	Tabletop	WARSIM	Sim
Panzer Grenadier 4th Edition*	Hex map	AK-47 Republic*	Tabletop	TACWAR*	Sim
A Victory Denied: Crisis at Smolensk*	Hex map	Skirmish Sangin*	Tabletop	TACSPIEL	Tabletop
Old School Tactical*	Hex map	War in Europe*	Hex map	C-WAM*	Tabletop
Assault: Tactical Combat Europe*	Hex map	Grey Storm, Red Steel*	Tabletop	JWARS*	Sim
No Middle Ground: Golan 1973*	Hex map	Cross Fire*	Tabletop	JCATS*	Sim
Advanced Squad Leader*	Hex map	Close Combat Series*	Sim	JICM*	Sim
Combat Commander Series*	Hex map	Panzer Campaigns: Sicily '43*	Sim	STORM*	Sim
Lock 'n Load Tactical Modern 4.1*	Hex map	Total War Series*	Sim	JSIMS	Sim
Disposable Heroes II*	Tabletop	Men at War: Assault Squad 2*	Sim	JSAF*	Sim

Table 3.5—Continued

Title	Type	Title	Type	Title	Type
Summer Lightning: Poland '39*	Hex map	Combat Mission Series*	Sim	Carmonette*	Sim
WWII Micro Squad 2d Edition*	Tabletop	Ultimate General: Civil War*	Sim	JANUS*	Sim
A Sergeant's War Updated Edition*	Tabletop	1944 Across the Rhine*	Sim	CASTFOREM	Sim
Dawn's Early Light: Red Hammer*	Hex map	Tank on Tank Digital*	Sim	SPARTAN I + II*	Sim
Battle Academy*	Sim	Strategic Command Series*	Sim	CAEN	Sim
Company of Heroes Series*	Sim	To End All Wars*	Sim	GRWSIM	Sim
Wargame: Red Dragon*	Sim	Achtung Panzer*	Sim	MTWS	Sim
Order of Battle Series	Sim	R-FLEX*	Tabletop	Combat XXI	Sim
War Games Rules 1925–75 Infantry*	Tabletop	RSAS	Sim	CES	Sim

NOTE: CAEN = Close Action Environment; JSAF = Joint Semi-Automated Forces; ModSAF = Modular Semi-Automated Forces; R-FLEX = RAND Framework for Live Exercises; CASTFOREM = Combined Arms and Support Task Force Evaluation Model; RSAS = RAND Strategic Assessment System; MTWS = MAGTF Tactical Wargame Simulation; GRWSIM = Ground Warfare Simulation; WARSIM = Warfare Simulation; CES = Combat Evaluation System; CBS = Corps Battle Simulation

2. Commercial simulation, or computer games from the platoon level to the battalion level
3. U.S. military tabletop games typically using hexagon maps and counters
4. U.S. military simulation from the squad level to the corps level

Complex commercial tabletop war games like *Lock 'n Load Tactical Modern Core Rules 4.1*, a company-level game using terrain models and figures, made will to fight part of the stochastic determination for tactical combat. In other words, will to fight figured at least in some way into every player decision and every combat outcome. Some games, like GHQ's *WWII Micro Squad*, place will to fight at the center of the game. GHQ created a cohesion system that rolls together leadership, morale, and other aspects of will to fight. This meta-cohesion system applies at each tactical fight, and it clearly influences the outcome of the game. *WWII Micro Squad* and a handful of other tabletop games represent the kind of aggressive adoption of will-to-fight modeling that might help make military simulation more realistic.[41]

Table 3.6 lists all of the inductive codes that emerged in the coding process. We also coded for product title, a subjective analyst rating of will to fight using a 1–5 Likert Scale (with 0 indicating "not included"), the production company or owning organization, the lead designer or developer, the year published, a description of the game environment (e.g., map, model, or simulation), unit depiction (e.g., counters or figures), echelon of play (e.g., platoon or corps), play era or genre (e.g., World War II or modern), and a binary code for human-in-the-loop or autonomous simulation. All codes in Table 3.6 are binary unless otherwise noted. Note that the term *morale* is used here because it emerged inductively in the product reviews.

We conducted a PCA of the 24 coded factors.[42] There was considerable variation between the factor groupings. We found very few consistent relationships between the factors. There was a close correlation in two groupings:

1. Will to fight (not) relevant to combat outcomes + will to fight (not) relevant to victory conditions + game or simulation type—U.S. military simulation
2. Culture affects will to fight (yes) + training affects will to fight (yes) + veterancy affects will to fight (yes) + cohesion affects will to fight (yes) + game or simulation type—commercial.

In plain language, military games and simulations did not make will to fight a significant factor in the outcome of combat, a campaign, or a war. Games that did

---

[41] Other games with more aggressive models include *A Sergeant's War: Updated Edition*, *Advanced Squad Leader*, and the Wargames Research Group's *War Games Rules 3000 BC to 1485 AD*. Other games, such as *Chain of Command*, *Old School Tactical*, *Combat Commander*, *Disposable Heroes*, *Up Front*, *Bolt Action!*, *Fireteam WWII*, *Cold War 3rd Edition*, *Grey Storm, Red Steel*, and *Battalions in Crisis!*, applied detailed tactical rule sets but did not feature will to fight as a central victory condition.

[42] This included dimension reduction and projecting cases into a constructed feature space.

Table 3.6
Inductive Codes Generated and Applied to Each Game or Simulation Product

Inductive Codes	
Will to fight in stochastic combat adjudication?	Maneuver affects will to fight?
Individual morale?	Surprise affects will to fight?
Unit morale?	Casualties affect will to fight?
Unit cohesion?	Climate and/or terrain affect will to fight?
Unit leadership?	Relevance to combat? Not/Minimal/Important/Essential
Suppression as a modifier?	Force or national morale?
Veterancy as a modifier?	Force or national cohesion?
Soldier competence as a modifier?	Force or national leadership?
Quality of equipment as a modifier?	Force or national fatigue?
Quality of training as a modifier?	Relevance to victory? Not/Indirect/Min./Important/Primary
Fatigue affects will to fight?	Casualties affect will to fight?
Culture modifies will to fight?	Climate and/or terrain affect will to fight?

include major will-to-fight factors like cohesion and training also included aspects of culture. These typically emerged as national modifiers based on the judgment of analysts. For example, World War II–era Japanese soldiers might have higher will to fight than Italian soldiers from the same era. Even these crude assumptions added depth and some realism to the games and simulations in which they were included. Culture and social identity stood out as important factors in the better will-to-fight simulations.

Figure 3.2 shows the will-to-fight system from Phil Barker's *War Games Rules 3000 BC to 1485 AD*. It links three aggregated factors—morale, cohesion, and fatigue—into a will-to-fight system. Each factor has shifting states ranging from eager, steady, and fresh, to demoralized, broken, and exhausted. Factor states change as battle grinds units down over time. Barker and the Wargames Research Group adopted a modern-day interpretation of Clausewitzean theory: "The purpose of battle historically was to destroy a rival political entity's power to resist."[43] Decisive conditions for victory are reached by a combination of force destruction and driving enemy units off the board by breaking their will to fight.

Commercial computer games were the most effective at representing will to fight, primarily because computers can run complex black box calculations in the background while players focus on the game. Many simulations replicated will to fight in

---

[43]   Phil Barker, *War Games Rules 3000 BC to 1485 AD*, version 7.5, UK: Wargames Research Group, 1992, p. 39.

Figure 3.2
War Games Rules 3000 BC to 1485 AD Will-to-Fight System

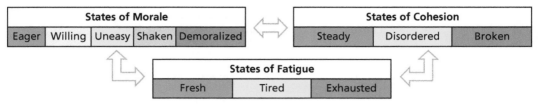

detail, bringing together the influences of factors like veterancy, skill levels, cohesion, morale, leadership, fatigue, surprise, and maneuver. We found that later iterations of *Close Combat* (e.g., *Panthers in the Fog* and *Gateway to Caen*) have some of the most thoughtful commercial will-to-fight systems. *Close Combat* remains one of the few commercial ground combat simulations at the tactical-operational level of war with a detailed individual will-to-fight system. Close contenders include *To End All Wars*, *Ultimate General: Civil War*, *Combat Mission* (series), *Total War* (series), *Strategic Command* (series), and *1944 Across the Rhine*. Each of these carefully and expertly incorporates will to fight as a central component of tactical battle and, to varying degrees, of the outcomes of campaigns and wars.

Together, commercial tabletop and computer games offer a dense menu of options for modeling will to fight ranging from simple tactical modifiers to holistic central gaming systems. The variety of definitions, scoring, and factor relationships makes it impossible to describe a typical commercial approach to will to fight. Instead, the commercial value for military war gaming and simulations experts is broken ground: Modeling theories, gaming systems, issues of play balance, and challenges finding the right degree of realism have been hashed out in hundreds of rule books and designer notes for over 40 years.

The increasing sophistication of computer gaming makes these existing commercial models relevant to modern simulation. In some cases the U.S. military has adopted commercial games outright.[44] In the past 20 years both the U.S. Army and the U.S. Marine Corps have used commercial computer games as training aids.[45] The Army Game Studio developed *America's Army*, which incorporates factors like courage and teamwork, and *Operation Overmatch*, a force-on-force soldier-level game.[46] The Marine

---

[44]   Army major Bruce E. Stanley made an impassioned plea for commercial gaming in his 1999 School of Advanced Military Studies thesis. Bruce E. Stanley, *Wargames, Training, and Decision-Making: Increasing the Experience of Army Leaders*, thesis, Fort Leavenworth, Kan.: U.S. Army Command and General Staff College, 1999.

[45]   Sabin, 2012, p. 90.

[46]   For more information, see U.S. Army, "America's Army Homepage," and Amy Robinson, "Gamers Shape Future Force: Army Seeks Soldiers' Input Through Online Gaming," Tradoc News Center, August 23, 2017.

Corps used *Close Combat* as a tactical decisionmaking simulation and helped develop *Close Combat Marine.*[47] At least one computer training simulation in use by the U.S. Army—Virtual Battlespace 3 (VBS3)—has a complex will-to-fight system. However, as of mid-2018, neither of the ground combat services nor the joint force has fully incorporated a will-to-fight model into war gaming or simulation. While our research was not comprehensive, it did show a major gap in a sample of the most prominent games and simulations.

None of the military war games or simulations we assessed gave priority to will to fight as the most or even one of the most important factors in war.[48] In fact, with the exception of a few limited experiments and an occasional nod to the suppressive effects of weapon fire or casualty loss ratios, none of these games or simulations includes a serious effort to model will to fight.[49] In the official military simulations we reviewed, holistic combat effectiveness was and is determined almost solely by calculating physical attributes and tactical actions: numbers of tanks, ranges of weapon systems, and flank attacks that exposed vulnerable armor.[50] Battle outcomes are effectively bereft of the dynamic human element. Except where suppression or basic casualty rules are present, orders are always followed without question or hesitation; infantry soldiers charge relentlessly forward, fighting to the last, no matter how desperate the situation; panic, routs, surrender, and heroism are practicably nonexistent. In the few cases where veterancy was acknowledged, it was assigned universally positive value.[51]

Our coding, while representing a nonrandom sample, generally agreed with *National Defense* analyst Michael Peck's 2003 lament that military simulations amounted to "firepower-fetish attrition models that award victory to whoever has the biggest guns, rather than giving equal weight to soft factors such as morale, fatigue

---

[47] For example: C. Neil Fitzpatrick III and Umit Ayvaz, *Training Methods and Tactical Decision-Making Simulations*, thesis, Monterey, Calif.: Naval Postgraduate School, 2007; Brendan B. McBreen, *Marine Close Combat Workbook*, Washington, D.C.: Marine Corps Institute, May 2002.

[48] We did not formally review VBS3, a commercial simulation presently in use by the DoD. Our informal, initial analysis of VBS3 indicates that it has a fairly complex will-to-fight component for its nonplayer agents. However, VBS3 is generally a human-in-the-loop simulation that places less emphasis on the autonomous behavior of individual agents or units. Therefore, the value of its will-to-fight system may be limited for large battle simulations that seek to quantify outcomes.

[49] U.S. Joint Forces Command, in coordination with the National Ground Intelligence Center (NGIC), conducted one of the most interesting experiments in 2004 using JWARS. This experiment showed that adding a will-to-fight component to a complex military simulation changed combat outcomes significantly. Paul J. Bross, *Measuring the "Will to Fight" in Simulation*, Suffolk, Va.: U.S. Joint Forces Command J-9, November 30, 2005.

[50] In some cases, will-to-fight considerations are buried in a larger combat score, but these attributes are usually fixed rather than dynamic; they may not lead to actions like surrender, hesitation, rout, or heroism.

[51] This was also true in commercial simulations, or games. In a gross oversimplification of reality, veteran units are always more capable than nonveteran units.

and cohesion."[52] While no game, model, or simulation can ever be truly realistic, the absence of will to fight leaves a glaring absence of realism. This risks defeating one of the central purposes of military war gaming and simulation: to help reduce uncertainty in order to inform practical decisionmaking.[53]

Counterarguments to the demand for increased will-to-fight realism emerged during our research. Several expert military simulation designers told our team that they had not pursued will-to-fight simulation because there was no demand from consumers: Military and civilian leaders were not asking for will to fight, the demand was not included in the modeling and simulations contracts, and so will to fight was effectively ignored.[54] These are certainly practical considerations. It is also true that simulating unpredictable behavioral factors makes it harder to understand the technical aspects of combat: It is much easier to understand why one tank defeats another tank when stochastic outcomes are reduced to quantifiable variables like range and armor penetration. Adding will to fight to games or simulations adds to complexity and reduces the predictability and replicability of outcomes, mirroring the all-too-disconcerting unpredictability of war. It is worth noting here that will to fight can be turned on or off in most simulations, so the drag on technical analysis has a simple fix for those seeking to avoid realistic complexities and concentrate only on more basic learning objectives.

A less practical and more compelling theme emerged as we reviewed hundreds of commercial game feedback websites and discussion threads and spent time talking with gamers: Will to fight makes computer-simulated soldiers and units do things the user does not want them to do (e.g., freeze, refuse orders, or flee), which is annoying and, therefore, often unwanted.[55] This sentiment also emerged in discussions with military simulation experts, albeit more subtly. War game and simulation designers take a risk when they try to incorporate will to fight. This risk must be acknowledged. But it is insufficient to offset the costly gap in realism that currently exists.

Renowned computer and systems engineer Jay Wright Forrester made a compelling argument in support of risk taking in the pursuit of realism in modeling. His argument about hard-to-quantify factors in systems analysis—quoted by RAND's Paul K.

---

[52]   Michael Peck, "Successful War Games Combine Both Civilian and Military Traits," *National Defense*, November 1, 2011. Note that Peck was writing for an industry journal representing an industry that stood to benefit from new investment in military simulation.

[53]   Both Peter Perla and Philip Sabin offer detailed analyses on the purposes of war gaming and simulation. See Sabin, 2012.

[54]   RAND engaged with five current military simulation design teams and several more independent or retired designers.

[55]   This mostly informal review was conducted as part of our game and simulation selection and testing process. For example, see Close Combat Series, homepage, undated; Steam Community, homepage, undated; and PAX-sims, homepage, undated.

Davis in a 1989 article lamenting the absence of "soft factors" in military simulation—is applicable to the continuing gap in will-to-fight modeling today:[56]

> Much of the behavior of systems rests on relationships and interactions that are believed, and probably correctly so, to be important but that for a long time will evade quantitative measure. Unless we take our best estimates of these relationships and include them in a system model, we are in effect saying they make no difference and can be omitted. It is far more serious to omit a relationship that is believed to be important than to include it at a low level of accuracy that fits a plausible range of uncertainty. If one believes a relationship to be important, he acts accordingly, and makes the best use he can of information available.

Thankfully, all military simulation is not entirely bereft of soft factor modeling. There have been intermittent official experiments with will to fight in military gaming and simulation, most recently at ARL.[57] The Center for Naval Analyses experimented with the EINStein system for the U.S. Marine Corps. EINStein replicated personalities for individual squad members and included "trigger states" for suppression, panic, fatigue, aggression, and proxies for cohesion.[58] EINStein demonstrated that complex individual agent behaviors can be thoughtfully and effectively applied. Simulation experts working with the Australian Army on a program called CROCADILE provided evidence that adding behavioral modifications to agents changed combat outcomes.[59] A 2004 experimental effort with JWARS stands out for its aggressiveness and its relevance to ongoing simulation development.

The 2004 JWARS Experiment
In 2004 the U.S. Joint Forces Command (JFCOM) and NGIC implemented a complex will-to-fight system into JWARS as part of the Unified Vision 04 exercise.[60] This

---

[56] Jay W. Forrester, *Urban Dynamics*, Cambridge, Mass.: The Massachusetts Institute of Technology Press, 1969, as quoted in Paul K. Davis, *Modeling of Soft Factors in the RAND Strategy Assessment System (RSAS)*, Santa Monica, Calif.: RAND Corporation, P-7538 1989a, p. 4.

[57] In mid-2017 the RAND will-to-fight research team engaged with the ARL team working on the Distributed Soldier Representation (DSR). ARL was seeking to implement will to fight into OneSAF for the U.S. Army.

[58] Andrew Ilachinski, *Artificial War: Multiagent-Based Simulation of Combat*, River Edge, N.J.: World Scientific Publishing Corporation, 2004, pp. 379–381; and Fredlake and Wang, 2008. EINStein stands for the *Enhanced ISAAC Neural Simulation Tool*. Ilachinski's book explains the EINStein experiments in explicit detail. They focused more on replicating complex systems and tactical decisionmaking than on will to fight, although the replication of individual agent behavior was complex and groundbreaking.

[59] Michael Barlow and Adam Easton, "CROCADILE—An Open, Extensible Agent-Based Distillation Engine," *Information and Security*, Vol. 8, No. 1, 2002, pp. 17–51. Recall again that "outcomes" in this context does not simply connote winning or losing.

[60] Like several other military simulations, including IWARS and JCATS, JWARS has a built-in capacity to model some individual agent and unit-level behaviors.

experiment sought to answer three questions, each of which has broader implications for the military modeling and simulation community:[61]

1. What is the impact of the "will to fight" on combat outcomes?
2. How sensitive is JWARS to the morale and cohesion "soft" factors?
3. Is it worth the cost and effort to integrate will to fight into JWARS?

The simulation team integrated an NGIC country factor model to give each unit a starting set of attributes that would serve as a baseline for will-to-fight behavior. These included capabilities like combat experience, training, and fire support, as well as factors more closely associated with will to fight, like leadership, morale, and cohesion.[62] Units from each country represented in the simulation were given an aggregated morale and cohesion factor (the "NGIC country factor") particular to that country. The NGIC country factor table represented many of the factors in our model but from the perspective of an entire national military force. It included esprit de corps ("pride"), discipline, state and societal support, and a unit morale factor. Units were ranked as elite, standard, or militia, and given a function factor of combat unit or combat support unit. Together with the country factor these scores allowed the designers to calculate how units would change their behavior in response to enemy fire and maneuver.

Experimenters reached the same conclusion about will-to-fight assessment and analysis as our research team. They wrote that there was no standard methodology to apply the factors in the model and that "while intelligence estimates may allow for the classification of a unit into one of the categories, the value set is strictly under the control of the analyst studying the problem at hand."[63] In other words, assessing will to fight for simulation required an explanatory and portable model.

In his assessment of the experiment, Paul J. Bross noted that, as of 2004, "soft factor" elements like morale and leadership were "seldom modeled explicitly in simulations at the campaign level." The experiment involved multiple scenario iterations and runs, and it produced some robust findings. Results showed that Blue fire suppression fixed Red forces in place, causing them to have to stand and fight rather than run, leading to higher casualties. This made sense to the military participants. Bross found that "we actually have a measure of what degree of influence is exerted upon the forces in the engagement rather than just the military semantics to rely upon."[64] In other words, simulating will to fight gave the military a quantifiable, and therefore tangible, output. Simulation helped move will to fight from an annoying, squishy factor that could be

---

[61]   Bross, 2005, p. 3. We corrected question 1 for grammar and abbreviated question 3.

[62]   Bross, 2005, p. 5. We included the NGIC model in our literature review; it informed the development of the model in Chapter Two.

[63]   Bross, 2005, p. 8.

[64]   Bross, 2005, p. 18.

easily overlooked to a calculation that generated a real and visible (albeit notional) change in outcome.

Bross delivered two important findings. First, adding will to fight produced "statistically and militarily significant effects" on the simulated combat agents. Second, even with a limited set of factors, adding will to fight "still yielded an immense difference in battlefield performance that affected both Red and Blue forces." In other words, at least for this experiment in a verified and validated joint U.S. military simulation, adding will to fight mattered a great deal. However, it does not appear that JFCOM moved this behavioral model forward.[65]

Testing Will to Fight in Simulation: Does It Make a Difference?

U.S. military organizations have made a few other limited efforts to incorporate will to fight into gaming and simulation. However, as of mid-2018 we were not able to identify a publicly available body of empirical, replicable testing sufficient to prove the value of full implementation of a will-to-fight model. We conducted experimental testing to help rectify the gap.

This section describes and presents results from our initial experimentation with will-to-fight behavioral modifications in computer-aided simulation using NetLogo and the Natick Soldier Research Development and Engineering Center (NSRDEC) IWARS (version 5.1.2). Design and execution of our experiments were informed by existing modeling and simulation, by the war game and simulation analysis presented in this chapter, and by discussions with designers and programmers. Appendix E provides detailed descriptions of model and code applied to IWARS.

Note that these experiments generate some precise quantitative results. This approach may appear contradictory to the argument that will to fight cannot be quantified. It is not. We argue that will to fight cannot be quantified in the real world. Games and simulations are only notional approximations of the real world. As long as these numbers are not applied literally to real people, then they have use: They help show differentiation between behaviors when variables like suppression are added to or removed from combat. Quantification here is a tool for understanding generalized notional dynamics, not a measuring device for real combat units.

Literature on military modeling and simulation was helpful in shaping experimental design.[66] As of mid-2018 the literature on incorporating will to fight into

---

[65]   The command was eliminated in 2011. Former JFCOM simulation groups continue to exist under the Joint Staff. Various elements of DoD continue to use JWARS as of mid-2018. For example, U.S. Navy Naval Air Warfare Center Aircraft Division offers JWARS as a Virtual Warfare Environment. See Naval Air Warfare Center Aircraft Division, homepage, undated.

[66]   For example: Davis, 1989a; Paul K. Davis, *Some Lessons Learned from Building Red Agents in the RAND Strategy Assessment System (RSAS)*, Santa Monica, Calif.: RAND Corporation, N-3003-OSD, 1989c; Richard W.

military simulation shows the following: (1) no agreed-on model exists, (2) there is reluctance in the simulation community to incorporate will to fight because it is complex and unpredictable, and (3) limited experiments always show differences between outcomes, depending on whether simulated will to fight is included.[67] Our experimentation builds from these published examples and seeks to further the incorporation of will to fight into military simulation.

We conducted two experiments in parallel with the development of the model presented in Chapter Two. Therefore, we could not test the finished RAND Arroyo Center model of tactical-operational will to fight in simulation. We instead took the preliminary step of testing a hypothesis developed during the initial literature review. Following our conclusion that will to fight always plays at least some role in determining the outcome of battle, we hypothesized that incorporating will to fight into computer simulation of battle would always change the outcome of simulated combat *to some extent*. That hypothesis (H[1]) is:

> H[1]: Comparative analysis of automated computer-simulated force-on-force combat using identical programs and scenarios will show that applying a will-to-fight behavioral modification model will always—to varying degrees—change agent behavior and overall combat results.

Our initial experiments in IWARS support the hypothesis in H[1], although these results would benefit from additional testing across various programs and scenarios.[68] We generated but did not test an additional, related hypothesis (H[2]) focused on war gaming not involving computer simulation (e.g., a tabletop game with counters or figures). It also assumes that human-in-the-loop game play, or the decisions of human gamers, would always change *to some extent* if they had to factor will-to-fight considerations into the stochastic behavior of their units.

> H[2]: Comparative analysis of tabletop, matrix, or other noncomputer-aided force-on-force war games using identical gaming systems and scenarios will show that

---

Pew and Anne S. Mavor, eds., *Representing Human Behavior in Military Simulations*, Washington, D.C.: National Academy Press, 1997; Larry J. Hutson, *A Representational Approach to Knowledge and Multiple Skill Levels for Broad Classes of Computer Generated Forces*, thesis, Wright-Patterson Air Force Base, Ohio: Air Force Institute of Technology, 1997; Barlow and Easton, 2002; Bross, 2005; Artelli, 2007; Spear and Baines, 2009; Kevin Fefferman, Manuel Diego, Chris Gaughan, Charneta Samms, Howard Borum, Jon Clegg, Joseph S. McDonnell, and Robert Leach, *A Study in the Implementation of a Distributed Soldier Representation*, ARL-TR-6985, Aberdeen Proving Ground, Md.: Army Research Laboratory, March 2015; and Byron R. Harder, *Automated Battle Planning for Combat Models with Maneuver and Fire Support*, thesis, Monterey, Calif.: Naval Postgraduate School, 2017.

[67] This finding was confirmed by our survey of current simulations and interviews with simulation experts, designers, and researchers between late 2016 and late 2017.

[68] We have not yet determined how much replication will be necessary to scientifically prove H[1]. However, initial experimentation in one program across more than one scenario with over 1,600 runs supported the hypothesis without exception.

applying a will-to-fight behavioral modification model will always—to varying degrees—change human player decisionmaking, the course of play, and the outcomes of games.

While it proved possible to test H[1] and produce clear, quantitative results, it will be far more difficult to test H[2] and generate replicable results. Because human decisionmaking is inconsistent from person to person and from instance to instance, generating replicable results from human-in-the-loop war gaming will require careful experiment design. RAND may pursue this experimentation in the future.

The next sections describe Steven Silver's Combat Psychological Model (CPM, or "The Silver Model"), our initial experimentation with IWARS, and then the inclusion of the Silver Model into IWARS for testing at the squad and platoon levels.

Introduction to the Silver Model

In this section we explain the modified Silver Model that we adapted and applied for our IWARS experiments. We used this model because it is one of the only existing published complex will-to-fight models designed for computer simulation; because it was readily available; and because we were able to discuss its origins, merits, applications, and limitations with the designer. This experiment does not constitute an endorsement of the Silver Model as a candidate for the universal will-to-fight model for the U.S. Army or Joint Force. It should be judged on its merits. Instead, we view its application as one step in the longer process of developing and incorporating a variation of the RAND Arroyo Center model, or a better model, into military simulation.

In the mid-1990s Microsoft Corporation and its subsidiary Atomic Games approached Steven Silver, a former U.S. Marine officer, U.S. Army National Guard officer, and combat psychologist with the U.S. Veterans Administration, to develop a psychological model for inclusion in a commercial tactical war game later published as *Close Combat*.[69] Leveraging his military experience, his training and experience as a psychologist, and his interest in military history, Silver developed what is alternatively called a trait-state or state-trait psychological behavioral model. Atomic Games chose to apply a much-simplified version of Silver's model in order to avoid excessive computer processing demands. But even with this simplified model, *Close Combat* expanded into a long-running series of games that set a high bar for the inclusion of will-to-fight factors in commercial gaming.[70]

---

[69]   Communications with Steven Silver by phone and email, 2017. Silver's model was published by then–Air Force captain Larry J. Hutson in Hutson, 1997. Also see David A. Van Veldhuizen and Larry J. Hutson, "A Design Methodology for Domain Independent Computer Generated Forces," *MAICS-97 Proceedings*, Dayton, Ohio: Wright State University, 1997.

[70]   Various companies have published at least 18 iterations of the game since 1996, and there are hundreds (and perhaps thousands) of individual developer modifications and scenarios. As of mid-2018 *Close Combat* is still under development by Matrix Games with a tentative edition titled *Close Combat: The Bloody First*. As of mid-2018, for additional information on the series, see Close Combat Series, homepage, undated.

State-trait is a psychological assessment model and approach designed to help understand individual behavior.[71] In the state-trait model each individual has traits that, together, constitute personality. Traits are semipermanent and can be changed over time or as the result of a traumatic experience. From moment to moment these traits exist as states. In a notional example, someone can have high *trait* of anxiety, but their actual *state* of anxiety changes from moment to moment, shifting from the standing trait level on a continuous basis. While there is no way to predict individual behavior, knowing someone's collective traits can, in very general terms, help forecast his or her likely reaction to certain situations.

A version of the original Silver Model is published in Hutson, 1997, and replicated in Appendix E of this report. We experimented with the original model in the Net-Logo open-source agent-based modeling computer program, identified some inconsistencies in performance, and modified the model for inclusion into IWARS. Modification was an iterative process done in communication with Silver and the IWARS team at NSRDEC. This description represents Silver's original model with some minor modifications.

Each individual soldier has eight traits: acquiescence, anger, anxiety, charisma, humor, independence, knowledge, and stability. These are quantified on a scale from 0 to 1 for purposes of simple computation. Traits are merged into combinatory states designed to model combat behavior for soldiers and leaders: (1) morale, (2) leadership, (3) squad leader leadership, (4) support, and (5) group support. Silver's original model includes situational stress, which modified behavior in several ways. A depiction of a soldier, his or her traits, and his or her individual and group-related (e.g., group support) states is shown in Figure 3.3.

The Silver Model adjusts the will to fight of soldiers in conflict situations based on events that characterize their local circumstances. Events affect individual traits and can be moderated by additional factors such as temporal duration (i.e., repeated effects or multipliers occurring if events persist beyond some threshold). Events may also have additional effects if a soldier's traits or states enter extreme ranges, which may make the soldier increasingly sensitive to additional events and display extreme behaviors, such as elevated combat effectiveness, hesitation, or panic.[72]

---

[71] Note that not all psychologists view this model as valid. It may or may not offer a good starting point for modeling will to fight, and our interviews with two psychologists suggested that the state-trait approach is somewhat dated. Silver developed his model in the mid-1990s. Nevertheless, state-trait has appeared extensively in psychological literature. See Charles Donald Spielberger, *Manual for the State-Trait Anxiety Inventory STAI (Form Y)*, Palo Alto, Calif.: Mind Garden, 1983; Peter J. Bieling, Martin M. Antony, and Richard P. Swinson, "The State-Trait Anxiety Inventory, Trait Version, Structure and Content Re-Examined," *Behaviour Research and Therapy*, No. 36, 1998, pp. 777–788; Norman S. Endler and Nancy Kocovski, "State and Trait Anxiety Revisited," *Anxiety Disorders*, No. 15, 2001, pp. 231–245; and Rolf Steyer, Manfred Schmitt, and Michael Eid, "Latent State-Trait Theory and Research in Personality Individual Differences," *European Journal of Personality*, No. 13, 1999, pp. 398–408.

[72] In the model, a soldier's traits and states are all on the interval of [0, 1].

Figure 3.3
A Notional Example of States and Traits in the Silver Model (CPM)

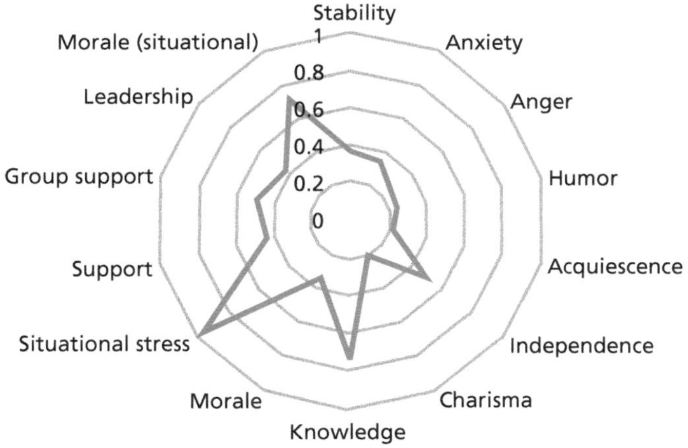

RAND RR2341A-3.3

Experiment 1: Silver Model in NetLogo

We implemented the Silver Model in NetLogo, replicating the state-trait framework based on Silver's original psychological theory. NetLogo is an open-source agent-based modeling framework commonly used for teaching computer programming and the modeling of complex systems, for scientific research, and for prototyping large-scale models using other modeling and simulation frameworks.[73] The operation of the NetLogo implementation of the model created a simple artificial military unit. The unit could be constructed of any size, meaning that users could model a single soldier or a group of arbitrarily large sizes.[74]

With the unit constructed, we tested behavioral reactions by adding user-selected events like direct or indirect fire. Many noncombat events are also available, such as having a new team member join the group, sleeping, eating a meal, receiving new clothing or equipment, and so on. In the simulation, the unit experiences selected events for specified durations of time. For example, a user might select that the unit experience heavy fire for 5 minutes or 15 minutes. Because events often have compounding effects based on their duration, choices of event interval sizes can have significant consequences on the overall experience of soldiers. With each event the soldiers adjust their states and semipermanent traits. Soldiers also maintain an action state that

---

[73]   For more information, see Uri Wilensky, "Netlogo Home Page," Center for Connected Learning and Computer-Based Modeling, Northwestern University, Evanston, Ill., 1999.

[74]   We found that the level of individual soldier detail in the Silver Model, and the uniformity of intraunit calculations and updating, makes it a poor candidate for large-scale simulation of thousands of soldiers, or complex and distributed military operations.

characterizes their behaviors with respect to their military effectiveness, action delays, and obedience. These additional properties characterize the manifest behaviors of will to fight. The soldiers may achieve elevated or degraded states of combat effectiveness based on their state, delay their actions out of fear, or be hesitant, disobedient, or even attack their leadership in times of extreme and prolonged situational stress.

Figure 3.4 shows changes in the overall traits of a 12-member military unit after 50 events of experiencing heavy fire, with each event registered for five minutes. The result is a military unit experiencing 250 minutes of heavy fire from an adversary. The dynamics of soldier traits in response to events show how the internal composition and will to fight of a unit can change because of its experiences. Change shows as an immediate increase in anxiety as a result of experiencing heavy fire. This upward movement was later followed by an increase in overall knowledge as the group learned from the experience and acquired improved soldiering skills by surviving the ordeal; competence has much lower durability in Silver's model than in the RAND Arroyo Center model.[75] Alternatively, the traits of humor, stability, anger, charisma, and independence all declined because of the events.

Figure 3.4
State Changes in Silver Model NetLogo Implementation

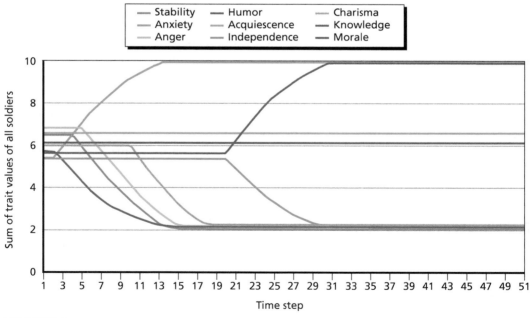

---

[75] This simulated set of events did not include the team taking any casualties.

Changes in the personal traits of the individuals resulted in unpredictability at the unit level. As the individuals in the military unit changed according to their experiences, the collective behavior of the unit became increasingly unpredictable. In the same scenario noted above, the 12-member unit displayed erratic behavior in response to the stresses of the heavy fire experience. In Figure 3.5 the unit started out with all 12 members complying with their leadership. However, two soldiers moved out of compliance and became hesitant and unresponsive to orders between time steps four and five. Subsequently, two soldiers oscillated periodically between continued hesitation and attacking their leadership ("frag") during the remainder of the simulation.

Finally, the unit experienced delays associated with their respective actions. A soldier experiencing a hesitation event fails to execute his or her order, while a soldier who is delayed will still perform the event once the time delay is accounted for. Total time lost to delays in the simulated pattern of events is shown in Figure 3.6.

It is important to remember that these graphs show aggregate unit behaviors. In each case, trait changes, obedience behaviors, and delays in action can all be monitored at the level of individual soldiers within the model. Once we corrected errors and implemented the Silver Model in NetLogo, we reimplemented the model in IWARS. First we conducted a limited experiment with suppression to test the simulation's behavioral modification capabilities. Both Experiment 2 and Experiment 3 generated useful and complementary results.

Figure 3.5
Obedience Events in Silver Model NetLogo Implementation

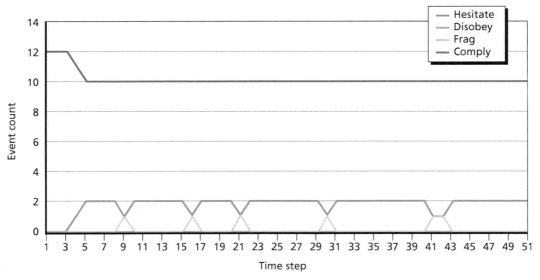

Figure 3.6
Total Sum of Order Delays in Silver Model NetLogo Implementation

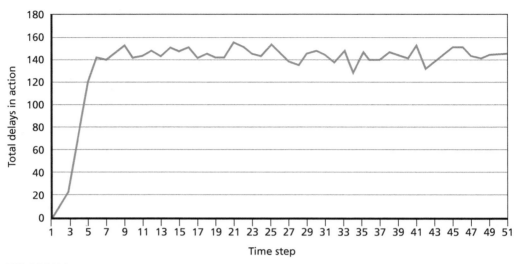

RAND RR2341A-3.6

Experiment 2: Suppression in IWARS

We conducted a separate, less complex experiment with suppression (Experiment 2) prior to the reimplementation of the Silver Model (Experiment 3). With the help of NSRDEC we used IWARS (version 5.1.2) to study how changes in a soldier's will to fight can affect the outcome of a simulated combat engagement. The purpose of Experiment 2 was to demonstrate that existing DoD ground combat simulations can effectively replicate will to fight, and to test hypothesis H[1], above. Suppression occurs when direct or indirect fire passes by or strikes near a soldier, triggering fear and possibly affecting will to fight. Suppression is a common proxy for will to fight. It is widely modeled in commercial games and simulations and occasionally modeled in U.S. military simulation. Previous research and experimentation informed our work.[76] Rather

---

[76]   For example: J. Milikan, M. Wong, and D. Grieger, "Suppression of Dismounted Soldiers: Towards Improving Dynamic Threat Assessment in Closed Loop Combat Simulations," conference paper, 20th International Conference on Modeling and Simulation, Adelaide, Australia, December 1–6, 2013; Gregory Ray Wilson, *Modeling and Evaluating U.S. Army Special Operations Forces Combat Attrition Using Janus (A)*, thesis, Monterey, Calif.: Naval Postgraduate School, 1995; General Research Corporation, *CARMONETTE Volume I General Description*, technical manual, McLean, Va.: Operations Analysis Division of General Research Corporation, November 1974; David Rowland, "Assessments of Combat Degradation," *RUSI Journal*, Vol. 131, No. 2, 1986, pp. 33–43; Charles L. Frame, Brian R. McEnany, and Kurt A. Kladivko, "Combat Operational Data Analysis: An Examination of World War II Suppression Data," *Human Behavior and Performance as Essential Ingredients in Realistic Modeling of Combat—MORIMOC II Volume 2*, proceedings, Alexandria, Va.: Military Operations Research Society, February 1989; U.S. Army Field Artillery School, *Can It Be Quantified?* proceedings from the Fort Sill Fire Suppression Symposium, Fort Sill, Ok.: Directorate of Combat Developments, January 14, 1980; and Fredlake and Wang, 2008.

than breaking new ground, the intent of this experiment was to provide transparent, comparative, and replicable research showing that adding even the simplest will-to-fight factor will always change combat simulation outcomes with all other factors being equal. Experiment 3 sought greater resolution and realism.

IWARS is a high-resolution, small-scale combat simulator that uses agent-based modeling to quantitatively measure the outcomes of tactical battles and to test specific soldier-level capabilities and stressors. It was originally designed by the Natick Soldier Center, the Army Materiel Systems Analysis Activity, and ARL to test Network Centric Warfare technologies at the soldier level. Squad-on-squad and basic platoon-on-platoon combat simulations in IWARS can be run on a moderately powerful laptop computer. Agents (soldiers) replicate physiological characteristics like heart rate, eyesight, core body temperature, and breathing, and some behavioral characteristics.[77]

The first part of Experiment 2 involved simple behavioral modification using existing components in the IWARS model. The simulation team at Natick built a suppression condition to show how proximate direct weapons fire might change the behavior of individual soldiers in a notional squad. They pitted two equal squads (Red and Blue) against one another in a 200-meter direct-fire engagement and conducted 20 runs each of a baseline scenario and a suppression-added scenario.[78] In the baseline scenario the supersoldiers fought to the death with no will-to-fight behavioral changes. In the suppression scenario, suppression effects were added to the Blue side only. A condition was added causing any soldier twice suppressed by enemy fire—determined by rounds passing within a certain distance from the soldier—to cease firing and flee. Table 3.7 shows the results from this initial experiment. There was a notable 1.95 difference in mean Red KIA and a 50-percent change in the ratio between Blue and Red KIA.

Table 3.7
IWARS Suppression Experiment 2 NSRDEC Results

Scenario	IWARS Runs	Mean Blue KIA	Mean Red KIA	Blue KIA <= Red KIA (%)
Baseline	20	7.60	7.80	50
Suppression	20	7.45	5.85	25
	DELTA:	0.15	1.95	50

---

[77] IWARS consists of four components: (1) Agent and Combat Models—can be added to each agent for three-dimensional simulation; (2) Mission Builder (Behavioral Engine)—customizable by the analyst; (3) Methodologies—customizable, establishes numerical relationships of and between objects like soldiers and bullets; (4) Battlefield Overlay—establishes objectives, waypoints, tripwires, node networks, and shielding objects. Each simulation can be initiated with a random seed and viewed in real time. Agent characteristics are stored during each simulation tick and can be retrieved. Force killed in action (KIA) tables allow the computation of odds ratios.

[78] IWARS uses a stochastic seed that is applied to all chance rolls during each run—that is, an element of "luck" is connected with the results in each simulation.

Figure 3.7
Blue Soldiers Reacting to Suppression in IWARS Experiment 2

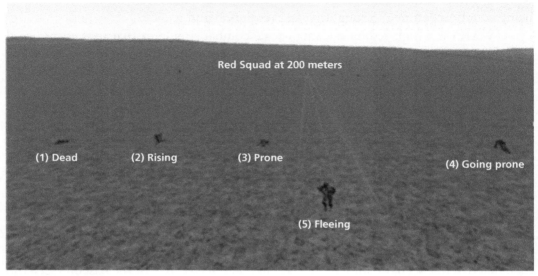

SOURCE: NSRDEC
RAND RR2341A-3.7

In the 2004 JWARS experiment, suppression caused soldiers to be pinned in the line of fire, thereby suffering greater casualties. Here suppression reduced casualties because it caused soldiers to flee (a different programmed behavioral outcome) and remove themselves from the line of fire. On the other side, Red casualties were reduced due to the consequent drop in Blue fire. Figure 3.7 shows an IWARS three-dimensional display screenshot from the initial suppression test. Blue Soldier 1 is dead. Soldier 2 has partly recovered from suppression and is in the process of rising back to a kneeling position to fire. Soldier 3 is prone due to suppression. Soldier 4 is in the process of going into the prone position. Soldier 5 is fleeing under Red fire due to suppression effects.

Building from this initial effort, RAND Arroyo Center expanded and altered the scenarios to test variations on suppression effects and to see whether changes in terrain or leadership roles might affect behavioral changes. We ran two series within Experiment 2 (Experiment 2, Series 1, and Experiment 2, Series 2) by adding behavioral modifiers to each soldier model, varying by side but keeping each soldier consistent within units. Results showed changes to the odds that one side or the other would win when compared with a baseline or no-suppression scenario. We tested for suppression as a proxy for will to fight and then tested for suppression against expert soldier will to fight. Expertise was generated by another proxy called Reduced Interaction Zones. This replicated the reduced vulnerability of expert soldiers to suppression by reducing the suppression cone around the soldier: Fewer bullets would affect the soldier's proxy will to fight. First runs were conducted at the squad level, and a final set of runs was conducted with a platoon-on-platoon scenario. Experiment 2, Series 1, had three variations:

Suppressed: All Blue agents are modified to have knowledge of their own suppression level. When munitions enter the Suppression Interaction Zone range, the agent is suppressed. This can press the agent to a Task Interruption state, leaving the agent *intimidated* and unable to engage in combat. The agent drops to a prone position. At the second suppression event the agent flees.

Reduced Interaction Zones: The Blue squad leader and fire team leaders are modified so that non-hit munitions must enter a Suppression Interaction Zone range around the agent that is half the model's normal suppression range, before causing suppression. The intended effect is to replicate higher *leader* resistance to suppression. All other Blue agents follow the Suppressed scenario model.

Fearless: The Blue squad and fire team leaders are modified so that they have no knowledge of their own suppression level. All Blue leaders continue to fight until incapacitated, while all other Blue agents follow the Suppressed scenario model.

We ran each scenario 100 times in two iterations each for a total of 600 runs compared with the supersoldier baseline scenario with no suppression or other behavioral modification. Results are presented in Table 3.8. Odds ratios show the likeliness multiplier of an outcome for a case of interest compared with a null case. Odds ratios are computed from the win/lose results of the scenario of interest and the results of the baseline scenario (in this case, 94 wins to 94 losses, ties excluded). For example, the Suppressed scenario showed a 3.67 times odds ratio to Blue loss (i.e., Blue was 3.67 times more likely to lose in the Suppressed scenario than in the baseline scenario) and a –58.5-percent change in Blue win chances. The Fearless scenario showed minimal change. Reduced Interaction Zones resulted in a 4.15 times odds ratio for Blue loss, a 43.9-percent drop in average Red KIA, a –25.1-percent change in average Blue KIA, and a –63.8-percent change in Blue win chances. All of these results contributed to the

Table 3.8
IWARS Suppression Experiment 2, RAND Series 1, Results

Scenario with Suppression *Versus Baseline Without Suppression*	Odds Ratio to Blue Loss	% Change in Average Red KIA	% Change in Average Blue KIA	% Change in Blue Wins
Suppressed	3.67	–21.4	5.6	–58.5
Fearless	1.17	–6.1	2.1	–10.6
Reduced Interaction Zones	4.15	–43.9	–25.1	–63.8

overall finding that H[1] is supported: Will to fight always, and sometimes significantly, changes combat outcomes.

We designed Experiment 2, Series 2, with the intent of removing determinism caused by the initial unit formation (how the squads deployed). In Series 2, Blue agents appeared in pseudorandom spawning areas and retreat was not allowed. A 15-second scenario delay was inserted to allow repositioning for cover after start. The triggering levels for Suppression and Task Interruption were raised. We tested two scenarios: (1) Varying Firing/Reload Delay Duration and (2) Varying Reduced Field of Regard Duration.[79] Each scenario imposed a gradual step-change increase in disruption to the Blue force from the baseline, resulting in changes to the odds of Blue victory. Results ranged from a 1.59 times change to a 13.14 times change in outcomes, with an average of 5.48 times change for all 25 step-change variations across 5,000 runs.[80] In other words, Series 2 showed that adding suppression led to an approximate 5.5 times odds change in victory outcome. Table 3.9 shows the averaged results from each of the three scenarios. Significant odds ratios are highlighted in red.

Series 1 and Series 2 of Experiment 2 showed that adding suppression to one side in an otherwise precisely equal simulated tactical fight always changes outcomes and usually changes them significantly. This was a basic effort designed to prove the on-off

Table 3.9
IWARS Suppression Experiment 2, RAND Series 2, Results

Step-Change	Average Blue KIA	Average Red KIA	Average Odds Ratio
Baseline	7.45	7.66	NA
When Varying Firing/Reload Delay Duration			
0–3.5	8.48	6.23	5.38
When Varying Reduced Field of Regard Duration			
0–30	8.58	6.17	7.67
When Varying Number of Affected BLUE Agents			
1–9	8.35	6.66	3.90

[79]   Varying Firing/Reload Delay Duration: All Blue agents have a fixed field of regard (FoR) change duration of 30 seconds while varying reload/firing delay from 0 to 3.5 seconds once suppressed. Horizontal FoR initializes at 150 degrees azimuth before reducing to 57 degrees azimuth. Once the duration under test elapses, the FoR then widens to 100 degrees azimuth. Vertical FoR remained at 50 degrees elevation under all situations. Varying Reduced Field of Regard Duration: All Blue agents have a fixed reload/firing delay of 0.5 seconds while varying FoR duration from 0 to 30 seconds.

[80]   Note that the 1.59× change resulted from suppression effects on only one Blue soldier in the squad.

value of will-to-fight proxy values.[81] Suppression is perhaps the simplest way to replicate will to fight. While we added some individual variation, soldier quality was replicated at only the most basic level with no other differentiation in will to fight. Suppression and quality are far from the only factors in war that affect will, but they are useful, if simple, proxies for initial experimentation. All of the 29 factors and 61 subfactors in the RAND Arroyo Center model are relevant to will to fight. While we have not tested the RAND Arroyo Center model in simulation, Experiment 3 adds complexity and realism with detailed agent- and unit-level psychological and behavioral modeling. The final part of Experiment 3 shows results from adding a will-to-fight model to both sides.

Experiment 3: Silver Model in IWARS
In this culminating experiment we further modified the Silver Model from Experiment 1 (NetLogo) and reimplemented it into IWARS. This gave each agent complex psychological and behavioral characteristics designed from the ground up to replicate will to fight. It also incorporated the collective, unit-level aspects in the Silver Model, allowing us to observe individual- and unit-level will-to-fight behavioral changes during simulated combat. While the Silver Model may not be immediately applicable for the U.S. military, it is sufficiently detailed and transparent for experimentation. This experiment also sought to show on-off changes against baseline scenarios. Series 1 implemented the Silver Model for Blue only across a variety of scenarios, while the shorter Series 2 implemented the Silver Model for both Red and Blue in an equal contest.

For Experiment 3, Series 1 and 2, we simplified the model for the IWARS experiments, reducing behavioral changes to (1) hesitate and (2) flee. This eliminated disobedience of orders and fragging, both of which we believed to be unhelpfully extreme for experimentation.[82] Hesitating soldiers had time delays to simulated firing and reloading of weapons. Silver originally modeled a wide array of combat stressors.[83] We reduced these to (1) nighttime; (2) reduced visibility; (3) attacked by inferior, equal size, or superior force; (4) team members killed (less than 10 percent, 10–40 percent, more

---

[81]   When values are turned "on" they are active. When they are turned "off" they are inactive. In this case, suppression is either on or off, and is therefore active or inactive. This also applies to the Silver Model: It is either on or off, active or inactive. When either suppression or the Silver Model is inactive it is removed entirely from the simulation, reverting the simulation to supersoldier status devoid of will-to-fight characteristics.

[82]   Fragging, or incidents of junior soldiers killing leaders, is uncommon. There may have been as many as 1,000 cases during the entire Vietnam War from the early 1960s through 1975, a war that probably involved nearly 3 million U.S. service members. *Fragging* may be a U.S. term, but it is not unique to the American military. Nonetheless, there is insufficient evidence to suggest that incident rates are sufficiently high in worldwide historical cases to warrant routine appearance in the Silver Model. See George Lepre, *Fragging: Why U.S. Soldiers Assaulted Their Officers in Vietnam*, Lubbock: Texas Tech University Press, 2011; and, for example, Gautam Navlakha, "A Force Stretched and Stressed," *Economic and Political Weekly*, Vol. 41, No. 46, 2006, pp. 4722–4724.

[83]   See Appendix E.

Figure 3.8
Silver Model (CPM) Process Flowchart

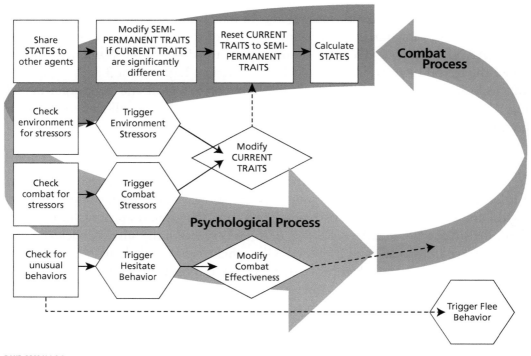

than 40 percent); and (5) squad leader killed. Additional, specific combat stressors were (1) intermittent indirect fire and (2) continuous indirect fire.

Figure 3.8 shows the Silver Model process applied in IWARS. Each agent has semipermanent traits and combat states. Routines check for inputs like suppression or observing a squad leader killed and then apply appropriate state changes based on pre-existing calculations in the model. Changes are based on thresholds: Preset high and low state levels for various traits lead to increases or reductions in behavior.

Experiment 3, Series 1: Silver Model Blue Side Only

Series 1 of Experiment 3 consisted of two iterations of 200 runs for three separate scenarios for a total of 1,200 runs. Each scenario in this series applied the Silver Model to the Blue side only but varied conditions in an attempt to identify factors most likely to influence outcome. In the *Blue Cover, Red Weak* scenario, Blue forces were placed in a tree line and we applied the nighttime, reduced visibility stressors, and no-armor conditions to Red. In the *Blue Cover, Red Equal* scenario, Blue remained in cover but we equipped both sides equally. In *Blue Red Equal*, both sides were identically equipped and in mirror image positions; the Silver Model was the only modifier. We then conducted a platoon-on-platoon scenario to test the capacity for IWARS and the model to

Table 3.10
RAND IWARS Experiment 3, Series 1, Silver Model Results for Blue Only

Scenario *With* Versus *Without* the Silver Model (CPM)	Odds Ratio to Blue Loss	% Change to Blue Fleeing	% Change to Blue Hesitating	% Change to Red Average KIA	% Change to Blue Average KIA
Blue Cover, Red Weak	2.06	24.3	4.3	2.0	3.7
Blue Cover, Red Equal	1.64	23.9	4.5	−2.5	6.3
Blue Red Equal	0.89	16.3	3.4	−6.5	−4.8
Platoon	1.37	11.6	6.6	−2.5	0.9

scale above squad level. We simulated one scenario of two equal platoons for 200 runs with some model changes.[84] Results are presented in Table 3.10. While the differences were not as dramatic as those from Experiment 2, they do show enough variation to reinforce the other evidence supporting our H^1 hypothesis. Significant changes from baseline (test runs without the Silver Model) are highlighted in red text.[85]

Across all scenarios for Series 1, the Silver Model caused an average of 19 percent of troops to flee and 4.7 percent of troops to hesitate, and increased Blue KIA by 1.5 percent. Here, the odds ratio to Blue loss is the likeliness multiplier that Blue will lose *with* the Silver Model applied compared with *without* for a specific scenario. Odds ratios greater than 1 indicate that Blue is more likely to lose with the Silver Model than without. In those scenarios Red agents continued to fire on retreating Blue agents; this occurred in at least half of all runs. Soldier hesitation resulting in a firing/reload delay occurred far less frequently (less than 25 percent of all runs) but would also contribute to Blue's disadvantage. The results of the *Blue Red Equal* scenario prompted the development and execution of the *Platoon* scenario. In addition to generating unit-level results, IWARS Experiment 3 generated thousands of data points for each individual soldier. Figure 3.9 shows an example of state changes to a squad leader's traits over the course of one simulation run. It shows marked increases in anxiety and anger, and fluctuations in stability, all of which collectively resulted in behavioral changes.

Figure 3.10 shows changes to the states of the same squad leader's traits and adds the red dashed and solid lines to represent the points at which the elevated anxiety and

---

[84] Changes include the following: Squad Leader (or superior officer) leadership was 0 if that leader was dead, 0.5 if alive; the random roll for a flee event was lowered from 50 percent to 10 percent; the update rate for combat events was raised to 30 seconds from 2 seconds; and Group Support was changed to the ratio of alive friendlies to all friendlies that are known to an agent (using the IWARS's perception and knowledge models).

[85] *Baseline* is a term used to describe the existing state of a simulation before modifications are added. Here we ran the baseline, or "will to fight: off," scenario a number of times to establish a consistent, smooth set of results from which we could identify deviation. We do not show baseline results in this chapter, instead describing results in terms of change from baseline.

Figure 3.9
Squad Leader State Value Changes to Traits over Time
in Experiment 3

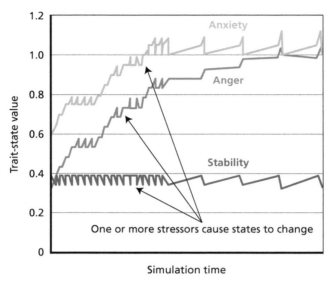

Figure 3.10
Squad Leader State Change Triggers Flight

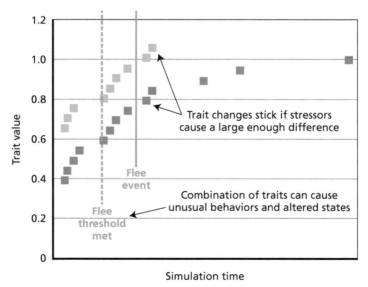

anger triggered a flight threshold and then flight behavior, with the gap between the two lines representing a delay between the change in disposition and the decision to flee.

We did not explicitly track postcombat trait changes. Silver originally intended these kinds of long-term effects on individual soldiers to help show change over the course of a campaign or a war. *Close Combat* replicates that with simpler modeling in campaign modes. Future experiments could set thresholds for permanent trait change, perhaps triggering them by intensity of change over time. Other commercial simulations also have agents that learn and change from battle to battle, although the underlying models tend to be less sophisticated.

Experiment 3, Series 2: Silver Model with Red and Blue Platoons Equal

Series 2 of Experiment 3 implemented the Silver Model into both Blue and Red platoons in a single equal scenario. Implementing for both sides was the next logical step after showing differentiation with Blue only. We expected to have reduced differentiation between Red and Blue behavior since the agents on both sides would have the same thresholds and behavioral changes for hesitation and flight. This expectation bore out. Series 2 did, however, generate behavioral change from baseline in every case. This was a further reinforcement of hypothesis H[1]. This series also showed a significant change in agents' psychological states even below breaking thresholds, a point we return to at the end of this section.

Following the pattern from Series 1 we narrowed behavioral changes based on trait-state variation to hesitation or flee. Two platoons deployed in equal formations on equal terrain and engaged in direct fire combat. Figure 3.11 depicts the two platoons facing off in open terrain in mirror-image skirmish lines. On the left, Soldier 1

Figure 3.11
Soldiers Reacting to Suppression in IWARS Experiment 3, Series 2

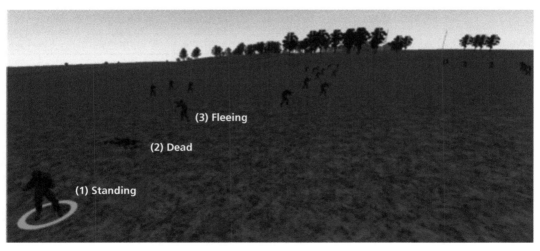

is standing, Soldier 2 is dead, and Soldier 3 is fleeing. We did not add kneeling as a behavior in this scenario.

We ran this single equal-force scenario 200 times. Based on total KIA at the end of the scenario, Blue won 80 and lost 114, with 6 ties. Over these 200 runs the total number of agents fleeing increased by 11.6 percent over baseline, and the total hesitations were 6.6 percent above baseline. In other words, with both sides replicating trait-state behavioral modification and facing only direct rifle fire, more than 1 in 10 soldiers exhibited behavior that would not have appeared in a supersoldier simulation. Table 3.11 presents the findings from this experiment, repeating the findings from the Platoon scenario from Experiment 3, Series 1, for comparison.[86]

We analyzed the initial margin from unusual behaviors by summing the difference of soldier traits from the threshold that must be exceeded for the entire platoon.[87] The result is a model-driven measure of initial "mental toughness" to resist temptations toward unusual behaviors that is then reduced as a soldier experiences combat. Figure 3.12 shows this initial distribution of margins for the flee behavior across all 200 runs. The unstructured scatter plot shows that, on average, Red and Blue experienced the same initial margins to unusual behaviors. This is because the random distribution of initial traits did not favor one force over the other. Changes in outcomes could then be driven by the combat experience itself.[88]

Overall, Series 2 showed modest change from the baseline. Putting aside the 11.6-percent change in flight behavior, some might consider a 1.10 odds ratio to Blue loss to be within an acceptable margin of error. It might follow that if the results were within the same margin of error as the baseline scenario, it is not worth adding will to fight to the simulation. However, it is important to keep in mind that these experi-

Table 3.11
IWARS Experiment 3, RAND Series 2, Silver Model Platoon Comparison

Silver Model (CPM)	Odds Ratio to Blue Loss	% Change to Blue Fleeing	% Change to Blue Hesitating	% Change to Red Average KIA	% Change to Blue Average KIA
Platoon (CPM: Blue only) (Series 1)	1.37	11.6	6.6	−2.5	0.9
Platoon (CPM: both sides) (Series 2)	1.10	11.8	6.9	−0.6	−0.2

[86]   Red odds ratio was 0.91×, 1.7 percent fled, and 6.0 percent hesitated.

[87]   For hesitation, the difference (Δ) of morale below 0.4, anxiety above 0.7, and acquiescence below 0.4. For flee, the Δ of morale below 0.5, anxiety above 0.8, and acquiescence below 0.5.

[88]   This would require, for example, a general additive model with binomial logit regression.

Figure 3.12
Comparison of Red and Blue Team Flee Margin Thresholds

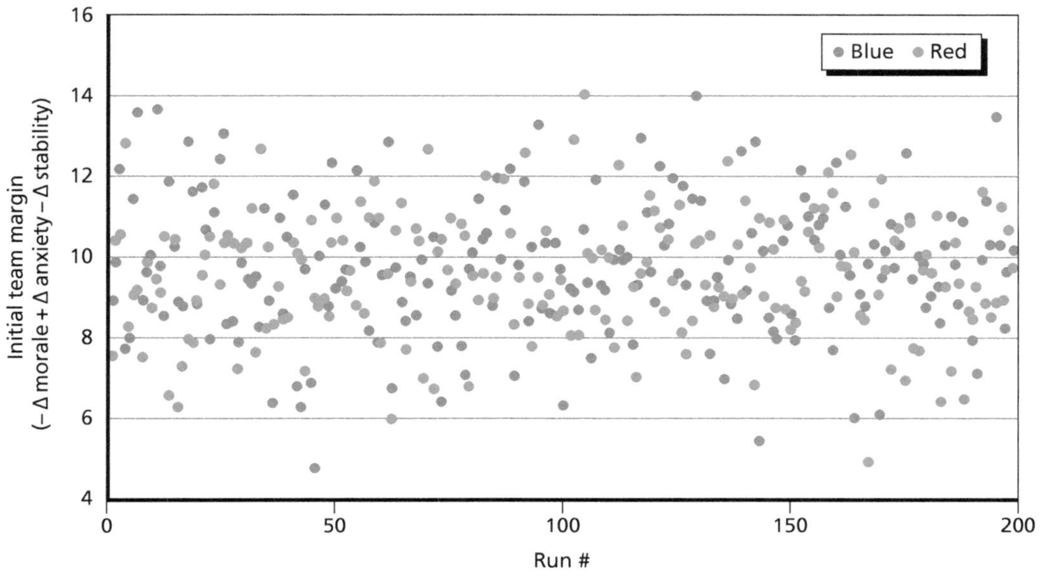

RAND *RR2341A-3.12*

ments test only the most basic combat conditions. None of the RAND Arroyo Center model factors were used to shape the going-in traits of the individual soldiers. These could vary significantly depending on soldier quality, identity, training, and other factors. In a more realistic scenario, each side would have differentiated profiles leading to greater differentiation and steeper changes in win-loss odds. More importantly, basic direct fire is by no means the only combat factor likely to affect will to fight. All of the adversary and exogenous factors listed earlier in this chapter—including artillery fire, sniper fire, chemical attack, cold weather, fatigue, and lack of sleep—could and should be modeled for more accurate simulation. If many other factors could lead to flight, hesitation, or heroic behavior, then the agent behavior in these experiments using this model is probably grossly understated for actual combat conditions.

Adding factors would probably exacerbate what we found to be overly sensitive behavioral response calculations in the Silver Model. While the relationships between the traits and behaviors generally make sense, the thresholds for behavioral change are probably too low to simulate a competent, modern conventional military force. For example, the number of incidents of flight seems excessive. One way to add nuance to the behavioral changes in the Silver Model would be to add gradations of behavioral change between hesitate and flee. Alternatively, the thresholds could be manually changed to make will to fight for each individual soldier, and collectively for the unit, more robust.

Summary of Gaming and Simulation Analysis and Experimentation

Results from our analysis of existing war games and simulations, interviews with game designers and program managers, and our game and simulation testing showed that will to fight is inadequately represented in official military models. If will to fight is one of the most important factors in war, and if it is absent or poorly represented in military gaming and simulation, then there is a dangerous gap in existing military games and simulations. It is possible that results from official military games and simulations are misleading, and have been for quite some time. Existing commercial examples, experimental models, and the new RAND Arroyo Center model can help fill the gap in short order. This is a concrete problem that can be solved in the near term.

Results from our simulation experiments support our first hypothesis (H[1]), suggesting that adding a will-to-fight component always, and sometimes significantly, changes outcomes.[89] Further experimentation with other simulations, models, and variables would be necessary to establish empirical proof. However, existing work by ARL, the Australian Army, the Center for Naval Analyses, JFCOM, and others shows that adding will to fight, or just basic individual personality components, into simulated agents generates meaningful change in results.[90] While we have not seen every experiment conducted with will to fight in simulation, there does not appear to be any existing evidence that contradicts H[1].

Based on the performance of the Silver Model it is safe to say that a more realistic experiment including more factors stimulating greater change in agents' trait-state would be likely to generate much greater behavioral changes and significantly different combat outcomes. Many of the agents that did not hesitate or flee in Experiment 3 were in a state of meta-stability, hovering somewhere just below the thresholds for dramatic behavior change. Results from Experiment 3 are likely just a foreshadowing

---

[89] There would always be an extremely small chance that stochastic determination of combat outcomes including will-to-fight variables would generate a null change from a baseline example or would not affect one outcome of combat (e.g., casualties) in any way. This would be more reflective of odd coincidence than general rule. It might occur more frequently when the number of agents and actions were strictly controlled (e.g., two agents firing 15 rounds each, and only at each other).

[90] Also see Victor Middleton, "Simulating Small Unit Military Operations with Agent-Based Models of Complex Adaptive Systems," in B. Johannson, S. Jain, J. Montoya-Torres, J. Hugan, and E. Yucesan, eds., *Proceedings of the 2010 Winter Simulation Conference*, 2010, pp. 119–134; Thomas M. Cioppa, Thomas W. Lucas, and Susan M. Sanchez, "Military Applications of Agent-Based Simulations," in R. G. Ingalls, M. D. Rossetti, J. S. Smith, and B. A. Peters, eds., *Proceedings of the 2004 Winter Simulation Conference*, 2004, pp. 171–180; Jonathan Gratch and Stacy Marsella, "Fight the Way You Train: The Role and Limits of Emotions in Training for Combat," *Brown Journal of World Affairs*, Vol. 63, No. 7, 2003, pp. 63–75; Rick Evertsz, Frank E. Ritter, Paolo Busetta, and Matteo Pedtrotti, "Realistic Behavior Variation in a BDI-Based Cognitive Architecture," *Proceedings of SimTec 2008*, Melbourne, Australia: SIAA Ltd., 2008; and Greg L. Zacharias, Jean MacMillan, and Susan B. Van Hemel, eds., *Behavioral Modeling and Simulation: From Individuals to Societies*, Washington, D.C.: The National Academies Press, 2008.

of the kind of paradigm changes likely to be achieved with a fine-tuned realistic will-to-fight combat model.

What do these results mean for the U.S. military? First, they set a demand signal for further research by military modeling and simulation experts. We assert that these findings make will to fight all but impossible to ignore for ongoing and future simulation development. Second, the finding that will to fight changes simulated combat outcomes reinforces the central findings of this report: Will to fight must not be ignored.

CHAPTER FOUR

Concluding Thoughts and a Note About Ongoing Research

On June 6, 1944, the U.S. Army landed thousands of soldiers directly into the Wehrmacht's beach defenses along the northern French coast. Army historian S. L. A. Marshall described the chaos, catastrophe, and courage on Omaha Beach as parts of the 116th Infantry Regiment, 29th Division, came ashore in Higgins boats. Before the boats reached shore, German shells ripped some of them apart. At least one boat coxswain had to be persuaded forward at gunpoint. When the ramps dropped on Able Company's lead boats, the Germans raked them with machine-gun fire, forcing soldiers to choose between almost instant death and piling over the gunwales to risk drowning under the weight of their own equipment. Many dove into the water, shedding helmets, rifles, and packs to avoid sinking like stones. As they made their way to the beach, unarmed and exhausted, German machine gunners were "shooting into the survivors as if from a roof top."[1] Marshall describes the scene only 15 minutes into the landing:

> Able Company has still not fired a weapon. No orders are being given by anyone. No words are spoken. The few able-bodied survivors move or not as they see fit. Merely to stay alive is a full-time job. The fight has become a rescue operation in which nothing counts but the force of a strong example.

Much of Baker Company suffered the same fate. Officers were cut down in seconds. Blood soaked the beach and turned the water red. Soldiers huddled against the narrow cover of logs and rocks. Attacking into the German machine guns seemed an insane proposition for the mostly unarmed, leaderless men. So they sat and waited for salvation. Meanwhile a few boats managed to land in relative safety. One of these carried LT Walter Taylor. With the other officers dead or severely wounded, he took over command of Baker Company.

Taylor first led a handful of men in quick action to destroy a German platoon. Then, with only 28 soldiers he attacked into the German defenses, following his original

---

[1] This description and all quotes are drawn from S. L. A. Marshall, "First Wave at Omaha Beach," *The Atlantic*, November 1960.

orders to seize part of the town above the bluffs. Driving forward aggressively, Taylor captured most of another German platoon and then fought off a counterattack that put his men at a 1:3 disadvantage. A sergeant serving under Taylor that day later said, "We saw no sign of fear in him. Watching him made men of us. Marching or fighting, he was leading." Marshall wrote:

> Taylor is a luminous figure in the story of D-Day, one of forty-seven immortals of Omaha who, by their dauntless initiative at widely separate points along the beach, saved the landing from total stagnation and disaster. Courage and luck are his in extraordinary measure.

Marshall's narrative puts will to fight at the fore. Some men fell apart, while others drove forward relentlessly. Happenstance put entire units in untenable positions: A boat landed in the wrong place and a platoon was rendered leaderless. Terrified, exhausted, and unarmed, its men scattered and believed themselves alone and unprotected by their friends or supporting units. Only a few hundred yards away another unit retained its cohesion. Brilliant leaders emerged to shore up the will to fight of a handful of men at just the right moment. Hidden in the unseen folds of Marshall's recounting are hundreds of instances of necessary mediocrity. Soldiers did their jobs, but without brilliance. Some leaders fell apart, or led poorly, but their men still drove forward. Training, discipline, a sense of professional identity, esprit de corps, love of their fellow soldiers, a belief in American ideological purpose and strategy, popular support for the war, and even hatred of the German soldiers drove our soldiers up the bluffs.

It would be difficult to read any version of the Omaha Beach story and believe that the right weapons or tactics alone won the day. This was an event driven in great part by human psychology and human agency. If the soldiers from the 116th Regiment had been automatons, they would have moved unhesitatingly forward rather than abandoning their equipment in the water, thus surviving to fight another day. Lieutenant Taylor would have followed a tactical subroutine demanding he build a 3:1 numerical advantage before attacking. Instead, these real-life soldiers made real-life human decisions based on their dispositions and decisions to fight.

On the other side, German soldiers did not unhesitatingly sit behind their machine guns. They faced the greatest landing fleet ever assembled in human history. Many of them probably knew they were fighting a hopeless delaying action. In his memoir of the battle, German machine gunner Heinrich Severloh recalls thinking, "Dear God, why have you abandoned me? . . . My only thought was, 'How can I get away from here?'"[2] But Severloh stayed and fought, as did thousands of other German

---

[2]   Published as Hein Severloh, *WN 62: Erinnerungen an Omaha Beach Normandie, 6. Juni 1944*, Germany, HEK Creativ Verlag, 2006; quotation in Glenn Frankel, "War and Emerging Remembrance: German Veterans Begin to Add Narrative Piece to WWII," *Washington Post*, July 24, 2004.

soldiers across the Normandy coast that day.[3] They probably did so for many reasons that would have been familiar to the Americans coming across the beach into the beaten zones of the German's fire: duty, honor, comradeship, nationalism, leadership, discipline, and training.[4]

Narratives of Omaha Beach and of the Russian-Chechen battle for Hill 776 described in Chapter One highlight the importance of the will to fight. But these narratives provide no clear answers to the fundamental question underlying all military histories: Why did one side win and the other side lose? It is not possible to know with certainty why Lieutenant Taylor led so effectively on June 6, 1944. It is impossible to know with any accuracy or precision how much his contribution mattered to the overall operation. Therefore, with the richness of Marshall's narrative rendered intangible, we are left with numbers and things. Messy human reality gives way to the neat and clean world of quantifiable data, and will to fight is relegated to easily overlooked one-paragraph doctrinal nods to Clausewitz.

A Better, If Messier, Way

Ignoring will to fight or paying it lip service will not make it go away. At the very least, will to fight is an inalienable partner to physical power in a conceptual double-helix model of combat effectiveness. Will to fight is central to the enduring nature of war. Its relevance can be masked by dynamic changes to the character of war, and it can be discarded as an errant, undefined variable by anyone seeking quantitative clarity in war. But as the Vietnam and Iraq cases show, avoiding will to fight in assessment, analysis, or operations courts avoidable failure. It is time for the U.S. military to rethink the way it applies its own theories of warfare. Or these theories should be revisited. Stating that will to fight is the most important factor in war and then seeking to avoid its messy complexity is illogical. Until accepted theory changes, will to fight should be embraced.

This will be difficult. We can quantify will to fight in simulations but we can never accurately quantify will to fight in the real world. Advisors, intelligence professionals, and leaders will require extra training and education. Even with a better understanding of will to fight, all assessments and analyses of will to fight will always be partly wrong. Perceptions of subjectivity will pervade, driving away some leaders who demand objectivity, precision, accuracy, and an Argus Panoptes–like, all-seeing vision of the battlefield. The argument to offset this kind of reasoning is simple: What we have now is worse, and, to paraphrase Jay Wright Forrester, it is better to include

---

[3]   Severloh defended aggressively for several hours and may have killed hundreds of Americans. He eventually fled when a U.S. destroyer began to shell his position. Severloh was captured by U.S. forces.

[4]   Some were certainly avowed Nazis, although most of the frontline units along the Normandy beaches were regular Wehrmacht and not the Waffen-SS units that were more likely to attract fanatical Nazis.

a critical variable at a low level of accuracy in a plausible range of uncertainty than to omit it entirely.

The good news is that we can improve the level of objectivity, accuracy, and precision to make will-to-fight assessments and analyses more reliable and more useful. Adopting a universal definition of will to fight is the first step. Collectively, the U.S. military should be able to describe what it claims to be the most important factor in war. Adopting a universal model of will to fight is the next logical step. A model will give advisors, intelligence analysts, leaders, and anyone else studying unit combat effectiveness a common anchor. It will provide a commonly agreed-on guide and a baseline for analysis. It can lend confidence to war gaming and simulation experts who too often shy away from soft-factor modeling. Perhaps most importantly, it will increase the confidence of skeptical consumers by tying findings to existing research.

Our model is designed to give the U.S. Army and the Joint Force a starting point for the development of a universal definition and model of will to fight. The model is purpose-built to be both grounded and flexible. It is derived from existing literature and research and provides what should be a defensible basis for official assessment and analysis of partner and adversary military units. However, it is also designed for portability and modification to meet the tailored needs of advisors, intelligence analysts, military leaders, planners, and other users. Ideally a universal joint model will have the same characteristics.

Summary of Recommendations

We identified three recommended actions that the U.S. Army and the Joint Force can take to improve understanding of will to fight, and to make this understanding practical for military and political leaders.

U.S. Army and Joint Force Should Adopt Universal Definition and Model of Will to Fight

It is unlikely that much progress will be made in improving the application of will to fight absent a definition and model that is accepted and used across the Joint Force. While this research was conducted for the U.S. Army, one service alone cannot shape the way the United States prepares for and prosecutes war. Both Army and joint doctrine and practice should fully incorporate will to fight in clear and detailed terms. All Army Doctrine Publications (ADPs) and Joint Publications that address warfighting (e.g., ADP 3-0 and JP 5-0) should define will to fight, explain how it applies to each aspect of warfighting, and describe ways to incorporate will-to-fight considerations. Methods for understanding and influencing will to fight should be developed and described in doctrinal, tactical, and technical manuals. Capstone doctrine should cement will to fight as an enduring and central factor of warfare. Will to fight should not be eliminated in future doctrine. Our definition and model are intended to serve as a starting point for the Army and, ultimately, the Joint Force, in the development of a universal standard.

Include Will to Fight in All Holistic Estimates of Ground Combat Effectiveness

If will to fight is an important, or perhaps the most important, factor in war, and if it is a necessary component of holistic combat effectiveness, then all efforts to assess or analyze the holistic combat effectiveness of a partner or adversary ground combat unit must include will to fight. This recommendation has significant implications for military planners, advisors, intelligence analysts, and commanders seeking to understand the likelihood of success in prospective combat. Methods and standards for determining holistic ground combat unit effectiveness should be changed accordingly. Assessment of partner effectiveness should include grounded estimates of disposition to fight derived from a universal definition and model. Advisors should be trained to assess will to fight, and forms used to analyze and illustrate combat effectiveness should include a structured section on will to fight. Analyses of adversary, or potential adversary, will to fight should be similarly grounded in order to meet standards for analytic integrity. Intelligence order of battle (OOB) analyses should include estimates of unit will to fight. Our research focused on ground combat, but this recommendation should also be considered for estimates of aerospace and naval units.

War Games and Simulations of Combat Should Include Will to Fight

If will to fight is a necessary and important part of determining holistic ground combat effectiveness, and if war games and simulations of force-on-force combat are intended to represent and understand relative combat effectiveness, then will to fight should be included in any war game or simulation that seeks to replicate or determine the outcome of force-on-force ground combat. Games and simulations that fail to consider will to fight, or do not seek to model it in sufficient detail, risk generating misleading play and results. Commercial games and simulations have demonstrated some useful models, and we show how will to fight can be incorporated into military simulation with IWARS. Our model is intended to provide a basis for incorporating will to fight into tabletop games as well as verified, validated, and accredited military simulations. The U.S. Army should incorporate will to fight into its OneSAF and WARSIM simulations. The Joint Force should incorporate will to fight into all current and prospective simulations of force-on-force ground combat.

Ongoing Research: Allied Will to Fight

This report builds from a wealth of existing research, but it is also a potential starting point for improving U.S. Army and Joint Force understanding of will to fight. Further research and refinement is needed. In late 2017 the sponsor of this research funded follow-on research focusing on partner will to fight at the national level. The RAND Arroyo Center team will continue to pursue experimentation and modeling improvements for military simulation.

Structured Literature Review Process and Findings

This appendix presents the initial results from our literature review. While it is written as a holistic response to our research question, it was only one of nine steps in a collective multimethod process. It generated an independent model of will to fight that was central to the development of our completed model, presented in Chapter Two. The literature-driven model is similar to, but in many ways substantively different from, the model generated by our broader research effort. We present our steps and provisional findings from this effort in the interest of transparency, but caution readers to remember that this appendix represents the initial work in an iterative, multimethod process.

As part of a research effort to answer the question *what is the will to fight* at the tactical and operational levels of war, we conducted a literature review of relevant studies. In the course of our review, we examined 202 total sources—mostly scholarly journal articles and books, but also some well-regarded histories and memoirs—which we considered potentially relevant to our study.[1] We characterized the literature and described the various factors this body of literature implicates in the will to fight throughout the body text of the report. In the rest of this appendix, we explain our data and methods, analytical findings, and insights.

Scope

Our goal for the literature review was to look broadly at prior research on will to fight across multiple disciplines. While we reviewed scholarly sources that were empirically grounded, our aim was not to assess each source but rather to build an aggregate picture of scholarship that we could cross-reference by variables such as disciplinary source, author national perspective, and study object (e.g., service, nation, or conflict). This mixed-method approach of building an aggregated review by variable allowed us to discover relevant relationships—for example, revenge is an important factor in will

---

[1] While it is common and useful to distinguish between tactical and operational levels of warfare, we note that these levels are intimately related, and thus any definition of will to fight relative to military members/units crosses both levels.

to fight for nonstate actors, but generally less important in historical cases describing the will to fight of Western conventional forces.

Initially we cast a fairly wide net for any study we thought might be relevant to our project. We quickly found that our first selection of literature needed to be pared down. Some literature was interesting but not directly relevant to our analysis.[2] After reviewing many studies that were at best peripherally relevant, we more strictly scoped out the review. Based on our initial survey of literature, we *tentatively* defined tactical-operational will to fight as *the determination of individuals in a military unit, or of the unit itself, to conduct a mission even under conditions of adversity, such as tactical disadvantage or lack of supply.* We later modified this definition to match findings from our multimethod research.

This tentative definition was useful to us in that it was narrow enough to eliminate much of the peripheral literature that was not directly relevant to the study, but also broad enough to capture the fullness of this critical human dimension in war. On the one hand, scoping this down to the determination of persons and units to continue the fight eliminates a wide swath of combat effectiveness and force-building literature. We take for granted that high levels of skill with advanced, well-maintained equipment are an important part of combat readiness, or that effective command and control systems increase combat effectiveness. But those examples, while important to combat outcomes, are clearly distinct from the willingness to use weapon systems, or respond to command and control output. On the other hand, will to fight is more than just combat motivation. While combat motivation is part of the larger whole of will to fight, we would point to the logistics soldier who is driving a fuel truck on day 28 of continuous operations, exhausted, hungry, and miserable, and still absolutely determined to accomplish the mission.

This scoping allowed us to discriminate between directly relevant and tangential sources. For example, a source that explored the relationship between reserve status and identity and the willingness to fight was included, whereas a study strictly limited to reserve status and retention was not. The result of this scoping exercise was that of the 202 sources we reviewed, we retained 110 for coding in our database.

---

[2]   Robert L. Grice and Lawrence C. Katz, *Cohesion in Military and Aviation Psychology: An Annotated Bibliography and Suggestions for US Army Aviation*, Fort Rucker, Ala.: Army Research Institute for the Behavioral and Social Sciences Fort Rucker Al Rotary-Wing Aviation Research Unit, ARI-TR-1166, 2005; Peter A. Hancock, Deborah R. Billings, Kristin E. Schaefer, Jessie Y. C. Chen, Ewart J. De Visser, and Raja Parasuraman, "A Meta-Analysis of Factors Affecting Trust in Human-Robot Interaction," *Human Factors*, Vol. 53, No. 5, 2011, pp. 517–527; and Meyer Kestnbaum, "Mars Revealed: The Entry of Ordinary People into War Among States," in Julia Adams, Elisabeth S. Clemens, and Ann Shola Orloff, eds., *Remaking Modernity: Politics, History, and Sociology*, Durham, N.C.: Duke University Press, 2005, pp. 13–29.

Method

Integrative Review

Integrative review is a summative literature review method that allows for broadly comprehensive framing of a particular issue or problem, and thus oriented toward practice and well suited to policy research.[3] Ensuring a well-thought-out and explicit set of criteria for inclusion and exclusion in the review enhances rigor in a study by ensuring appropriate coverage of a fairly novel or unstudied problem (i.e., the factors of determination in the will to fight).[4]

We used a five-step process in our review, allowing for both analytic insight and synthesis of diverse approaches to the problem (e.g., both theory and applied literature)[5]:

- *Factor identification.* We started with a broad overview of literature to better understand the factors that affect will to fight, which we suspected might be a complex construct, and used that as the basis to formulate specific inclusion/exclusion criteria for the review. An example of exclusion criteria was our choice to exclude literature solely applicable to concepts such as cohesion, retention, or general combat effectiveness. An example of inclusion criteria was literature relevant to the continued commitment to battles or operations in the face of significant adversity. This step included multiple members of the research team contributing potentially relevant literature, and the generation of potential keywords for searches.
- *Literature search.* Individual researchers conducted a wider, criteria-based search for potentially relevant literature based on the inclusion/exclusion criteria in the factor identification step.[6] While the majority of sources we reviewed came from peer-reviewed academic journals or from academic presses, we did review some popular histories and memoirs. For such works, we included foundational works cited by later scholars, as well as sources that added national and cultural diversity to our review. Researchers also included potential subcategories for organizing the review into a more useful, annotated document.
- *Data evaluation.* We engaged in team evaluation of potential sources, with team-based decisions to include/exclude sources. New sources gave us an inductive way to expand and improve our original a priori set of search terms. For example, we

---

[3]   Robin Whittemore and Kathleen Knafl, "The Integrative Review: Updated Methodology," *Journal of Advanced Nursing*, Vol. 52, No. 5, 2005, pp. 546–553.

[4]   David N. Boote and Penny Beile, "Scholars Before Researchers: On the Centrality of the Dissertation Literature Review in Research Preparation," *Educational Researcher*, Vol. 34, No. 6, 2005, pp. 3–15.

[5]   Adapted from Whittemore and Knafl, 2005.

[6]   Databases searched include ScienceDirect, SAGE, Academic Search Complete, PsychARTICLES, Business Source Complete, JSTOR, Defense Technical Information Center, and University of Chicago Press Journals.

found that "why they fight" and "why they fought" were two useful terms of art for finding additional literature that was directly relevant to the study. This led to iterations of steps 2 and 3. We iterated until we reached a saturation point (unable to find new, relevant sources that met our criteria).

- *Data analysis.* We reviewed each entry to extract relevant data, applying codes using software (see below) as well as making our own, analytical observations. This also included synthetic observations, building possible new knowledge by connecting distinct but related data in our sources.
- *Modeling.* We synthesized our research into a model of the problem, both in the form of this report and in a conceptual model of how the will to fight operates.

Literature Review Software

To enhance rigor in our review, we used a collaborative mixed-method software environment called Dedoose.[7] Dedoose is an analytic software environment that leverages the strengths of both quantitative and qualitative approaches to data analysis to describe qualitative data through the application of codes. *Codes* in this sense means a label for discovered patterns in data, allowing us to organize and count those codes as they are applied to data, and map them to the quantitative descriptors of sources.[8] In this case:

- **Qualitative codes:** After reviewing a study, we used qualitative codes on relevant claims about the will to fight, such as motivations to continue operations under adversity, enabling and diminishing factors affecting fighting will, potential measures of will to fight, and the countries and services discussed in the study.
- **Quantitative descriptors:** We also recorded demographic data about each study, such as the study language, first author's home country, principal disciplinary perspective in the study, study methods, study era, and the national culture the study focused on.[9]

Cross-referring qualitative codes and quantitative demographics allowed us to richly characterize the findings in our review against the traits of the studies. For example, one of the least applied qualitative codes in our study was for economic motivations. When we cross-correlated economic motivations with descriptors, we found that economic motivations occurred only in studies about nonstate actors such as the

---

[7]   Dedoose Version 8.0.35, web application for managing, analyzing, and presenting qualitative and mixed method research data, 2018, Los Angeles, Calif.: SocioCultural Research Consultants, LLC.

[8]   Eli Lieber, "Mixing Qualitative and Quantitative Methods: Insights into Design and Analysis Issues," *Journal of Ethnographic and Qualitative Research*, Vol. 3, No. 4, 2009, pp. 218–227.

[9]   In addition, we initially tried to collect demographic information on theoretical perspectives informing the study (e.g., theories of human agency, organizational theory, and psychological trait theories). However, more than half of the studies had no explicit theoretical commitments, and thus we discarded this attempt.

Colombian insurgency Fuerzas Armadas Revolucionarias de Colombia. The ability to both describe the findings in these studies and count their demographics meant we could build a holistic picture of this body of literature and summarize relationships such as that between economic motivation and nonstate actors' will to fight.

As this is a cloud-based service, we were able to collaborate in the same digital project space, with real-time visibility of each other's work.[10] This improved our ability to refine the coding framework, discover relationships, and enhance rigor in our review and coding through a shared view of other team members' coding. We did this by developing coding criteria, with inclusion, exclusion, and disambiguation criteria. This allowed team members to code based on explicit coding guidance rather than intuition. We enhanced this by conducting coding reconciliation meetings to further develop a robust shared understanding of our coding protocol.[11] When we did have a particular concern over relevance, inclusion, or disambiguation of an argument for a will-to-fight factor, we were able to share that item and come to a team decision.

Literature Review Limitations

Our primary limitation in this study was around language: We confined our review to English-language scholarship. So, for example, while there is existing French scholarship on the will to fight, our research team did not have the translation capacity to incorporate such scholarship, at least not with the kind of accuracy and rigor used in our English-language research. Likewise, we think there is likely relevant Russian-language and Mandarin Chinese–language scholarship that could have informed our model, but because of labor/translation constraints could not be included.

Existing Scholarship on the Will to Fight

In our first broad review of potentially relevant literature, we found that while there was some obvious agreement—cohesion and leadership seemed clearly implicated in the will to fight—there were many other potentially relevant factors as well. We suspected therefore that the will to fight might be a complex construct, potentially weighted so that, depending on the circumstances, some factors might be more important than others. To extract such complexity, we carefully reviewed relevant scholarly literature to identify and then code what the field positively identified as contributing to the will to fight (e.g., we did not code when an author argued that a *factor* does not contribute).

---

[10]   Software and data storage offered as a remote service, accessible through a browser window; in contrast to stand-alone software installed separately on individual computers.

[11]   Robert G. Orwin and Jack L. Vevea, "Evaluating Coding Decisions," in Harris Cooper, Larry V. Hedges, and Jeffrey C. Valentine, eds., *The Handbook of Research Synthesis and Meta-Analysis II*, New York: Russell Sage Foundation, 2009, pp. 177–203.

Applying a code when we found a claim about what goes into will to fight allowed the team to build a summative and interpretive structure out of a large literature set.[12] We could then both qualify the literature and count how often a given factor was offered, and whether there were relationships between the factors and their sources. We note here that our claim is not that frequency of mention for a factor automatically means it is more important in understanding fighting will. But in the particular step of characterizing what the field has to say overall, counts matter: That various kinds of cohesion were mentioned as factors in 71 distinct sources, that ideology was cited 32 times, and that communication appeared as a factor in only 3 sources are critical to characterizing existing scholarship.

We note here that coding for this content involved analytical choices about granularity. As an example, leadership was discussed as a factor, but at different levels of granularity: mostly as a top-level factor, but occasionally specified by a type of leadership (e.g., transactional or charismatic). In that case, we decided it made more sense to treat subvarieties of distinct factors as wholes—for example, different leadership styles as a single factor of leadership or both social and physical punishments as coercion.

Explicit Models of the Will to Fight

The literature we reviewed generally indicated the importance of one or more factors supporting or enhancing the will to fight, and we have mined these sources to gather the field's aggregate sense of those factors to support our own attempt to model the will to fight. However, we also encountered explicit, formal models of the will to fight. These range from complex psychological factor models with embedded psychometric measures to broader conceptual models for factors, their context, and interrelations.[13] We present a sample of some of these formal models below, chosen to illustrate the range of different models in this area.

Fighter-Spirit Model

As we noted earlier, U.S. scholarship has strongly featured cohesion guided by leadership as the most important factors in explaining the will to fight. A good example of a cohesion plus leadership model is Smith's (1983) explicitly quantitative Fighter-Spirit model. This complex psychological factor model argues for two primary sets of interactions (leadership and cohesion) that result in "fighter spirit."

1.   Leadership: The first set of interactions is at the company level between the company command leadership climate and the example that officers set for their subordinates. Interestingly, in this model lower educational standards improve fighter spirit—Smith (1983) argued that less educated soldiers had

[12]   Thérèse Kairuz, K. Crump, and A. O'Brien, "Tools for Data Collection and Analysis," *Pharmaceutical Journal*, Vol. 278, 2007, p. 372.

[13]   Smith, 1983; van den Aker, Duel, and Soeters, 2016.

lower expectations/higher satisfaction with military life, and thus improved relationships with leaders.

2. Cohesion: Along with the leadership factor, vertical and peer cohesion (which we combine into "social cohesion") leads to a rating for fighter spirit.

Figure A.1 illustrates the relationship between Smith's (1983) variables.

Figure A.1
Fighter-Spirit Model

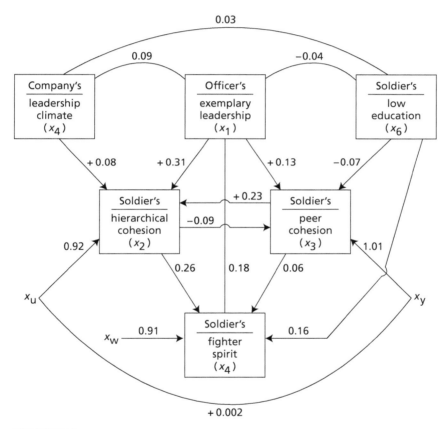

Dutch Organizational Support Model

Another will-to-fight model that seeks to quantify the relationship between various factors is van den Aker, Duel, and Soeters's (2016) study of Dutch combat veterans since the end of World War II. The study is based on a survey of motivations and conditions as reported by 2,101 veterans and active duty soldiers, and found two main sets of factors: trust across operational dimensions (i.e., unit and organizational cohesion, self-confidence, and trust in materiel and weapons) and a psychosocial sense of support from within the organization and wider civil society. Figure A.2 shows this model.

Figure A.2
Dutch Organizational Support Model

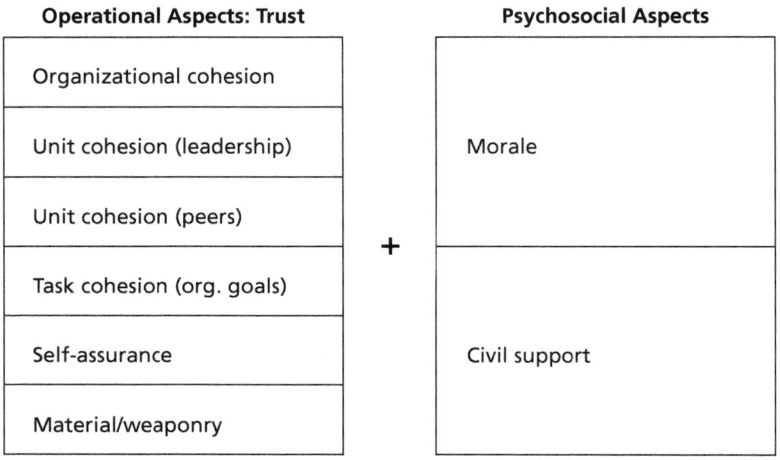

Operational Aspects: Trust		Psychosocial Aspects
Organizational cohesion		
Unit cohesion (leadership)		Morale
Unit cohesion (peers)	**+**	
Task cohesion (org. goals)		
Self-assurance		Civil support
Material/weaponry		

RAND RR2341A-A.2

Terrorist Will-to-Fight Model

While the majority of will-to-fight literature examines state military power, nonstate actors/terrorists were also addressed. The single source we found that directly addresses breaking an enemy's will to fight argues for a personal and sociocultural understanding of terrorists' motivations.[14] The following formula represents terrorists' will to fight (w_t) as a function of beliefs about values (how and why a person should live and die, in relation to the rest of his or her social group), their desire for revenge on behalf of that group, their personal sense of identity and meaning, and broader sociocultural support for fighting:

$$w_t = f(b + r + s)_t \, c_t$$

where

1. b denotes the summation of all beliefs (religious, ideological, ethnic, and values) at time t;
2. r is the desire for revenge at time t;
3. s is the summation of the desires for satisfaction (renown, joy, and finances) at time t; and
4. c represents culture at time t.

> With some initial values, $b0$ for belief, $r0$ for the desire for revenge, and $s0$ for the desire of satisfaction, the value of w_t can be calculated over time for each $t \in \_\{1,2,3,...\}$.[15]

---

[14] Paulo E. Santa Barba, *Breaking Terrorists' Will to Fight*, Monterey, Calif.: Naval Postgraduate, 2014.

[15] Barba, 2014.

In the terrorist will-to-fight model, when w_t crosses a minimum threshold value (contextual to a given time and place), terrorists are willing to fight and will engage in violence. But a reduction in any or all of the variables in the w_t function—for example, the desire for revenge—will lower a terrorist's will to fight, hopefully to below the violence threshold.

Analysis of Current Scholarship on the Will to Fight

Our analysis of existing scholarship on the will to fight shows a strong bias that elevates cohesion above all other factors. Ultimately, we were able to synthesize this literature into a unified model that accounts for the complex motivations and enablers previously studied. In the rest of this appendix we describe the review and findings, and then present the unified literature model synthesized from the review.

Description of the Review

We studied 202 scholarly sources potentially relevant to understanding the will to fight, ultimately retaining 110 of those sources for inclusion in the coded review. We used the review of the 92 sources we did not code to inform our broader research. Reasons for excluding sources from the coding process varied: Some had insufficient detail, while others did not directly address our research objectives. Our review was entirely of English-language studies, and overwhelmingly from U.S. and UK/Commonwealth scholars.[16]

Focused on U.S. and Western European Militaries

We further note that scholarship on the will to fight that we reviewed focuses almost exclusively on the United States and Western European countries. This may reflect historical and material realities. U.S. and UK forces have been much more engaged in combat in the last century than, say, South Africa. We tracked "national culture" because we noted that while there were some truly multinational studies, by and large our sources were on a single force from a specific country, for example, U.S. Army soldiers, Israeli Defense Force members, People's Liberation Armed Force, or ARVN members. One important choice we made was to include nonstate actors under a common heading. Clearly such forces do not share a national culture per se, but they did seem to share structural similarities.

Thus an important caveat to our study is that there is a source bias toward the West. While there is broad consensus on the importance of cohesion in will to fight,

---

[16]   As we read through the literature, we saw so much commonality between descriptions of the will to fight for British and Canadian forces that we created a broad "UK/Commonwealth" category to capture cultural similarities. While the majority of this literature was on British forces, we also found analyses of the will to fight in Canadian, Scottish, and New Zealand forces.

this may reflect a Western bias. For example, we note that revenge appears in all three of the studies we read that focused on nonstate actors—the relative infrequency of revenge cited as a factor may be a result of bias in the literature toward Western militaries, which are built on cohesion, ideological commitment, unit morale, and esprit de corps.

Factors Affecting Will to Fight: Motivation and Enabling and Diminishing Influences

As we read through the existing literature on will to fight, we found that we could divide the factors we encountered into motivations and enabling and diminishing influences. So, for example, while vertical cohesion (loyalty and mutuality between leaders and their unit members) was a motivation to stay in the fight, good leadership itself was an enabler, channeling and structuring unit efforts. In the following sections, we list motivations and enabling factors (which are diminishing or detracting influences if they are missing or working in the wrong direction, like poor leadership), ranked by total number of studies that included that factor.

Will-to-Fight Enablers and Obstacles

In addition to motivating factors, we found enablers and obstacles to generating and sustaining the will to fight. Studies generally focused only on enablers, but we infer that the absence or opposite of a factor could be a diminishing influence: If good leadership helps structure unit behavior in ways that enable fighting will, then poor leadership would detract from it.

A Model of Will to Fight Derived from the Literature

As noted earlier, will-to-fight literature has primarily been conducted by U.S. and UK scholars on Western European and U.S. military forces, and so while we can say that some factors (e.g., cohesion, leadership, esprit, and personal morale) were mentioned much more frequently than others (e.g., doctrine, economic motivation, and revenge), we cannot generalize relative importance from the above frequency counts. Instead, our analysis supports the idea that rather than being a stable construct, will to fight is a variable construct and depends on context and culture. We do not feel it is possible or useful to create a weighted model that elevates some factors above others in importance. Instead, we propose to consolidate the identified factors into a more usable and coherent whole. This allows for a flexible, context-sensitive model that can be applied locally to understand and assess both partner and enemy will to fight. This model includes both motivations and enablers, and attempts to visually represent these factors within the social contexts that will to fight occurs in (see Figure A.3). All of the factors in this tentative model were derived from the literature alone, and not from any other sources. Therefore, this model is a literature review model and does not represent the nine-part multimethod research effort conducted through mid-2018.

Figure A.3
Tentative Consolidated Model Derived Only from Literature Review

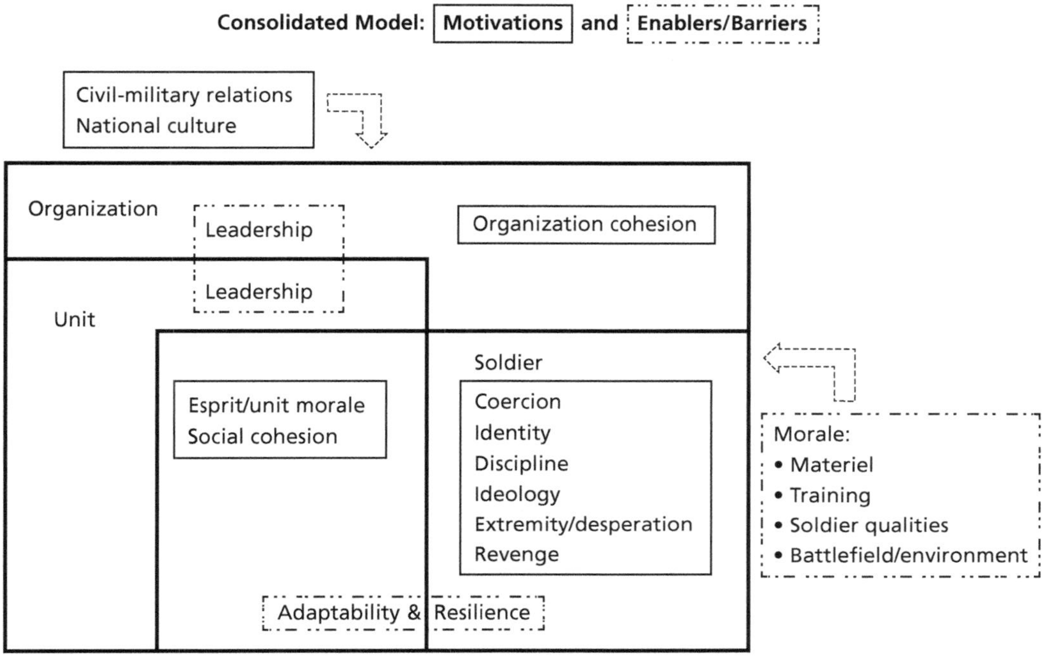

Consolidated Model: | Motivations | and | Enablers/Barriers |

RAND RR2341A-A.3

Summary: A Complex Construct Bigger Than Cohesion

We found that the will to fight is a complex construct. While U.S. research on the subject has strongly emphasized cohesion, a very thorough reading of the literature, especially when extended to other militaries, shows multiple factors for will to fight that vary by context and culture. We found that these multiple factors can be usefully conceived as either *motivations* or *enablers*: *reasons why* soldiers and units are willing to continue the fight and operate under extremely adverse conditions, and the *means* by which those reasons are harnessed to tactical and operational ends. Finally, we think that a consolidated model that covers the range of factors can be useful to the Army not only for assessing partner and enemy will to fight but also for assessing or degrading their will to fight.

Table A.1 provides codes and definitions for the literature review coding process. We consolidated some of the codes that repeated in order to shorten the table. For example, variations of coercion appeared several times.

Table A.1
Literature Review Codes and Descriptions

Code	Description
Motivation	Reasons for fighting: why does an individual want to fight?
Service component	Identify specific service, if relevant
Coercion	Combat motivations that involve fear, compulsion, punishment, and external threats to elicit obedience
Cohesion	Top-level code for cohesion and cohesiveness, and their variations (e.g. task cohesion, social cohesion, organizational cohesion)
Task cohesion	Instrumental or task cohesion, a commitment to collective goals, or a willingness to sacrifice to achieve the mission
Trust	Trust along multiple dimensions: interpersonal demonstrated trust, confidence in skills or training, confidence in the institution, etc.
Social cohesion (primary)	Horizontal/vertical cohesion, amity, comradeship, trust, mutuality, often called "peer" and "leader" in the standard military cohesion model
Organizational cohesion (secondary)	Service/regimental cohesion to the larger organization often called "organizational" and "institutional" in the standard military cohesion model
Role theory	The performance of organizational roles
National	Unit/personal commitment to the larger nation, shared national culture, membership, and identity as an enabler, not motivation
Discipline	Willingness to be subject to military authority and regulation. May also be referred to as obedience, submission, or habituation
Esprit and unit morale	Esprit de corps, élan, and unit pride, the concepts that point to the fighting spirit of a unit and an ardor or eagerness to pursue a cause or task, confidence in battle prowess/success, and concepts of elite membership
Life-threat, extremity, desperation	Fear of death/self-preservation, a sense of utter extremity, or no other options, when you fight because your back is to the wall; individual, unit, or national survival
Revenge	Combat motivations and willingness to fight that spring from a desire for revenge (e.g., to avenge or free [perceived] oppressed people, or get revenge for the death of comrades)
Economic	Monetary, economic, subsistence as a reason to fight
Identity and self satisfaction	When personal identity, personal meaning-making/sense of self, and the search for satisfaction (renown, joy, or financial incentives) are implicated in the will to fight
Personal identity	Sense of how personal identity or search for meaning/satisfaction motivates a willingness to fight
Social identity	Attachment to performing roles and operating according to group ideals and norms, and the performance of culture (e.g., local identities such as village or county, or group acculturated identities)
Ideological commitment	Any commitment to a cause or belief system, whether it be a religion, an ideology (including perceived legitimacy of a cause), or values, for which members are willing to fight

Table A.1—Continued

Code	Description
Enablers and obstacles	Factors that can enhance, leverage, or improve the will to fight, or by their absence degrade it
Doctrine	Relationship between doctrine/how doctrine is taught and will to fight
Adaptability and resilience	Individual or unit resilience/adaptability that allows for the continuation of fighting, and the ability to bounce back from stressors that would weaken the will to fight
Personal adaptability/ resilience	Adaptability and resilience at the individual level
Group adaptability/ resilience	Adaptability and resilience at the group (unit) level
Battlefield and environmental conditions	How external factors beyond the person/unit/service affect the will to fight, including the enemy, battlefield lethality, weather/terrain, etc.
Civil-military	Relationship between members and the larger national context, as it pertains to the will to fight
Reserve component	Reservists and differences between reservists and active forces
Conscription and volunteer force building	Effects of the end of conscription, or how conscription/volunteer force structures affect the will to fight
Leadership	Leadership as instrumental to the creation of leveraging will to fight, combat effectiveness, and mission accomplishment
Materiel	Indications that materiel/logistics are relevant to the ability to sustain operations under adversity
Morale	Attitude or affect toward unit/service/effort; includes sense of well-being, job/life satisfaction, confidence in leadership, and general outlook
Soldier quality and capabilities	Individual soldier qualities like stability, fitness, and aggression, and capabilities like social interaction, individual skills
Training and skills	Training at all levels: personal, small unit, and operational units as well as the resulting skills that come from training related to will to fight
Research characteristics	Characteristics of the objects of analysis in a study, e.g. country or service being examined
Understanding will to fight	Specific research findings offering analytical insight into will to fight
Combat effectiveness/ performance	How combat effectiveness is implicated in will to fight
Measures	Identified published measures to help understand will to fight
Building/sustaining will to fight	Description of ways to create or sustain will to fight
Attacking/degrading will to fight	Description of ways to attack or degrade will to fight

Coded Case Study Procedures and Results

Historical case analysis was an essential part of our nine-part multimethod research effort. Our researchers brought their expertise with specific cases to bear in support of each analytic effort. The separate analyses of the Vietnam War and Russian will to fight influenced the development of our model. We also conducted a formal case coding analysis to identify factors to include in the model, and to determine whether there might be a single factor that always determines will to fight. This appendix presents the methodology and findings from the case coding analysis. It is important to note up front that we did not use statistical analysis or any quantitative methodology when conducting our case analysis or comparison. The coding process and results had informative and qualitative value rather than empirical value. The coding matrix is too large to be presented here; it will be provided on request once this report is published. Results cannot be released due to sensitivities with participant anonymity, but we do hope to eventually release results from a more robust sample of cases and a refined coding effort.

We began our case coding in parallel with the coded literature review. While it would have been ideal to apply our model to the cases, research sequencing led us to develop codes based on our initial literature review. We identified 58 tactical-operational coding questions designed to help characterize the will to fight of a single side in a single conventional warfare case. We amassed these questions in an iterative group process leveraging the informed subjective expert opinion of the coders. These questions are listed in Table B.1. Instructions to the coders also included detailed explanations of the coding process and objectives. Coders were required to assign a confidence level of 1–4 for each code to describe their confidence in the accuracy of their response, a narrative rationale for each code, specific examples of will to fight tied to the code, and then areas of significant expert disagreement, citation, and process comments to help the coding team improve the instrument for prospective follow-on iterations. Note that we used terms like *morale* that emerged in the literature but that we did not include in our finished model.

We selected 14 cases from the Correlates of War database, bracketing conventional warfare cases between World War I and 2017. In addition to limiting scope and scale, we also sought out cases that were well recorded and cases in which the two main

Table B.1
Questions for Tactical-Operational Will-to-Fight Case Coding

Code
On a scale of 1–4, rate the overall stakes in the conflict as perceived at the operational and tactical levels.
Was success or failure believed to be existential for the assessed organization? **yes** or **no**
On a scale of 1–4, how high was troop motivation to succeed in the mission?
Were defections **very common** (20% or more), **common** (10–20%), **uncommon** (5–10%) or **rare** (0–5%)?
On a scale of 1–4, rate the overall quality of leadership.
On a scale of 1–4, rate the quality of operational leadership at the **organizational** level.
On a scale of 1–4, rate the quality of operational leadership at the **unit** level.
Did soldiers view their direct leadership as **legitimate** or **illegitimate** and **competent** or **incompetent**?
Did soldiers view higher levels of service leadership as **legitimate** or **illegitimate, competent** or **incompetent**?
Do members of the military see the government as legitimate? **yes** or **no**
On a scale of 1–4, rate the overall adequacy of resources and effectiveness of systems.
Did the country in question have adequate national resources to achieve operational objectives? **yes** or **no**
Was operational supply **adequate** or **inadequate** within the campaign?
Is corruption corrosive to function and legitimacy of organization?
Is the military's defense planning system **fully functional, somewhat functional,** or **not functional**?
Is the military's procurement and budgeting systems **fully functional, somewhat functional,** or **not functional**?
Is the military's personnel planning system **fully functional, somewhat functional,** or **not functional**?
Does the military perform basic services for its personnel? **yes** or **no**
Is there a functioning military justice system? **yes** or **no**
Are punishments for violating rules **harsh, fair,** or **lenient**?
Is the military command culture **merit-based** or **influence-based**?
Was a perception of low pay a source of distraction? **yes** or **no**
Were the basic needs of the unit being met? **yes** or **no**
Were there special units that were better/better supported than regular units? **yes** or **no**
(If yes to "special units" above) Did special treatment, caste, create animosity? **yes** or **no**
On a scale of 1–4, rate overall cohesion.
Was lateral organizational cohesion between similar units (e.g. brigade to brigade) **tight, loose,** or **nonexistent**?
Was vertical cohesion between units and higher command **tight, loose,** or **nonexistent**?
How was military obedience obtained in the organization: **coercion, cohesion,** or **behavioral norms,** or a **mix**?
Is horizontal cohesion in average units **strong, adequate, weak** or **nonexistent**?

Table B.1—Continued

Code

Is vertical cohesion in average units **strong, adequate, weak,** or **nonexistent?**

On a scale of 1–4, rate overall morale.

On a scale of 1–4, rate **organizational morale**.

On a scale of 1–4, rate quality of overall training.

Did troops believe their combat training was **adequate** or **inadequate?**

Were the unit's battle tactics appropriate to the mission, enemy, terrain and available equipment? **yes** or **no**

On a scale of 1–4, rate quality of overall C3I (Command, Control, Communications, and Intelligence).

One a scale of 1–4, how effective is **command** and **control** at senior levels?

One a scale of 1–4, how effective is **command** and **control** throughout the military more broadly?

One a scale of 1–4, how effective is **communications** among units and with headquarters?

One a scale of 1–4, how effective is intelligence collection and sharing among units and with headquarters?

One a scale of 1–4, rate the quality of the military's overall fighting power compared with the adversary's?

Was the adversary **aggressive, defensive** or **passive?**

Was the adversary **better equipped, less well equipped,** or **similarly equipped?**

How did the org. respond to adversary atrocities? **United against adversary, no impact, created fissures**

Is the adversary's overall fighting power **more powerful, equal to,** or **less powerful** than the organization?

Did the adversary employ effective psychological messaging against the fighting force in question? **yes** or **no**

Did the adversary **accept** or **reject and/or abuse** defectors?

Did the adversary have adequate equipment to achieve their operational objective? **yes** or **no**

Did the adversary experience **ethnic, sectarian, or regional animosities** at the hands of the country in question?

Did the operation (or war) **succeed** or **fail** from the perspective of this (coded) side?

Did the country experience **ethnic, sectarian,** or **regional animosities** at the hands of the adversary?

Were individual units geographically **tightly grouped, moderately dispersed,** or **widely distributed?**

Did the country experience **ethnic,** and/or **sectarian,** and/or **regional animosities** at the hands of the adversary?

Did soldiers harbor personal hatred toward their adversary? **yes** or **no**

(If yes to above) Was this hatred **situational** or **long-standing?**

Is there civilian control of the military? **yes** or **no**

Does the military have greater influence than civilian institutions in government decisions? **yes** or **no**

Did organization have history of **winning** wars, **losing** wars, or **no substantive history?**

combatants were somewhat evenly matched in size. This effectively restricted our selection to the mid to late twentieth century. We coded each case and developed useful findings from ten of these cases. Findings in this appendix are derived from these ten coded cases:[1]

1.   Vietnam War: Army of the Republic of Vietnam
2.   Vietnam War: People's Army of Vietnam
3.   Iran-Iraq War: Iraqi Army
4.   Korean War: Republic of Korea Army
5.   World War I: Russian Army
6.   World War I: German Army
7.   World War I: French Army
8.   World War II: Russian Army
9.   World War II: German Army
10. World War II: French Army

Coding a war case involves assigning values to a selected range of factors and determining their relevance to the outcome of the war (and, ideally, to each other). Previous examples of RAND war coding include *How Insurgencies End* (2010) and *Victory Has a Thousand Fathers* (2010).[2] Because wars tend to last for several years, it can be problematic to assign a single value to a single factor for an entire war case. For example, while American societal and state-level will to fight in the Vietnam War was quite low by 1973, it was actually high in the early- to mid-1960s. To account for change over time we coded each case three times: (1) at the beginning of the war, (2) at the coder-defined turning point of the war, and (3) at the end of the war. For example, in the case of Vietnam, we coded the American ground force deployments in 1965 as the beginning of the conventional war, the Tet Offensive in 1968 as the turning point, and the fall of Saigon to the PAVN in 1975 as the end of the war.

Coding is a subjective process that requires consistent, well-informed judgment from the coders. To improve the reliability of our coding process, we enlisted the aid of several case experts: Gregory Daddis and Kevin Boylan for the Vietnam War, RAND Middle East expert Andrew Parasiliti for the Iran-Iraq War, RAND World Wars expert Jasen Castillo, and for the Korean War, In Hyo Seol, a National Defense University Fellow from the Republic of Korea and a researcher at the Korean Institute for Defense Analyses. We conducted an intercoder reliability test on the Vietnam War with four researchers, two internal to RAND and two external. Each researcher coded

---

[1]   We coded but did not analyze (1) World War I: Austria-Hungary, (2) World War I: Italy, (3) Russia in Chechnya, and (4) Chechnya against Russia.

[2]   Ben Connable and Martin Libicki, *How Insurgencies End*, Santa Monica, Calif.: RAND Corporation, MG-965, 2010; Christopher Paul, Colin P. Clarke, and Beth Grill, *Victory Has a Thousand Fathers: Sources of Success in Counterinsurgency*, Santa Monica, Calif.: RAND Corporation, MG-964, 2010.

the case separately, and we then compared the pairwise answers to identify similarities and differences with the intent of determining the likely impact of coder bias and differentiation in coder expertise. Results from this test were inconclusive, suggesting significant and unhelpful variation in coder analysis.[3] This in turn contributed to our ultimate decision to discard the quantitative findings from our coding effort.

Coding 60 questions three times across each case generated 180 codes per case for 14 cases for 2,520 data points. Only ten of the coded cases provided data we believed to be sufficiently clean and accurate for analysis. Two generated data that we deemed to be inaccurate, one was determined ex post facto to be an inappropriate case selection, and one generated incomplete data. To analyze the results from these remaining 1,800 coded data points, we converted all text to UTF-8 standard, created question property files to standardize questions according to category, cleaned the data for coding and entry errors, created a mini-model question list, created a case object for storing ingested data, converted case studies into a bit matrix data structure, and then completed the generation of the full dataset.[4] This involved reducing the set of questions on each case to cover their high-level factors. For example, rather than include multiple questions on specific types of cohesion (vertical, horizontal, etc.), we used the single, aggregate code for overall cohesion. This allowed for a reduced set of codes/features that described each case.

For each bit matrix we performed a PCA for dimensional reduction. This process reveals the complexity of the data and the number of dimensions needed to characterize the results. We then built a covariance matrix to see which factors, or variables, move together and which opposed one another. We then conducted pairwise distance measures. This involved creating matrices based on comparisons of similarities between variables across all ten cases.[5]

The purpose of all this data processing was to determine (1) the complexity of will to fight and (2) of all coding queries, which had the highest correspondence to high will to fight and conflict outcomes? Our PCA analyzed the data in sets of questions designed to help isolate important variables and variable relationships.

Our results—based on a small n and not statistically significant—suggest that will to fight is complex and highly multidimensional. In other words, several dimensions of

---

[3]   Ideally we would have used these inconclusive results to adjust our coding process. However, we did not receive results from two participants until late in the research process. We were not afforded the time or resources to revisit our coding process at that point. The intercoder reliability effort was not conclusive.

[4]   Bit matrix is a technique for reducing data to a matrix of all 0s and 1s, allowing for a wider range of distance-based and topic measures to be used to analyze data. The general approach is that a single question, Q1, that might be answered as High, Medium, or Low can be converted into three columns, Q1_High, Q1_Medium, and Q1_Low, where cases that were coded with a High would place a 1 in the Q1_High column, 0s in the others, and so on.

[5]   This involved Hamming distance, or simple binary matching; Jaccard distance, or binary matching accounting for the set size of used features; and cosine distance, or an analysis of the vectors in space (do variables point in the same direction?).

variable relationships would be required to explain variation, in contrast to less complex cases in which the first dimension can usually explain at least 50 percent of variation. Nothing in the data helped us identify points of divergence or convergence. This analysis suggests that will to fight is, unsurprisingly, increasingly complex as more data are considered.

Simple models of will to fight may have the most power to show differentiation. However, based on our reading of the literature, these simple models tend to be predicated on nearly tautological assumptions about the relevance of unitary factors. Cohesion is the best contemporary example of this approach. Some studies of cohesion might be summarized as follows: Cohesion matters most to will to fight; therefore we will focus our analysis on cohesion; and our analysis shows that cohesion matters most. Not all analyses of cohesion or other prospective unitary factors take this approach; some do, but others are more nuanced and thoughtful. We did not find examples of empirical small-set data analyses on will to fight that produced sufficiently replicable or generalizable data to suggest the existence of a unitary will-to-fight factor.

There were some correlations in the coded case study data. We found high will to fight to be associated with state and national issues of economic independence, social and political indoctrination (or coercive discipline and ideology), government willingness to take risks, high cohesion within the military, merit-based culture, and taking the operational offensive against a defensive adversary. Low will to fight was associated with incompetence of leadership, regardless of the legitimacy of government. History mattered: A history of poor leadership and military failure suggested low will to fight. Economic dependency, situational and temporary hatred of the adversary, and low military cohesion also correlated with low will to fight. We were surprised to find that legitimacy of leadership and military obedience had no discernible relationship with will to fight in any direction.

These correlations were interesting, but they should not be used to draw conclusions about will to fight. Ten cases compose an insufficient sample to produce generalizable findings. The weakness of the statistical results suggests the lack of a unitary factor and the importance of looking at will to fight holistically. However, once again the small n case set precludes a firm finding. We can say that no one part of the nine-part multimethod approach identified a generalizable unitary factor, but we cannot definitively say that one does not exist.

What, then, were we able to glean from this effort? First and foremost the process of thinking through the coding questions and reading the cases with an eye toward will to fight was highly informative for our qualitative analysis of will to fight. As one of our external participants noted, "You are asking the right questions."[6] While the case set was unhelpfully small, the depth of analysis—60 questions and 180 codes for each case, as well as required source data, detailed response explanations for each code,

---

[6]   Contracted case study participant, quote provided in person to the lead author of the report, 2017.

and analyst insights regarding the value of each response to will to fight—generated a wealth of analysis for each case. Asking these questions required team members to examine them in detail, revealing interesting and informative case-specific information for each of the 60 questions. Will to fight is normally woven into historical literature; sometimes it stands out, while in other cases it is one of many variables. Focusing specifically on will to fight shined a light on questions that are often unasked or under-appreciated, or at least insufficiently compared.

We discerned several trends in will-to-fight cases from this effort, none of which can be generalized but all of which should help inform the design of follow-on research questions and methods. We present these with the understanding that they are anecdotal rather than scientifically generalizable conclusions:

- Will-to-fight cases should be examined and described using some kind of longitudinal format rather than in fixed, declarative terms. Will to fight changed to varying degrees over the course of the war in each case we examined. Understanding these changes may be essential to rooting out the most important factors in each case.
- In the cases we examined, historico-cultural context was exceptionally important in understanding will to fight at the societal, state, and organizational levels of analysis. In the Vietnam War case the differences between northern and southern history and cultural context had a clear and perhaps decisive impact on comparative will to fight.
- There do not appear to be any unitary theories that explain will to fight in any one case. Factors that appeared to have the most influence on will to fight changed significantly from case to case.
- Even the most conventional, head-to-head combat cases that lent themselves to the most detailed quantitative and mechanistic analyses had significant will-to-fight components. The ebb of French will to fight in the later stages of World War I changed a battlefield dynamic that otherwise looked fairly evenly matched.

This effort set a baseline for future case study analysis, perhaps helping other researchers to refine case coding of will to fight into a more streamlined and digestible format. Most importantly, the case study effort informed the development of the RAND Arroyo Center model: It helped us refine, describe, and isolate the factors.

American Military Doctrine and the Will to Fight

As we argue in the body text of this report, neither the Army nor the Marine Corps has settled on an agreed-on model for will to fight. Neither service has found a way to address will to fight of ally and enemy forces. For the U.S. military, the lack of external focus is partly mitigated by episodes of acute self-examination and correction: American officials have made significant, if sometimes uneven, efforts to sustain and improve *American* will to fight over the past half century. U.S. Army and Marine Corps emphasis on leadership, realistic training, mission-type orders, esprit de corps, discipline, and morale all stems in part from an array of French, British, and officially sponsored American analyses of will to fight.[1] These efforts include S. L. A. Marshall's and Samuel A. Stouffer's works for the U.S. Army during and after World War II, Trevor N. Dupuy's extensive combat effectiveness studies, and Charles C. Moskos's analysis of American will to fight in the Vietnam War.[2]

The Army went on to sponsor further research into force morale and cohesion, particularly after the Vietnam War and during the initial period of the All-Volunteer Force.[3] This interest and effort are reflected in the surge in morale and cohesion literature in the late 1970s and early 1980s. The present RAND Arroyo Center study is also

---

[1] Mission-type orders, or simply mission orders, are military operation orders given with purposeful concision. They state what needs to be done and why it needs to be done, often in a single sentence. Units tasked with the mission are then given leeway to determine the best way to accomplish it and to adapt to changing battlefield conditions as needed.

[2] Kellett, 1982, describes a range of other studies sponsored by the U.S. military from World War II through the end of the Vietnam War. Our literature review brings to light additional studies that occurred after Kellett published *Combat Motivation*. See S. L. A. Marshall, *Men Against Fire: The Problem of Battle Command in Future War*, Washington, D.C.: U.S. War Department, 1947; Samuel A. Stouffer, Arthur A. Lumsdaine, Marion Harper Lumsdaine, Robin M. Williams, Jr., M. Brewster Smith, Irving L. Janis, Shirley A. Star, and Leonard S. Cottrell, Jr., *The American Soldier: Combat and Its Aftermath*, Princeton, N.J.: Princeton University Press, 1949; Dupuy and Hammerman, 1980; Moskos, 1975.

[3] These studies included development and brief implementation of the Cohesion, Operational Readiness, Training (COHORT) system in the early 1980s, sponsorship of Guy Siebold's cohesion analysis in the late 1980s, and a range of other studies. See Monte D. Smith and Joseph D. Hagman, *Personnel Stabilization and Cohesion: A Summary of Key Literature Findings*, Alexandria, Va.: Army Research Laboratory, 2004; Guy L. Siebold, "The Evolution of the Measurement of Cohesion," *Military Psychology*, Vol. 11, No. 1, 1999, pp. 5–26.

testament to the Army's interest in rectifying gaps in military practice. Marine Corps efforts to assess internal and external will to fight have generally paralleled those of the Army, and included focused efforts to build a holistic understanding of combat effectiveness.[4]

Despite all of these post–World War II efforts, including all of the intellectual contributions of adaptive and free-thinking American military officers in the 1970s and 1980s and the many incidents of individual brilliance at all levels of command, contemporary American land force adoption of will-to-fight theory for allies and adversaries amounts to lip service. The reasons for this failure appear to be twofold: the persistent complexity and intangibility of will to fight, and the equally persistent lure of the tangible, and therefore manageable, aspects of war.

World War II to the 1980s

Capstone military doctrine provides a window into the contemporaneous thoughts of senior military leaders. It tells the force what matters, and—often by omission—what does not. Prior to World War II, *in doctrine*, the U.S. Army and, to a lesser extent, the U.S. Marine Corps embraced many of the principles espoused in Clausewitz's *On War*.[5] Morale figured prominently in Army Brigadier General Arthur L. Wagner's 1895 *Organization and Tactics*. This was one of the most influential late nineteenth-century U.S. Army manuals on warfare. Wagner cites Clausewitz as a source.[6] Army manuals during World War I tended to offer technical instruction rather than broad observations on war, but field regulations between the world wars emphasized the human element in war, most likely as a result of the Army's experiences in trenches in France.

Postwar lessons began to filter into the 1923 version of the *Field Service Regulations*: "Infantry fighting power rests upon the basis of morale."[7] Interwar Army manu-

---

For an explanation of the All-Volunteer Force, see Richard N. Cooper, *Military Manpower and the All-Volunteer Force*, Santa Monica, Calif.: RAND Corporation, R-1450-ARPA, 1977.

[4] This is a reference to the adoption of maneuver warfare theory by the Army in the mid to late 1970s, and then by the Marine Corps from the late 1980s through the early 1990s. This section provides further detail on maneuver theory. In the mid to late 1970s the Defense Advanced Research Project Agency helped the Marine Corps conduct a detailed, multiyear analysis of military effectiveness that included aspects of will to fight. See Richard E. Hayes, Paul C. Davis, John J. Hayes, Farid Abolfathi, and Bill Harvey, *Measurement of Unit Effectiveness in Marine Corps Infantry Battalions*, Washington, D.C.: DARPA, October 31, 1977.

[5] Prior to World War II the Marine Corps often relied on Army doctrinal and training manuals. It published a landing force manual in 1939 that focused on amphibious doctrine. The *Small Wars Manual* published in 1940 devoted considerable space to aspects of will to fight, but this manual was not widely disseminated or adopted by the Marine Corps. U.S. Marine Corps, *Small Wars Manual*, Washington, D.C.: Government Printing Office, 1940.

[6] Arthur L. Wagner, *Organization and Tactics*, Kansas City, Mo.: Hudson-Kimberly Publishing Co., 1895, p. XIV. Wagner was a captain at the time. For a review of various manuals and theories, see John L. Romjue, *American Army Doctrine for the Post-Cold War*, Fort Leavenworth, Kan.: U.S. Army Training and Doctrine Command, 1997.

[7] U.S. Army, *Field Service Regulations*, Washington, D.C.: Government Printing Office, 1923, p. 11.

als described warfare as a tool of political effort designed to break the enemy's "will to war." By 1939 the Army was arguing for the centrality of the human over physical and technical factors:[8]

> Man is the fundamental instrument in war; other instruments may change but he remains a constant factor. Unless his behavior and elemental attributes are understood, gross mistakes will be made in planning operations and in troop leading. . . . In spite of advances in technique, the worth of the *individual* man is still decisive. . . . The *combat value* of a unit is determined by the soldierly qualities of its leader and members and its "will to fight."

However, the Army went on to describe intelligence as a technical task designed to identify enemy equipment and movements.[9] Enemy will to fight mattered, but Army officers were expected to focus primarily on the will to fight of their own forces. Even when the manual emphasized the importance of the enemy's will to fight, it suggested that not much could be done to assess enemy will unless a "reliable index of these factors has been gained through previous combat."[10] In other words, assessing enemy will to fight is hard, and no standardized measure exists. The manual does not address ally will to fight.

Nonetheless, a doctrinal focus on morale, leadership, and will was effectively sustained through the end of the war. In 1944 the Army wrote, "The combat value of a unit is determined in great measure by the soldierly qualities of its leaders and members and its will to fight."[11] Figure C.1 depicts the representation of will to fight in a sample of Army manuals from 1895 through 1944. This is a fairly representative cycle of the broader ebb and flow of will to fight in Western military thought.

After World War II the United States became embroiled in a seemingly endless series of complex, ill-defined, and frustrating interventions in places such as Korea, Vietnam, Lebanon, and El Salvador. American officers stymied by the inability to achieve strategic victory had to satisfy higher echelon demands for progress with anything that smacked of tangible results. This trend started during the stalemate period of the Korean War and hit its first peak during the Vietnam War.[12] From the early 1960s through the end of the Vietnam War in 1975, the tactical, tangible, and often misleading or irrelevant data of war—numbers of enemy killed, miles of highway open

---

[8] U.S. Army, *Tentative Field Service Regulations: Operations*, FM 100-5, Washington, D.C.: Government Printing Office, 1939, pp. 29–31; emphasis in original. These pages also emphasized the destruction of enemy forces.

[9] U.S. Army, 1939, p. 38.

[10] U.S. Army, 1939, p. 58.

[11] U.S. Army, *Field Service Regulation: Operations*, FM 100-5, Washington, D.C.: War Department, 1944, p. 29.

[12] Scott Sigmund Gartner and Marissa Edmund Myers, "Body Counts and 'Success' in the Vietnam and Korean Wars," *Journal of Interdisciplinary History*, Vol. 25, No. 3, 1994, pp. 377–395.

Figure C.1
Changing Emphasis on Will to Fight in U.S. Army Manuals, 1895–1944

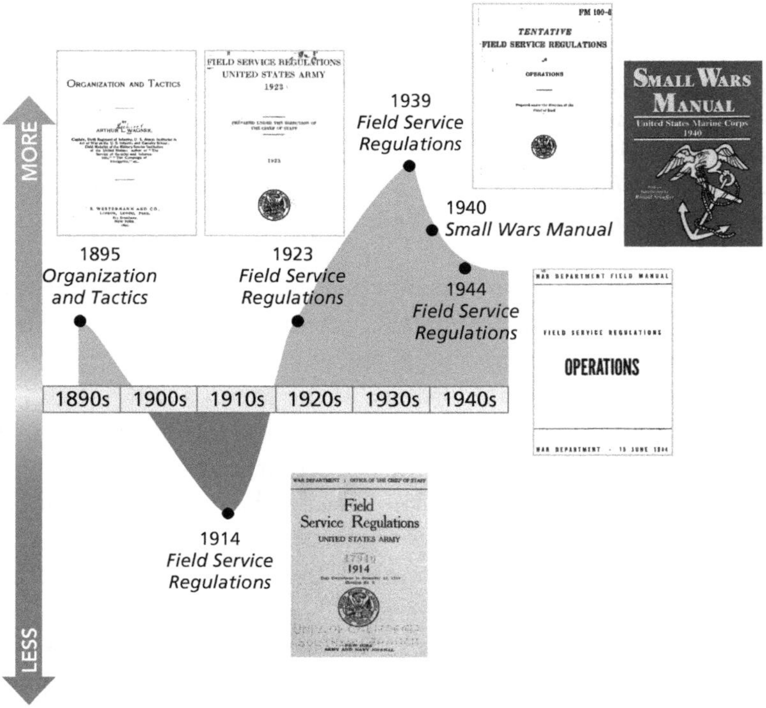

to traffic, and even total bars of soap distributed to the population—drove operational intelligence and analyses.[13]

Army and Marine veterans of the Vietnam War, sobered by America's first strategic defeat since the War of 1812, saw the postwar period as a chance to realign doctrine and practice with the unchanging nature of war.[14] This short-lived, uneven, and incomplete renaissance of will to fight offers lessons for current practice.

From the beginning of World War II through the mid-1970s, U.S. Army doctrine accepted that will to fight was at least of coequal importance to the role of physical force.[15] This was the Army's position in the 1949 version of *Operations*: "The ultimate

---

[13] Connable, 2012; Emily Mushen and Jonathan Schroden, *Are We Winning? A Brief History of Military Operations Assessment*, Alexandria, Va.: Center for Naval Analyses, September 2014. Chapter Three of this report addresses the U.S. military's failure to effectively convey the importance of partner or adversary will to fight in Vietnam.

[14] Suzanne C. Nielsen, *The U.S. Army's Post-Vietnam Recovery and the Dynamics of Change in Military Organizations*, Carlisle, Pa.: U.S. Army War College Strategic Studies Institute, September 2010.

[15] Robert A. Doughty, *The Evolution of US Army Tactical Doctrine, 1946–76*, Leavenworth Paper No. 1, Fort Leavenworth, Kan.: U.S. Army Combat Studies Institute, August 1979. Language from the 1939 version of FM 100-5 survived through the 1941, 1943, and 1944 versions, with changes thereafter.

objective of all military operations is the destruction of the enemy's armed forces *and* his will to fight."[16] Explicit mention of will to fight disappeared from *Operations* in 1968. But this version, written at the height of the Vietnam War, stated, "Despite advances in technology, man remains the most essential element on the battlefield." In the same 1968 manual the Army recognized that there were "certain intangibles" that would affect the outcome of battle, including enemy "will to resist," but that there was "no precise method" for understanding these intangibles. Understanding of the internal Army will to fight was clearer. For the 1968 Army, combat power derived from physical means as well as discipline, morale, and esprit de corps, all elements of will to fight.[17] Will to fight mattered, but not more than any other factor in war. The same was generally true for the Marine Corps.[18]

The U.S. Army took a different turn in the mid-1970s. Soviet conventional power was blossoming in eastern Europe as NATO nations struggled through economic doldrums and social upheaval. It looked like the United States and its allies might actually lose a prospective conventional war in Europe, or be forced into a cataclysmic nuclear exchange. Post-Vietnam morale in the Army and Marine Corps was low. One year after the United States withdrew from Vietnam the Army wrote a new doctrine called Active Defense. This new capstone doctrine all but eliminated will to fight from the Army's conceptualization of warfare.[19] The 1976 and 1977 versions of *Operations* did not even seek to define the term *will to fight*.[20] Morale, cohesion, and other human aspects of warfare were mentioned in passing, and primarily with a focus on the Army rather than on allied forces or on the enemy. Active Defense was met with severe critique.[21] It represented a nadir in doctrinal thought from which the Army would quickly recover. Debates over maneuver warfare, led by outsider William S. Lind, Army officers Donn A. Starry and Huba Wass de Czege, and Marine officers including G. I. Wilson, Alfred M. Gray, and John F. Schmitt, fed the reemergence of will to fight in doctrine.[22]

---

[16]   U.S. Army, *Operations*, FM 100-5, Washington, D.C.: Department of the Army, 1949, p. 80; Bill Benson, "The Evolution of Army Doctrine for Success in the 21st Century," *Military Review*, March–April 2012, pp. 2–12; emphasis added.

[17]   U.S. Army, *Operations*, FM 100-5, Washington, D.C.: Department of the Army, 1968, pp. 3-1, 3-5.

[18]   This was due in great part to the fact that the Marine Corps often relied on Army field manuals.

[19]   The best analysis of this doctrinal shift can be found in Paul H. Herbert, *Deciding What Has to Be Done: General William E. DePuy and the 1976 Edition of FM 100-5, Operations*, Leavenworth Paper No. 16, Fort Leavenworth, Kan.: U.S. Army Combat Studies Institute, July 1988.

[20]   U.S. Army, *Operations*, FM 100-5, Washington, D.C.: Department of the Army, 1977.

[21]   Jeffrey W. Long, *The Evolution of U.S. Army Doctrine: From Active Defense to AirLand Battle and Beyond*, thesis, Fort Leavenworth, Kan.: U.S. Army Command and General Staff College, 1991.

[22]   Huba Wass de Czege, "How to Change an Army," *Military Review*, Vol. 64, No. 11, November 1984, pp. 32–49; William S. Lind, *Maneuver Warfare Handbook*, New York: Westview Press, 1985; G. I. Wilson, Michael D. Wyly, William S. Lind, and B. E. Trainor, "The 'Maneuver Warfare' Concept," *Marine Corps Gazette*, Vol. 65, No. 4, April 1981, pp. 49–54; Fideleon Damian, *The Road to FMFM 1: The United States Marine Corps and*

Maneuver Warfare Versus the RMA: The RMA Wins

Maneuver warfare brought Clausewitzean theory and will to fight to the fore. Lind explained maneuver warfare as an embrace of the unchanging nature of war: All war is complex, dynamic, uncertain, and, most importantly, it is fundamentally a contest of opposing, independent wills. As he put it to the Marine Corps in 1980, "The objective is the enemy's mind not his body."[23] Maneuver warfare was offered as an operational approach, rather than an attrition approach or a technical solution, to Soviet conventional dominance in Europe. A smaller U.S. ground combat force could defeat the Soviet Army by identifying its center of gravity, using combined arms and maneuver to place it on the horns of a dilemma, thereby forcing it to break or surrender. Maneuver warfare emerged in parallel to the RMA, a theory weighted toward technological and information advances rather than the human aspects of war.[24] Parallel theoretical debate led to a parallel struggle for control of military doctrine. After a brief shining moment from 1989 through 1993, RMA all but eliminated maneuver warfare and will to fight.

Will to Fight in Post-Vietnam Army Doctrine and the Brick Wall of the RMA

In 1982 GEN Donn A. Starry, commander of the U.S. Army Training and Doctrine Command, adopted parts of maneuver warfare theory in one of the periodic revisions to *Operations*, FM 100-5. He reversed Active Defense and instituted the Army's groundbreaking *AirLand Battle* doctrine.[25] Starry and his doctrine writers took a middle-ground approach, adopting and emphasizing some elements of Clausewitz—operational maneuver, mission-type orders, and tempo—while incorporating aspects of will to fight as lesser included concepts.[26] Even with all of the contemporaneous

---

Maneuver Warfare Doctrine, 1979–1989, thesis, Manhattan: Kansas State University, 2008; and John F. Schmitt, "The Great FMFM 1 Debate: Is There Anything New Here?" *Marine Corps Gazette*, Vol. 73, No. 11, November 1989, pp. 25–26.

[23]   William S. Lind, "Defining Maneuver Warfare for the Marine Corps," *Marine Corps Gazette*, Vol. 64, No. 3, March 1980, p. 56.

[24]   For descriptions and analyses of the RMA, see William A. Owens, "The Emerging U.S. System-of-Systems," *Strategic Forum*, Institute for National Strategic Studies, No. 63, February 1996; U.S. Joint Chiefs of Staff, *Joint Vision 2010*, Washington, D.C.: Joint Staff, May 30, 2000; Williamson Murray, "Thinking About Revolutions in Military Affairs," *Joint Forces Quarterly*, Summer 1997, pp. 69–76; Sabine Collmer, *Information as a Key Resource: The Influence of RMA and Network-Centric Operations on the Transformation of the German Armed Forces*, Garmisch, Germany: George C. Marshall European Center for Security Studies, February 2007, pp. 6–10; Lothar Ibrugger, *The Revolution in Military Affairs: Special Report*, NATO Parliamentary Assembly, Science and Technology Committee, November 1998; and Barry R. Schneider and Lawrence E. Grinter, eds., *Battlefield of the Future: 21st Century Warfare Issues*, 3rd ed., Montgomery, Ala.: Air University Press, 1998.

[25]   U.S. Army, *Operations*, FM 100-5, Washington, D.C.: Headquarters Department of the Army, August 20, 1982; Donn A. Starry, "To Change an Army," *Military Review*, Vol. 63, No. 3, March 1983, pp. 20–31.

[26]   For a full accounting of this development process, see John L. Romjue, *From Active Defense to AirLand Battle: The Development of Army Doctrine, 1973–1982*, Fort Monroe, Va.: U.S. Army Training and Doctrine Command, June 1984.

emphasis on maneuver warfare, will to fight reemerged in Army doctrine only as one of those "intangible factors" that might or might not be most important in deciding the outcome of war. *AirLand Battle* was simply a return to the Army's post–World War II understanding of will to fight as *an* important, but not necessarily as *the most* important, factor in war. But this was a clear improvement over Active Defense.

AirLand Battle saw one update in 1986 and then foundered on two unpublished draft revisions. Starry's take on will to fight lasted until the next major revision of *Operations* in 1993.[27] The 1993 version of the Army's most important doctrinal manual was written just after the vivid, one-sided success in Operation Desert Storm in 1991. In the Vietnam War the United States lost to a far less well-equipped army. In Desert Storm a large, well-equipped enemy army broke and ran in the face of a sweeping combined arms invasion. Lightning victory against the Iraqi Army offered a stark, and what should have been a lasting, example of the value of breaking enemy will to fight. The post–Desert Storm period marked a rebirth for the U.S. Army and, at least in writing, a deeper embrace of will-to-fight concepts.[28] For the first time since World War II the Army defined will to fight: "Will is the disposition to act towards achievement of a desired end state. It is an expression of determination, the articulation of choice and desire."[29] The Army went on to frame war in Clausewitzean terms:[30]

> *War is a contest of wills.* Combat power is the product of military forces and their will to fight. When will is lacking, so is combat power; when will is strong, it multiplies the effectiveness of military forces. *Ultimately, the focus of all combat operations must be to the enemy's will.* Break his will and he is defeated. When he no longer wants to fight, he cannot fight. Conversely, if his will remains strong, even though physically weakened and materially depleted, he remains a formidable opponent.

Later in the same manual the Army takes this approach to will to fight a step further. It seeks to explain the sources of will to fight and takes a clear and uncompromising position on the ultimate source of will to fight. Ostensibly this applies to the U.S. Army, allied armies, and adversaries:[31]

---

[27]   The 1986 version of *Operations* did not provide any substantive changes regarding will to fight. According to Army major Jeff W. Karohs, two later unpublished drafts did not include mention of moral factors or will to fight. He wrote, "[T]he moral domain is not addressed to any great extent in either of two recent official drafts." Jeff W. Karohs, *AirLand Battle-Future—A Hop, Skip, or Jump?*, monograph, Fort Leavenworth, Kan.: U.S. Army Command and General Staff College, December 15, 1990, p. 5.

[28]   For an examination of this period, see Michael McCormick, *The New FM 100-5: A Return to Operational Art*, monograph, Fort Leavenworth, Kan.: U.S. Army School of Advanced Military Studies, April 18, 1997.

[29]   U.S. Army, 1993, p. 6-7

[30]   U.S. Army, 1993, p. 6-7; emphasis added.

[31]   U.S. Army, 1993, p. 6-7.

Leaders are the main source of will. They inspire their soldiers with the desire to win, to accomplish the mission, and to persevere in the face of all difficulties. When the will of the enemy commander is broken, his force quickly disintegrates. Analyzing and attacking the underpinnings of his will therefore is key to victory.

It is not clear how the Army came to such a singular and decisive conclusion. While the renewed emphasis on will to fight was, from our perspective, welcomed and helpful, it is not proven that leaders are the main source of will in every case. There are many cases where leadership appeared to be the key element in will to fight, but there is no causal proof to support this explanation of will to fight. Our research shows that good leadership is primarily an enabler of will to fight. But it is not true that units inevitably disintegrate when commanders break. There are many instances in both twentieth- and twenty-first-century warfare when commanders have broken in combat but units have carried on with new commanders—including noncommissioned officers—in charge. This example is from the Vietnam War:[32]

> During a battalion-size search and destroy mission, an infantry company was ambushed by a VC [Viet Cong] battalion at approximately 1000 hours. In the initial contact, the company commander and artillery forward observer were killed. The company first sergeant notified the company executive officer. . . . The executive officer crawled into a B-52 shellhole and refused to command the company. . . . The first sergeant assumed command of the company through the entire action.

In this case the unit fought on; later the executive officer was relieved and the first sergeant was awarded a medal. While the definitive statements on leadership and will to fight may have been unsubstantiated, the concept helped draw the Army back toward the human aspects of war. Army doctrine writers pressed forward in an unpublished 1998 draft of *Operations*, this time including morale as a "principle of operations."[33] But neither this principle nor the brief 1993 embrace of will to fight would survive the RMA.[34] Will to fight hit a plateau in 1993 and then fell from grace.

By the mid-1990s, promises to concretize war had temporarily reburied Clausewitz and will to fight. Some wished for a more permanent interment. In 1995 Steven Metz of the Army War College wrote a scathing indictment of Clausewitz, the enduring nature of war, and by necessary inclusion the preeminence of will to fight:[35]

---

[32]   Thomas V. Draude, *When Should a Commander Be Relieved: A Study of Combat Reliefs of Commanders of Battalions and Lower Units During the Vietnam Era*, Fort Leavenworth, Kan.: U.S. Army Command and General Staff College, June 11, 1976, p. 44.

[33]   See Russell W. Glenn, "No More Principles of War?" *Parameters*, Spring 1998, pp. 48–66.

[34]   See Harry K. Lesser, Jr., *The Revolution in Military Affairs and Its Effect on the Future Army*, thesis, Newport, R.I.: U.S. Naval War College, 1994. Lesser, then a U.S. Army colonel, argued that the RMA constituted a necessary step beyond maneuver warfare, and that "knowledge warfare" made maneuver warfare obsolete.

[35]   Steven Metz, "A Wake for Clausewitz: Toward a Philosophy of 21st Century Warfare," *Parameters*, Vol. 24, 1994–1995, p. 126.

Like adoration for some family elder, the veneration heaped on Clausewitz seems to grow even as his power to explain the world declines. . . . *On War* is treated like holy script from which quotations are plucked to legitimize all sorts of policies and programs. But enough! It is time to hold a wake so that strategists can pay their respects to Clausewitz and then move on, leaving him to rest among the historians.

For Metz and other RMA proponents, technology in the form of advanced information systems and precision strikes would change what they saw as the not-so-enduring nature of war.[36] Human factors like will to fight would be far less relevant than the technical and material aspects of warfare.[37] In this view, Desert Storm was a lesson in the dominance of technology rather than in the importance of will to fight.[38] Most RMA publications barely mentioned the human aspect of war, or they described ways in which technology would obviate or overwhelm human inputs to combat.[39] Table C.1 shows how the RMA differs from maneuver warfare theory in its application of basic Clausewitzean theories about the enduring nature of war and will

Table C.1
Comparison of Will-to-Fight Tenets in Maneuver Warfare and the RMA

Warfighting Concept	Maneuver Warfare	RMA
High-tempo, pinpoint attacks are most successful	✔	✔
Maneuver can disrupt enemy command, control	✔	✔
War is a contest of opposing, independent wills	✔	✖
Will to fight is the preeminent factor in war	✔	✖
Military effectiveness is primarily a matter of will	✔	✖
Winning necessitates understanding adversary will	✔	–

---

[36] Some RMA advocates might dispute this argument. This represents subjective expert opinion. See Eliot A. Cohen, "A Revolution in Warfare," *Foreign Affairs*, Vol. 75, No. 2, March–April 1996, pp. 37–54; Connable, 2012, Appendix E.

[37] Others, like Martin Van Creveld, argued that will to fight mattered but only for supposedly irrational insurgent and terrorist fanatics against who (in Metz's interpretation of Van Creveld's work) would negate the very concepts of deterrence and conflict resolution. Metz, 1994–1995, p. 132.

[38] This theory is directly contradicted by official postwar analysis. Thomas A. Keaney and Eliot A. Cohen, *Gulf War Air Power Survey: Summary Report*, Washington, D.C.: U.S. Air Force, 1993, pp. 235–251.

[39] For example, *Joint Vision 2010* allows for the importance of human factors only in irregular war, when "we cannot bring our technological capabilities fully to bear." Even in this case, physical aspects of war take priority over "moral strengths." U.S. Joint Chiefs of Staff, 2000, p. 27. For a critique of this approach, see Scott Stephenson, "The Revolution in Military Affairs: 12 Observations on an Out-of-Fashion Idea," *Military Review*, May-June 2010, pp. 38–46. Some RMA advocates misinterpreted Clausewitz, arguing that he represented physical defeat of the military as the ultimate purpose of war. For example: John A. Warden III, "Air Theory for the Twenty-First Century," in Schneider and Grinter, 1998, pp. 103–124.

to fight. Other than inconsistent recognition of the importance of enemy will to fight as a possible center of gravity, the RMA almost completely deemphasized will to fight. Italicized warfighting concepts specifically address will to fight.[40]

The RMA was an explicit reinforcement of the American predilection to seek tangible explanations for warfare that might avoid the complexity of the Clausewitzean human element. By the time the Army published its next version of *Operations* in 2001—at the peak of RMA fervor and on the verge of the 9/11 attacks—will to fight had once again been relegated to a narrow, secondary consideration.[41]

Maneuver Warfare and Will to Fight in the Marine Corps

While the Marines contemplated maneuver warfare as early as 1979, their experimentation lagged slightly behind the Army's throughout the 1980s.[42] The Marines made up for this lag with a wholehearted embrace of maneuver theory beginning in 1989. Building from *Warfighting*, the Marine Corps enshrined maneuver warfare in a slew of unabashedly Clausewitzean doctrinal publications.[43] Marine leaders like Alfred M. Gray gave extensive leeway to writers like John F. Schmitt, who in turn translated the canonical interpretation of will to fight into the Marine Corps' new warfighting "philosophy."[44] By the early 1990s, maneuver and will to fight were the central tenets of Marine doctrine.

Some Marine officers welcomed this new approach. Others were turned off by the more esoteric aspects of maneuver warfare.[45] Maneuver theory suffered from its association with unfamiliar and, for some, off-putting German terms like *Schwerpunkt* (center of gravity) and *Fingerspitzengefuehl* (fingertip feel, or combat intuition). These exotic words made for interesting schoolhouse discussion, but for some they proved hard to translate into practical techniques and procedures. Linguistic association with the German Wehrmacht and, perhaps unfairly, with the Nazis did not help.[46] Some of the more extreme incantations by maneuver warfare proponents tended to leave offi-

---

[40]   This table is aggregated from all of the sources on both theories cited throughout this report.

[41]   U.S. Army, *Operations*, FM 3-0, Washington, D.C.: Headquarters, Department of the Army, June 2001.

[42]   For a chronology of professional Marine Corps articles on maneuver warfare, see Kenneth F. McKenzie, Jr., "On the Verge of a New Era: The Marine Corps and Maneuver Warfare," *Marine Corps Gazette*, Vol. 77, No. 7, July 1993, p. 65.

[43]   These include *Warfighting*, as well as subsequent publications in a series on leadership, command and control, campaigning, intelligence, and logistics. Each of these warfighting publications is derived from Clausewitzean theory.

[44]   Then-commandant of the Marine Corps Charles C. Krulak described maneuver warfare as the Corps' warfighting philosophy in the 1997 version of Marine Corps Doctrinal Publication-1 (MCDP-1), Foreword.

[45]   For example: Andrew D. Walker, "An Alternative to Maneuver Warfare," *Marine Corps Gazette*, Vol. 75, No. 11, November 1991, pp. 48–51; Gary W. Anderson, "When Maneuver Fails," *Marine Corps Gazette*, Vol. 73, No. 4, April 1989, pp. 57–59. Also see Terriff, 2006.

[46]   William S. Lind, "Why the German Example?" *Marine Corps Gazette*, Vol. 66, No. 6, June 1982, pp. 59–63.

cers and noncommissioned officers cold to the surging re-embrace of Clausewitz: The idea of winning without fighting—an arguably excessive interpretation of his theory—seemed fantastical.[47] Mentions of Clausewitz began to elicit some audible groans in Marine Corps classrooms.[48] Efforts to embrace and understand ally and enemy will to fight remained anemic throughout the 1990s.

Practice never truly matched doctrine in either the Army or the Marine Corps during the heights of will-to-fight discourse. Heady promises of an RMA essentially blunted wholesale implementation of maneuver warfare in the 1990s.[49] Then doctrine gave way as well. By the early 2000s, the act of achieving temporary, tactical effects like destroying vehicles, shattering command and control nodes, or killing individual soldiers—all of which can contribute to breaking enemy will—had become an end unto itself.[50]

Will-to-Fight Doctrine and Practice: Post-9/11 and Current Issues

Army doctrine sidelined will to fight in the 2001 FM 3-0, and then dropped it completely in the Army's 2011–2012 capstone doctrinal series.[51] Clausewitz and will to fight returned to capstone doctrine in ADP 3-0 in 2016. Figure C.2 extends Figure C.1 to show the ebb and flow of the doctrinal emphasis on will to fight in the Army and the Marine Corps from 1895 through 2017.

---

[47] B. A. Friedman, "Maneuver Warfare: A Defense," *Marine Corps Gazette*, Vol. 98, No. 12, 2014, pp. 26–29; Jeffrey J. Lloyd, "Our Warfighting Philosophy," *Marine Corps Gazette*, Vol. 73, No. 11, November 1989, pp. 24–25; Richard D. Hooker, Jr., "The Mythology Surrounding Maneuver Warfare," *Parameters*, Spring 1993, p. 32; Connable, 2016, Chapter Seven. Also see G. S. Lauer, *Maneuver Warfare Theory: Creating a Tactically Unbalanced Fleet Marine Force?* Fort Leavenworth, Kan.: U.S. Army School of Advanced Military Studies, December 24, 1990.

[48] This is a direct observation of the lead author of this report, who served as a U.S. Marine from 1988 through 2009.

[49] For example: Connable, 2012, Appendix E; Michael S. Chmielewski, "Maybe It's Time to Reconsider Maneuver Warfare," *Marine Corps Gazette*, Vol. 86, No. 8, 2002, pp. 65–67.

[50] For example: Connable, 2012, Appendix E; and U.S. Joint Forces Command, 2006. The latter publication is an example of effects-based operations theory turned to practice. It does not mention will to fight, mentions morale only in passing, and quotes Clausewitz but not about will to fight. Joint doctrine has never fully embraced will to fight, most likely as a residual artifact of the RMA. As of mid-2018, joint military doctrine does not even define the term *will to fight*. It defines *morale* only in terms of recreation.

[51] ADP 1-0 briefly mentions enemy cohesion on page 2-2. ADRP 3-0, a reference publication, mentions *will to fight* three times and the *contest of wills* once, all in passing. U.S. Army, *The Army*, ADP 1-0, Washington, D.C.: Headquarters, Department of the Army, September 2012g; U.S. Army, *Intelligence*, ADP 2-0, Washington, D.C.: Headquarters, Department of the Army, August 2012d; U.S. Army, 2012f; U.S. Army, *Unified Land Operations*, ADP 3-0, Washington, D.C.: Headquarters, Department of the Army, October 2011; U.S. Army, *Unified Land Operations*, ADRP 3-0, Washington, D.C.: Headquarters, Department of the Army, May 2012a; and U.S. Army, *The Operations Process*, ADP 5-0, Washington, D.C.: Headquarters, Department of the Army, May 2012b. Also see U.S. Army, *Operations*, FM 3-0, Washington, D.C.: Headquarters, Department of the Army, February 2008a.

Figure C.2
Changing Emphasis on Will to Fight in Army and Marine Doctrine, 1895–2017

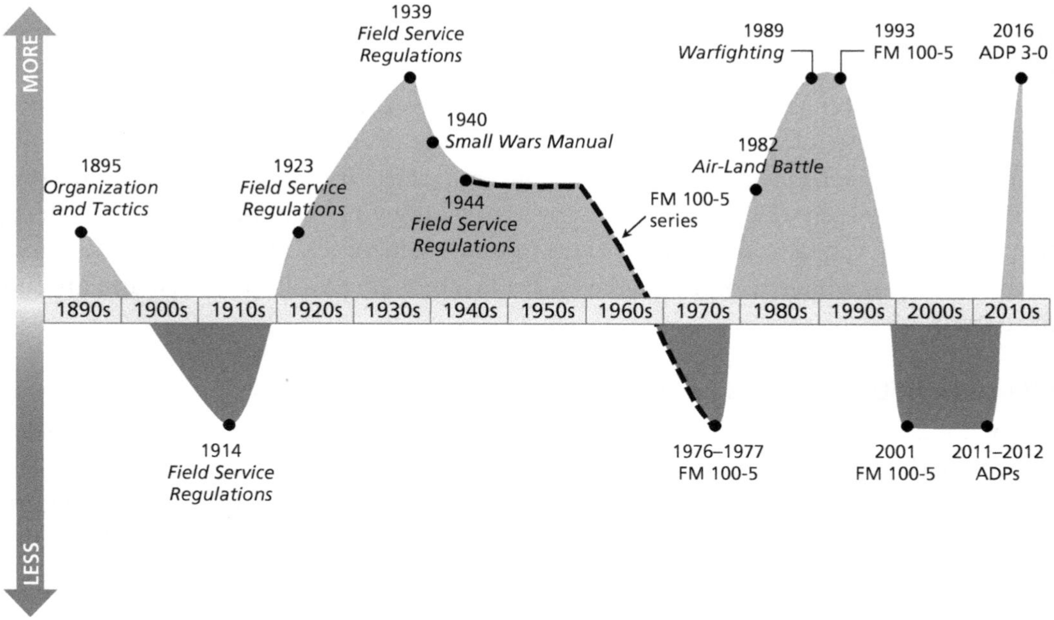

NOTE: FSR = Field Service Regulation
RAND RR2341A-C.2

It is not clear whether the reintroduction of will to fight in ADP 3-0 marks a paradigm shift for Army doctrine; as this research was concluding, there had been no updates to the remaining ADPs. *Warfighting* lives on as the Marines' philosophy of warfighting, but in a 2015 article, Daniel Grazier and William Lind argued that the Marine Corps gave up on maneuver warfare shortly after it was implemented: "With General Gray's retirement, that is where the effort largely stopped."[52] Gray retired in 1991. This argument may be overstated, but our initial assessment shows that the essential element of maneuver warfare theory—will to fight—played only a minor and sometimes negligible part in advisor or intelligence assessment practices.

Will to Fight in Conventional Force Advising

Both services generally failed to develop consistent and grounded methods for assessing ally will to fight. Post–Vietnam War dynamics were unhelpful: The conventional advisor community all but disappeared at the end of the Vietnam War.[53] Conventional

---

[52]   Daniel Grazier and William S. Lind, "Maneuver Warfare: Making It Real in the Marine Corps," *Marine Corps Gazette*, Vol. 99, No. 4, April 2015, p. 24. Also see Friedman, 2014.

[53]   Conventional forces advisors are from conventional, or general purpose, forces units rather than from special operations forces like the U.S. Army Special Forces (SF) or U.S. Marine Corps Raiders.

advisors did not reemerge until the early 2000s to support operations in Afghanistan and Iraq.[54] Consequently, many crucial advisor lessons from the Vietnam War were never incorporated into conventional forces doctrine.[55] Initial surveys of advisor practices suggest that almost no headway was made in assessing the will to fight of allied conventional forces.[56] Advisor assessments in the 2000s in Afghanistan and Iraq focused on building ally physical capabilities and reducing enemy manpower.[57] In 2009 the Army, summarizing lessons from Afghanistan and Iraq, wrote: "SFA must build the morale and confidence of the FSF [Foreign Security Force]."[58] It suggests a go-slow approach to build morale, but does not define morale, suggest how it should be assessed, or make any mention of the broader concept of will to fight.

For example, there was no structured effort to assess the will to fight of the Afghan National Security Forces (ANSF) between 2002 and 2010. For the first eight years of the war, advisors used a variety of color-coded checklists that ignored or buried human aspects of combat effectiveness.[59] In mid-2010 the advisors began to use the new Commanders Unit Assessment Tool (CUAT).[60] The first versions of this assessment tool

---

[54] This was not true of the special operations advisor community. U.S. SF routinely assessed partner will to fight. However, even the best of these assessments (typically written within the Special Operations Debrief and Retrieval System [SODARS]) tended to be unstructured, presented as parts of long narratives on multiple subjects, and difficult for those outside the SF or intelligence communities to obtain. Doctrine for SF advising tends to be restricted and cannot be referenced in this report. For example: U.S. Army, *Army Special Operations Forces Foreign Internal Defense*, FM 3-05.137, Washington, D.C.: Headquarters, Department of the Army, June 2008b, restricted distribution.

[55] For example: Remi Hajjar, "What Lessons Did We Learn (or Re-Learn) About Military Advising After 9/11?" *Military Review*, November-December 2014, pp. 63–75.

[56] This assessment will be refined in follow-on research planned for FY2018. For a summary of contemporary conventional forces advising, see Joshua J. Potter, *American Advisors: Security Forces Assistance Model in the Long War*, Fort Leavenworth, Kan.: U.S. Army Combat Studies Institute Press, 2011. This approximately 100-page report does not mention will to fight, morale, cohesion, or esprit, but does briefly discuss discipline and spends considerable space on leadership.

[57] This is made clear in recent histories of advising in Iraq and Afghanistan, as well as in the methods used to assess Iraqi and Afghan security forces. See U.S. Department of Defense, *Assessment of Afghan National Security Forces Metrics*, Washington, D.C.: DoD Inspector General, February 20, 2013; Pace L. Jaworsky, "Conventional Advising: A Tactical Leader's Assessment of a Strategic Initiative," *Armor*, January–March 2013, pp. 23–37.

[58] U.S. Army, *Security Force Assistance*, FM 3-07.1, Washington, D.C.: Headquarters, Department of the Army, May 2009, p. 2-6. More checklists and slightly more detail are provided in the manual on foreign internal defense (FID), but FID is primarily an SF mission. U.S. Army, *Army Special Operations Forces Foreign Internal Defense*, ATP 3-05.2, Washington, D.C.: Headquarters, Department of the Army, August 2015.

[59] For an example of the Training and Readiness Assessment Tool (TRAT), see Combined Security Transition Command-Afghanistan, "The Training Readiness Assessment Tool," *The Enduring Ledger*, April 2009, p. 18.

[60] The "U" in CUAT can also stand for *Update*. Karl Gingrich, Matthew Shane, and Matthew Durkin, "Measuring Quality of the ANSF," *Phalanx*, March 2011, p. 22. Previous iterations were the Capabilities Milestone system and the TRAT. Also see Adam Mausner, *Reforming ANSF Metrics: Improving the CUAT System*, Washington, D.C.: Center for Strategic and International Studies, August 2010; Terrence K. Kelly, Nora Bensahel, and

made little or no mention of will to fight.[61] In a later version advisors were asked to rate "unit morale" and, separately, "ANSF will to fight."[62] However, it is not clear from our research whether advisors had explanations of these terms, rating guidance, or training to assess will to fight.

Will to Fight in Military Intelligence Analysis

From 2001 through 2017 the Army and Marine Corps military intelligence communities neglected to aggressively pursue or publish methods for analyzing enemy will to fight. For example, neither the 2004 nor the 2010 version of the Army military intelligence field manual mentions will to fight. Both make only brief and oblique references to associated terms like *morale*.[63] Marine Corps intelligence manuals encourage the use of intelligence to find and analyze ways to break enemy cohesion, but do not define cohesion.[64] The 2004 and 2016 versions of the Marine Corps intelligence production and analysis manual provide a structured OOB assessment tool that includes assessment of *combat effectiveness*, which it defines as the "ability to perform intended mission or function expressed in a percentage." It does not suggest how this percentage might be derived or what role will to fight might play in describing combat effectiveness. Figure C.3 depicts this assessment tool.[65]

Our research suggests that the efforts of the advisor and intelligence communities to codify assessments of will to fight amount to an inconsistent series of checklists built on choppy one- or two-word explanations.[66] These brief explanations reveal little or no connection to theory or historical lessons. They leave it to each individual practitioner to define, understand, and explain will to fight in a way that might resonate

---

Olga Oliker, *Security Force Assistance in Afghanistan: Identifying Lessons for Future Efforts*, Santa Monica, Calif.: RAND Corporation, MG-1066-A, 2011.

[61]   CUAT data are classified or restricted. The blank form is unclassified. International Security Assistance Force (ISAF), *Instruction Manual for the Commander's Update Assessment Tool Located in CIDNE*, Kabul, Afghanistan: International Security Assistance Force, November 14, 2010.

[62]   Special Inspector General for Afghanistan Reconstruction, *Afghan National Security Forces: Actions Needed to Improve Plans for Sustaining Capability Assessment Efforts*, SIGAR 14-33 Audit Report, Washington, D.C.: Special Inspector General for Afghanistan Reconstruction, February 2014, p. 14.

[63]   U.S. Army, *Intelligence*, FM 2-0, Washington, D.C.: Headquarters, Department of the Army, May 2004; U.S. Army, *Intelligence*, FM 2-0, Washington, D.C.: Headquarters, Department of the Army, March 2010.

[64]   U.S. Marine Corps, *MAGTF Intelligence Production and Analysis*, MCTP 2-10B, Washington, D.C.: Headquarters, U.S. Marine Corps, May 2, 2016.

[65]   U.S. Marine Corps, *MAGTF Intelligence Production and Analysis*, Washington, D.C.: Headquarters, U.S. Marine Corps, July 13, 2004, p. 3-10. This table is identical in the 2016 version of the manual.

[66]   For example: U.S. Army and U.S. Marine Corps, *Intelligence Preparation of the Battlefield/Battlespace*, ATP 2-01.3/MCRP 2-3A, Washington, D.C.: Headquarters, Departments of the Army and Marine Corps, November 2014, p. 5-13. On pages 5-20 and 5-21 this manual suggests understanding discipline and honor in irregular organizations, but does not explain why these factors matter, how they should be assessed, or how they might be explained.

Figure C.3
Sample 2004 Marine Corps Order of Battle Intelligence Assessment

PARENT FORMATION								
Service		Formation or Unit Name		Alternative Name		Role		Superior Formation	
HQ Location Name		HQ Location Coordinates		Combat Effectiveness		Allegiance		Commander's Last Name	

SUBORDINATE FORMATIONS/UNITS									
Serial Number	Subordinate Unit or Formation Name	Location Coordinates	Role	Signature Equipment	Equipment Quantity	Commander's Last Name	Personnel Strength	Combat Effectiveness	Record Date/Update

Record Evaluation and Source	Remarks

SOURCE: U.S. Marine Corps, *MAGTF Intelligence Production and Analysis*, 2004, pp. 3–10
RAND *RR2341A-C.3*

with military commanders and political leaders, who in turn tend to view such assessments as unreliably subjective, unanchored in fact or theory, and therefore unreliable.[67] Absence of a structured assessment method for will to fight has continually affected the way commanders understand the forces on the battlefield. Impacts of this gap in understanding are immeasurable, but the gaps are plain to see.

Off-Ramping of Human Aspects of Military Operations

Development of advisor and intelligence will-to-fight assessment methods were also limited by partial diversion of responsibilities. Throughout the 2001–2017 time frame the information operations (Military Information Support Operations [MISO]) community took shape and began to absorb tasks that involved the term *influence*.[68] Any nonquantifiable issues involving the ways people think were dropped into the MISO bin, partially relieving the advisor and intelligence communities of the need to develop will-to-fight assessment methods. For example, as of December 2016, one of the primary duties of an Army information operations officer is to identify and understand

---

[67] See Connable, 2012, Chapters One, Five, Six, and Eight.

[68] The Army's official explanation of MISO includes the purpose to "create effects" intended to "influence, disrupt, corrupt, or usurp enemy or adversary decision making." U.S. Army, *Information Operations*, FM 3-13, Washington, D.C.: Headquarters, Department of the Army, December 2016c, p. 1-1.

"threat morale."[69] Whatever did not fall under information support operations was lumped in with culture and human terrain, and then for a time into the Human Terrain System.[70] By 2012, when the United States had withdrawn from Iraq and was drawing down from its surge in Afghanistan, nearly everything having to do with will to fight had been isolated from, or watered down in, advisor, intelligence, and operations processes of the conventional Army and Marine Corps.

Summary

Doctrine has been called the last refuge of the unimaginative.[71] But even if it is rarely applied as written, doctrine signals many things to a military force. It conveys an overarching theory of warfare. It lets soldiers know what leaders consider to be important or unimportant. It sets guideposts for training and military education. Doctrine generally sets the course for military acquisition by establishing requirements for different kinds of equipment and technology. Military doctrine that ignores or underplays the importance of will to fight signals an emphasis on hard-factor warfare. It encourages the kind of mechanistic thinking that undermined U.S. strategy in Vietnam and led to the overly enthusiastic promises of the RMA. Mechanistic thinking that ignores the human element of warfare sets the stage for anything from limited failure to outright catastrophe in future wars. American ground force doctrine should consistently include and emphasize the importance of will to fight as a central pillar of warfare and warfighting.

The Army's 2016 ADP 3-0 is a step in the right direction. The Joint Force should take similar steps to cement the importance of will to fight in its capstone doctrine and to proliferate will-to-fight concepts across its other doctrinal publications. Both the Army and the Marine Corps should take inventory of capstone doctrine and field manuals to identify places where will to fight can be incorporated and emphasized. However, no firm steps should be taken until the services and the Joint Force have defined and set standards for understanding will to fight. This starts with a definition and a model.

---

[69] U.S. Army, 2016c, p. 4-9. The Marine Corps expects the intelligence team to provide information on enemy morale, but does not define morale or offer options as to how it might be exploited. U.S. Marine Corps, *Marine Air-Ground Task Force Information Operations*, MCWP 3-40.4, Washington, D.C.: Headquarters, U.S. Marine Corps, July 9, 2003. In the July 1, 2013, version of this manual, morale is simply listed as something that might be manipulated by information operations to degrade enemy effectiveness. U.S. Marine Corps, *Marine Air-Ground Task Force Information Operations*, MCWP 3-40.4, Washington, D.C.: Headquarters, U.S. Marine Corps, July 1, 2013, p. 1-5. Neither Marine manual mentions will to fight or other associated terms.

[70] For example: Yvette Clinton, Virginia Foran-Cain, Julia Voelker McQuaid, Catherine E. Norman, and William H. Sims, *Congressionally Directed Assessment of the Human Terrain System*, Alexandria, Va.: Center for Naval Analyses, November 2011.

[71] This insight is attributed to Secretary of State James N. Mattis, undated. See John Spencer, "What Is Army Doctrine?" *Modern War Institute*, March 21, 2016.

Interview Questions and Representative Quotes

Throughout the course of our research we engaged subject matter experts from a variety of fields, including military history, psychology, psychiatry, anthropology, social science, regional history, modeling, war gaming, and simulation. Several of the 68 experts we interviewed were senior military leaders, including flag officers in U.S. and allied ground combat organizations. Our researchers tailored discussions to match the expertise of the discussant. Some discussions were highly technical. We generally sought to address the following questions:

1. How do you think about will to fight in the context of your work?
2. How do you define will to fight?
3. What are the key factors associated with will to fight?
4. Which of these factors is most important and why?
5. Based on your definitions, what are some good examples of will to fight?
6. How does a country influence the will of allies and adversaries?

We incorporated the information obtained from these expert engagements throughout the report. Some of the most important responses helped us think through our modeling process, our evaluation of the Silver Model, and war game and simulation design. Military experts and historians provided some interesting thoughts directly related to the above questions. The remainder of this appendix presents an anonymized sample of these quotes. All quotes are drawn from professional discussions with experts conducted from late 2016 through 2017 in the United States and in the United Kingdom. We include a one-word cue at the beginning of each quote, relating each back to the RAND Arroyo Center model or the combat factors from Chapter Three. Quotes are presented in alphabetical order by subject.

Adversary: Remember Sun Tzu's dictum about the enemy and the golden bridge. Give him a golden bridge that allows him to run away with no shame!

Assessment: Nothing in our annual reporting system accounts for cunning, aggression, or other intangible factors associated with will to fight.

Casualties: If you are in the fight, the way to destroy someone's will to fight is by killing a lot of their friends. Destroying the units.

Casualties: We're going to have to look at our training and get people to understand much higher casualty rates.

Coercion: If you're more afraid of your commanders than the enemy, that is a coercive element of will to fight. There's a different calculus if you get captured and put in a POW camp, you're fed and clothed and kept dry whereas your commanders could shoot you in the back.

Cohesion: Because warfare is the domain of uncertainty, death and fear, to motivate individuals and groups to fight and overcome the fear of death, the only source of motivation is the bond between soldiers. Bonds between soldiers equal cohesion and stand for special bonds of friendship and the motivation arising from them.

Cohesion: Cohesion is extremely important. Even when the other things fail, even when there isn't as clear a national purpose, cohesion goes a long way.

Cohesion: No question that it's important but it's not as important as military mythology makes it.

Cohesion: Task cohesion exists when people believe their fellow soldiers can perform and have their back. It can have a positive impact on morale and feed into soldiers' willingness to perform their tasks. . . . Cohesion and morale are not the same thing.

Cohesion: When people use cohesion to mean will to fight, they underestimate the other factors. They emphasize the friendship factor while dismissing or ignoring the other factors. The training has taken over and colonized that space of motivation to the point where it influences cohesion and those friendships.

Definition: Don't confuse what we learned from our engagement in Iraq and Afghanistan with will-to-fight requirements in potential future conflicts. What we did in Afghanistan was willingness to face an adversary. The context of will to fight is different from the willingness to operate.

Definition: Will to fight is essentially the willingness of both commanders and soldiers to put themselves in hazard to accomplish a mission.

Definition: Will to fight is preparedness to put oneself in harm's way and use lethal force.

Discipline: It's an instinct of what you need to have, what you want to do. Fear makes discipline fragile as consequences shift from punishment to death.

Discipline: Self-discipline is the most important ingredient in will to fight. If you have to enforce discipline then you are probably going to lose will to fight in combat.

Factors: The factors of will to fight are (1) morale, (2) leadership, (3) confidence and capability, (4) self-belief, (5) pride, (6) mateship, or the human bond, (7) belief in a cause or a team, and (8) a sense of duty. You have to create training scenarios in which these are tested.

Factors: The most important factors are, in order, (1) the quality of the noncommissioned officers, (2) training of troops, (3) esprit de corps, and (4) resources like firepower and air support, (5) troops must have an offensive spirit, and (6) they must have good small unit leadership.

Individual: At some stage, no matter how much kit you have, it will come down to an individual soldier. Close hand-to-hand aspects of fighting make the difference for infantry soldiers.

Morale: Morale is probably an important component of will to fight but I don't think it's necessarily the case that high morale units are necessarily more willing to fight.

Morale: Morale is synonymous with will to fight. . . . Morale gets associated with happiness, but analytically, whether an individual or unit is happy, I'm not sure that has any analytical relevance whatsoever in measuring morale.

Motivation: It's all about matehood—no one buries people saying they did it for country. He did it for his mates.

Motivation: The motivation of the soldier is the single most important factor in war.

Motivation: The things that motivate soldiers to be willing to go on the battlefield and risk their lives are (a) a greater purpose or belief, (b) that they can be victorious rather quickly, (c) that they and their buddies are qualified to do the job. There's an underlying belief that the country is behind them. I think people are far less willing to fight what they see are unpopular wars.

Motivation: There are four potential ways to motivate soldiers: (1) cohesion, or the personal obligation to friends and comrades; (2) training them; (3) ideological/ political; (4) discipline, or "if you don't fight you're punished (coercion)." In history, those four factors play a variable role in soldiers fighting.

Risk: In Afghanistan, shared risk with the Afghans was an important aspect. If one is expecting the Afghans to fight then we need to be with them. They were, in theory, fighting for their own country, we were fighting for a foreign land. They were laissez-faire; their risk appetite was more than ours.

Risk: We have to encourage leaders who are willing to take risks. It is easy to relieve people in command during combat. It is much harder to do so in peacetime. How do we develop the right characteristics for war needed in leaders, in peacetime?

Strategy: Our guys will fight for a sense of duty. . . . But does the national objective resonate with me and am I passionate about it?

Training: Most propensity to fight, and to fight well, comes from training. Good training, well delivered, with depth of frequency and currency. People fight well if they know what to do in the circumstances. At that point battle is no longer a paralyzing noise; it is stimulation for action.

Training: Training needs to address combat ethos and fighting spirit: giving people the confidence that if they had to go to war they are better than the opponent.

Training: Where you want to focus is training. In a professional force, the will to fight is based in the training of units which inculcates a capability to fight. If you're good at it, you might be more willing. But what happens at training is the relationships between soldiers start to change. Deep friendships emerge. They are professional bonds which bring with them a special form of solidarity and the obligation to fight well and bravely. . . . Bonds in training make high levels of will to fight.

Silver Model (CPM) Technical Details

This technical appendix presents the original Silver Model (CPM) as published in Hutson, 1997, and in consultation with Silver in mid-2017 correspondence and phone calls. It then presents programming guidelines for the implementation of the Silver Model into IWARS.

Original Silver Model (CPM)

This section presents the original model in verbatim text drawn from Hutson, 1997. Note that we changed several of these factors and calculations during our IWARS experiments. Table E.1 depicts the original trait-states and their definitions. Table E.2 provides the basic calculations showing how environmental inputs are combined with traits to generate state changes. Figure E.1 presents the calculations for the aggregated morale, support, and leadership traits.

Table E.1
Original Silver Model Trait-States

Trait-States	Definition
Stability	Emotional "governor" ~ self-control
Anxiety	Inherent fearfulness
Anger	Emotion of anger and aggressiveness
Humor	Emotional "bounce-back" for morale
Acquiescence	Willingness to obey orders
Independence	Ability to function without leaders
Charisma	Attractiveness of personality to others
Knowledge	Familiarity with weapons, equipment

Table E.2
Original Silver Model Aggregated States

Aggregated States	Definition
Situational stress	Ratio of friendly-enemy modified by friendly and enemy fire + Fatigue
Support	Ability to support the team, equal to Stability + Humor + Acquiescence
Group support	Group average of all individuals' support states within the group
Leadership	Independence + Charisma + Anger + Knowledge
Morale	Stability + Anxiety + Anger + Humor modified by group support + situational stress + leadership

Figure E.1
Original Silver Model Morale, Support, and Leadership Calculations

$$\text{\textbf{trait} Morale} = \frac{Stability + Anxiety + \dfrac{Anger}{2}}{3.5}$$

$$\text{\textbf{trait} Support} = \frac{Stability + Humor + Acquiescence}{3}$$

$$\text{\textbf{trait} Leadership} = \frac{Independence + Charisma + Knowledge + Stability + Morale}{5}$$

RAND RR2341A-E.1

Precombat traits are modified into states at the start of the simulation, then further modified as the scenario evolves. Morale is an important state, modified with leader's leadership and group support in Figure E.2.

Figure E.2
Original Silver Model State Morale Calculation

$$\text{\textbf{state} } Morale =$$

$$\frac{trait\ Morale + \dfrac{Leader's\ Leadership + Group\ Support}{2}}{2}$$

RAND RR2341A-E.2

States are modified by many battlefield variables consisting of exogenous events like sniper fire or conditions like reduced visibility. Table E.3 presents these modifiers. The numbers in the boxes represent step changes to trait-state by incident.

Table E.3
Original Silver Model Battlefield Variables

Event	Stab.	Anx.	Ang.	Hum.	Acq.	Ind.	Char.	Knw.
New team member	−0.05	.05		−0.05	−0.05			
Nighttime conditions		0.10	−0.01	−0.02	0.02	−0.02	−0.01	
Reduced visibility		0.05	−0.01	−0.01	0.01	−0.01		
Indirect fire/intermittent		0.01	0.01					
Indirect fire/continuous[a]		0.03	0.02	−0.01	−0.01			
Sniper fire		0.02	0.01		−0.01			0.01
Light fire/ineffective	0.05	−0.01	−0.01	−0.02			0.01	
Moderate fire	−0.03	0.08	−0.02	−0.02	−0.02		−0.01	0.01
Heavy fire	−0.05	0.12	−0.04	−0.10	−0.05	−0.01	−0.01	0.01
Ambushed	−0.03	0.10[a]	−0.02	−0.20	−0.04		−0.03	0.01
Minefield	−0.02	0.05	0.01	−0.01	−0.03		−0.02	0.01
Attack by inferior force		0.05	0.08		0.01		0.01	0.01
Attack by equal force		0.06	0.02	−0.01				0.01
Attack by superior force	−0.01	0.06	−0.01	−0.02	−0.01		−0.01	0.01
Attack by overwhelming force		0.10[b]	−0.01	−0.10	−0.04	−0.02	−0.02	0.01
Ambush an inferior force		0.02	0.10	0.02	0.02		0.01	0.01
Ambush an equal force		0.03	0.10		0.01			0.01
Ambush a superior force		0.04	0.10	−0.01			−0.01	0.01
Support fire on call			0.10	0.02	0.05	0.04	0.02	
Close quarters combat	0.01	−0.02	0.01	0.01	0.01			0.01
See dead enemy	−0.01	0.02	0.01	0.01	0.01			0.01
See wounded enemy	−0.01	0.01	0.03					0.01

NOTE: [a] Every 15 minutes; [b] Every 30 minutes.

States are also modified at the group level, with group elements modifying individual-level trait-states. Table E.4 presents the group elements.

There are also stress reducer variables that can lower unhelpful changes in trait-state conditions. Stress reducers can be immediate or timed. These are depicted in Tables E.5 and E.6.

Table E.4
Original Silver Model Group Elements

Event	Stab.	Anx.	Ang.	Hum.	Acq.	Ind.	Char.	Knw.
Team member wounded (team casualty rate [TCR]≤10%)	−0.02	0.02	0.02	−0.01				
Team member wounded (10%<TCR<40%)	−0.03	0.04	0.04	−0.02	−0.01	−0.01		
Team member wounded (TCR≥40%)	−0.04	0.05	0.04	−0.05	−0.02	−0.02		
Team member killed (TCR≤10%)	−0.04	0.04	0.04	−0.02		−0.01		
Team member killed (10%<TCR<40%)	−0.05	0.05	0.05	−0.05	−0.02	−0.02		
Team member killed (TCR≥40%)	−0.06	−0.07	0.05	−0.10	−0.03	−0.03		
Team leader wounded	−0.04	0.05	0.03	−0.05	−0.03			
Team leader killed	−0.08	0.10	0.03	−0.20	−0.05	0.02		
Incorrect order given	−0.03	0.05	0.05	−0.02	−0.09	0.01		

Table E.5
Original Silver Model Stress Reduction Variables (Immediate)

Event	Stab.	Anx.[a]	Ang.	Hum.	Acq.	Ind.	Char.	Knw.
Issued more effective equipment		−0.05						
Issued new clothing				0.05				
Successful defense		−0.05	−0.01	0.05	0.03		0.01	0.01
Successful attack	−0.02	−0.06	0.04	0.05	0.04		0.01	0.01
Eating a meal	0.01	−0.10	−0.01	0.02	0.01		0.01	

NOTE: [a] If value>70, effects are doubled.

Table E.6
Original Silver Model Stress Reduction Variables (Timed)

Event (every 30 min.)	Stab.	Anx.[a]	Ang.	Hum.	Acq.	Ind.	Char.	Knw.
Sleep	0.01	−0.03	−0.02	0.01	0.01			
Issued new clothing	0.01	−0.03	−0.02	0.01	0.01			
Successful defense	0.01	−0.02	−0.01	0.01	0.01			

NOTE: [a] If value>70, effects are doubled.

Figure E.3
Original Silver Model Changes in Performance

(Anxiety>0.70) ∧ (Anger<0.50) → *action delay X random seconds*

(Anxiety>0.85) ∧ (Anger<0.80) → *action delay X + 10 seconds*

(Morale>0.80) → *increased accuracy and weapons effectiveness* / (Morale<0.50) → *reduced accuracy and weapons effectiveness*

(Morale<0.40) ∧ (Anxiety>0.70) ∧ (Acquiescence<0.40) → *hesitate*

(Morale<0.40) ∧ (Anxiety>0.80) ∧ (Acquiescence<0.35) ∧ (Support<0.50) ∧ (Leadership<0.50) ∧ (Random>0.50) → *disobey*

(Morale<0.50) ∧ (Anxiety>0.80) ∧ (Stability<0.50) ∧ (Support<0.40) ∧ (Leadership<0.40) ∧ (Random>0.50) → *flee*

(Support>0.85) ∧ (Morale>0.60) ∧ (Anger>0.70) ∧ (Independence>0.75) ∧ (Random>0.50) → *heroism*

RAND *RR2341A-E.3*

Finally, state changes result in behavioral changes. Soldiers suffer from delays in performance, or they are more accurate or more courageous, or they disobey orders or flee. Figure E.3 presents the performance change calculations. Actions that degrade performance are in red. Actions that improve performance are in green.

Programming the Silver Model (CPM) into IWARS

This section provides programmer notes from RAND Arroyo Center's IWARS Silver Model, or CPM experiment. For the sake of brevity we refer to the model as CPM throughout this section.

IWARS version 5.1.2 uses a drag-and-drop scripting language with mathematical syntax that allows basic computation and Boolean comparisons. This programming is completed within the Mission Builder interface. The IWARS User Guide provides a basic introduction to the Mission Builder, which is normally used to drive combat actions. This appendix serves to explain how an additional agent framework can be built without needing the software vendor to build a proprietary module. For clarity, key functions are *italicized*.

Figure E.4 represents an IWARS's CPM implementation. *Missions* are containers that hold agent decision trees called *activity groups*, can be assigned to any agent, and are built from three main components: boxes are *activities* that employ *skills*, lines are conditional *transitions*, and circles represent *start/end* points that can be controlled with Boolean events.[1] Agent-owned variables exist as *Activity Parameters* or *Knowledge Parameters*; there are no global variables that can be shared among agents, but *knowledge parameters* can be shared between missions. Table E.7 lists *skills* frequently used in CPM.

---

[1]   The *interrupt* and *end controllers* did not respond as expected in this version of IWARS.

Figure E.4
IWARS Implementation Table

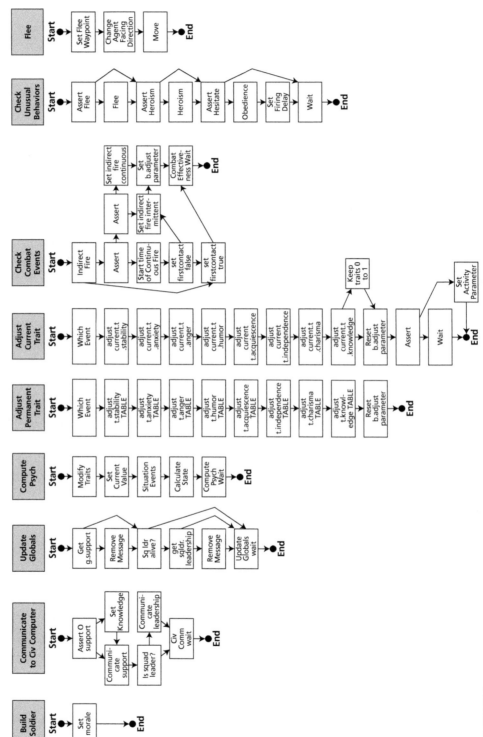

Table E.7
Skills Frequently Used in IWARS Implementation

Assert	1. Ask if a certain event is true to cause a branch in the activity group
Communicate	1. Transmit agent-owned variables to other agents
Evaluate	1. Perform a computation (e.g., ratio of RED to BLUE forces) or syntax (e.g., selecting an item from a list)
Set Activity (Knowledge) Parameter	1. Storing CPM trait and state variables 2. Changing the hesitate variable 3. Changing a Boolean to TRUE to trigger an event such as updating traits or receiving a message
Wait	1. Cause hesitation between fires 2. Act as an update rate by causing an activity group delay

All *activity groups* run simultaneously with each tick of the simulation clock. This lists the key *activity groups* for CPM. An additional nonplayer agent named the civilian computer was used to allow sharing of global variables by using the *communicate* skill. Table E.8, below, lists the key activity groups for CPM.

Table E.8
Key Activity Groups Used for CPM

Adjust current traits	Updates current traits when a stressor is triggered. Normalizes all current traits on a 0 to 1 scale before executing again.
Check combat effectiveness	Uses IWARS' *Suppression Level* model to trigger the indirect fire (intermittent) stressor when an agent is under fire. If *Suppression Level* was elevated for more than 60 seconds, the indirect fire (continuous) stressor was triggered.
Check unusual behaviors	Uses the *Assert skill* to see if traits are sufficient to trigger combat behavior changes. Flee and Hesitate were both implemented with a Boolean trigger and time variable increment respectively.
Communicate to civ computer	Send an agent's Support state to the Civilian Computer in order to compute and disseminate the Group Support state. See Figure E.6 for how the Civilian Computer accomplishes this.
Compute psych	Main CPM activity group. Permanent traits are first modified if the magnitude of elevation or depression of current traits is greater than 0.02; see Figure E.7. Current traits are returned to the permanent trait level, effectively removing any transient stressor effects. Environmental stressors are then checked and effects applied; see Figure E.8. Lastly, states are computed using the *Set Activity Parameter skill* before the *Wait skill* delays repeating the process.
Flee	Triggered by the Flee Boolean; causes the affected agent to face and move towards a retreat waypoint.
Update globals	Obtain the Group Support state and the Squad Leader's Leadership state (if alive).

Scripting Specifics and Difficulties

Although there is no detailed syntax manual for scripting in Mission Builder, complex functions are still possible with workarounds. IWARS scenario files contain all scripts in an XML-like format that can be edited directly with a text editor. However, rigorous syntax and nesting rules can cause loading or runtime faults, requiring careful manipulation by the programmer.

What follows are `code` examples (for clarity, `courier font` indicates syntax and ⇒ indicates a programmer action) to assist other researchers should they choose IWARS as their modeling and simulation platform. Scripts are entered in the *Value* field for each skill using the *Expression Builder* interface. Generally, any value is only stored once the programmer clicks on the entered value. In addition, before a *decimal*, *integer*, *time*, and so on, value is entered, the programmer has to specify the data type at the prompt:

```
[...]  ⇒  [Decimal]
```

Extracting Variables from Communication Messages

Other than the built-in message types, unique message types can be created to pass variables as included pieces of data. Use the dropdown menu under the *Message To Send* property, type in the unique message name, and select, as in Figure E.5. *Message Data* may then be entered, also with a unique *Name*. *Activities* can be triggered when a specific *Message* is received. To extract data:

```
Get [Text] from [Message] Message ⇒
Get group.support from Group Support Message
```

Figure E.5
Communication Skill Detail

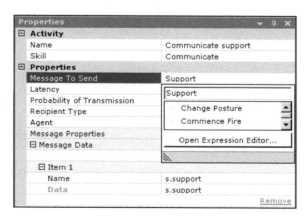

RAND *RR2341A-E.5*

Storing and Extracting Values from Lists

Lists allow the programmer to store multiple values of any data type. The first index is 1 and can store many values. To build a list, use a comma to add additional values:

$$[\ldots] \Rightarrow [\ldots] \text{ , } \Rightarrow [\ldots] \text{ , } [\ldots]$$

To retrieve the second item from a *Decimal List* called list.event.anxiety:

```
[...] → Select [...] ⇒ [Decimal List] → Select [Integer] ⇒
            list.event.anxiety → Select 2
```

Evaluating Complex Expressions

Because all syntax entries must originate from the dropdown menus in *Expression Builder*, otherwise straightforward values such as the ratio of RED agents and BLUE agents (for calculation of the situational stress state) may require additional syntax to achieve. In addition, some mathematical operators will work only with the *Decimal* data type and require conversion. The IWARS User Guide notes that the order of how expressions are added is essential to performing the correct computation; expressions are added by simply adding a mathematical operator (e.g., +, -, /, *) or a syntax that forces a data type such as Decimal. An example of how to build the ratio of RED and BLUE agents follows:

```
[...] → Count ⇒
[Agent List] → Count ⇒
'All Agents → Count' – [...] ⇒
'All Agents → Count' – [...] ⇒
'All Agents → Count' – 'Number of [...] who are Dead' ⇒
'All Agents → Count' – 'Number of Red who are Dead' – [...] ⇒
'All Agents → Count' – 'Number of Red who are Dead' – [Decimal] ⇒
'All Agents → Count' – 'Number of Red who are Dead' – '5' ⇒
'All Agents → Count – Number of Red who are Dead – 5' as Decimal ⇒
'All Agents → Count – Number of Red who are Dead – 5 as Decimal' / [...] ⇒
```

... and finally [2]

```
'All Agents → Count – Number of Red who are Dead – 5 as Decimal' /
        '5 – Number of Blue who are Dead as Decimal'
```

---

[2]   A shorter and more universal way to get this ratio:
```
'1 – Percentage of Red who are Dead' / '1 – Percentage of Blue who are Dead'
```

Other Lessons Learned

Most other expressions are straightforward to build for those with a programming background. *Activity Parameters* can be modified by assigning a new value added to the original *Activity Parameter* itself, If…Then…Else statements nest as expected, and there are many useful commands too numerous to list here. Designed for agent actions such as combat (see Figures E.8 and E.10), fairly complex scenarios can be created to include complex movement paths along node networks, sharing of Opposing Force positions, and even calls for artillery support. However, some additional caveats are worth noting. *Start controllers* using *Time* values should use greater-than operators instead of equal signs. Booleans can trigger *activities* but the programmer is able to only crudely control the flow of many events, especially the receipt and data extraction of *communications*. Lastly, without a robust exception-handling process, *Mission Builder* is prone to errors, and debugging requires close examination of simulation results vice tracing execution errors. Figures E.8 through E.9 show how environmental stressors are triggered and two combat routine examples.

Figure E.6
How the Civilian Computer Computes and Communicates

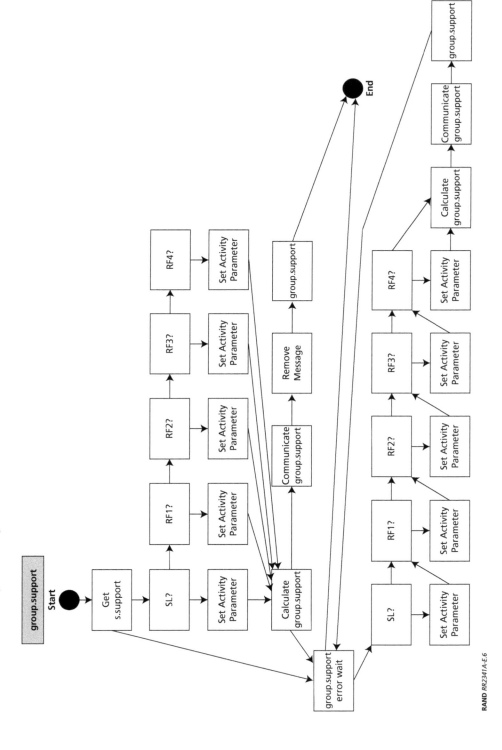

Figure E.7
How Permanent Traits Are Adjusted

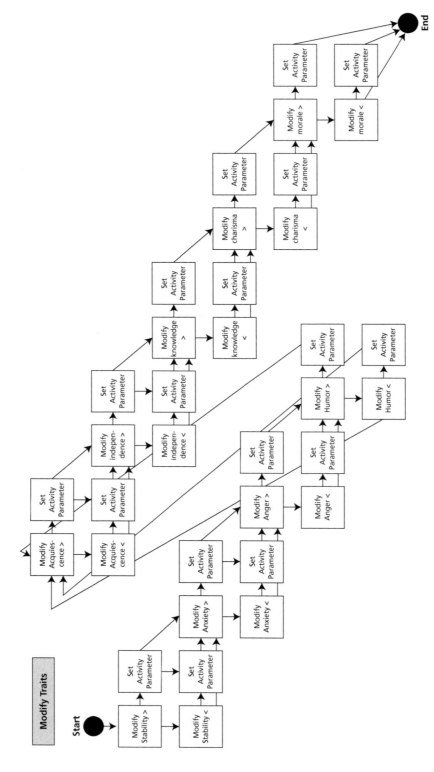

RAND RR2341A-E.7

Figure E.8
How Environmental Stressors Are Triggered

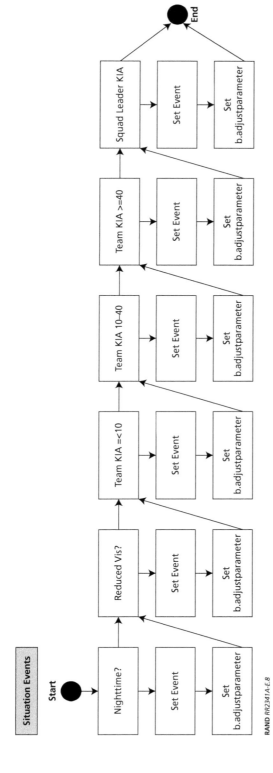

RAND *RR2341A-E.8*

Figure E.9
Combat Routine

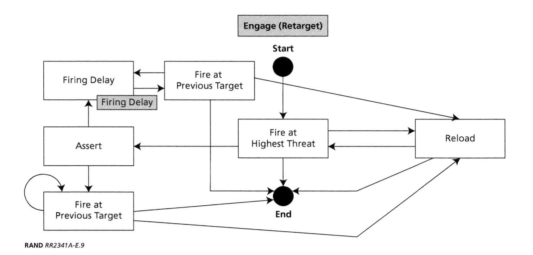

Figure E.10
Red Combat

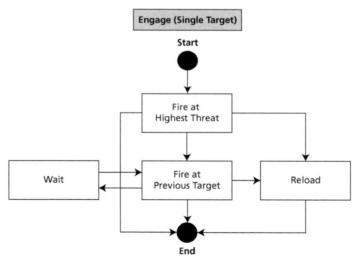

Bibliography

We have included some sources that were not explicitly referenced in the body of the report. These sources were included in our literature review. We cite them here so they may be readily available to interested readers.

Abbas, Yassir, and Dan Trombley, "Inside the Collapse of the Iraqi Army's 2d Division," *War on the Rocks*, July 1, 2014. As of July 3, 2017:
https://warontherocks.com/2014/07/inside-the-collapse-of-the-iraqi-armys-2nd-division/

Ackoff, Russell, "Towards a System of Systems Concepts," *Management Science*, Vol. 17, No. 11, 1971, pp. 661–671.

Ahrenfeldt, Robert H., *Psychiatry in the British Army in the Second World War*, London: Routledge and Kegan Paul Limited, 1958.

Allen, John P., and John T. Hazer, *Development of a Field-Oriented Measure of Soldier Morale*, Fort Benjamin Harrison, Ind.: Army Research Institute for the Behavioral and Social Sciences, December 1981.

Alpass, Fiona, Nigel Long, Carol MacDonald, and Kerry Chamberlain, "The Moskos Institution-Occupation Model: Effects on Individual Work Related Perceptions and Experiences in the Military," *JPMS: Journal of Political and Military Sociology*, Vol. 27, No. 1, 1999, pp. 67–80.

Anderson, Gary W., "When Maneuver Fails," *Marine Corps Gazette*, Vol. 73, No. 4, April 1989, pp. 57–59.

Anzulovic, James Venceslav, Jr., *The Russian Record of the Winter War, 1939–1940: An Analytical Study of Soviet Records of the War with Finland from 30 November 1939 to 12 March 1940*, dissertation, College Park: University of Maryland, 1968.

Arango, Tim, and Ceylon Yeginsu, "With Army in Disarray, a Pillar of Modern Turkey Lies Broken," *New York Times*, July 28, 2016. As of April 3, 2018:
https://www.nytimes.com/2016/07/29/world/europe/turkey-military-coup.html

Artelli, Michael J., *Modeling and Analysis of Resolve and Morale for the "Long War,"* thesis, Wright-Patterson Air Force Base, Ohio: Air Institute of Technology, 2007.

Atran, Scott, Hammad Sheikh, and Angel Gomez, "Devoted Actors Sacrifice for Close Comrades and Sacred Cause," *Proceedings of the National Academy of Sciences*, Vol. 111, No. 50, 2014, pp. 17702–17703.

Barba, Paulo E. Santa, *Breaking Terrorists' Will to Fight*, Monterey, Calif.: Naval Postgraduate, 2014.

Bar-Joseph, Uri, *The 1973 Yom Kippur War*, Israel Studies: An Anthology, Jewish Virtual Library Publications, May 2009. As of March 15, 2018:
http://www.jewishvirtuallibrary.org/israel-studies-an-anthology-the-yom-kippur-war

Barker, Phil, *War Games Rules 3000 BC to 1485 AD*, version 7.5, UK: Wargames Research Group, 1992.

Barlow, Michael, and Adam Easton, "CROCADILE—An Open, Extensible Agent-Based Distillation Engine," *Information and Security*, Vol. 8, No. 1, 2002, pp. 17–51.

Bartone, Paul T., "Resilience Under Military Operational Stress: Can Leaders Influence Hardiness?" *Military Psychology*, No. 18 (supplemental), 2006, pp. 131–148.

Bartone, Paul T., Robert R. Roland, James J. Picano, and Thomas J. Williams, "Psychological Hardiness Predicts Success in U.S. Army Special Forces Candidates," *International Journal of Selection and Assessment*, Vol. 16, No. 1, March 2008, pp. 78–81.

Bartov, Omer, "The Conduct of War: Soldiers and the Barbarization of Warfare," *Journal of Modern History*, Vol. 64, 1992, pp. S32–S45.

Bass, Bernard M., Bruce J. Avolio, Dong I. Jung, and Yair Berson, "Predicting Unit Performance by Assessing Transformational and Transactional Leadership," *Journal of Applied Psychology*, Vol. 88, No. 2, 2003, p. 207.

Bassford, Christopher, *Clausewitz in English: The Reception of Clausewitz in Britain and America, 1815–1945*, Oxford: Oxford University Press, 1994.

Basu, Moni, "Survey: Veterans Say Afghanistan, Iraq Wars Not Worth It," *CNN*, October 5, 2011.

Baynes, John, *Morale: A Study of Men and Courage*, Garden City Park, N.Y.: Avery Publishing Group, Inc., 1988 (1967).

Beaumont, Roger A., and William P. Snyder, "Combat Effectiveness: Paradigms and Paradoxes," in Sarkesian, 1980, pp. 20–56.

Belenky, Gregory, ed., *Contemporary Studies in Combat Psychiatry*, New York: Greenwood Press, 1987.

Ben-Dor, Gabriel, Ami Pedahzur, Daphna Canetti-Nisim, Eran Zaidise, Arie Perliger, and Shai Bermanis, "I Versus We: Collective and Individual Factors of Reserve Service Motivation During War and Peace," *Armed Forces and Society*, Vol. 34, No. 4, 2008, pp. 565–592.

Bennett, Bruce W., Arthur M. Bullock, Daniel B. Fox, Carl M. Jones, John Schrader, Robert Weissler, and Barry A. Wilson, *JICM 1.0 Summary*, Santa Monica, Calif.: RAND Corporation, MR-383-NA, 1994. As of March 21, 2018:
https://www.rand.org/pubs/monograph_reports/MR383.html

Bennett, Bruce W., Carl M. Jones, Arthur M. Bullock, and Paul K. Davis, *Main Theater Modeling in the RAND Strategy Assessment System (3.0)*, Santa Monica, Calif.: RAND Corporation, N-2743-NA, 1988. As of March 21, 2018:
https://www.rand.org/pubs/notes/N2743.html

Ben-Shalom, Uzi, and Yizhaq Benbenisty, "Coping Styles and Combat Motivation During Operations: An IDF Case Study," *Armed Forces and Society*, Vol. 42, No. 4, 2016, pp. 655–674.

Benson, Bill, "The Evolution of Army Doctrine for Success in the 21st Century," *Military Review*, March–April 2012, pp. 2–12.

Bercuson, David J., "Up from the Ashes: The Re-Professionalization of the Canadian Forces After the Somalia Affair," *Canadian Military Journal*, Vol. 9, No. 3, 2009, pp. 31–39.

Betz, David J., *Civil-Military Relations in Russia and Eastern Europe*, London: RoutledgeCurzon, 2004.

Bidwell, Shelford, *Modern Warfare: A Study of Men, Weapons and Theories*, London: Allen Lane, 1973.

Bieling, Peter J., Martin M. Antony, and Richard P. Swinson, "The State-Trait Anxiety Inventory, Trait Version, Structure and Content Re-Examined," *Behaviour Research and Therapy*, No. 36, 1998, pp. 777–788.

Binkley, John, "Clausewitz and Subjective Civilian Control: An Analysis of Clausewitz's Views on the Role of the Military Advisor in the Development of National Policy," *Armed Forces and Society*, Vol. 42, No. 2, 2016, pp. 251–275.

Blalock, H. M., Jr., ed., *Causal Models in the Social Sciences*, 2nd ed., New York: Aldine de Gruyter, 1985.

Bloom, William, *Personal Identity, National Identity, and International Relations*, Cambridge: Cambridge University Press, 1990.

Boldovici, John A., David W. Bessemer, and Amy E. Bolton, *The Elements of Training Evaluation*, Alexandria, Va.: Army Research Institute, 2001.

Bonura, Michael A., *French Thought and the American Military Mind: A History of French Influence on the American Way of Warfare from 1814 Through 1941*, thesis, Tallahassee: Florida State University, 2008.

Boote, David N., and Penny Beile, "Scholars Before Researchers: On the Centrality of the Dissertation Literature Review in Research Preparation," *Educational Researcher*, Vol. 34, No. 6, 2005, pp. 3–15.

Bracken, Jerome, "Lanchester Models of the Ardennes Campaign," *Naval Research Logistics*, Vol. 42, 1995, pp. 559–577.

Brennan, Richard R., Jr., Charles P. Ries, Larry Hanauer, Ben Connable, Terrence K. Kelly, Michael J. McNerney, Stephanie Young, Jason Campbell, and K. Scott McMahon, *Ending the U.S. War in Iraq: The Final Transition, Operational Maneuver, and Disestablishment of the United States Forces-Iraq*, Santa Monica, Calif.: RAND Corporation, RR-232-USFI, 2013. As of March 23, 2018: https://www.rand.org/pubs/research_reports/RR232.html

Brigham, Robert K., *ARVN: Life and Death in the South Vietnamese Army*, Lawrence, Kan.: University Press of Kansas, 2006.

British Broadcasting Corporation, "1975: Vietnam's President Thieu Resigns," April 21, 1975.

———, "Iraq General Says Planned U.S. Troop Pullout 'Too Soon,'" August 12, 2010. As of June 30, 2017: http://www.bbc.com/news/world-middle-east-10947918

Britt, T. W., *Responsibility, Morale, and Commitment During Military Operations,* Heidelberg, Germany: Army Medical Research Unit Europe, 1996.

Brocheux, Pierre, and Daniel Hémery, *Indochina: An Ambiguous Colonization 1858–1954*, Berkeley: University of California Press, 2009.

Bross, Paul J., *Measuring the "Will to Fight" in Simulation*, Suffolk, Va.: U.S. Joint Forces Command J-9, November 30, 2005.

Builder, Carl H., *The Masks of War: American Military Styles in Strategy and Analysis*, Baltimore: Johns Hopkins University Press, 1989.

Burke, Peter J., Timothy J. Owens, Richard T. Serpe, and Peggy A. Thoits, eds., *Advances in Identity Theory and Research*, Boston: Springer, 2003.

Cafferata, Hector, "Commandant's Message: 235th Birthday of the Marine Corps." As of August 18, 2017:
https://www.youtube.com/watch?v=5-jRvs69yzs

Camfield, Thomas M., " 'Will to Win'—The U.S. Army Troop Morale Program of World War I," *Military Affairs*, Vol. 41, No. 3, October 1977, pp. 125–128.

Campbell, James E., Dennis E. Longsine, Donald Shirah, and Dennis J. Anderson, *System of Systems Modeling and Analysis*, SAND2005-0020, Albuquerque, N.M.: Sandia National Laboratories, 2005.

Campise, Rick L., Schuyler K. Geller, and Mary E. Campise, "Combat Stress," in Kennedy and Zillmer, 2006, pp. 215–240.

Carver, George A., Jr., "The Real Revolution in South Vietnam," *Foreign Affairs*, Vol. 43, No. 3, 1965, pp. 387–408.

Castillo, Jasen J., *Endurance and War: The National Sources of Military Cohesion*, Stanford, Calif.: Stanford University Press, 2014.

Catignani, Sergio, "Motivating Soldiers: The Example of the Israeli Defense Forces," *Parameters*, Vol. 34, No. 3, 2004, p. 108.

Chacho, T. M., "Why Did They Fight? American Airborne Units in World War II," *Defence Studies*, Vol. 1, No. 3, 2001, pp. 59–94.

Chamberlain, Robert, "The Mud of Verdun: Falkenhayn and the Future of American Landpower," *Military Review*, July-August 2016, pp. 78–87.

China Military (website). As of November 11, 2017:
http://english.chinamil.com.cn

Chmielewski, Michael S., "Maybe It's Time to Reconsider Maneuver Warfare," *Marine Corps Gazette*, Vol. 86, No. 8, 2002, pp. 65–67.

Chulov, Martin, "Post-War Iraq: 'Everybody Is Corrupt, from Top to Bottom, Including Me,' " *The Guardian*, February 19, 2016. As of April 3, 2018:
https://www.theguardian.com/world/2016/feb/19/post-war-iraq-corruption-oil-prices-revenues

Cioppa, Thomas M., Thomas W. Lucas, and Susan M. Sanchez, "Military Applications of Agent-Based Simulations," in R. G. Ingalls, M. D. Rossetti, J. S. Smith, and B. A. Peters, eds., *Proceedings of the 2004 Winter Simulation Conference*, 2004, pp. 171–180. As of April 19, 2018:
https://calhoun.nps.edu/bitstream/handle/10945/35333/020.pdf?sequence=1

Clausewitz, Carl Von, *On War*, trans. J. J. Graham, 1873. As of February 16, 2017:
https://www.clausewitz.com/readings/OnWar1873/BK1ch01.html

Clinton, Yvette, Virginia Foran-Cain, Julia Voelker McQuaid, Catherine E. Norman, and William H. Sims, *Congressionally Directed Assessment of the Human Terrain System*, Alexandria, Va.: Center for Naval Analyses, November 2011.

Clodfelter, Mark, "Aiming to Break Will: America's World War II Bombing of German Morale and Its Ramifications," *Journal of Strategic Studies*, Vol. 33, No. 3, 2010, pp. 401–435.

Close Combat Series, homepage, undated. As of April 18, 2018:
http://www.closecombatseries.net/CCS/

Cohen, Avner, "The Last Nuclear Moment," *New York Times*, October 6, 2003. As of April 3, 2018:
https://www.nytimes.com/2003/10/06/opinion/the-last-nuclear-moment.html

Cohen, Eliot A., "A Revolution in Warfare," *Foreign Affairs*, Vol. 75, No. 2, March–April 1996, pp. 37–54.

Collmer, Sabine, *Information as a Key Resource: The Influence of RMA and Network-Centric Operations on the Transformation of the German Armed Forces*, Garmisch, Germany: George C. Marshall European Center for Security Studies, February 2007.

Combined Security Transition Command-Afghanistan, "The Training Readiness Assessment Tool," *The Enduring Ledger*, April 2009, p.18.

Congressional Medal of Honor Society, "Cafferata, Hector A., Jr." As of August 18, 2017: http://www.cmohs.org/recipient-detail/3091/cafferata-hector-a-jr.php

Connable, Ben, *Embracing the Fog of War: Assessment and Metrics in Counterinsurgency*, Santa Monica, Calif.: RAND Corporation, MG-1086, 2012. As of March 16, 2018: https://www.rand.org/pubs/monographs/MG1086.html

———, *Warrior-Maverick Culture: The Evolution of Adaptability in the U.S. Marine Corps*, doctoral thesis, London: King's College London, 2016.

———, *Redesigning Strategy for Irregular War: Improving Strategic Design for Planners and Policymakers to Help Defeat Groups Like the Islamic State*, Santa Monica, Calif.: RAND Corporation, WR-1172-OSD, 2017.

Connable, Ben, and Martin Libicki, *How Insurgencies End*, Santa Monica, Calif.: RAND Corporation, MG-965, 2010. As of March 16, 2018: https://www.rand.org/pubs/monographs/MG965.html

Cooper, Richard N., *Military Manpower and the All-Volunteer Force*, Santa Monica, Calif.: RAND Corporation, R-1450-ARPA, 1977. As of March 16, 2018: https://www.rand.org/pubs/reports/R1450.html

Czarniawska-Joerges, Barbara, *Exploring Complex Organizations: A Cultural Perspective*, Newberry Park, Calif.: Sage Publications, 1992.

Damian, Fideleon, *The Road to FMFM 1: The United States Marine Corps and Maneuver Warfare Doctrine, 1979–1989*, thesis, Manhattan: Kansas State University, 2008.

D'Andrade, Roy G., "Schemas and Motivation," in D'Andrade and Strauss, 1992, pp. 23–44.

D'Andrade, Roy G., and Claudia Strauss, eds., *Human Motives and Cultural Models*, Cambridge: Cambridge University Press, 1992.

Davies, Christie, "Itali sunt imbelles," *Journal of Strategic Studies*, Vol. 5, No. 2, 1982, pp. 266–269.

Davis, Lorraine B., ed., "War Psychiatry," in Russ Zajtchuk, ed., *Textbook of Military Medicine*, Washington, D.C.: TTM Publications, U.S. Army Office of the Surgeon General, 1995. As of April 19, 2018: https://fas.org/irp/doddir/milmed/warpsychiatry.pdf

Davis, Paul K., *Modeling of Soft Factors in the RAND Strategy Assessment System (RSAS)*, Santa Monica, Calif.: RAND Corporation, P-7538, 1989a. As of March 16, 2018: https://www.rand.org/pubs/papers/P7538.html

———, *The Role of Uncertainty in Assessing the NATO/Pact Central Region Balance*, Santa Monica, Calif.: RAND Corporation, N-2839-RC, 1989b. As of March 21, 2018: https://www.rand.org/pubs/notes/N2839.html

———, *Some Lessons Learned from Building Red Agents in the RAND Strategy Assessment System (RSAS)*, Santa Monica, Calif.: RAND Corporation, N-3003-OSD, 1989c. As of March 16, 2018: https://www.rand.org/pubs/notes/N3003.html

Davis, Paul K., and James H. Bigelow, *Experiments in Multiresolution Modeling (MRM)*, Santa Monica, Calif.: RAND Corporation, MR-1004-DARPA, 1998. As of March 16, 2018: https://www.rand.org/pubs/monograph_reports/MR1004.html

Davis, Paul K., and Donald Blumenthal, *The Base of Sand Problem: A White Paper on the State of Military Combat Modeling*, Santa Monica, Calif.: RAND Corporation, N-3148-OSD/DARPA, 1991. As of March 16, 2018: https://www.rand.org/pubs/notes/N3148.html

Davis, Paul K., and James A. Winnefeld, *The RAND Strategy Assessment Center: An Overview and Interim Conclusions About Utility and Development Options*, Santa Monica, Calif.: RAND Corporation, R-2945-DNA, 1983. As of March 16, 2018: https://www.rand.org/pubs/reports/R2945.html

Dedoose Version 8.0.35, web application for managing, analyzing, and presenting qualitative and mixed method research data, Los Angeles, Calif.: SocioCultural Research Consultants, LLC, 2018. As of April 5, 2018: www.dedoose.com

Democratic Republic of Vietnam, *The Thieu Regime Put to the Test: 1973–1975*, Hanoi, D.R.V.: Foreign Language Publishing House, 1975.

Denton, Frank H., *Some Effects of Military Operations on Viet Cong Attitudes*, Santa Monica, Calif.: RAND Corporation, RM-4966-1-ISA/ARPA, 1966. As of March 16, 2018: https://www.rand.org/pubs/research_memoranda/RM4966-1.html

De Tavernier, Johan, "The Historical Roots of Personalism: From Renouvier's Le Personnalisme, Mounier's Manifeste au service du personnalisme, and Maritain's Humanisme integral to Janssens' Personne et Societe," *Ethical Perspectives*, Vol. 16, No. 3, 2009, pp. 361–392.

de Weerd, H. A., ed., *Selected Speeches and Statements of General of the Army George C. Marshall*, New York: De Capo Press, 1973.

Director of Central Intelligence, *The Performance of the Intelligence Community Before the Arab-Israeli War of October 1973: A Preliminary Post-Mortem Report*, declassified intelligence assessment, Washington, D.C.: Intelligence Community Staff, December 1973.

Dong Van Khuyen, *The RVNAF*, Washington, D.C.: Center of Military History, 1980.

Doughty, Robert A., *The Evolution of US Army Tactical Doctrine, 1946–76*, Leavenworth Paper No. 1, Fort Leavenworth, Kan.: U.S. Army Combat Studies Institute, August 1979.

Draude, Thomas V., *When Should a Commander Be Relieved: A Study of Combat Reliefs of Commanders of Battalions and Lower Units During the Vietnam Era*, Fort Leavenworth, Kan.: U.S. Army Command and General Staff College, June 11, 1976.

Drury, Bob, and Tom Clavin, *The Last Stand of Fox Company*, New York: Atlantic Monthly Press, 2009.

du Picq, Ardant, *Battle Studies: Ancient and Modern Battle*, trans., John R. Greely and Robert C. Cotton, New York: The Macmillan Company, 1921.

Dupuy, Trevor N., and Gay M. Hammerman, *Soldier Capability—Army Combat Effectiveness (SCACE): Volume III, Historical Combat Data and Analysis*, Dunn Loring, Va.: Historical Evaluation and Research Organization, December 1980.

Durant, Henry, "Morale and Its Measurement," *American Journal of Sociology*, Vol. 47, No. 3, November 1941, pp. 406–414.

Dyches, Karmon D., James A. Anderson, and Kristin N. Saboe, "Modeling the Indirect Association of Combat Exposure with Anger and Aggression During Combat Deployment: The Moderating Role of Morale," *Military Psychology*, Vol. 29, No. 4, 2017, pp. 260–270.

Echevarria II, Antulio J., "War, Politics, and the RMA—The Legacy of Clausewitz," *Joint Forces Quarterly*, Winter 1995–1996, pp. 76–80.

Edwards, Peter, "Mort pour la France: Conflict and Commemoration in France After the First World War," *University of Sussex Journal of Contemporary History*, Vol. 1, 2000, pp. 1–11.

Egbert, Robert L., Tor Meeland, Victor B. Cline, Edward W. Forgy, Martin W. Spickler, and Charles Brown, *Fighter 1: An Analysis of Combat Fighters and Non-Fighters*, Technical Report 44, Monterey, Calif.: U.S. Army Leadership Human Research Unit, December 1957.

Elliott, David W. P., and Mai Elliott, *Documents of an Elite Viet Cong Delta Unit: The Demolition Platoon of the 514th Battalion: Part Four: Political Indoctrination and Military Training*, Santa Monica, Calif.: RAND Corporation, RM-5851-ISA/ARPA, 1969. As of March 23, 2018: https://www.rand.org/pubs/research_memoranda/RM5851.html

Endler, Norman S., and Nancy Kocovski, "State and Trait Anxiety Revisited," *Anxiety Disorders*, No. 15, 2001, pp. 231–245.

English, Allan D., *Understanding Military Culture: A Canadian Perspective*, Ithaca, N.Y.: McGill-Queens University Press, 2004.

English, John A., *A Perspective on Infantry*, New York: Praeger Publishers, 1981.

Evertsz, Rick, Frank E. Ritter, Paolo Busetta, and Matteo Pedtrotti, "Realistic Behavior Variation in a BDI-Based Cognitive Architecture," *Proceedings of SimTec 2008*, Melbourne, Australia: SIAA Ltd., 2008.

Falkenhayn, Erich von, *The German General Staff and Its Decisions, 1914–1916*, New York: Dodd, Mead, and Company, Inc., 1920 (1919).

Fefferman, Kevin, Manuel Diego, Chris Gaughan, Charneta Samms, Howard Borum, Jon Clegg, Joseph S. McDonnell, and Robert Leach, *A Study in the Implementation of a Distributed Soldier Representation*, ARL-TR-6985, Aberdeen Proving Ground, Md.: Army Research Laboratory, March 2015.

Fehrenbach, T. R., *This Kind of War: The Classic Korean War History*, Washington, D.C.: Brassey's, 1994 (1963).

Fennell, J., "Courage and Cowardice in the North African Campaign: The Eighth Army and Defeat in the Summer of 1942," *War in History*, Vol. 20, No. 1, 2013, pp. 99–122.

Fine, Saul, Judith Goldenberg, and Yair Noam, "Integrity Testing and the Prediction of Counterproductive Behaviours in the Military," *Journal of Occupational and Organizational Psychology*, No. 89, 2016, pp. 198–218.

Fitzpatrick III, C. Neil, and Umit Ayvaz, *Training Methods and Tactical Decision-Making Simulations*, thesis, Monterey, Calif.: Naval Postgraduate School, 2007.

Flammer, Philip M., "Conflicting Loyalties and the American Military Ethic," *American Behavioral Scientist*, Vol. 19, No. 5, May–June 1976, pp. 589–604.

Foch, Ferdinand, *The Principles of War*, trans. Hilaire Belloc, New York: Henry Holt and Company, 1920. As of April 9, 2018: https://archive.org/details/principlesofwar00foch

Foley, Robert T., *German Strategy and the Path to Verdun: Erich Von Falkenhayn and the Development of Attrition, 1870–1916*, Cambridge: Cambridge University Press, 2005.

Ford, Douglas, "British Intelligence on Japanese Army Morale During the Pacific War: Logical Analysis or Racial Stereotyping," *Journal of Military History*, Vol. 69, No. 2, April 2005, pp. 439–474.

Ford, Gerald R., Address Before a Joint Session of the Congress Reporting on United States Foreign Policy, The American Presidency Project, The White House, April 10, 1975.

Forrester, Jay W., *Urban Dynamics*, Cambridge, Mass.: The Massachusetts Institute of Technology Press, 1969, as quoted in Davis, 1989.

Frame, Charles L., Brian R. McEnany, and Kurt A. Kladivko, "Combat Operational Data Analysis: An Examination of World War II Suppression Data," *Human Behavior and Performance as Essential Ingredients in Realistic Modeling of Combat—MORIMOC II Volume 2*, proceedings, Alexandria, Va.: Military Operations Research Society, February 1989.

Frank, Joseph Allan, and George A. Reaves, *Seeing the Elephant: Raw Recruits at the Battle of Shiloh*, Urbana: University of Illinois Press, 2003.

Frankel, Glenn, "War and Emerging Remembrance: German Veterans Begin to Add Narrative Piece to WWII," *Washington Post*, July 24, 2004, p. A01. As of April 3, 2018: http://www.washingtonpost.com/wp-dyn/articles/A10191-2004Jul23.html

Fredlake, Christopher P., and Kai Wang, *EINStein Goes to War: A Primer on Ground Combat Models*, Alexandria, Va.: Center for Naval Analyses, September 2008.

Friedman, B. A., "Maneuver Warfare: A Defense," *Marine Corps Gazette*, Vol. 98, No. 12, 2014, pp. 26–29.

Friedman, Russell, and John W. James, "The Myth of the Stages of Dying, Death, and Grief," *Skeptic*, Vol. 14, No. 2, 2008, pp. 25–37.

Gabel, Christopher R., and James H. Willbanks, eds., *Great Commanders*, Fort Leavenworth, Kan.: Combat Studies Institute Press, 2012.

Gachter, Simon, and Jonathan F. Schulz, "Intrinsic Honesty and the Prevalence of Rule Violations across Societies," letter, *Nature*, Vol. 531, March 24, 2016, pp. 496–499, with additional data pages.

Gal, Reuven, "Unit Morale: From a Theoretical Puzzle to an Empirical Illustration—An Israeli Example," *Journal of Applied Social Psychology*, Vol. 16, No. 6, 1986, pp. 549–564.

———, "Combat Stress as an Opportunity: The Case of Heroism," in Belenky, 1987, pp. 31–46.

Gal, Reuven, and Franklin D. Jones, "A Psychological Model of Combat Stress," in Russ Zajtchuk, ed., *Textbook of Military Medicine, Part I: War Psychiatry*, Falls Church, Va.: Office of the Surgeon General of the United States of America, 1995, pp. 133–148.

García-Guiu, Carlos, Miguel Moya, Fernando Molero, and Juan Antonio Moriano, "Transformational Leadership and Group Potency in Small Military Units: The Mediating Role of Group Identification and Cohesion," *Revista de Psicología del Trabajo y de las Organizaciones*, Vol. 32, No. 3, 2016, pp. 145–152.

Gartner, Scott Sigmund, and Marissa Edmund Myers, "Body Counts and 'Success' in the Vietnam and Korean Wars," *Journal of Interdisciplinary History*, Vol. 25, No. 3, 1994, pp. 377–395.

Gawrych, George W., *The 1973 Arab-Israeli War: The Albatross of Decisive Victory*, Leavenworth Papers Number 21, Fort Leavenworth, Kan.: Combat Studies Institute, U.S. Army Command and General Staff College, 1996.

General Research Corporation, *CARMONETTE Volume I General Description*, technical manual, McLean, Va.: Operations Analysis Division of General Research Corporation, November 1974.

Gibson, Stephen, and Susan Condor, "State Institutions and Social Identity: National Representation in Soldiers' and Civilians' Interview Talk Concerning Military Service," *British Journal of Social Psychology*, Vol. 48, No. 2, June 2009, pp. 313–336.

Giles, Lionel, trans., *Sun Tzu on the Art of War: The Oldest Military Treatise in the World*, London: Luzac, 1910. As of April 19, 2018:
http://classics.mit.edu/Tzu/artwar.html

Gingrich, Karl, Matthew Shane, and Matthew Durkin, "Measuring Quality of the ANSF," *Phalanx*, March 2011, pp. 22–24.

Glenn, Russell W., "No More Principles of War?" *Parameters*, Spring 1998, pp. 48–66.

Glick, Stephen P., and L. Ian Charters, "War, Games, and Military History," *Journal of Contemporary History*, Vol. 18, No. 4, October 1983, pp. 567–582.

Gordon, Michael R., and Eric Schmitt, "Russia's Military Drills near NATO Border Raise Fears of Aggression," *New York Times*, July 31, 2017. As of April 3, 2018:
https://www.nytimes.com/2017/07/31/world/europe/russia-military-exercise-zapad-west.html

Granovetter, Mark, "Threshold Models of Collective Behavior," *American Journal of Sociology*, Vol. 83, No. 6, May 1978, pp. 1420–1443.

Gratch, Jonathan, and Stacy Marsella, "Fight the Way You Train: The Role and Limits of Emotions in Training for Combat," *Brown Journal of World Affairs*, Vol. 63, No. 7, 2003, pp. 63–75.

Grazier, Daniel, and William S. Lind, "Maneuver Warfare: Making It Real in the Marine Corps," *Marine Corps Gazette*, Vol. 99, No. 4, April 2015, pp. 24–27.

Green, Kimberly T., Patrick S. Calhoun, and Michelle F. Dennis, "Exploration of the Resilience Construct in Posttraumatic Stress Disorder Severity and Functional Correlates in Military Combat Veterans Who Have Served Since September 11, 2001," *Journal of Clinical Psychiatry*, Vol. 71, No. 7, July 2010, pp. 823–830.

Gregory, Shaun, and James Revill, "The Role of the Military in the Cohesion and Stability of Pakistan," *Contemporary South Asia*, Vol. 16, No. 1, March 2008, pp. 39–61.

Grice, Robert L., and Lawrence C. Katz, *Cohesion in Military and Aviation Psychology: An Annotated Bibliography and Suggestions for US Army Aviation*, Fort Rucker, Ala.: Army Research Institute for the Behavioral and Social Sciences Fort Rucker Al Rotary-Wing Aviation Research Unit, No. ARI-TR-1166, 2005.

Griffith, James, "Measurement of Group Cohesion in U.S. Army," *Basic and Applied Social Psychology*, Vol. 9, No. 2, 1988, pp. 149–171.

———, "Multilevel Analysis of Cohesion's Relation to Stress, Well-Being, Identification, Disintegration, and Perceived Combat Readiness," *Military Psychology*, Vol. 14, No. 3, 2002, pp. 217–239.

———, "What Do the Soldiers Say? Needed Ingredients for Determining Unit Readiness," *Armed Forces and Society*, Vol. 32, No. 3, 2006, pp. 367–388.

Grinker, Roy R., and John P. Spiegel, *Men under Stress*, Philadelphia: The Blakiston Company, 1945.

Grossman, Dave, *On Killing: The Psychological Cost of Learning to Kill in War and Society*, Boston: Little, Brown, and Company, 1995.

Gupta, Sanjeev, Luiz de Mello, and Raju Sharan, "Corruption and Military Spending," *European Journal of Political Economy*, Vol. 17, 2001, pp. 749–777.

Hajjar, Remi, "What Lessons Did We Learn (or Re-Learn) About Military Advising After 9/11?" *Military Review*, November–December 2014, pp. 63–75.

Hancock, Peter A., Deborah R. Billings, Kristin E. Schaefer, Jessie Y. C. Chen, Ewart J. De Visser, and Raja Parasuraman, "A Meta-Analysis of Factors Affecting Trust in Human-Robot Interaction," *Human Factors*, Vol. 53, No. 5, 2011, pp. 517–527.

Harder, Byron R., *Automated Battle Planning for Combat Models with Maneuver and Fire Support*, thesis, Monterey, Calif.: Naval Postgraduate School, 2017.

Hardy, Ben, *Morale: Definitions, Dimensions, and Measurement*, doctoral thesis, Cambridge: Cambridge Judge Business School, 2009.

Harré, Rom, and Fathali M. Moghaddam, eds., *Questioning Causality: Scientific Explorations of Cause and Consequence Across Social Contexts*, Santa Barbara, Calif.: Praeger, 2016.

Harte, Julia, "The Fraud of War: U.S. Troops in Iraq and Afghanistan Have Stolen Tens of Millions Through Bribery, Theft, and Rigged Contracts," *Slate*, May 5, 2015. As of April 3, 2018: http://www.slate.com/articles/news_and_politics/politics/2015/05/u_s_troops_have_stolen_tens_of_millions_in_iraq_and_afghanistan_center_for.html

Haslam, Diana R., and Peter Abraham, "Sleep Loss and Military Performance," in Belenky, 1987, pp. 167–184.

Hata, Ikuhiko, "From Consideration to Contempt: The Changing Nature of Japanese Military and Popular Perceptions of Prisoners of War Through the Ages," in Bob Moore and Kent Fedorowich, eds., *Prisoners of War and Their Captors in World War II*, Washington, D.C.: Berg Press, 1996, pp. 253–276.

Hauser, William L., "The Will to Fight," in Sarkesian, 1980, pp. 186–211.

Hayes, Richard E., Paul C. Davis, John J. Hayes, Farid Abolfathi, and Bill Harvey, *Measurement of Unit Effectiveness in Marine Corps Infantry Battalions*, Washington, D.C.: DARPA, October 31, 1977.

Hegi, Benjamin P., *Extermination Warfare? The Conduct of the Second Marine Division at Saipan*, thesis, Denton: University of North Texas, 2008.

Henderson, William Darryl, *Cohesion: The Human Element in Combat*, Washington, D.C.: National Defense University Press, 1985.

Henriksen, Rune, "Warriors in Combat—What Makes People Actively Fight in Combat?" *Journal of Strategic Studies*, Vol. 30, No. 2, 2007, pp. 187–223.

Henriksen, Rune, and Anthony Vinci, "Combat Motivation in Non-State Armed Groups," *Terrorism and Political Violence*, Vol. 20, No. 1, 2007, pp. 87–109.

Herbert, Paul H., *Deciding What Has to Be Done: General William E. DePuy and the 1976 Edition of FM 100-5, Operations*, Leavenworth Paper No. 16, Fort Leavenworth, Kan.: U.S. Army Combat Studies Institute, July 1988.

Herrera, Natalia, and Douglas Porch. " 'Like Going to a Fiesta'—The Role of Female Fighters in Colombia's FARC-EP," *Small Wars and Insurgencies*, Vol. 19, No. 4, 2008, pp. 609–634.

Herspring, Dale R., "Undermining Combat Readiness in the Russian Military, 1992–2005," *Armed Forces & Society*, Vol. 32, No. 4, 2006, pp. 513–531.

Heuser, Beatrice, *Reading Clausewitz*, London: Pimlico, 2002.

Hiroi, Taeko, and Sawa Omori, "Causes and Triggers of Coups d'état: An Event History Analysis," *Politics and Policy*, Vol. 41, No. 1, 2013, pp. 39–64.

Hitlin, Steven, "Values as the Core of Personal Identity: Drawing Links Between Two Theories of Self," *Social Psychology Quarterly*, Vol. 66, No. 2, June 2003, pp. 118–137.

Hocking, William Ernest, "The Nature of Morale," *American Journal of Sociology*, Vol. 47, No. 3, November 1941, pp. 302–320.

Hogg, Michael A., Deborah J. Terry, and Katherine M. White, "A Tale of Two Theories: A Critical Comparison of Identity Theory with Social Identity Theory," *Social Psychology Quarterly*, Vol. 58, No. 4, December 1995, pp. 255–269.

Holmes, Richard, *Acts of War: The Behavior of Men in Battle*, New York: The Free Press, 1985.

Honig, Jan Willem, "Avoiding War, Inviting Defeat: The Srebrenica Crisis, July 1995," *Journal of Contingencies and Crisis Management*, Vol. 9, No. 4, December 2001, pp. 200–210.

Hooker, Richard D., Jr., "The Mythology Surrounding Maneuver Warfare," *Parameters*, Spring 1993, pp. 27–38.

Horne, Alistair, *The Price of Glory: Verdun 1916*, New York: St. Martin's Press, 1962.

———, "The Legend of Verdun," *NewStatesman*, February 17, 2016. As of April 3, 2018: https://www.newstatesman.com/politics/uk/2016/02/legend-verdun

Huddy, Leonie, "From Social to Political Identity: A Critical Examination of Social Identity Theory," *Political Psychology*, Vol. 22, No. 1, March 2001, pp. 127–156.

Hulswit, Menno, "Causality and Causation: The Inadequacy of the Received View," undated manuscript.

Hutson, Larry J., *A Representational Approach to Knowledge and Multiple Skill Levels for Broad Classes of Computer Generated Forces*, thesis, Wright-Patterson Air Force Base, Ohio: Air Force Institute of Technology, 1997.

Hyllengren, Peder, "Military Leaders' Adaptability in Unexpected Situations," *Military Psychology*, Vol. 29, No. 4, 2017, pp. 245–259.

Ibrugger, Lothar, *The Revolution in Military Affairs: Special Report*, NATO Parliamentary Assembly, Science and Technology Committee, November 1998.

Ilachinski, Andrew, *Artificial War: Multiagent-Based Simulation of Combat*, River Edge, N.J.: World Scientific Publishing Corporation, 2004.

International Security Assistance Force (ISAF), *Instruction Manual for the Commander's Update Assessment Tool Located in CIDNE*, Kabul, Afghanistan: International Security Assistance Force, November 14, 2010.

Jaffe, Greg, and Loveday Morris, "Defense Secretary Carter: Iraqis Lack 'Will to Fight' to Defeat Islamic State," *Washington Post*, May 24, 2015. As of April 3, 2018: https://www.washingtonpost.com/politics/defense-secretary-carter-iraqis-need-will-to-fight-to-defeat-islamic-state/2015/05/24/1f189454-022e-11e5-bc72-f3e16bf50bb6_story.html?utm_term=.0fede8c04cd7

Jankowski, Paul, *Verdun: The Longest Battle of the Great War*, New York: Oxford University Press, 2013.

Janowitz, Morris, *On Social Organization and Social Control*, Chicago: The University of Chicago Press, 1991.

Jaworsky, Pace L., "Conventional Advising: A Tactical Leader's Assessment of a Strategic Initiative," *Armor*, January–March 2013, pp. 23–37.

Joes, Anthony James, *The War for South Vietnam: 1954–1975*, rev. ed. Westport, Conn.: Praeger Publishers, 2001.

Johnson, Stuart, Martin C. Libicki, and Gregory F. Treverton, eds., *New Challenges, New Tools for Defense Decisionmaking*, Santa Monica, Calif.: RAND Corporation, MR-1576-RC, 2003. As of March 23, 2018:
https://www.rand.org/pubs/monograph_reports/MR1576.html

Johnson, Stuart E., John E. Peters, Karin E. Kitchens, Aaron Martin, and Jordan R. Fischbach, *A Review of the Army's Modular Force Structure*, Santa Monica, Calif.: RAND Corporation, TR-927-2-OSD, 2012. As of March 19, 2018:
https://www.rand.org/pubs/technical_reports/TR927-2.html

Jones, Edgar, "The Psychology of Killing: The Combat Experience of British Soldiers During the First World War," *Journal of Contemporary History*, Vol. 41, No. 2, 2006, pp. 229–246.

Jozwiak, S. J., *Military Unit Cohesion: The Mechanics and Why Some Programs Evolve and Others Dissolve*, Quantico, Va.: Marine Corps University, 1999.

Kahn, Herman, and Irwin Mann, *Techniques of Systems Analysis*, Santa Monica, Calif.: RAND Corporation, RM-1829-1-PR, 1957. As of March 19, 2018:
https://www.rand.org/pubs/research_memoranda/RM1829-1.html

———, *War Gaming*, Santa Monica, Calif.: RAND Corporation, 1957. As of April 19, 2018:
https://www.rand.org/pubs/papers/P1167.html

Kairuz, Thérése, K. Crump, and A. O'Brien, "Tools for Data Collection and Analysis," *Pharmaceutical Journal*, Vol. 278, 2007, pp. 371–377.

Kamarck, Kristy N., *Diversity, Inclusion, and Equal Opportunity in the Armed Services: Background and Issues for Congress*, Congressional Research Service, October 24, 2017.

Karnow, Stanley, "Giap Remembers," *New York Times*, June 24, 1990. As of April 3, 2018:
https://www.nytimes.com/1990/06/24/magazine/giap-remembers.html

Karohs, Jeff W., *AirLand Battle-Future—A Hop, Skip, or Jump?*, monograph, Fort Leavenworth, Kan.: U.S. Army Command and General Staff College, December 15, 1990.

Kay, Lindell, "Marine Accused of Stealing $1M in Gov't Property," *The Daily News* (Jacksonville, N.C.), March 4, 2013. As of April 3, 2018:
https://www.military.com/daily-news/2013/03/04/marine-accused-of-stealing-1m-in-government-property.html

Keaney, Thomas A., and Eliot A. Cohen, *Gulf War Air Power Survey: Summary Report*, Washington, D.C.: U.S. Air Force, 1993.

Keegan, John, *The Face of Battle*, New York: Viking Penguin Incorporated, 1976.

Keene, Jennifer Diane, "Intelligence and Morale in the Army of a Democracy," *Military Psychology*, Vol. 6, No. 4, 1994, pp. 235–253.

Kellen, Konrad, *Conversations with Enemy Soldiers in Late 1968/Early 1969: A Study of Motivation and Morale*, Santa Monica, Calif.: RAND Corporation, RM-6131-1-ISA/ARPA, 1970. As of March 19, 2018:
https://www.rand.org/pubs/research_memoranda/RM6131-1.html

Kellett, Anthony, *Combat Motivation: The Behavior of Soldiers in Battle*, Hingham, Mass.: Kluwer Boston, Inc., 1982.

Kelly, Terrence K., Nora Bensahel, and Olga Oliker, *Security Force Assistance in Afghanistan: Identifying Lessons for Future Efforts*, Santa Monica, Calif.: RAND Corporation, MG-1066-A, 2011. As of March 22, 2018:
https://www.rand.org/pubs/monographs/MG1066.html

Kendzierski, Deborah, and Daniel J. Whitaker, "The Role of Self-Schema in Linking Intentions with Behavior," *Personality and Social Psychology Bulletin*, Vol. 23, No. 2, 1997, pp. 139–147.

Kennedy, Carrie H., and Eric A. Zillmer, eds., *Military Psychology: Clinical and Operational Applications*, New York: The Guilford Press, 2006.

Kestnbaum, Meyer, "Mars Revealed: The Entry of Ordinary People into War Among States," in Julia Adams, Elisabeth S. Clemens, and Ann Shola Orloff, eds., *Remaking Modernity: Politics, History, and Sociology*, Durham, N.C.: Duke University Press, 2005, pp. 13–29.

Kier, Elizabeth, "Culture and Military Doctrine: France Between the Wars," *International Security*, Vol. 19, No. 4, Spring 1995, pp. 65–93.

King, Anthony, "The Word of Command: Communication and Cohesion in the Military," *Armed Forces and Society*, Vol. 32, No. 4, 2006, pp. 493–512.

———, "On Cohesion," in Anthony King, ed., *Frontline: Combat and Cohesion in the Twenty-First Century*, Oxford: Oxford University Press, 2015, pp. 3–23.

———, "On Combat Effectiveness in the Infantry Platoon: Beyond the Primary Group Thesis," *Security Studies*, Vol. 25, No. 4, 2016, pp. 699–728.

King, Lynda A., Daniel W. King, Dawne S. Vogt, Jeffrey Knight, and Rita E. Samper, "Deployment Risk and Resilience Inventory: A Collection of Measures for Studying Deployment-Related Experiences of Military Personnel and Veterans," *Military Psychology*, Vol. 18, No. 2, pp. 89–120.

Kreiner, Glen E., Elaine C. Hollensbe, and Mathew L. Sheep, "On the Edge of Identity: Boundary Dynamics at the Interface of Individual and Organizational Identities," *Human Relations*, Vol. 59, No. 10, 2006, pp. 1315–1341.

Lang, Andrew F., "Upon the Altar of Our Country: Confederate Identity, Nationalism, and Morale in Harrison County, Texas, 1860–1865," *Civil War History*, Vol. 55, No. 2, 2009, pp. 278–306.

Lauer, G. S., *Maneuver Warfare Theory: Creating a Tactically Unbalanced Fleet Marine Force?* Fort Leavenworth, Kan.: U.S. Army School of Advanced Military Studies, December 24, 1990.

Lepre, George, *Fragging: Why U.S. Soldiers Assaulted Their Officers in Vietnam*, Lubbock, Tex.: Texas Tech University Press, 2011.

Lesser, Harry K., Jr., *The Revolution in Military Affairs and Its Effect on the Future Army*, thesis, Newport, R.I.: U.S. Naval War College, 1994.

Li, Jennifer J., Tracy C. McCausland, Lawrence M. Hanser, Andrew M. Naber, and Judith Babcock LaValley, *Enhancing Professionalism in the U.S. Air Force*, Santa Monica, Calif.: RAND Corporation, RR-1721-AF, 2017. As of March 19, 2018:
https://www.rand.org/pubs/research_reports/RR1721.html

Li, Ji, Jane Moy, Kevin Lam, and W. L. Chris Chu, "Institutional Pillars and Corruption at the Societal Level," *Journal of Business Ethics*, Vol. 83, No. 3, 2008, pp. 327–339.

Lieber, Eli, "Mixing Qualitative and Quantitative Methods: Insights into Design and Analysis Issues," *Journal of Ethnographic and Qualitative Research*, Vol. 3, No. 4, 2009, pp. 218–227.

Lind, William S., "Defining Maneuver Warfare for the Marine Corps," *Marine Corps Gazette*, Vol. 64, No. 3, March 1980, pp. 55–58.

———, "Why the German Example?" *Marine Corps Gazette*, Vol. 66, No. 6, June 1982, pp. 59–63.

———, *Maneuver Warfare Handbook*, New York: Westview Press, 1985.

Linde, Charlotte, *Working the Past: Narrative and Institutional Memory*, Oxford: Oxford University Press, 2009.

Lloyd, Jeffrey J., "Our Warfighting Philosophy," *Marine Corps Gazette*, Vol. 73, No. 11, November 1989, pp. 24–25.

Long, Jeffrey W., *The Evolution of U.S. Army Doctrine: From Active Defense to AirLand Battle and Beyond*, thesis, Fort Leavenworth, Kan.: U.S. Army Command and General Staff College, 1991.

Losh, Elizabeth, "Playing Defense: Gender, Just War, and Game Design," in Pat Harrigan and Matthew G. Kirschenbaum, eds., *Zones of Control: Perspectives on Wargaming*, Cambridge, Mass.: The Massachusetts Institute of Technology, 2016, pp. 355–369.

Love, Ricardo M., *Psychological Resilience: Preparing Our Soldiers for War*, Carlisle, Pa.: U.S. Army War College, 2011.

Lyall, Jason, "Forced to Fight: Coercion, Blocking Detachments, and Tradeoffs in Military Effectiveness," unpublished research paper, December 15, 2015.

———, "Why Armies Break: Explaining Mass Desertion in Conventional War," unpublished research paper, November 9, 2016.

MacCoun, Robert J., "What Is Known About Unit Cohesion and Military Performance," in Bernard Rostker et al., eds., *Sexual Orientation and U.S. Military Personnel Policy: Options and Assessment*, Santa Monica, Calif.: RAND Corporation, MR-323-OSD, 1993, pp. 283–331. As of March 19, 2018: https://www.rand.org/pubs/monograph_reports/MR323.html

MacCoun, Robert J., Elizabeth Kier, and Aaron Belkin, "Does Social Cohesion Determine Motivation in Combat? An Old Question with an Old Answer," *Armed Forces & Society*, Vol. 32, No. 4, 2006, pp. 646–654.

Maclachlan, Karolina, "How Corruption Undermines NATO Operations," *DefenseOne*, December 2, 2015. As of April 3, 2018: http://www.defenseone.com/ideas/2015/12/how-corruption-undermines-nato-operations/124148/

Mael, Fred A., and Cathie E. Alderks, "Leadership Team Cohesion and Subordinate Work Unit Morale and Performance," *Military Psychology*, Vol. 5, No. 3, 1993, pp. 141–158.

Maklak, Alena, "Dedovshchina on Trial: Some Evidence Concerning the Last Soviet Generation of 'Sons' and 'Grandfathers,'" *Nationalities Papers*, Vol. 43, No. 5, 2015, pp. 682–699.

Manning, Frederick J., "Morale and Cohesion in Military Psychiatry," in Russ Zajtchuk, ed., *Textbook of Military Medicine*, Washington, D.C.: TTM Publications, U.S. Army Office of the Surgeon General, 1995.

Marcellino, William M, "Talk Like a Marine: USMC Linguistic Acculturation and Civil–Military Argument," *Discourse Studies*, Vol. 16, No. 3, 2014, pp. 385–405.

Markwick, Roger D., and Euridice Charon Cardona, *Soviet Women on the Frontline in the Second World War*, New York: Palgrave Macmillan, 2012.

Marshall, S. L. A., *Men Against Fire: The Problem of Battle Command in Future War*, Washington, D.C.: U.S. War Department, 1947.

———, "First Wave at Omaha Beach," *The Atlantic*, November 1960. As of April 3, 2018: https://www.theatlantic.com/magazine/archive/1960/11/first-wave-at-omaha-beach/303365/

Mausner, Adam, *Reforming ANSF Metrics: Improving the CUAT System*, Washington, D.C.: Center for Strategic and International Studies, August 2010.

McBreen, Brendan B., *Marine Close Combat Workbook*, Washington, D.C.: Marine Corps Institute, May 2002.

McCormick, Michael, *The New FM 100-5: A Return to Operational Art*, monograph, Fort Leavenworth, Kan.: U.S. Army School of Advanced Military Studies, April 18, 1997.

McDonnell, Joseph S., "Distributed Soldier Representation: M&S Representations of the Human Dimensions of the Soldier," presentation, NDIA Annual Systems Engineering Conference 2015, Orlando, Fla.: U.S. Army Research Laboratory, October 26–29, 2015.

McHale, Shawn Frederick, *Print and Power: Confucianism, Communism, and Buddhism in the Making of Modern Vietnam*, Honolulu: University of Hawaii Press, 2004 (reprint by Munshiram Manoharlal Publishers Pvt. Ltd., India, 2010).

McHugh, Francis J., *Fundamentals of War Gaming*, Newport, R.I.: U.S. Naval War College, March 1, 1966.

McKenzie, Kenneth F., Jr., "On the Verge of a New Era: The Marine Corps and Maneuver Warfare," *Marine Corps Gazette*, Vol. 77, No. 7, July 1993, pp. 63–67.

McMaster, H. R., *Dereliction of Duty: Lyndon Johnson, Robert McNamara, the Joint Chiefs of Staff, and the Lies That Led to Vietnam*, New York: HarperCollins, 1997.

McPherson, James M., *For Cause and Comrades: Why Men Fought in the Civil War*, New York: Oxford University Press, 1997.

Meerloo, Joost A. M., "Mental Danger, Stress and Fear: Part II. Man and His Morale," *Journal of Nervous and Mental Disease*, Vol. 125, No. 3, July–September 1957, pp. 357–379.

Menninger, W. Walter, "The Meaning of Morale: A Peace Corps Model," in D. P. Moynihan, ed., *Business and Society in Change*, New York: American Telegraph and Telephone Company, 1975.

Meredith, Lisa S., Cathy D. Sherbourne, Sarah Gaillot, Lydia Hansell, Hans V. Ritschard, Andrew M. Parker, and Glenda Wrenn, *Promoting Psychological Resilience in the U.S. Military*, Santa Monica, Calif.: RAND Corporation, MG-996-OSD, 2011. As of March 20, 2018: https://www.rand.org/pubs/monographs/MG996.html

Metz, Steven, "A Wake for Clausewitz: Toward a Philosophy of 21st Century Warfare," *Parameters*, Vol. 24, 1994–1995, pp. 126–132.

Middlekauff, Robert, "Why Men Fought in the American Revolution," *Huntington Library Quarterly*, Vol. 43, No. 2, 1980, pp.135–148.

Middleton, Victor, "Simulating Small Unit Military Operations with Agent-Based Models of Complex Adaptive Systems," in B. Johannson, S. Jain, J. Montoya-Torres, J. Hugan, and E. Yucesan, eds., *Proceedings of the 2010 Winter Simulation Conference*, 2010, pp. 119–134. As of April 19, 2018: https://www.informs-sim.org/wsc10papers/013.pdf

Milikan, J., M. Wong, and D. Grieger, "Suppression of Dismounted Soldiers: Towards Improving Dynamic Threat Assessment in Closed Loop Combat Simulations," conference paper, 20th International Conference on Modeling and Simulation, Adelaide, Australia, December 1–6, 2013.

Miller, Delbert C., and Neil J. Salkind, *Handbook of Research Design and Social Measurement*, 6th ed., Thousand Oaks, Calif.: Sage Publications, 2002.

Millett, Allan R., Williamson Murray, and Kenneth H. Watman, "The Effectiveness of Military Organizations," *International Security*, Vol. 11, No. 1, 1986, pp. 37–71.

Mitchell, Edward J., "Inequality and Insurgency: A Statistical Study of South Vietnam," *World Politics*, Vol. 23, No. 3, 1968, pp. 421–438.

Montgomery, Bernard Law, *The Memoirs of the Field-Marshal the Viscount Montgomery of Alamein, K.G.*, Cleveland, Ohio: World Publishing Company, 1958.

Montgomery, Field-Marshal Viscount, "Morale in Battle," *British Medical Journal*, Vol. 2, No. 4479, 1946, pp. 702–704.

Lord Moran (Charles McMoran Wilson), *The Anatomy of Courage*, New York: Carroll and Graf Publishers, 2007 (1945).

Morse, Janice M., "Principles of Mixed Methods and Multimethod Research Design," in Abbas Tashakkori and Charles Teddlie, eds., *Handbook of Mixed Methods in Social and Behavioral Research*, Thousand Oaks, Calif.: Sage Publications, 2003, pp. 189–208.

Moskos, Charles C., "The American Combat Soldier in Vietnam," *Journal of Social Issues*, Vol. 31, No. 4, 1975, pp. 25–37.

Mountcastle, John W., *Flame On: U.S. Incendiary Weapons, 1918–1945*, Mechanicsburg, Pa.: Stackpole Books, 1999.

Murray, Williamson, "Thinking About Revolutions in Military Affairs," *Joint Forces Quarterly*, Summer 1997, pp. 69–76.

Mushen, Emily, and Jonathan Schroden, *Are We Winning? A Brief History of Military Operations Assessment*, Alexandria, Va.: Center for Naval Analyses, September 2014.

Naval Air Warfare Center Aircraft Division, homepage, undated. As of October 13, 2017: http://www.navair.navy.mil/nawcad/index.cfm?fuseaction=home.get_content&key= 82A2BCDF-DD8A-4C40-BA9D-D4BE7977A222&highlight=jwars

Navlakha, Gautam, "A Force Stretched and Stressed," *Economic and Political Weekly*, Vol. 41, No. 46, 2006, pp. 4722–4724.

Neufeld, Jacob, and George M. Watson, Jr., "A Brief Survey of POWs in Twentieth Century Wars," *Air Power History*, Vol. 60, No. 2, 2013, pp. 34-45.

Newell, Thomas, *The Use of Special Operations Forces in Combating Terrorist Financing*, thesis, Monterey, Calif.: Naval Postgraduate School, 2006.

Newport, Frank, and Joseph Carroll, "Iraq Versus Vietnam: A Comparison of Public Opinion," *Gallup News Service*, August 24, 2006. As of April 3, 2018: http://news.gallup.com/poll/18097/iraq-versus-vietnam-comparison-public-opinion.aspx

Nguyen Tien Hung and Jerrold L. Schecter, *The Palace File: The Remarkable Story of the Secret Letters from Nixon and Ford to the President of South Vietnam and the American Promises That Were Never Kept*, New York: Harper and Row Publishers, Inc., 1985.

Nielsen, Suzanne C., *The U.S. Army's Post-Vietnam Recovery and the Dynamics of Change in Military Organizations*, Carlisle, Pa.: U.S. Army War College Strategic Studies Institute, September 2010.

O'Connor, Seini, and Ronald Fisher, "Predicting Societal Corruption Across Time," *Journal of Cross-Cultural Psychology*, Vol. 43, No. 4, 2012, pp. 644–659.

Orwin, Robert G., and Jack L. Vevea, "Evaluating Coding Decisions," in Harris Cooper, Larry V. Hedges, and Jeffrey C. Valentine, eds., *The Handbook of Research Synthesis and Meta-Analysis, Second Edition*, New York: Russell Sage Foundation, 2009, pp. 177–203.

Owens, William A., "The Emerging U.S. System-of-Systems," *Strategic Forum*, Institute for National Strategic Studies, No. 63, February 1996.

Palmer, Bruce, Jr., "U.S. Intelligence and Vietnam," declassified article, *Studies in Intelligence*, Vol. 28, Special Edition, 1984.

Palmisano, Michael, *With Friends, Family, and Conviction: Combat Motivation in British and Canadian Soldiers Fighting the First World War*, thesis, Boulder: University of Colorado, 2012.

Pamuk, Humeyra, and Gareth Jones, "Turkish Military a Fractured Force After Attempted Coup," *Reuters*, July 26, 2016. As of April 3, 2018:
https://www.reuters.com/article/us-turkey-security-military-insight/turkish-military-a-fractured-force-after-attempted-coup-idUSKCN10619L?il=0

Pardee RAND Graduate School, "Methods Centers at Pardee RAND: RAND Center for Gaming." As of April 9, 2018:
https://www.prgs.edu/research/methods-centers/gaming.html

Paul, Christopher, Colin P. Clarke, and Beth Grill, *Victory Has a Thousand Fathers: Sources of Success in Counterinsurgency*, Santa Monica, Calif.: RAND Corporation, MG-964, 2010. As of March 19, 2018:
https://www.rand.org/pubs/monographs/MG964.html

PAXsims, homepage, undated. As of April 18, 2018:
https://paxsims.wordpress.com

Peck, Michael, "Successful War Games Combine Both Civilian and Military Traits," *National Defense*, November 1, 2011. As of April 3, 2018:
http://www.opanalytics.ca/npscourse/Successful%20War%20Games%20Combine%20Both%20Civilian%20and%20Military%20Traits.pdf

Perry, Warren, "The Nature and Significance of Discipline," *The Australian Quarterly*, Vol. 13, No. 4, December 1941, pp. 99–103.

Petersen, Michael B., *The Vietnam Cauldron: Defense Intelligence in the War for Southeast Asia*, Washington, D.C.: Defense Intelligence Agency, 2012.

Peterson, Nolan, "Ukraine's War Against Putin-Backed Rebels Is Being Undermined by Corruption," *Newsweek*, August 13, 2017. As of April 3, 2018:
http://www.newsweek.com/ukraines-war-against-putin-backed-rebels-being-undermined-corruption-649756

Pew, Richard W., and Anne S. Mavor, eds., *Representing Human Behavior in Military Simulations*, Washington, D.C.: National Academy Press, 1997.

Pivarski, Jim, Collin Bennett, and Robert L. Grossman, *Deploying Analytics with the Portable Format for Analytics (PFA)*, River Forest, Ill.: Open Data Group, Inc., undated.

Pollock, Kenneth M., *Arabs at War: Military Effectiveness, 1948–1991*, Lincoln: University of Nebraska Press, 2002.

Posen, Barry R., *The Source of Military Doctrine: France, Britain, and Germany Between the World Wars*, Ithaca, N.Y.: Cornell University Press, 2014.

Potter, Joshua J., *American Advisors: Security Forces Assistance Model in the Long War*, Fort Leavenworth, Kan.: U.S. Army Combat Studies Institute Press, 2011.

"Profile: North Korean Leader Kim Jong-un," *BBC*, August 29, 2017.

Quade, E. S., *Military Systems Analysis*, Santa Monica, Calif.: RAND Corporation, RM-3452-PR, 1963. As of March 19, 2018:
https://www.rand.org/pubs/research_memoranda/RM3452.html

Rabinovich, Abraham, "Yom Kippur War: Against the Odds," *Jewish Journal*, September 11, 2013. As of April 3, 2018:
http://jewishjournal.com/opinion/121475/

Reese, Roger R., "Lessons of the Winter War: A Study in the Military Effectiveness of the Red Army, 1939–1940," *Journal of Military History*, Vol. 72, No. 3, July 2008, pp. 824–852.

Reuters, "Chinese Military Corruption Has Gotten So Bad That It Could Undermine the Country's Ability to Wage War," May 7, 2015. As of April 3, 2018: http://www.businessinsider.com/r-china-military-says-some-not-taking-graft-fight-seriously-2015-5

Reynolds, Craig W., "Flocks, Herds, and Schools: A Distributed Behavioral Model," *Computer Graphics*, Vol. 21, No. 4, July 1987, pp. 25–34.

Reynolds, Francis J., Allen L. Churchill, and Francis Trevelyan Miller, *The Story of the Great War: History of the European War from Official Sources*, New York: P. F. Collier and Sons, 1916.

Richardson, F. M., *Fighting Spirit: Psychological Factors in War*, New Delhi, India: Nahtraj Publishers, 2009 (1978).

Robinson, Amy, "Gamers Shape Future Force: Army Seeks Soldiers' Input Through Online Gaming," Tradoc News Center, August 23, 2017. As of October 16, 2017: http://tradocnews.org/tag/army-game-studio/

Robinson, Paul, " 'Ready to Kill but Not to Die': NATO Strategy in Kosovo," *International Journal*, Vol. 54, No. 4, Autumn 1999, pp. 671–682.

Roccas, Sonia, and Marilynn B. Brewer, "Social Identity Complexity," *Personality and Social Psychology Review*, Vol. 6, No. 2, 2002, pp. 88–106.

Rodrigues-Goulard, Fernando, "Combat Motivation," *Military Review*, November–December 2006, pp. 93–96.

Romjue, John L., *From Active Defense to AirLand Battle: The Development of Army Doctrine, 1973–1982*, Fort Monroe, Va.: U.S. Army Training and Doctrine Command, June 1984.

———, *American Army Doctrine for the Post-Cold War*, Fort Leavenworth, Kan.: U.S. Army Training and Doctrine Command, 1997.

Rosenau, William, Ralph Espach, Román D. Ortiz, and Natalia Herrera, "Why They Join, Why They Fight, and Why They Leave: Learning from Colombia's Database of Demobilized Militants," *Terrorism and Political Violence*, Vol. 26, No. 2, 2014, pp. 277–285.

Rowland, David, "Assessments of Combat Degradation," *RUSI Journal*, Vol. 131, No. 2, 1986, pp. 33–43.

Roy, Kaushik, "Discipline and Morale of the African, British and Indian Army Units in Burma and India During World War II: July 1943 to August 1945," *Modern Asian Studies*, Vol. 44, No. 6, 2010, pp. 1255–1282.

Royal Navy, "Royal Marines." As of November 11, 2017: https://www.royalnavy.mod.uk/our-organisation/the-fighting-arms/royal-marines

Ruffa, Chiara, "Cohesion, Political Motivation, and Military Performance in the Italian Alpini," in Anthony King, ed., *Frontline: Combat and Cohesion in the Twenty-First Century*, Oxford: Oxford University Press, 2015, pp. 250–265.

Rush, Robert S., "A Different Perspective: Cohesion, Morale, and Operational Effectiveness in the German Army, Fali 1944," *Armed Forces and Society*, Vol. 25, No. 3, 2016, pp. 477–508.

Russ, Martin, *Breakout: The Chosin Reservoir Campaign, Korea 1950*, New York: Fromm International Publishing, 1999.

Saad, Lydia, "Republicans and Democrats Disagree on Iraq War, but Support Troops," *Gallup News Service*, September 28, 2006. As of April 3, 2018: http://news.gallup.com/poll/24760/republicans-democrats-disagree-iraq-war-support-troops.aspx

Sabin, Philip, *Simulating War: Studying Conflict Through Simulation Games*, London: Bloomsbury Academic, 2012.

Sanders, Charles W., Jr., *No Other Law: The French Army and the Doctrine of the Offensive*, Santa Monica, Calif.: RAND Corporation, P-7331, 1987. As of March 19, 2018: https://www.rand.org/pubs/papers/P7331.html

Sarkesian, Sam C., "Combat Effectiveness," in Sarkesian, *Combat Effectiveness*, 1980, pp. 8–18.

Sarkesian, Sam C., ed., *Combat Effectiveness: Cohesion, Stress, and the Volunteer Military*, Beverly Hills, Calif.: Sage Publications, 1980.

Savage, Paul L., and Richard A. Gabriel, "Cohesion and Disintegration in the American Army: An Alternative Perspective," *Armed Forces and Society*, Vol. 2, No. 3, 1976, pp. 340–376.

Schaffer, Marvin B., *Lanchester Models of Guerrilla Engagements*, Santa Monica, Calif.: RAND Corporation, RM-5053-ARPA, 1967. As of March 19, 2018: https://www.rand.org/pubs/research_memoranda/RM5053.html

Schaubroeck, John M., Ann Chunyan Peng, Laura T. Riolli, and Everett S. Spain, "Resilience to Traumatic Exposure Among Soldiers Deployed in Combat," *Journal of Occupational Health Psychology*, Vol. 16, No. 1, 2011, pp. 18–37.

Scher, Adam, "The Collapse of the Iraqi Army's Will to Fight: A Lack of Motivation, Training, or Force Generation?" *Army Press Online Journal*, February 19, 2016. As of March 19, 2018: http://www.armyupress.army.mil/Journals/Military-Review/Online-Exclusive/2016-Online-Exclusive-Articles/Collapse-of-the-Iraqi-Army/

Schiavenza, Matt, "Why Iraq's Military Has No Will to Fight," *The Atlantic*, May 25, 2015. As of April 3, 2018: https://www.theatlantic.com/international/archive/2015/05/why-iraqs-military-has-no-will-to-fight/394067/

Schmitt, John F., "The Great FMFM 1 Debate: Is There Anything New Here?" *Marine Corps Gazette*, Vol. 73, No. 11, November 1989, pp. 25–26.

Schneider, Barry R., and Lawrence E. Grinter, eds., *Battlefield of the Future: 21st Century Warfare Issues*, 3rd ed., Montgomery, Ala.: Air University Press, 1998.

Schrage, Michael, "The Sword of Science," interview with Robert Cooper, *Washington Post*, October 9, 1983.

Severloh, Hein, *WN 62: Erinnerungen an Omaha Beach Normandie, 6. Juni 1944*, Germany, HEK Creativ Verlag, 2006.

Shah, Nirav B., Donna H. Rhodes, and Daniel E. Hastings, *Systems of Systems and Emergent System Context*, occasional paper #85, Cambridge, Mass.: Massachusetts Institute of Technology, undated.

Shamir, Boas, Esther Brainin, Eliav Zakay, and Micha Popper, "Perceived Combat Readiness as Collective Efficacy: Individual- and Group-Level Analysis," *Military Psychology*, Vol. 12, No. 2, 2000, pp. 105–119.

Shanker, Thom, "Study Says Faster Medical Evacuation Was Lifesaver for U.S. Troops," *New York Times*, September 30, 2015. As of April 3, 2018: https://www.nytimes.com/2015/10/01/us/politics/study-says-faster-medical-evacuation-was-lifesaver-for-us-troops.html

Shils, Edward A., and Morris Janowitz, "Cohesion and Disintegration in the Wehrmacht in World War II," *Public Opinion Quarterly*, Vol. 12, No. 2, 1948, pp. 280–315.

Shirley, W., *Moral: The Most Important Factor in War*, London: Sifton, Praed & Company, 1916.

Siebold, Guy L., "The Evolution of the Measurement of Cohesion," *Military Psychology*, Vol. 11, No. 1, 1999, pp. 5–26.

———, "Military Group Cohesion," *Military Life: The Psychology of Serving in Peace and Combat*, Vol. 1, 2006, pp. 185–201.

———, "The Essence of Military Group Cohesion," *Armed Forces and Society*, Vol. 33, No. 2, 2007, pp. 286–295.

Smith, Monte D., and Joseph D. Hagman, *Personnel Stabilization and Cohesion: A Summary of Key Literature Findings*, Alexandria, Va.: Army Research Laboratory, 2004.

Smith, Robert B., "Why Soldiers Fight. Part I. Leadership, Cohesion and Fighter Spirit," *Quality and Quantity*, Vol. 18, No. 1, 1983, pp. 1–32.

Smith, Roger, "The Long History of Gaming in Military Training," *Simulation Gaming*, Vol. 41, No. 1, February 2010, pp. 6–19.

Snider, Don M., "An Uninformed Debate on Military Culture," *Orbis*, Vol. 43, No. 1, 1999, pp. 11–26.

Sorley, Lewis, ed., *The Abrams Tapes: 1968–1972*, Lubbock: Texas Tech University Press, 2004.

Spear, Laura, and Vincent Baines, "An Initial Conceptual Model for Morale Factors," *Proceedings of the 18th Conference on Behavior Representation in Modeling and Simulation*, Sundance, Utah: Social Computing Behavioral Cultural Modeling & Prediction and Behavior Organization, 2009, pp. 31–38.

Specht, Robert D., *War Games*, Santa Monica, Calif.: RAND Corporation, P-1041, 1957. As of March 19, 2018:
https://www.rand.org/pubs/papers/P1041.html

Special Inspector General for Afghanistan Reconstruction, *Afghan National Security Forces: Actions Needed to Improve Plans for Sustaining Capability Assessment Efforts*, SIGAR 14-33 Audit Report, Washington, D.C., February 2014.

Spencer, John, "What Is Army Doctrine?" *Modern War Institute*, March 21, 2016. As of April 3, 2018:
https://mwi.usma.edu/what-is-army-doctrine/

Spielberger, Charles Donald, *Manual for the State-Trait Anxiety Inventory STAI (Form Y)*, Palo Alto, Calif.: Mind Garden, 1983.

Stafford-Clark, David, "Morale and Flying Experience: Results of a Wartime Study," *British Journal of Psychiatry*, Vol. 95, No. 398, 1949, pp. 10–50.

Stanley, Bruce E., *Wargames, Training, and Decision-Making: Increasing the Experience of Army Leaders*, thesis, Fort Leavenworth, Kan.: U.S. Army Command and General Staff College, 1999.

Starry, Donn A., "To Change an Army," *Military Review*, Vol. 63, No. 3, March 1983, pp. 20–31.

Steam Community, homepage, undated. As of April 18, 2018:
https://steamcommunity.com

Steenkamp, Maria M., William P. Nash, and Brett T. Litz, "Post-Traumatic Stress Disorder: Review of the Comprehensive Soldier Fitness Program," *American Journal of Preventive Medicine*, Vol. 44, No. 5, May 2013, pp. 507–512.

Stephens, Elizabeth, "Caught on the Hop: The Yom Kippur War," *History Today*, October 2008, pp. 44–50.

Stephenson, Scott, "The Revolution in Military Affairs: 12 Observations on an Out-of-Fashion Idea," *Military Review*, May–June 2010, pp. 38–46.

Stern, Paul C., "Why Do People Sacrifice for Their Nations?" *Political Psychology*, Vol. 16, No. 2, 1995, pp. 217–235.

Stets, Jan E., and Peter J. Burke, "Identity Theory and Social Identity Theory," *Social Psychology Quarterly*, Vol. 63, No. 3, September 2000, pp. 224–237.

Stewart, Nora Kinzer, *Mates and Muchachos: Unit Cohesion in the Falklands/Malvinas War*, McLean, Va.: Brassey's (U.S.), Inc., 1991.

Steyer, Rolf, Manfred Schmitt, and Michael Eid, "Latent State-Trait Theory and Research in Personality Individual Differences," *European Journal of Personality*, No. 13, 1999, pp. 398–408.

Stokes, James W., and Louis E. Banderet, "Psychological Aspects of Chemical Defense and Warfare," *Military Psychology*, Vol. 9, No. 4, 1997, pp. 395–415.

Storr, Jim, *The Human Face of War*, London: Continuum UK, 2009.

Stouffer, Samuel A., Arthur A. Lumsdaine, Marion Harper Lumsdaine, Robin M. Williams, Jr., M. Brewster Smith, Irving L. Janis, Shirley A. Star, and Leonard S. Cottrell, Jr., *The American Soldier: Combat and Its Aftermath*, Princeton, N.J.: Princeton University Press, 1949.

———, "The American Soldier: Combat and Its Aftermath," *Studies in Social Psychology in World War II*, Vol. 2, 1949.

Strachan, Hew, "Training, Morale and Modern War," *Journal of Contemporary History*, Vol. 41, No. 2, 2006, pp. 211–227.

Strauss, Claudia, "Models and Motives," in D'Andrade and Strauss, 1992, pp. 1–20.

Sullivan, Harry Stack, "Psychiatric Aspects of Morale," *American Journal of Sociology*, Vol. 47, No. 3, November 1941, pp. 277–301.

Swank, Roy L., and Walter E. Marchand, "Combat Neuroses: Development of Combat Exhaustion," *Archives of Neurology and Psychiatry*, Vol. 55, No. 3, 1946, pp. 236–247.

Tanielian, Terri, and Lisa H. Jaycox, eds., *Invisible Wounds of War: Psychological and Cognitive Injuries, Their Consequences, and Services to Assist Recovery*, Santa Monica, Calif.: RAND Corporation, MG-720-CCF, 2008. As of March 19, 2018:
https://www.rand.org/pubs/monographs/MG720.html

Taylor, K. W., ed., *Voices from the Second Republic of South Vietnam (1967–1975)*, Ithaca, N.Y.: Cornell University Press, 2014.

Taylor, Marcus K., Amanda E. Markham, Jared P. Reis, Genieleah A. Padilla, Eric G. Potterat, Sean P. A. Drummond, and Lilianne R. Mujica-Parodi, "Physical Fitness Influences Stress Reactions to Extreme Military Training," *Military Medicine*, Vol. 173, No. 8, 2008, pp. 738–742.

Tellis, Ashley J., Janice Bially, Christopher Layne, and Melissa McPherson, *Measuring National Power in the Postindustrial Age*, Santa Monica, Calif.: RAND Corporation, MR-1110-A, 2000. As of March 19, 2018:
https://www.rand.org/pubs/monograph_reports/MR1110.html

Terriff, Terry, "'Innovate or Die': Organizational Culture and the Origins of Maneuver Warfare in the United States Marine Corps," *Journal of Strategic Studies*, Vol. 29, No. 3, 2006, pp. 475–503.

Tharoor, Ishaan, "Why the Iraqi Army Keeps Failing," *Washington Post*, May 19, 2015. As of April 3, 2018:
https://www.washingtonpost.com/news/worldviews/wp/2015/05/19/why-the-iraqi-army-keeps-failing/?utm_term=.ad5add351bc4

Toomepuu, Juri, *Soldier Capability-Army Combat Effectiveness (SCACE) Study*, Fort Benjamin Harrison, Ind.: Army Soldier Support Center, 1980.

Troxel, Wendy M., Regina A. Shih, Eric Pedersen, Lily Geyer, Michael P. Fisher, Beth Ann Griffin, Ann C. Haas, Jeremy R. Kurz, and Paul S. Steinberg, *Sleep in the Military: Promoting Healthy Sleep Among U.S. Servicemembers*, Santa Monica, Calif.: RAND Corporation, RR-739, 2015. As of March 19, 2018:
https://www.rand.org/pubs/research_reports/RR739.html

UK Ministry of Defence, *Army Doctrine Primer*, AC 71954, Swindon, UK: Development, Concepts, and Doctrine Centre, 2011.

Ulio, James A., "Military Morale," *American Journal of Sociology*, Vol. 47, No. 3, November 1941, pp. 321–330.

U.S. Army, *Field Service Regulations*, Washington, D.C.: Government Printing Office, 1923.

———, *Tentative Field Service Regulations: Operations*, FM 100-5, Washington, D.C.: Government Printing Office, 1939.

———, *Field Service Regulation: Operations*, FM 100-5, Washington, D.C.: War Department, 1944.

———, *Operations*, FM 100-5, Washington, D.C.: Department of the Army, 1949.

———, *Operations*, FM 100-5, Washington, D.C.: Department of the Army, 1968.

———, *Operations*, FM 100-5, Washington, D.C.: Department of the Army, 1977.

———, *Operations*, FM 100-5, Washington, D.C.: Headquarters Department of the Army, August 20, 1982.

———, *Operations*, Washington, D.C.: Headquarters, Department of the Army, June 1993.

———, *Operations*, FM 3-0, Washington, D.C.: Headquarters, Department of the Army, June 2001.

———, *Intelligence*, FM 2-0, Washington, D.C.: Headquarters, Department of the Army, May 2004.

———, *Operations*, FM 3-0, Washington, D.C.: Headquarters, Department of the Army, February 2008a.

———, *Army Special Operations Forces Foreign Internal Defense*, FM 3-05.137, Washington, D.C.: Headquarters, Department of the Army, June 2008b, restricted distribution.

———, *Security Force Assistance*, FM 3-07.1, Washington, D.C.: Headquarters, Department of the Army, May 2009.

———, *Intelligence*, FM 2-0, Washington, D.C.: Headquarters, Department of the Army, March 2010.

———, *Unified Land Operations*, ADP 3-0, Washington, D.C.: Headquarters, Department of the Army, October 2011.

———, *Unified Land Operations*, ADRP 3-0, Washington, D.C.: Headquarters, Department of the Army, May 2012a.

———, *The Operations Process*, ADP 5-0, Washington, D.C.: Headquarters, Department of the Army, May 2012b.

———, *Army Leadership*, ADRP 6-22, Washington, D.C., Headquarters, Department of the Army, August 2012c.

————, *Intelligence*, ADP 2-0, Washington, D.C.: Headquarters, Department of the Army, August 2012d.

————, *Training Units and Developing Leaders*, ADRP 7-0, Washington, D.C.: Headquarters, Department of the Army, August 2012e.

————, *Offense and Defense*, ADP 3-90, Washington, D.C.: Headquarters, Department of the Army, 2012f.

————, *The Army*, ADP 1-0, Washington, D.C.: Headquarters, Department of the Army, September 2012g.

————, *Doctrine Primer*, ADP 1-01, Washington, D.C.: Headquarters, Department of the Army, September 2014.

————, *Army Special Operations Forces Foreign Internal Defense*, ATP 3-05.2, Washington, D.C.: Headquarters, Department of the Army, August 2015.

————, *Armor and Mechanized Infantry Team*, ATP 3-90.1, Washington, D.C.: Headquarters, Department of the Army, January 2016a.

————, *Operations*, ADP 3-0, Washington, D.C.: Headquarters, Department of the Army, November 2016b.

————, *Information Operations*, FM 3-13, Washington, D.C.: Headquarters, Department of the Army, December 2016c.

————, "*America's Army* Homepage." As of October 16, 2017:
https://www.americasarmy.com

————, "Special Forces." As of November 19, 2017:
https://www.goarmy.com/special-forces/team-members.html

U.S. Army and U.S. Marine Corps, *Intelligence Preparation of the Battlefield/Battlespace*, ATP 2-01.3/MCRP 2-3A, Washington, D.C.: Headquarters, Departments of the Army and Marine Corps, November 2014.

U.S. Army Field Artillery School, *Can It Be Quantified?* proceedings from the Fort Sill Fire Suppression Symposium, Fort Sill, Ok.: Directorate of Combat Developments, January 14, 1980.

U.S. Central Intelligence Agency, *Post-Geneva Outlook in Indochina*, National Intelligence Estimate Number 63-5-54, Washington, D.C.: Director of Central Intelligence, August 3, 1954.

————, *Prospects for North and South Vietnam, 26 May 1959*, National Intelligence Estimate 63-59, Washington, D.C.: Directorate of Intelligence, May 26, 1959.

————, *The Outlook for North Vietnam*, SNIE 14.3-64, Washington, D.C.: Director of Central Intelligence, March 4, 1964.

————, *The Vietnamese Communists Will to Persist*, memorandum, Director of Central Intelligence, August 26, 1966.

————, *Special Assessment on Vietnam*, Washington, D.C.: CIA, May 24, 1967.

————, *The Attitudes of North Vietnamese Leaders Towards Fighting and Negotiating*, Washington, D.C.: CIA, March 25, 1968.

————, *The Outlook from Hanoi: Factors Affecting North Vietnam's Policy on the War in Vietnam*, Special National Intelligence Estimate 14.3-70, Washington, D.C.: Director of Central Intelligence, February 5, 1970.

———, *WSAG Principals: Middle East War*, declassified memorandum, Washington, D.C.: The White House, October 17, 1973.

———, *The Likelihood of a Major North Vietnamese Offensive Against South Vietnam Before June 30, 1975*, National Intelligence Estimate 14.3-1-74, Washington, D.C.: Director of Central Intelligence, May 23, 1974.

U.S. Department of Defense, *Assessment of Afghan National Security Forces Metrics*, Washington, D.C.: DoD Inspector General, February 20, 2013.

U.S. Department of Defense, Active Duty Military Strength by Service, website. As of March 29, 2018:
https://www.dmdc.osd.mil/appj/dwp/dwp_reports.jsp

U.S. Department of State, *ARVN Morale Study: November 1974*, Saigon, R.V.N.: U.S. Embassy, November 1974.

U.S. Joint Chiefs of Staff, *Joint Vision 2010*, Washington, D.C.: Joint Staff, May 30, 2000.

———, *Major Combat Operations Joint Operating Concept*, Version 2.0, Washington, D.C.: Joint Staff, December 2006.

———, *Doctrine for the Armed Forces of the United States*, Joint Publication 1, Washington, D.C.: Joint Staff, March 25, 2013.

———, *Joint Concept for Human Aspects of Military Operations (JC-HAMO)*, Washington, D.C.: Joint Staff, October 19, 2016.

U.S. Joint Forces Command, *Commander's Handbook for an Effects-Based Approach to Operations*, Suffolk, Va.: Joint Warfighting Center, February 24, 2006.

U.S. Marine Corps, *Small Wars Manual*, Washington, D.C.: Government Printing Office, 1940.

———, *Warfighting*, MCDP-1, Washington, D.C.: Headquarters, U.S. Marine Corps, 1997.

———, *Leading Marines*, MCWP 6-11, Washington, D.C.: Headquarters, U.S. Marine Corps, 2002. As of April 13, 2018:
http://www.marines.mil/Portals/59/Publications/MCWP%206-11%20Leading%20Marine.pdf

———, *Marine Air-Ground Task Force Information Operations*, MCWP 3-40.4, Washington, D.C.: Headquarters, U.S. Marine Corps, July 9, 2003.

———, *MAGTF Intelligence Production and Analysis*, Washington, D.C.: Headquarters, U.S. Marine Corps, July 13, 2004.

———, *Marine Air-Ground Task Force Information Operations*, MCWP 3-40.4, Washington, D.C.: Headquarters, U.S. Marine Corps, July 1, 2013.

———, *MAGTF Intelligence Production and Analysis*, MCTP 2-10B, Washington, D.C.: Headquarters, U.S. Marine Corps, May 2, 2016.

U.S. Pacific Fleet, *Japanese Army Discipline and Morale*, Special Translation Number 76, Pearl Harbor, Hawaii: Commander in Chief Pacific, July 7, 1945.

Vaitkus, Mark, and James Griffith, "An Evaluation of Unit Replacement on Unit Cohesion and Individual Morale in the U.S. Army All-Volunteer Force," *Military Psychology*, Vol. 2, No. 4, 1990, pp. 221–239.

van den Aker, Peter, Jacco Duel, and Joseph Soeters, "Combat Motivation and Combat Action: Dutch Soldiers in Operations Since the Second World War; A Research Note," *Armed Forces and Society*, Vol. 42, No.1, 2016, pp. 211–225.

van der Dennen, Johan M. G., "Combat Motivation," *Peace Review: A Journal of Social Justice*, No. 17, 2005, pp. 81–89.

Vandergriff, Donald, and Stephen Webber, eds., *Mission Command: The Who, What, Where, When, and Why*, self-published, 2017.

Vandersteen, Kurt P., *Classical Theories and the Will to Fight*, Leavenworth, Kan.: Army Command and General Staff College Fort, 2001.

Van Veldhuizen, David A., and Larry J. Hutson, "A Design Methodology for Domain Independent Computer Generated Forces," *MAICS-97 Proceedings*, Dayton, Ohio: Wright State University, 1997.

Vauvilliers, Jean, "Pour une théorie générale de l'esprit de corps," *La Revue Administrative*, No. 347, September 2005, pp. 489–498.

Veith, George T., and Merle L. Pribbenow II, " 'Fighting Is an Art': The Army of the Republic of Vietnam's Defense of Xuan Loc, 9–21 April, 1975," *Journal of Military History*, Vol. 68, No. 1, January 2004, pp. 163–213.

Wagner, Arthur L., *Organization and Tactics*, Kansas City, Mo.: Hudson-Kimberly Publishing Co., 1895.

Walker, Andrew D., "An Alternative to Maneuver Warfare," *Marine Corps Gazette*, Vol. 75, No. 11, November 1991, pp. 48–51.

Walker, Mark, "Mattis: Success in Iraq Now a Test of Wills," *San Diego Union Tribune*, August 22, 2006. As of April 3, 2018:
http://www.sandiegouniontribune.com/sdut-mattis-success-in-iraq-now-a-test-of-wills-2006aug22-story.html

Wansink, Brian, Collin R. Payne, and Koert van Ittersum, "Profiling the Heroic Leader: Empirical Lessons from Combat-Decorated Veterans of World War II," *The Leadership Quarterly*, No. 19, 2008, pp. 547–555.

Warden, John A., III, "Air Theory for the Twenty-First Century," in Schneider and Grinter, 1998, pp. 103–124.

Wass de Czege, Huba, "How to Change an Army," *Military Review*, Vol. 64, No. 11, November 1984, pp. 32–49.

Watson, Bruce Allen, *When Soldiers Quit: Studies in Military Disintegration*, Westport, Conn.: Greenwood Publishing Group, 1997.

Watt, Richard, *Dare Call It Treason*, New York: Simon and Schuster, 1963.

Whitlock, Craig, " 'Fat Leonard' Probe Expands to Ensnare More Than 60 Admirals," *Washington Post*, November 5, 2017. As of April 3, 2018:
https://www.washingtonpost.com/investigations/fat-leonard-scandal-expands-to-ensnare-more-than-60-admirals/2017/11/05/f6a12678-be5d-11e7-97d9-bdab5a0ab381_story.html?utm_term=.58770955ca7d

Whitmore, John K., "Social Organization and Confucian Thought in Vietnam," *Journal of Southeast Asian Studies*, Vol. 15, No. 2, September 1984, pp. 296–306.

Whittemore, Robin, and Kathleen Knafl, "The Integrative Review: Updated Methodology," *Journal of Advanced Nursing*, Vol. 52, No. 5, 2005, pp. 546–553.

Wiest, Andrew, *Vietnam's Forgotten Army: Heroism and Betrayal in the ARVN*, New York: New York University Press, 2008.

Wilbanks, James H., *Xuan Loc: The Final Battle Vietnam, 1975*, conference paper, New Orleans, La.: Popular Culture Association, 2000.

Wilensky, Uri, "Netlogo Home Page," Center for Connected Learning and Computer-Based Modeling, Northwestern University, Evanston, Ill., 1999. As of April 9, 2018: https://ccl.northwestern.edu/netlogo/

Wilmoth, Michael D., and Peter G. Tsouras, "ULUS-KERT: An Airborne Company's Last Stand," *Military Review*, July–August 2001. As of April 3, 2018: https://thesaker.is/ulus-kert-an-airborne-companys-last-stand/

Wilson, G. I., Michael D. Wyly, William S. Lind, and B. E. Trainor, "The 'Maneuver Warfare' Concept," *Marine Corps Gazette*, Vol. 65, No. 4, April 1981, pp. 49–54.

Wilson, Gregory Ray, *Modeling and Evaluating U.S. Army Special Operations Forces Combat Attrition Using Janus (A)*, thesis, Monterey, Calif.: Naval Postgraduate School, 1995.

Wilson, Ramey L., *Building Partner Capacity and Strengthening Security Through Medical Security Force Assistance*, thesis, Monterey, Calif.: Naval Postgraduate School, 2013.

Wong, Leonard, Thomas A. Kolditz, Raymond A. Millen, and Terrence M. Potter, *Why They Fight: Combat Motivation in the Iraq War*, Carlisle Barracks, Pa.: Army War College Strategic Studies Institute, 2003.

Woodside, Alexander, "History, Structure, and Revolution in Vietnam," *International Political Science Review*, Vol. 10, No. 2, 1989, pp. 143–157.

Woodward, Rachel, and K. Neil Jenkings, "Military Identities in the Situated Accounts of British Military Personnel," *Sociology*, Vol. 45, No. 2, 2011, pp. 252–268.

Zacharias, Greg L., Jean MacMillan, and Susan B. Van Hemel, eds., *Behavioral Modeling and Simulation: From Individuals to Societies*, Washington, D.C.: The National Academies Press, 2008.

Zhukov, Georgy Konstantinovich, *The Memoirs of Marshal Zhukov*, trans., Jonathan Cape, London: Jonathan Cape Ltd., 1971 (1969).

Lightning Source UK Ltd.
Milton Keynes UK
UKHW051255220722
406239UK00013B/468